CHRIST'S
GLOBE-TROTTER

CHRIST'S GLOBE-TROTTER

The Legacy of Edward (Ted) Pollock

Ted Pollock
with Beverly Reeve

Providence House Publishers
PROVIDENCE PUBLISHING CORPORATION
FRANKLIN, TENNESSEE

Printed in the United States of America

09   08   07   06   05   1   2   3   4   5

Library of Congress Control Number: 2005904466

ISBN: 1-57736-337-X

Author sketch by Ruth Eliot
Maps by Bill Pollock
Cover design by Joey McNair and Ross Chirico/Chirico Design Associates
Page design by Hope Seth

PROVIDENCE HOUSE PUBLISHERS
an imprint of
Providence Publishing Corporation
238 Seaboard Lane • Franklin, Tennessee 37067
www.providence-publishing.com
800-321-5692

*Without a high school or college education,
I was not qualified to become a missionary.
Even though I lacked the requirements,
many of the men and women
mentioned throughout this book had faith in me.
With appreciation, I dedicate this book to you.*

*So many of you want to be a part of my team,
but can't physically go with me on the mission field.
You are my wide prayer support.
With appreciation, I dedicate this book to you.*

*None of my mission projects would have been possible
without the understanding and support of
my wife, Dolly, and our children.
With appreciation, I dedicate this book to you.*

*I take none of the credit.
Ultimately, I give God the glory.
I dedicate this book to Him.*

CONTENTS

ILLUSTRATIONS AND MAPS

PREFACE

My interest in travel was stimulated at an early age by stories that I heard from missionaries working in Egypt and China. I dreamed of becoming a missionary in a foreign country and prayed that God would show me the way. After I dropped out of school in the seventh grade, the dream began to fade. Since the missionaries I knew were doctors, nurses, teachers, and preachers, I did not believe there was a place for an uneducated handyman on the mission field.

As an adult, I remained active in the church. The thought of serving the church in some way still remained with me, and I prayed that God would help me find a wife who shared my sense of calling. I had to wait until I was twenty-seven years old before God introduced me to Dolly. She too felt called to church service, but since she could not afford to go to college, she believed the only way she could serve the church would be to marry a preacher. For this reason she was not sure she wanted to marry me.

This book is the story of our response to God's call to the mission field. It is the story of the way God provided the job opportunities that would prepare us for the unique service for which we were called. It is also a story about the family, friends, and church members who nurtured our early faith, provided support and learning opportunities, and stood behind us during the years we were on the mission field.

Looking back, I have lived as a disciple of Jesus Christ in very difficult circumstances. I wanted to live and work in any country where I could be most useful to the glory of God. I was switching from one country to another—each with its own language, culture, and currency. It was an exciting life and a rewarding one. But God did not promise it would be an easy life. He did promise He would be with us, and He always was.

Although our life as missionary builders was one of hardship and sacrifice, it was our life and our work, and we would not have exchanged it for anything. To us it seemed like we were doing so little, and yet people say much was being accomplished. It really wasn't us, but the thoughts, support, and prayers of our friends back home that kept God working through us.

As you read your Bible you will find that many of the men did not choose the job that God called them for. Moses didn't want to lead the children of Israel out of Egypt. Jonah used every excuse he could think of to get out of going to Nineveh. Paul had to be struck down and blinded before he was willing to do what God wanted. I do not believe that I had anymore to do with my going to the mission field than these men had to do with the job for which God called them. God had a plan for me just as He has for each of you. Many times I felt inadequate to do the work God called me to do, but I learned that God was more interested in my availability than He was in my abilities.

I didn't consciously plan to save every single piece of mission memorabilia in order to write a book. In haste, all of it was thrown into one room of the basement in our Canonsburg, Pennsylvania, house. Then in 1982, as part of our move to Rochester, New York, we loaded the memorabilia into a U-Haul and dumped it into the barn on our son's lot next to ours. I have been cleaning it out ever since.

In the last half century I have seen Christ perform many miracles. Today I am able to look back on a life packed with more high adventure than most people could fit into a dozen lifetimes. It is my hope as you read this story that you will realize God has a unique job for you, too, and that you will respond when the opportunity comes.

Many people with whom I have worked are now gone. But God has given me so much work to do and I am so far behind, I feel like I can never die.

CHRIST'S
GLOBE-TROTTER

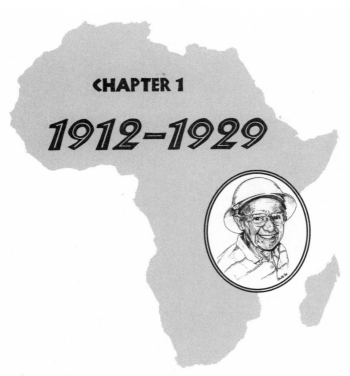

CHAPTER 1

1912–1929

Time past can be revisited by memory, and at my stage of life I am what my children call a frequent flyer to that place, with many miles to my account. I am glad to take any of them along, should they care to go.

—*from David Freeman,* One of Us

IN THE BEGINNING

As I celebrated my eighty-sixth birthday, I had just finished touring Alaska, the only state in which I had not set foot. I had visited the first forty-eight before the last two became states. I've also been in fifty-two countries. I like to travel. However, I don't like traveling as a tourist; rather, I like having a purpose for my trips. As a mission builder for the Presbyterian Church, I have done construction and community development projects in twelve countries. Many of my friends call me "Christ's Globe-Trotter."

I was born Edward Oliver Pollock on November 7, 1912. In those days women didn't go to the hospital to have babies. So I was born in the big old house we shared with Mama's parents

3

that stood at the top of North Central Avenue in Canonsburg, a little burg in western Pennsylvania. Around the turn of the century, oil was discovered in Canonsburg, and as a boy, I remember counting eighty-seven oil derricks from our back porch. Papa was a teamster, a guy who drove a team of horses or mules. He traveled throughout the United States and Canada driving teams for the pipeline companies that built oil and gas lines across the middle of North America. But eventually Papa decided he wanted to be near home, so he and Mama became partners in the operation of a livery stable in Midway, Pennsylvania. Mama and Papa soon discovered that they couldn't make a living running the livery stable, especially with the advent of the automobile, so Papa returned to driving horses.

Some of my earliest memories include going down the hill to the stables with Papa on Sunday afternoons to feed and water the teams. But Papa's employer eventually switched from livery to trucks, and in 1918, Papa got his driver's license (an oval metal pin that had to be worn when driving) and started driving a White two-ton truck. How proud I was riding in the cab of this truck in the Armistice Day parade wearing a soldier's uniform that my mother had made! Most of the hauling that Papa did for the transfer company was local, allowing him to be home to help Mama with my upbringing.

Papa's driver's license

In those days, Mama and Papa seldom attended church. Because of the expenses generated by all the children, it was often necessary for Papa to work on Sundays while Mama stayed home with the babies. As a young child, I walked down the hill from my home to Greenside Avenue Presbyterian Church in Canonsburg, where my grandfather, aunts, and uncles attended, and where I was baptized.

My first grade teacher, Emma McPeake, also had taught my mother and grandfather. I didn't do well my first year of school in 1918, partly because I had severe eczema on my hands which was aggravated by chalk dust from the blackboards. My tale was that I was allergic to school.

Due to an astigmatism, it wasn't long before I got my first pair of glasses. Back then none of the children wore glasses, and the boys immediately labeled me "four eyes." My eyes were changing so fast that the doctor recommended I stay out of school for a year. Besides the astigmatism and eczema, I also had typical childhood diseases like measles, mumps, whooping cough, and chicken pox, causing me to be absent a total of fifty-seven days during that first school year. In my mind, I was a poor, sickly kid.

At the age of seven I lived with my Aunt Jean and Uncle Bill in Midway, Ohio. I was Aunt Jean's pet, and she was happy to have me live with her and Uncle Bill while I took a recess from school for a year due to my astigmatism.

After I returned to school, my performance wasn't any better. In a classroom of fifty students, I strategically placed myself in the last row where I could hide behind my big geography book and watch the steeplejack make repairs on the Catholic church across the street. My bashfulness, dislike for following orders, and lack of interest in my schoolwork all contributed to spending two years in some grades.

In 1925, Mama and Papa bought a coal-heated, two-bedroom house next door to the home where I was born. At this time there were six children in our family. The siblings shared one bedroom—my three sisters in a bed on one side of the room and my brother Clark and I shared a bed on the other side. Baby brother Jim slept in Mama and Papa's room. Since there was no bathroom in this house, weekly baths each Saturday night were taken in a pan of water in front of a little gas stove in the bedroom.

My brother Jack joined the family in 1926, Harry was born in 1928, Dorothy in 1931, Will in 1934, and Pat in 1938, for a total of eleven children. During this period I helped Papa add a bathroom and another bedroom to our house. We tore down the old barn in the backyard and built a playhouse for the kids—a six-by-twelve-foot area for the girls and the same for the boys.

Store-bought toys were not nearly as common back then as they are today. At nine and ten years of age, I mowed lawns in order to buy a hammer and various other tools, and started making toys. First I made dollhouses for my sisters, and later I constructed cookie cutters shaped from soldered metal with a handle attached. One winter, some of my friends and I built a bobsled big enough for all of us to ride and started making jigsaw puzzles using a jigsaw that was crafted from an old sewing machine. After I had my shop, I made box hockey and table polo for the boys and girls in the Young People Christian Union Group (YPCU) in my church and repaired Yankee jumpers, a single ski with a seat attached, for the neighbor kids.

I had many different jobs in my youth, and when I was twelve, one of them was delivering handbills. In those days there was no such thing as bulk mail, so advertisers hired kids to distribute the "bills" to each house. On a good day, I could earn one dollar and fifty cents.

Boy Scouts played a big part in my life. Joining in 1925, I remained active in the organization until the 1940s. Even though I only attained second class rank and earned but one merit badge (carpentry), Scouts toughened me.

Scouting introduced me to diary keeping, and I have kept a diary ever since I left for the mission field in 1947. Today I continue to make daily diary entries and have over eighty-five diaries filled.

One Boy Scout project was learning to braid bull leather whips—the longest was sixteen feet. A buddy of mine, who was adept with the whip, could light a match by striking it in my hand. I still have a scar on my arm where he misjudged.

Through my early years I served in a number of roles in Scouting, including Cubmaster for a pack that met in my shop every Saturday evening. I taught knots that I had learned from my dad, lashing, and many of the pioneering skills that I would later use on the mission field.

Reflecting back, I'm sure I learned more from Scouting than from school. In fact, my Scoutmaster, Tom Jones, was one of three people who played a major role in shaping my life. Many times through the years I have used my Scouting skills and referred to merit badge pamphlets when out on the mission field. Today I am still registered as a member of the National Association of Presbyterian Scouters (NAPS).

A review of my early diaries indicates that four activities occupied much of my time: Sunday school, Young People Christian Union Group, Scouting, and listening to the radio. The radio was a Crosby Pup, a one-tube set with earphones which I bought in 1925 with money I had earned from doing odd jobs. I can remember the many times I listened to the radio late into the night to see how many stations I could locate. On December 18, 1925, my diary revealed that I was able to locate sixty-six stations on my Crosby Pup.

Mama's brother, Uncle Jim, lived with his parents (my grandparents), Grandma and Grandpa Coleman, in the house next to ours. Edward White Coleman, my mom's father and one of my namesakes, worked in his dad's drugstore where Bradbury's *Memory Work of Pharmacy, 1889*, was used for mixing up medicinal recipes. In 1920, the requirements changed and disqualified Grandpa from dispensing medicine.

Grandpa Coleman had a loom in his basement, and many people tore up rags, rolled them into balls, and brought them to him to be woven into rugs. Later he taught me to do the weaving and eventually I had the loom in my own shop. This skill was later put to use on some of my African mission trips.

In 1927, I started to work in Pollock's Shoe Store owned by my father's cousin. Besides working Saturdays, I worked for an hour before school sweeping up the store and front sidewalk and then returned after school for several hours. My main job was to clean up the store and bail the old boxes, but I also sold shoes when the store was busy. There was a shoe repair shop in the store and, by helping the shoemaker, I learned how to half-sole and do other repairs. Many times since then I used this skill to repair Dolly's and my shoes.

When I turned sixteen, my seventh grade teacher told me I was wasting my time in school and suggested that I stop attending. It took me a few months, but early in 1929, I finally convinced Papa to let me drop out of school.

In 1930, Uncle Jim bought an old lab building from the Standard Chemical Works in Canonsburg. I tore down this building and used the lumber to build a shop for Uncle Jim between our two houses. Uncle Jim bought and sold antiques on the side and used this shop to display his inventory. Often he hired me to strip the old finishes off the furniture.

As payment for the demolition of the old lab, I was given some of the lumber and built an eighteen-by-eighteen-foot shop for myself in Papa and Mama's backyard. Eventually, I put a loft in this shop and moved in. It was very cold sleeping in the unheated shop during the winter, so I built in a chimney and a hot blast stove.

In 1946, when Uncle Jim decided to move, I bought his property and took over his shop.

My other namesake is my dad's father, Oliver Collins Pollock. One of my very first jobs was working on Grandpa Pollock's farm during the summers. The farm was used mostly to raise food for the family, but it also had a few cows and chickens. Without refrigeration, there was no way to keep milk. Instead, the cream was separated from the milk with a hand crank separator, stored in the springhouse, and used to churn butter. The butter and eggs were taken by horse and buggy into town each Saturday to their regular customers. For my pay at the end of each summer, Grandpa took me into town to Pollock's Shoe Store to buy a new pair of shoes.

Grandpa and I hoed rows of corn and other vegetables together. When we finished a row, we would sit in the shade and rest while he told me stories of his army days. Grandpa graduated from Westminster College in New Wilmington, Pennsylvania, and was in his second year of seminary when he dropped out of school to join the army. From 1875 to 1880, he participated in all of the last major Indian battles, except for the Battle of Little Big Horn. At the Battle of Little Big Horn, where Custer was massacred, Grandpa was sent three miles away to fetch supplies and possibly saved from meeting his fate.

Fighting against Sitting Bull and Crazy Horse, he was present at Fort Robinson the day Crazy Horse was killed. According to Joseph McFarland's book, *20th Century History of the City of Washington and Washington County*, Grandpa had met many of the legends of the West, including Buffalo Bill, Wild Bill, and Texas Jack.[1]

At the age of seventeen, I worked on Grandpa's farm cutting trees for pit posts that were used to shore up coal mine shafts. I walked three miles out to the farm in the morning, cut posts all day, and walked home in the evening.

In those days people walked a lot more than they do today. We walked to get where we wanted to go, and we walked for fun. That same year I joined a walking contest sponsored by

Pollock's Shoe Store. Each contestant was provided with a walking meter to measure how far he walked in a week. In my diary, I recorded that I walked nine miles on Monday, nine on Tuesday, nine on Wednesday, and eleven on Thursday. Friday night my buddy and I decided that we needed to accumulate more miles, so we started using the Scout pace of walking fifty steps, then running fifty steps. We continued well into the night, covering forty-two miles. Before the contest ended on Saturday, we walked an additional twenty-eight miles, only to discover that the postman, with his twice-daily delivery route, beat us out.

With no television or radio for entertainment, it was a big event when Chautauqua, a traveling cultural program, came to town each year. Chautauqua had evening programs that included lectures, plays, and music, besides the special programs for kids in the mornings. Sites were selected so the cast could rotate among several towns in the same area. The Scouts volunteered to set up their tents and do the ushering.

One year, instead of using the train, the Chautauqua crew began moving tents and equipment by truck. When I was asked if I wanted to replace one of the crew boys, Uncle Jim drove me over to Hartville, Ohio, to join the crew. From Hartville, the crew traveled to Ripley, Ohio; on to Richmond, Indiana; and finished the season in La Crosse, Wisconsin. From La Crosse, we had to take the tents back to Kansas City to be stored for the winter, and from there, I took a bus home. I didn't get paid, but it was a chance to travel and learn about rigging, the logistics of planning, and getting a job done on schedule.

I was introduced at an early age to the Canonsburg Historical Society (now known as the Jefferson College Historical Society). Members of the Pollock family, including my grandfather, Oliver Collins Pollock, had been involved with Jefferson College. The 125th anniversary of Canonsburg was celebrated in 1927, and a year later, the society organized an antique and historical exhibit in the Old College Building at

Jefferson College to raise funds to make improvements to the building. Uncle Jim, active in the historical society, provided the antiques and hired me to be the daytime watchman while the display was open to the public. In the years that followed, I became an active member of the society and assisted them in trying to preserve the items in the museum and the college book collection. I am still a member today.

CHAPTER 2

1930-1946

"I've gone to the school of experience; 24 hours a day, 7 days a week, no holidays, no vacations, and I'm never going to graduate."

—*Theodore Roosevelt*

LEARNING BY DOING

I dropped out of school in 1929 during the beginning of the Great Depression. Companies weren't hiring, and not wanting to sit idle, I started riding with my dad on the trucks from the transfer company.

One day is especially vivid in my memory. This particular day, from morning to night, I helped the transfer company move my Uncle Bill and Aunt Jean from Canonsburg to Brownsville, Pennsylvania. Upon my return that night, even though exhausted, I volunteered to help unload a boxcar of flour, truck it across town, and stack it in the basement of the local bakery. By the end of my twenty-hour day, I could hardly trudge up the hill to go home. I fell into bed with my clothes on and immediately dropped off to sleep. Not expecting to be paid for this work, I was surprised when I received a paycheck, and even more surprised when the transfer company offered me a part-time job.

Chuck Campbell, one of the owners of the transfer company, was also associated with several other companies. This allowed Chuck to move me around from one company to another. Much of my work involved loading and unloading trucks, but I also worked with the crew transporting material for bridge construction. Since this was before the time of hydraulic braking systems, someone had to ride on the trailer to work the hand brake. In winter this was a very cold job and wasn't any more pleasant on a hot summer day when the brake wheel burned the hand when touched. Chuck was one of my role models, and I learned a lot from him and his crews during these years.

One interesting project the transfer company was involved in during this time was the removal of an old bridge. We lifted the bridge off its foundations and rotated it ninety degrees in order to lower it onto barges in the river below. Then the bridge was floated downriver to a new location where it was shortened and placed on a new foundation.

Normally I earned forty cents an hour working for the transfer company, but there were years during this time when the company didn't have enough money to cover payroll. The married men were paid first. Pay didn't come regularly, but I didn't care. My aim wasn't to get rich. I took jobs because I thought they were interesting and hoped that I would learn from them. Typically I worked long, 12-hour days (occasionally 20 hours), with 117 hours the most I ever worked in one week. Long hours were required to get the jobs done, so catnaps replaced any long stretches of sleep.

In 1933, I traveled for the first time by airplane—from Pittsburgh to Chicago to the World's Fair. At one of the exhibits, I was intrigued when introduced to closed circuit television. During a tour of Chicago, I saw a series of statues that had the verse inscribed on them: "Time goes, you say? Ah no! Alas, Time stays. We go." I've used this quote many times through the years.

Besides working part-time for the transfer company during these early years, I also worked in my shop over lunch breaks doing simple repairs for friends and neighbors. I was always busy, and there were many weeks when I worked all night in order to complete a job by the date I had promised. I wasn't doing the work just for the money but mainly because so many people needed help. One of my old accounting books shows that I earned only $365.75 in 1935, and that included my pay from the transfer company. In those days, there were many people who couldn't afford to pay me, so I often made exchanges for the work I did. For example, if I reupholstered a couch for a family and discovered that they could not pay the full price, I would accept goods for the balance.

Since we bathed only on Saturdays in those days, we were very dirty by the end of the work week. Work pants were worn until they fell apart and were never washed. We owned two work shirts and wore one for a full week before washing it. Leather leggings and bib overalls helped to protect our clothing.

One of my regular customers was Doc Johnston. At first I washed windows for him, but it wasn't long before I was called upon to take care of a variety of jobs around his office/apartment building. No money exchanged hands. I worked there from the time I was fourteen years old until I left on my first trip to Africa, and initially was paid with free medical service for my family. As I took on more of his work, eventually he owed me more than I owed him.

On its first floor, my workshop had a six-foot-by-six-foot office, only big enough to hold my rolltop desk and swivel chair. Eventually I added a sleep loft and acquired an old pedal organ to put in the loft under the eaves. One of the neighborhood guys could play the organ, and we bought song sheets for the group to sing along. We also had an old Scout bugle, and many of the young people started to hang around the shop in the evening to sing or listen to the radio and play cards.

I called my shop Pollock's Everything and used the logo, "We specialize in the impossible." Pollock's Everything's core business was restoring antiques, reupholstering, and custom building furniture. If I couldn't do the job, I was sure one of my buddies could. I relied on Theodore Roosevelt's suggestion: If someone asks if you can do something, say, "Certainly I can!" and then figure out how to do it.

When I needed extra help in my shop, I hired my brothers, friends, and neighborhood kids. When they weren't working for me, some of the kids often stopped by to visit or make games and toys. Also, the young people from the church came by to make lawn decorations, candleholders, and other items, which they sold to raise money for church projects.

In the early thirties, I joined Chartiers United Presbyterian Church, just two blocks away from Greenside in Canonsburg. Most of my friends were members of Chartiers, and I liked attending the same church.

In 1936, I built my first baptismal font and dedicated it as a memorial to the pioneer families who started Chartiers. In following years, I built three more baptismal fonts for Presbyterian churches: two in Pennsylvania and one in Ohio.

My trip with Chautauqua back in 1930 stirred my desire to travel. In 1936, I bought my first car—a secondhand Plymouth for $250. Starting in 1937, I bought a new Plymouth every year for the next four years. This cost me $25 a month. With the purchase of a car, I began a practice that I continued into the early 1940s: I worked for five months and then took a month off to travel. In the summers I traveled north or west and in the winters I headed south.

I was active in the United Presbyterian youth programs and every summer took a carload of young people to the YPCU National Conference. In 1936, the conference was held in Northfield, Massachusetts. Before the conference, we took a trip to Lake Placid and drove up through New England to Montreal. From there, we came south to the conference in Northfield, Massachusetts, then stopped in New York City for a day on the way home. This was considered a big trip in those days.

In 1937, I started working for Donaldson Supply and Equipment as yard foreman and worked there for approximately two years. I did special millwork for Donaldson's in my shop and continued doing odd jobs around town, including refinishing and reupholstering furniture.

In the summer of 1937, the YPCU conference was held at Muskingum College in New Concord, Ohio. After the conference, I went out west, following the old Route 66 to New Mexico and visited many of the Indian tribes in that area.

That winter I drove south into the Carolinas. This trip was sort of a working vacation since I was yard foreman at Donaldson's Supply and visited plywood mills that were their suppliers. This set the pattern for future trips. From then on, my vacations were used to gather new ideas and information that would be useful in my work. On a trip to Williamsburg, I learned about blacksmithing, which brought back memories of the blacksmith shop on my grandfather's farm in the 1920s where I turned the crank for the bellows. (To this day, my favorite poem is "The Blacksmith" by Henry Longfellow.)

It was during this time that I first started to tithe. While making twenty-five dollars a week in the lumberyard, I put one dollar in the church offering, gave one dollar to Dr. Al Pollock, my grandmother's cousin (a missionary in Egypt whose salary was paid by the YPCU at Chartiers United Presbyterian Church), and fifty cents in the Sunday school collection.

My brother Clark, sister Jean, and a friend went with me to the YPCU conference in Aimes, Iowa, the summer of 1938. After the conference, we visited the Grand Canyon. Actually, as

I look back, these trips provided the education in geography and U.S. history that I had missed in school. And, of course, the YPCU conferences provided good education in religion and missions.

In January 1939, I drove to Florida to visit Freddy Ashe, a friend from Canonsburg who was attending Miami University in Coral Gables. He shared an apartment with his roommate, and I stayed with the two of them. Since they were both members of the Pi Delta Sigma fraternity, I spent a good deal of time with the fellows from the fraternity and helped them set up for the Kampus King Kapers Dance at the Biltmore Hotel. I was made the first and only honorary member of Pi Delta Sig (it went national in 1940, and the name changed to Kappa Sigma). From Miami University, I traveled to Key West before heading home. I returned to Florida the next two winters and stayed in the fraternity house but never had enough money to buy a fraternity ring.

The YPCU conference in 1939 was held at Penn State and my brother Jim traveled over to State College with me. We were both short of money so I borrowed five dollars from my sister for the gas and we camped outside under the bleachers. It was at this conference that I heard Don McClure, a pioneer United Presbyterian evangelist, speak for the first time. (Don spent fifty years in the Sudan and Ethiopia and was martyred in Ethiopia in 1977.)

From 1929 until 1939, I continued to work part-time for the Transfer Company. Late in 1939, I was involved in a couple of jobs that gave me great hands-on experience. The first of these was the moving of the presses and equipment of the Daily Notes Publishing Company, which published the Canonsburg newspaper. The other job was helping to move Charlie Khuns' dry cleaning shop. My job was setting up and aligning the shafts and belts that powered the washing machines and clothes extractors (as clothes dryers were called back then) and getting them all to work properly.

One fun job we had in those years was the conversion of an old apple orchard warehouse into a roller-skating rink. We added bathrooms to the building and converted an old boiler into the heat supply. After we finished sanding the floor, the fun part was putting on skates and testing it to make sure there were no bumps.

At this same site, I continued to learn by doing and helped build a house from an old corn crib. The ground under the crib was mostly shale, and hand digging the basement was slow going. I used the knowledge gained from this experience several years later when digging a basement under a house at Murray Hill, Pennsylvania, and again on a mission project in Addis Ababa, Ethiopia.

I liked being challenged and was like a sponge soaking up new ideas. As I passed the high school one day, I noticed several guys trying to climb the flagpole. The rope had broken and the janitor had offered five dollars to the person who could climb the pole and put up a new one. I went to my shop and made climbing stirrups out of pieces of rope and old saddle stirrups. I returned to the school, and using my homemade stirrups and a girth hitch, worked my way to the top of the eighty-foot pole, replaced the rope, and collected the five dollars. After that, I was offered jobs replacing ropes and painting two other flagpoles in town. The worst of these jobs was replacing a rope on a cold, windy day in November in order to fly the flag on Armistice Day.

In the early 1940s, I accepted the job of re-pointing the brick on the front of Chartiers United Presbyterian Church. My ladders weren't tall enough to reach the top of the wall, so I accomplished the job by lowering myself down the face of the building in a barrel.

I also took the job of painting the steeple of Chartiers. I made a small platform for my eight-foot ladder that fit on top of the belfry roof. By standing at the top of the stepladder, I could just reach to paint the tip of the steeple. OSHA would never have approved.

In the summer of 1940, the YPCU held its conference at Estes Park, Colorado. After dropping off my brother Clark at the conference, I continued across the mountains to visit a friend who was working at the Grand Lake Ranger Station for the summer. One day, donned in my cowboy hat, shirt, and boots, I drove from the ranger station over to see Clark in Estes Park and happened to notice a pretty young lady who had come to pick up her mail. She smiled. I smiled back. Eventually she asked if I had a horse. I replied, "We can soon find one." I rented two horses from the livery stable and we went riding.

Her name was Dolly Marie Kelly, a graduate from Toronto High School, Toronto, Ohio. She was one of the delegates at the conference from Steubenville, Ohio, and a leader of YPCU. Dolly and five of her friends from their presbytery made a bet on the way to the conference. Which of the girls would be lucky enough to meet the first cowboy? Dolly won the bet and met the first cowboy . . . but he happened to be from Pennsylvania.

In the fall of 1940 I made many fifty-mile trips from Canonsburg to Dolly's home and, after knowing her for one year, we married on August 21, 1941, at the pastor's home in Richmond, Ohio. She was twenty, and I, twenty-eight. On our one-month honeymoon (which cost $250) we traveled from Ft. Wayne, Indiana; continued on to East Chicago, Illinois; Lake Geneva, Wisconsin; La Crosse, Wisconsin (stopping at the 1941 YPCU conference in Lake Geneva, Wisconsin); and out through Idaho and Washington. Our trip eventually led down to Los Angeles, and back across the Grand Canyon, Texas, and Louisiana.

Dolly was the daughter of a poor Lithuanian family who arrived in the United States a few years before she was born on October 17, 1919. Her father worked in the coal mines in Pennsylvania and later did a little farming in Ohio. Her mother died in childbirth when Dolly was seven years old. She had four sisters and four brothers but two of her brothers died at an early age. After her mother's death, the baby, Nancy, was sent to live with other relatives, and Dolly's oldest sister, Virginia, took over the responsibility of keeping the rest of the family together.

Because the other children teased these poor kids with the funny-sounding family name, they had it changed to Kelly at the recommendation of one of their teachers. Actually they weren't sure of their real family name. Since neither her mother nor father could read or write, they used whatever variation of their family name that was easiest for the person writing it.

The Depression years were particularly hard for them. Her father could not find work, so they had to survive on what they could raise on the farm that he rented. They often had to supplement their diet with edible weeds like lambs quarters, pig weed, and beet greens that they found in the area. Later this knowledge became very useful to us on the mission field in Africa. Dolly's parents were Catholic, but since the only church nearby was the Knoxville Presbyterian Church, she and her bothers and sisters attended there.

One story that Dolly told of her childhood was the day she and her brother Cookie (Edwin) were walking to school in a rainstorm and both were struck by lightning. They were knocked unconscious but did not appear to receive any other injuries. However, we have always wondered if this lightning strike caused the slow-growing brain tumor Dolly developed in later years.

By the time Dolly started high school, her oldest sister, Virginia, had married and moved to Toronto, Ohio. Eventually Dolly moved in with Virginia and attended Toronto High School. After she graduated from high school in 1937, Dolly returned home to her father, two brothers and sister, and took care of the old farmhouse equiped with only a woodstove in the kitchen.

This book is *our* story. Without Dolly I could not have done the things I have done. When I was young, I prayed to God to help me find the right woman for my wife. God chose carefully for me. I had dated a lot of girls before I met Dolly, but not one of them could have put up with the hardships on the mission fields. Furthermore, Dolly had skills and abilities that I lacked that were needed to complete our assignments. She was my partner in every way. She made a home for the family out of every mud shack, chicken coop, or tent that we lived in. In addition to being wife, mother, and teacher for our kids, she was secretary, accountant, and business manager for all of the construction projects we did on the mission field. In this story

Dolly and Ted—"She was my partner in every way"

you will see that she was the force that pushed me forward in God's service when I hesitated.

Our first child Eddie Jr. was born on May 13, 1942, in the Canonsburg Hospital, followed shortly by daughter Penny on December 13, 1943. Penny's birth was particularly difficult for Dolly. Dr. Johnston thought Dolly would die because she hemorrhaged on the delivery table for two hours. Afterward, Dolly told of an out-of-body experience in which she saw Jesus. Jesus informed her that she could stay or she could come back to me. If she chose to come back, life would be difficult. She said she couldn't leave me alone with the two babies.

Eddie and Penny kept Dolly busy, but she helped out around the shop when she could. When World War II started, my brothers joined the armed services. Since I was married and had children, I wasn't near the top of the draft list. I discussed enlisting with the chairman of the draft board, and he responded, "Would you be more useful to the country in the army or in a defense plant?" I went to work as an electrical/mechanical maintenance man at the Alcoa plant in Canonsburg, servicing the electric forklifts and other electric vehicles used there.

After VE day in 1945, the plant closed down. I got reassigned to another plant and was given a job as a first-class electrician at Mare Island Navy Yard in California. I worked on some of the navy ships that had been damaged by kamikaze pilots in the ongoing war with Japan. Although I had no experience working on ships, I was made the foreman of a crew. By studying the blueprints before starting work each day, I had no trouble handling the job.

After four months in California, the war ended and we returned to Canonsburg. Doc Johnston and others in town had jobs they wanted done, so Dolly and I reopened Pollock's Everything in January 1946 and hired my brothers upon their return from military service.

THE CALL

"You did not choose me, but I chose you . . ." (John 15:16 RSV).

There were three men who had a great deal of influence on me while I was growing up: Tom Jones, Bob Malone, and Dr. Don Spencer. Tom Jones, a postal clerk, was very active in the church and a charter member of the Boy Scouts of America. Naturally he was the one who introduced me to Scouting and provided leadership for our troop. Bob Malone was a mail carrier and our Sunday school teacher. If I wasn't at Sunday school, he would send me a postcard to let me know that I was missed. Dr. Spencer was the pastor of Chartiers Church and nurtured my interest in missions. In 1934, he took a group of young people down to Frenchburg and Ezel, mission projects in the mountains of Kentucky.

As a boy of seven, I can remember sitting on my Grandma's porch listening to Dr. Al Pollock talk about his mission work in Egypt. (Al and James Pollock, my grandmother's cousins, were both mission doctors in Egypt.) Hearing his stories made me wonder if there was any possibility that someday I, too, would be fortunate enough to do work in the mission field.

In my early years, I had many contacts with those involved in mission work. One of my neighbors was the editor of the *Junior Missionary Magazine,* and for five to six years in the 1920s, I was a member of the Junior Missionary Society. Also in Canonsburg, there was a missionary to China who communicated with me and made mission life more real by sending postcards from her mission site. Through these contacts, I came to believe that missionaries were preachers, teachers, and doctors, and, after I dropped out of school in the seventh grade, my dream of becoming one began to fade.

Dolly also felt called to church service. The one way she could serve the church with only a high school education was to marry a preacher. This was a serious issue with her when deciding if she would accept my proposal of marriage. To her dying days, she still contended that she never really said "yes!"

We were a young couple called to church service but didn't know how to answer. We did the only thing we knew to do. We became active in Chartiers United Presbyterian Church in Canonsburg, working with the young people and serving in many other capacities: trustee and Scouting for me, and mission circle and teaching Sunday school for Dolly.

When we reopened Pollock's Everything with my brothers in January 1946, Dolly managed the accounts and billing. She had no training or experience, but her younger sister, Nancy, who was living with us and going to business college, showed Dolly how to set up the books and maintain them. In hindsight, I can see that this was the last bit of training we needed to do the job on the mission field that God had in mind for us. In my spare time, I was busy making racks for communion cups, holders for hymnal numbers, and folding screens for Sunday school for the church.

One night we went to hear the legendary Presbyterian missionary to Africa, Dr. Don McClure, speak at the Washington Presbytery spring YPCU conference in Pennsylvania. After the meeting, we went up to meet him and Dolly revealed that she really envied what he was doing. We shook hands and had a brief conversation. Don asked why we envied him and his work, and we explained that we felt called to the mission field but didn't have anything to offer but our two hands. I was not a doctor or a preacher; in fact, I hadn't made it past the seventh grade. He asked, "What do you do?" I told him about Pollock's Everything, describing the masonry, electric, and carpentry work. Don's enthusiastic response was, "I build houses and they fall down. Besides, I should be out preaching. If you feel God is calling you, come out and help us."

Dolly and I went on a family camping trip to Niagara Falls and up to Bar Harbor, Maine, with my brothers Jack, Harry, and Jim that July. Throughout the vacation, the conversation returned to the discussion we had with Don McClure. Don said that if we felt called, we should come out to the Sudan to help. We both felt called, but how do you go about answering the call? Whom should we tell? Where do we apply?

After our return from vacation, I went to Pittsburgh to purchase upholstering supplies for the shop and decided to stop by the United Presbyterian bookstore on Ninth Street. I told Mr. Fletcher, the manager of the store, about "our call" that we didn't know how to answer. Mr. Fletcher said he wasn't sure, but that he would call the chairperson of the woman's board who had offices on Ninth Street in Pittsburgh. The chairperson gave me the phone number of Dr. Glenn Reed, corresponding secretary for the United Presbyterian Board of Foreign Missions in Philadelphia. Glenn sent applications but warned us not to get our hopes up too high since the board was considering two men with college degrees. The board had never sent out a missionary without at least a high school degree, and had never sent a family out for a short term. We would be the exception to the rule.

With help from our church, we filled out as much of the application forms that we could. Part of the forms required references from a professor or teacher so I sought out Mary Wilson, my second grade teacher in 1920, to ask for assistance with filling in the information on my schooling.

In September 1946, it was timely that Glenn Reed came to interview me while I was in the middle of putting in a dental office for Doc Johnston's son. From the work that I was doing in the dentist's office, it was evident to Glenn that I was well qualified for the job of mission builder.

The cry came out from one town member in Canonsburg, "Take anybody but don't take Ted Pollock!" Canonsburg knew me for all the work I had done in the town: the big oak counters in the library, the front of the movie theater and the frames for advertising the shows, the wiring of speakers in the music shop, the shelves and counters in the men's store, the improvements to the beauty parlor, and the repair of the church steeple. And in Doc Johnston's building (his office and five apartments), I took care of everything except surgery.

When the Board of Foreign Missions confirmed our appointment to the South Sudan mission field to supervise the building of foreign mission schools, they also decided to send two young men to help me. Ken Rasmussen and Robb McLaughlin, buddies in their middle year at the Pittsburgh Theological Seminary, agreed to take a break from their studies and go to the mission field. Robb had grown up in Egypt, and his parents were there at this time.

After his appointment, Ken spent some time at my shop helping select the tools we would take along to the Sudan. The board told us that we shouldn't expect to find any tools there, so we tried to plan for everything. The board also agreed to let me take my car and trailer. We would all eventually travel together to our first assignment.

On October 6, we received board approval for our appointment to the South Sudan and I immediately began to close down the work in my shop. My brothers took over some of the business.

Dolly wrote in her journal, ". . . and there were many reasons why we should not go, even why we could not go, but we went because God had a plan for us."

In December 1946, we received a letter from the treasurer of the Board of Foreign Missions saying he did not think he would be able to get us on a ship before January. On a Friday night, however, he called and asked, "If I can get you on the *Citadel Victory*, will you be ready to go on Monday morning?"

At eight o'clock Saturday morning, December 14, he called to say that we were on! We all had just gotten our last typhoid shots and none of us were feeling too well, but I told him we would be there. We hurried to pack, and finished loading the trailer around midnight. Packing for a three- to five-year term in the tropics with Eddie, age four, and Penny Sue, age three, was a real challenge.

In the past two months, we had gotten shots, visas, passports, and crated up two tons of supplies in the trailer. Since I had no birth certificate, the only way to verify my birth date for my passport was from my baptismal certificate.

On a Sunday morning around 9:00 A.M., we left Canonsburg, Pennsylvania, heading for the Sudan mission fields and stopped to pick up Ken Rasmussen and his wife in Pittsburgh. It was windy and snowing heavily. The treasurer of the Board of Foreign Missions was concerned that we would get stuck on the Pennsylvania Turnpike and asked us to call him regularly to report our progress. The drive was slow and difficult. We didn't reach the Brooklyn Navy Yard until 4:00 A.M. Monday. Even though we were tightly squeezed in and uncomfortable, all six of us managed to sleep a couple of hours in the car after our arrival.

While eating breakfast in the little restaurant on the docks at the Navy Yard, Dolly became upset at the filthy surroundings. She would soon learn to put up with a lot worse conditions on the mission field. After breakfast we took a cab across town to get yellow fever shots. The car, trailer, and freight were loaded on Monday, but the boat did not sail until Tuesday morning, freeing us up for a day in New York City. In the city, Robb McLaughlin and Dr. Bob Gordon, with his wife and baby daughter, joined us. We had all been assigned to the South Sudan. Besides the crew, the only others on the ship were a wealthy Indian who had come to the United States for an operation, his personal physician, and servant.

The *Citadel Victory*, one of the old navy Victory ships built for World War II, was a tramp freighter that was taken over by the Merchant Marines after the war. Its maximum cargo was eight thousand tons, but on this trip we only had a load of five thousand, made up mostly of new cars, tobacco, paper, mail, and, of course, our equipment. Our quarters were in the aft end of the ship, the end the gunners used during the war. With the guns removed, we had our own private deck. All the men on board were in one room and the ladies in another. Because there was more freight than passengers, we not only ate in the officers' dining room but had run of the entire ship. This supplied me with many odd jobs helping the crew where I could.

Leaving New York harbor, disappointment set in when heavy fog prevented us from seeing the Statue of Liberty. The crew encouraged us not to fret, for they reassured us that we would appreciate her that much more on the return trip.

Sailing down the coast to Newport News, Virginia, the weather was rough, with some of the waves spraying up on the bridge. Here, we stayed overnight while tobacco, mail, and paper were loaded, allowing us a little more time in the States to do our last minute shopping. With so few on board, our Sunday church services were very informal but inspirational just the same, with Ken and Robb leading the service.

While docked at Newport News, the officers learned that there would be children on board for Christmas and rushed uptown by taxi to buy toys. Penny and Eddie were delighted with their large assortment of gifts. When the crew heard I didn't have time to paint Eddie's wooden toolbox, they quickly took it to their shop and turned it into a cheery bright red just in time for the holiday.

After our ten-day trip crossing the Atlantic, we entered the Mediterranean Sea on December 28. Our first sight of land was the formidable Atlas Mountains of northern Africa. Upon entering the Strait of Gibraltar, we suffered another disappointment. It was around nine o'clock at night and was too dark to see the Rock of Gibraltar except for a few lights at its base. It wasn't long before we saw the lights of Tangier and Tetrain in Morocco.

The Mediterranean sailing weather was just as calm as the Atlantic, and because the wind was with us, we made even better time. The porpoises were an unusual sight in the water as they played tag with the ship. From the bow of the ship, the phosphorus in the water made them look bright silver in the moonlight. The porpoises not only kept up with the ship traveling seventeen knots per hour, but swam back and forth in the spray and surf beside it.

Upon entering the harbor at Alexandria, Egypt, we waited until the inspection officers and native police, more numerous than flies, came aboard. The police didn't appear to have any purpose other than inquiring if any of the passengers had cigarettes or chocolate that they might be willing to relinquish. Even if the police couldn't speak English, they could all say "cigarettes" and "chocolate."

We hadn't dropped anchor for more that a few minutes before the local merchants spotted the American flag and a whole fleet of sailboats surrounded us carrying loads of everything from trinkets to furniture. They didn't make much for their morning's work from us missionaries who had no money. They didn't give up easily, however, but just kept sailing round and round the ship, cutting their prices each time with no success.

The manpower was fascinating! The native Arabs of Egypt came out in droves, barefooted and in every type of dress, to load our huge crates into their tiny four-wheeled carts. While chanting, they pushed their fully loaded carts up a fairly steep incline with a truck crate. Then they unloaded a whole boatload of coal, carrying it in baskets on their shoulders, to boxcars three hundred yards away. With arguments every few minutes, the fellow that could talk the loudest and the longest and could make the most motions with his hands without being interrupted was usually the winner. Egypt had more policemen and less order than I had seen anywhere and almost every street was marked, "Absolutely No Admittance."

Normally Haifa, Palestine, was only a day's travel; however, because of the presence of the king of Arabia and his royal launch here, it took two days before we were able to get into the port. Eventually we got ashore shortly after the royal procession had been on parade and just in time to see the picturesque array of military uniforms: the British tommies, the Arabian army with their draped hats, the Egyptians with the red tarboosh (flat-topped tasseled caps), and many others we couldn't identify.

Our ship was moored in the shadow of Mount Carmel where Elijah beheaded the priests of Baal, and when we got ashore, we climbed the mountain. Every time Eddie saw a hole in the rock he would insist, "This is the rock that Elijah struck to get his water," although the fact that it was not the exact spot made no difference to him.

Haifa looked how the English cities must have looked during the war, with its barbed wire entanglements. On our way to the post office, we walked for a block between two rows of barbed wire—and ran directly into the mouth of a rifle. Upon reaching the post office, we were searched for explosives before permitted to enter.

From Haifa we sailed for Port Said, Egypt, on the longest canal in the world, the Suez (104 miles long and 39 feet deep). If possible, the peddlers here were worse than in Alexandria. If you didn't have money, they were willing to take your shirt or any other article of clothing. It was our luck again, as with the Statue of Liberty and the Rock of Gibraltar, to enter the canal at midnight. However, with a beautiful full moon, we enjoyed the first part of the canal by moonlight. With the ships anchored at the mouth, the palm trees in the distance, and the ripples of the water reflecting the moon's rays, it was worth the wait.

Toward morning the fog was bad, and we had to anchor to keep from hitting a sand bar or another ship. The surrounding country was mostly sand with a highway running along the canal. Where the banks of the canal were higher, it was interesting to watch the natives walking along the shore, pulling their sailboats when the wind didn't strike their sails. The canal was very narrow, with shifting sands that had to be dredged out at least once a month, but we traveled through on our own power.

It was noon of the following day before we entered the Red Sea. We made full speed ahead for Jeddah, Saudi Arabia. Somewhere in the night we passed Mount Sinai, again missing an important site due to darkness.

The port at Jeddah on the Red Sea had anchoring space for only two or three ships, and we were unable to dock to unload some of our freight. Even anchoring in port was dangerous because of the many coral reefs. Our cargo, which was mostly generators, cars, and trucks, was taken ashore on small sailboats. Each piece had to be balanced perfectly or the boat would capsize. Very few of the new cars, even in crates, reached their destination intact. The most pitiful sights were what we called the "scavenger men," natives in dugouts who rowed around the ship waiting for garbage to be thrown out. First they fished out tin cans and drained them, then wrung salt water from any scraps of bread.

We remained at Jeddah a full week waiting to have our freight unloaded and weren't permitted to go ashore. While waiting in the harbor, we had big excitement when Robb and Ken hooked a shark using a homemade meat hook, some fishing line made from clothesline, and a piece of ham for bait. As is often the case, the shark's size grew every time it was mentioned, from five to twenty feet. Unfortunately the line wasn't heavy enough to hold the load, and while they were trying to wear him out, the shark took the line too near the blade of the prop and the line was severed. The shark refused to come near the hook again no matter how tempting the smell of the ham.

We passengers found plenty to do while at Jeddah that week. One day the natives were unloading some large generators for the minister of finance, and we discovered that all the stevedores (dock workers) were afraid to touch the generators for fear of losing their heads if any were broken. So our boys, not knowing the man nor fearing him, went down into the hold and unloaded the generators.

After crossing the Red Sea, we landed at Port Sudan, Sudan, on January 17, 1947, exactly one month from the day we left the Brooklyn Navy Yard. With seven thousand miles of water crossed, we were reluctant to leave the ship. All the officers had been very hospitable and it seemed so much like home. Fried chicken and all the trimmings were served at the farewell dinner held in our honor. Ken and I repaired the ice cream freezer so we could enjoy ice cream, too. The officers were generous and offered us anything on the ship we wanted— except for one particular anchor. We decided to take the small emergency generator that was aboard, since it had never been used and most likely never would be. It would be perfect for supplying electricity to one of our mission compounds, and we carried it off with our luggage.

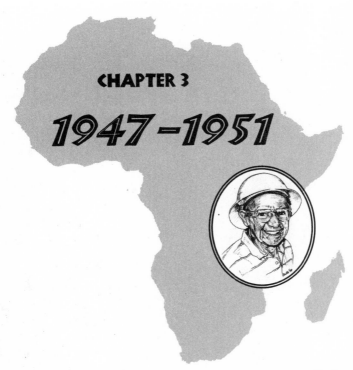

CHAPTER 3

1947-1951

"*Brothers, think of what you were when you were called. Not many were of noble birth. But God chose the foolish things of the world to shame the wise.*"

—*1 Corinthians 1:26–27 (NIV)*

SHORT TERM—SOUTH SUDAN

DOLEIB HILL, OBEL, AND WANGLEL

Port Sudan, Sudan, was the most modern port we had visited outside of the United States. Sweaters were needed only in the mornings on the beautiful, balmy spring days. We found all the old English customs here, with people dressing more formal for a late dinner and having tea three times a day. Fish was the popular dish. Like tea, we had fish three times a day—every day. It was served as a course by itself, even without bread or butter—just plain fish. We stayed at the Red Sea Hotel for four days, cleared customs, and then caught a train south to Khartoum, the capital of Sudan. It was a distance of five hundred miles and trains ran only twice a week. Unfortunately, our car and trailer were delayed clearing customs and didn't keep up with us.

On our way to the American Mission station in Khartoum, we saw large herds of camel, small donkeys, goats, black sheep, and even a few water buffalo. Our stay at the mission in Khartoum was pleasant, but rushed. We had very little time to gather supplies before leaving for the South Sudan where so little was available.

We suffered a big disappointment when discovering that Robb and Ken would not be stationed with us at Doleib Hill. Robb was assigned to Wanglel, a new station 132 miles west of Doleib Hill, where we were taking over from the Church Missionary Society of England (CMS). Here he was to build a home for Dr. Robert Gordon and his family, and Ken was sent to Atar to build a storeroom and workshop at the government school there. I was to join Ken the following season. Regardless of our suspicion that this separation would tremendously slow down our building plans, the Board of Foreign Missions felt it was best at this time.

With our steamer traveling three miles an hour up the beautiful Nile, our trip was very restful. At this time of the year the Nile was still flooded and the marsh grasses, or sudd as it is called, had torn loose and floated downstream. In the marshes along the banks, there were all sorts of flowers, including white water lilies with bright gold centers. Several hippos, large flocks of birds, and a few monkeys amused us along the way.

We thought we would be able to make the whole trip with the family in perfect health, but as was the misfortune of most new missionaries, the children became ill. We were met at the boat by Dr. Ronald Trudinger and discovered that both children had a slight attack of bronchitis. With the doctor's care, it wasn't long before they were feeling well again.

A permit issued by the Sudanese government was required to enter the closed district of the Anglo-Egyptian Upper Nile Province in the South Sudan. On January 31, 1947, we reached Malakal, the capital of the Upper Nile Province and the connecting link between the Arabic in the north and the pagan tribes of the south. We were only fifteen miles from our final destination, but those last fifteen miles proved to be most adventuresome.

The mission navy truck was loaded with our baggage and other gear as we started for Doleib Hill (site of the oldest United Presbyterian Church mission work in the South Sudan), our final destination. Due to flooding, the road was closed, so we traveled over fields and around many of the bridges which were badly in need of repair. Most of these bridges just spanned ravines that were dry and not terribly deep.

About five miles from our station, the waters of the Sobat River, a Nile tributary, had not yet receded to the river bed. We unloaded all our baggage and requested that the natives help carry our trunks to the other side of the flooded area. The natives informed us that the water was approximately two hundred yards wide and only knee-deep, and since the sun was quite hot, we thought it would feel refreshing to wade across. We took off our shoes, rolled up our pant legs, and proceeded. However, to our dismay, when we were halfway across we discovered that the tall natives' knees were considerably farther from the ground than ours.

Once across the flooded area, Rev. Bill Adair from Doleib Hill met us with a pickup truck to haul our load the final five miles. Since the truck could carry only half the load, we left the other half behind and continued on.

Our arrival at Doleib Hill was celebrated with a tasty dinner. After dinner, Bill and Robb started back to retrieve the goods that had been left behind. But, as often was the case in this land of rough terrain, it wasn't long before their truck became stubborn, and stopped. With all the energy they exerted, Bill, Robb, and the natives wore themselves out trying to push the truck. Eventually the decision was made to walk back to the station at Doleib Hill, leaving one native behind overnight to protect our goods.

Back at Doleib Hill, Bill left by bicycle to take mosquito netting and a blanket to the native watching over our bags. Robb and I returned to retrieve the truck. There was plenty of manpower available and when the natives pushed, we managed to bring the truck, badly in need of repair, back to the station. With the few old tools that we could find, we cleaned the carburetor and made gaskets out of pieces of heavy paper. By dusk we had the truck running fairly well—but it was still without lights.

As we started back to Doleib Hill I held a flashlight out the window while Robb drove over a trail of a road that we had seen only once before. Little did we know it would have been easier to travel over the expansive fields rather than attempt to navigate the incredibly muddy roads, and before long we got stuck. Robb put the truck in reverse, but the wheels did nothing but spin. Thoughts of being out in the open for the night without mosquito netting, provisions, or bedding raced through our heads.

Fortunately, a group of natives came along and, seeing our dilemma, offered to give us a push. The car started up and, instead of using the muddy road, we crossed through a field to where we left our baggage. After loading the baggage, we drove back to Doleib Hill in the dark with no lights. Safe at home we remarked, "What a day!"

Sudan, an Arabic word meaning "country of the blacks" is the largest country in Africa (one-third the size of continental United States) and is divided into provinces like Canada. According to a report written in 1956 by Edwin Fairman, D.D., titled *Facts about the Sudan*: "the nature of the country varies from desert in the north, through steppe and grassland in central Sudan, to tropical jungle in the south." The climate is tropical with two distinct seasons: a rainy season in summer and a dry season in winter. "The amount of rain and the length of the rainy season increase uniformly from the north to south . . . Average annual rainfall ranges between forty-seven inches in the extreme south to less than four inches on the Egyptian border," Fairman continued.

According to Fairman, northern Sudan in summer is one of the hottest regions in the world. In central Sudan, severe dust storms called haboobs are frequent during the rainy season. Sandstorms associated with bursts of cold air from the north occur during the dry winter months. The South Sudan is home to savannahs, forests, and swamps. "At one point the White Nile all but loses itself in a 3,000 square mile patch of papyrus and mud which the Sudanese boast is the biggest and most impenetrable swamp on earth," Edwin Fairman and Winburn Thomas state in their book, *Africa and the United Presbyterian*.[1]

Northern Sudan is mostly Moslem where Arabic is spoken and is the most developed part of the country. Here, Khartoum, the capital, is the largest modern city. In contrast, approximately one-third of the population of the Sudan lives in the south where individual tribal languages are spoken and primitive paganism is practiced.

In her journal Dolly described our new home at the Upper Nile Mission:

> *Our home and work were located in the great savannah land where wild animals still roamed and rivers were full of fish. Going south up the Nile the scenery became stark and haunting and was still tribal with drums throbbing at night as they had since the beginning of time. The swamp lands in southern Sudan were one of the largest in the world, choked full of ancient papyrus. The grasses grew ten feet high on the plains during the six months of the rainy season. These swamps were also full of mosquitoes and it was no joke that*

the hum of the mosquitoes were so loud that it drowned out the roar of the lion.

In February 1947, Dr. Alfred Heasty (an evangelist at Doleib Hill working on New Testament translations) described the condition of Doleib Hill in his building report to the Forty-second General Meeting of the Sudan Missionary Association: "The building program was slowed and ordinary repair work delayed," he stated. Floodwater prevented us from acquiring building materials and getting sand and poles from the native forest. They were unable to cut bamboo and all the brick was underwater. There were no builders or thatchers and the clinic was in need of extensive repairs.

Many problems? No, in my eyes there were many opportunities! I wanted the hard jobs, ones that challenged me and ones I had to rely on God for the answers. I would say, "If it is an easy job, let someone else do it."

After World War II, the Presbyterian Church sent out scores of missionaries and all of them needed houses, schools, and clinics. My title was mission builder, and my goal was to take the responsibility for construction away from the doctors, preachers, and teachers, freeing them to do the tasks for which they were trained. Instead of building their own homes and churches, preachers could spend their time in translation and evangelism, and instead of building hospitals and schools, doctors could heal the sick. As an industrial missionary I would pave the way for other missionaries to come.

There were no lumberyards from which to order a yard of cement or sand, no trained men to lay a corner, and no electricians. So we hired and trained Africans in all of the skills necessary for modern building. Since the natives were unable to read or write and since they spoke a mixture of five different languages, it was necessary for them to quickly learn a sign language. The easiest way to teach them was to show them.

"One of the first and hardest things we had to learn," Dolly stated in her diary, "was that we could not supply all their material needs. Nor are we meant to since their way of life is so different from ours." Yet it was difficult when, for the first time, Dolly saw an African mother, so thin that the skin seemed to be stretched over her bones. The corner of a dirty cloth thrown over the mother's one shoulder was the only covering for the baby. The baby's swollen eyes were stuck tight with pus and his face was covered with flies. Dolly's first impulse was to take the child into our home, but there were hundreds in the same condition. Our job would be to tell them of Christ's saving love and a better way of living—not just supply their material needs.

DOLEIB HILL

I had plenty to do at Doleib Hill. There was very little in the compound that wasn't badly in need of repairs. Our goal was to build two temporary houses to ease the shortage and build a school before the heavy rains set in. All this depended on whether bricks arrived in time.

First, we repaired the windmill on the compound at Doleib Hill and made it operable. Next, we repaired the launch to be ready to travel during the rains. Bees, more vicious than the American kind, were a constant problem in the buildings and on the launch. Even though we were dressed in heavy clothing and wore hats with netting over our heads, the launch was so thick with bees that they got underneath our clothing. If they were unable to get underneath, they stung right through.

One time, after an attack, I canoed back to shore from the launch and ran through the brush hoping to free myself from the bees. It didn't help. I enclosed myself in our double-screened door and had Dolly spray me down. All together I had approximately four or five hundred stingers in my clothes and about half of these had entered my arms. Riddled with holes, there was very little skin left on my forearms. I was very ill for a few hours, with vomiting, cramps, swelling, and severe pain, and was near death. Again, Dr. Trudinger came to the rescue and injected me with some form of magic antidote. Thankfully, it all cleared up in a few days and Robb and I were out at the launch again trying to get revenge. We eventually had the launch practically bee-free.

Because the housing shortage was worse than ever, we lived with Dr. Heasty in a one-room "snake house" with a sleeping veranda. Living up to its name, we killed a six-foot spitting cobra just outside the front door. Besides snakes, it was also exciting to chase and shoot crocodiles. Every few days we would hear the natives shouting out a warning that there was a crocodile in the river, and we would grab our guns and dash down to investigate.

Our first native church service at Doleib Hill was held in a brick building with thatched roof and concrete floor and preached in Shilluk, the language of one of the Nilotic tribes. Everyone sat directly on the concrete except for the foreigners; we were given pads and cushions to make the crude sitting arrangements more bearable.

Nilotic was the name given to the three tall, black, naked tribes (Shilluk, Nuer, and Dinka) who lived along the banks of the Upper Nile River where their grandfathers' fathers had lived many years ago. The Nilotics were proud of their dark skins that protected them from the hot sun, and clothes were unimportant to them. According to a booklet titled, "We Nilotics" (Vernacular Teacher Training Center, American Mission, Obel, Upper Nile Province, Anglo-Egyptian Sudan, 1951), cattle was their wealth and from the age of nine, they lived in cattle camps for three to four months each year. For the duration of the year they returned to their villages to hunt, fish, and work the fields.

These Nilotics believed in a supreme being, but it was far from our Christian concept of God. Tribal Sudanese were, for the most part, primitive pagan people who feared superstition and whose lives were inseparable from folklore, fetishism, and taboos. Witchcraft was prevalent, and the witch doctors administered the vilest concoctions with dancing and incantations.

At a village next to Doleib Hill, the Shilluks had the largest gathering ever—their annual dance in honor of the spirits of their dead ancestors. It lasted two days and two nights. They were dressed in very colorful costumes of leopard skins, white cloths, and their brightest colored sashes and headdresses. Many had their hair painted with a bright red brick dust that looked like red beads resting on their short clipped curly hair.

Their faces and ears were painted very artistically with all sorts of designs and colors, and their camel-haired white wigs really shook when they danced. Some of their hats with spangles, feathers, and bells were enough to make our womenfolk in the States envious. Most all the warriors carried at least two spears shined to perfection, a snake club, and a shield. Cowbells were tied to their ankles and the tribesmen produced surprisingly good music by blowing through huge rams' horns with gourds attached to the ends. We regretted that we were unable to tape record the music to complement the photos we had taken.

Normally our cook at Doleib Hill, the chief of the village, was quiet and humble at his work, so we were surprised to see him look ferocious as he led his tribe in dance. One of my builders had written the theme song that the natives chanted to the beat of the tom-toms. Unfortunately, our presence eventually attracted about as much attention as the dance, preventing us from seeing the dancers.

On many of our more adventurous trips in the South Sudan, Dolly and the children were left behind for their own protection. One such trip was to the Three Trees site at Atar. Ken Rasmussen planned to be stationed at Atar during the dry season to build a teacher's home and storeroom. We were to be stationed there with him the following year to construct buildings for a teachers' training school.

Ken, a few of the native workers, and I started out quite early on a typical Sudanese road and arrived at the east side of Khor Atar (*khor* is the name for a small stream that empties into the Nile). But due to the floods, its size had increased to approximately one thousand feet across. With the winds blowing and high waves washing on the shore, it was impossible to attempt crossing the khor in a dugout (a hollowed-out log) to get to our site at Three Trees on the other side. Besides, the dugout had a reputation of rolling over easily.

We waited an hour until the winds subsided and then started across. We had gone only a short distance before the waves were splashing in our faces and over the sides of the dugout. With nothing available to use, the natives cupped their hands and started to bail, but it wasn't long before we were sitting in several inches of water. Finally, we made it across the khor and hiked three miles through grassland along the shore to get to Three Trees. The grass had been burned off, and with the three large trees and the scenic view out over the khor, it was a beautiful site for a school. The next dry season we were scheduled to start construction of the thirty brick buildings for the teachers' training school at Three Trees.

Easter 1947 arrived, our first in the Sudan, but it didn't seem the same as previous Easters. Often Dolly made her own hats, but this year she wasn't donning a new one. In fact, she didn't have any new clothes, but she looked sweet in her blue dress just the same.

By the beginning of April, our building program in the Sudan was in full swing at Doleib Hill. The long Sudan/Anglo-Egyptian war and the record-breaking flood that year had caused an acute shortage of building material, making it necessary to build with local supplies. Our schedule was tight since the rainy season started in May.

The first job, nearly completed by this time, was the temporary house made of mud walls and thatched roof started by Dr. Heasty. To make the walls, a one-foot layer of mud was added daily and allowed to dry until the desired height was reached. Because of the lack of screening, the veranda was not completed. The sleeping porch, doors, and windows were screened, however, and safe from the prevalent malaria mosquito.

Our second temporary house at Doleib Hill was also nearly completed. It lacked only screening and two-by-fours for the verandas. The grass roof on the cattle barn was in poor condition so we replaced it. We also built four new thatch huts to be used at the clinic for the patients who were unable to go home after being treated. We hadn't planned on any of these projects prior to coming to the Sudan.

". . . all precedent and previous customs have been shattered to a million bits," said Dr. Albert Roode, a mission doctor at Doleib Hill, in his article titled, "Facts from the Foreign Field," for the *Christian Union Herald* (Presbyterian weekly publication). Dr. Roode continued:

> When Ted arrived, since there was so much building to do and most of the dry season had passed, there was need of drastic action. Workmen were hired right and left; two shifts a day were started and strangest of all, Ted did more work than any two workmen together. . . .

> One morning a man came to the clinic hardly able to walk, but a complete examination failed to find the cause. He had some cuts on his back over the site of the pain which he had made to let out the pain, but that had failed to relieve him. After much questioning, I found out that he had been digging the foundation of the school building and of his own accord decided to race with Ted. He kept up with Ted and Ted tells

me he removed a lot of dirt in a short time. I understand the contest ended with a draw, the only difference being that Ted went to work as usual the next morning whereas the native came to the clinic.[2]

Our most urgent need was for a schoolhouse at Doleib Hill. Part of Dr. Roode's house had been used as the old school, but at the time, all we had was a two-room building of mud and thatch to accommodate a hundred boys in five different grades for the beginning of school the first of May. We started building an eighteen-by-eighty-foot-long, three-room brick building for the boys. The walls were brick red with cement floors and a thatch roof. The ends were circular (more in keeping with native architecture) and much easier to thatch than a square building. I only had one worker who had experience laying brick, and he was trying to teach his skills to four more workers. The workmen did not understand what I meant by a straight line or a level surface since they had never seen a plumb line or a level before. Needless to say, each worker had to be supervised constantly.

We needed to build a garage for our trucks (a one-and-a-half ton Ford and a three-ton Studebaker) before the rains came.

*Natives mixing mud
with bare feet*

Due to scarcity of material, the garage would be built from a composite of different types of mud, cow dung, grass, and water and mixed by the natives in a large pit with their bare feet. It had to be just the right consistency.

We were told there was no sand available near Doleib Hill and that the government had been hauling its supply three hundred miles upriver by barge. Thankfully, Bill discovered a good sandbank only four miles from our station, and in about two weeks, we hauled seventy-five tons of sand to our site. When the government heard of our site, it indicated it would have to investigate and approve it, but we had already hauled enough for our needs for the year. We also had two crews of men hauling gravel (limestone nuggets) by dugout from along the banks of the river.

In order to purchase brick for our school we had to travel forty miles over very poor roads. On one of our trips to inquire about buying brick, we saw a herd of giraffes and stopped to study them. Two of the more curious bulls strolled over within one hundred feet of us. Unfortunately, we didn't have our cameras. We did have our guns, but since it cost a hundred pounds or more for a license for each giraffe, we didn't bother to use them. I had a resident license which allowed me to shoot animals such as antelope (including a large type called *tiang*), water buffalo, and gazelle, but the elephant and giraffe required a special license.

We were fortunate to get the brick, but compared to brick in the States, it was a very poor grade, of various shapes and sizes, and very difficult to lay. This explained why most of the living quarters here were made of mud. Eventually we arranged to have the brick transported by sailboat twenty-five miles down the Sobat River.

Native women did most of the heavy work at Doleib Hill. Since water for the mortar had to be carried about a quarter of a mile from the river, there was a continuous train of women

Pit saw cutting lumber for frames

making their way between the palms with five-gallon gas tins full of water on top their heads. The women used a round "doughnut" between the load and their heads to soften the burden. Through years of carrying heavy loads in this fashion, these women had developed extremely strong neck muscles. In fact, most could carry twice the weight on her head that one man could carry with both arms. We used approximately four or five hundred gallons of water per day, and with the extreme heat and dryness, it evaporated very quickly.

We had no lumber for school doors and windows at this time, so we used a pit saw (a six-foot, two-man, cross-cut saw) to rip two dead eucalyptus trees into boards for the frames. The trees were about fifty feet tall and fifteen inches in diameter, so there was enough wood for fifteen windows and three door frames.

The logs used to make the trusses for the school building were cut in the woods about twenty-five miles away. The rest of the framework was made of bamboo which was raised and cut on the compound. Our supply of bamboo had to be cut ahead of time and soaked in the river to prevent the wood borers and white ants (termites) from devouring it so quickly.

The rope we used to tie the bamboo together was made of a fine grade of grass that grew on the plains all around Doleib Hill and usually could be purchased at the village. But for this project we were using far more rope than the people had to sell, so we made our own. The workers took the grass, laid it in damp sand, rolled it between their hands, and twisted it into a grass rope. This rope was used to tie the grass to the trusses on the thatched roof.

Normally by this time of year, all the grasses would have dried off and been burned. But due to the flooded area at the mouth of the Sobat River, we still had plenty of grass that was green and were able to cut and haul enough for all our thatching needs.

Because of the intense heat in the afternoons it was the custom to work from 6:00 A.M. to 2:00 P.M., with no one working after two in the afternoon. But with the pressing need to complete the building before the rains, we now had a second shift of workers starting at 2:00 P.M. and working until 6:00 P.M.—the beginning of the twelve-hour day! It was something unheard of in this country.

The news of a crash of a large (for that time) DC–3 passenger plane ten miles south of Malakal was an exciting event at Doleib Hill. One evening around dark, we had a phone call from the local airport in Malakal asking if we had seen a plane that was a half hour overdue. Actually, our houseboy had seen it flying very low a short time after sunset. It wasn't long before we received word by native messenger from the captain of the plane saying they had been forced to land, belly in the grass.

Except for a few minor injuries, all passengers were safe. We notified the airport and started out to the crash site by truck with the messenger acting as our guide. About five miles from our station, the guide instructed us to leave the road and follow the light of a large fire in the distance. At first we thought it was a grass fire, and drove a couple of miles over *dura* (millet; a grain that was used almost exclusively in their diet with corn) fields and Sudan grasses nearly as high as the truck. But eventually we could see the fire and realized it was the plane in flames.

The starboard motor had failed when the plane was only nine minutes from its destination, but since the failed motor was the one that generated the power for the radio, the pilot could not notify the airport. The pilot had crash-landed with the wheels up and the plane burst into flames on impact.

The plane was carrying twenty-one passengers and four officers, the youngest only six weeks old and the daughter of missionary parents from southern Rhodesia. Amazingly, everyone was able to escape before the fire became too great and luckily there were no explosions. Only half the luggage was salvaged and many passports were lost.

Local natives with their spears, beads, and painted faces appeared on the scene within fifteen minutes after the crash. Knowing little of life in central Africa, the frightened passengers perhaps thought they would be used for stew meat by morning! But it wasn't long before the passengers realized the natives were friendly.

After our truck arrived at the crash site, I took all the passengers to the rest house at Malakal. Since the insurance company was located in South Africa and would never bother to salvage the plane, it became part of the mission property. Even though the center of the plane was completely burned, the wings and tail were intact, enabling us to bring them back to Doleib Hill piece by piece.

I live by the motto, "Waste not, want not." Some of the aluminum salvaged from the plane was used for sink tops, ladders, tables, and chairs in the temporary houses at Doleib Hill. The heavy rods were used for reinforcement of some of

Ken Rasmussen bringing in the fuselage

the buildings. Using ingenuity, I constructed a coffee table with the round aluminum nose of the airplane as its center.

By May, spring had arrived in the Sudan, but it was quite different from spring in the United States. Instead of a relief from cold weather, we were looking forward to a break in the heat. The fruit trees had just completed one crop and were coming out in full blossom again.

The "R.P.M." boys (the builders who were on the job: Rasmussen, Pollock, and McLaughlin) felt that the work was progressing quite well. Ken Rasmussen was still at Atar building a storeroom and workshop in preparation for the thirty buildings I would erect the next dry season, and Robb McLaughlin was nearly finished with the temporary house at Wanglel.

The building program progressed satisfactorily at Doleib Hill, but we did not finish our school as soon as we expected. Due to a delayed shipment from Khartoum, we ran out of cement. When the cement finally arrived, we were able to start school as scheduled with the boys using temporary rooms for their classes.

We laid a cornerstone for our first building on April 25, 1947, but since there were no corners in this round-ended building, we laid it in a doorway. This was the one and only time we laid a cornerstone during our construction in the South Sudan.

The Shilluk minister of our local church led a short dedication service. There were 130 boys in our school that year (48 of them were first-year boys), and many of them lived on the compound in our school boy huts. We did not have the peace and quiet that we had when we first arrived at the Hill, but it was rather nice with boys underfoot, singing their native songs in the evenings. What a racket the dried palm leaves made when the boys tried to knock the tagua nuts off the Doleib palms with long bamboo poles. Their excited laughter followed when one of the nuts dropped.

Many crocodiles made their homes in the Sobat River, and we feared for the school boys' safety when they bathed. To ease our fears, we built a crocodile barricade of woven bamboo tied together with wire to protect the boys. The river was low at this time, which made it easier for us to put the barricade up along its edge until the rainy season returned.

The boys were quite a study. Some wore the snow-white native muslin cloths that the mission had given them tied in a knot over their left shoulder (the closest thing they had to a school uniform), while others dyed theirs red with brick dust. Then there were many of them who wore only the outfits that nature presented them, embellishing with a few brightly colored beads.

A hunting trip supplied us with an oribi (small tan-colored antelope), two tiang, and a waterbuck that we donated for the celebration of the completion of the school. At the end of May, we had the big feed for the workmen. A few of the workers started the food prep in the morning, and, using dura, simsim oil (sesame seed oil), onions, and salt, they cooked meat and made a stew. A planting dance for the surrounding villages preceded the feast and there was much merriment.

Robb McLaughlin was working at Wanglel among the Nuers (one of the Nilotic tribes) with just a few tools on loan to him, waiting for his to arrive from the United States. When the tools arrived, I decided to deliver them to him. To do so meant driving over one of the worst roads imaginable.

Not surprisingly, the first night on my way to Wanglel, I got stuck in the mud. With no Motel 6 waiting with the light on, I was lucky to have my bedroll and mosquito net along to use for my outdoor accommodations. Upon awakening in the morning, it was a shock to discover that the strange noise over-head was a flock of buzzards, or the African equivalent, circling over me and excited for their next meal. I knew I was hungry, but I didn't think I was that far gone!

After having a can of beans for breakfast, I was back on the road. A stretch of rough, wet road that obviously had been

The R.P.M.: Ted Pollock, Robb McLaughlin, and Ken Rasmussen

trampled by a herd of elephants was a challenge, but I eventually arrived at Wanglel. With the few tools Robb had and
nothing but native materials—mud, poles, bamboo, and
grasses—he was doing a respectable job of house building.
Wanglel's location opened up exposure to a large number of
people, but the compound needed work and the buildings
were temporary.

Another day, another adventure! Two ladies, a nurse and a
teacher, arrived at Doleib Hill on their way back to Nasir
Station (mission station on the Sobat River). They were told
there would be no province steamer going to Nasir before some
time in June. Since the road had been reported open for a week,
we decided to try to get the girls through by truck. As Sudan
roads go, the first half of the trip was not bad, but it wasn't
long before we ran into swamplands. The original road was
swamp that had not drained, but the narrow strip of higher
ground along the river's edge was dry. We followed this strip of
ground by watching for tire tracks that had been made by a
truck passing through earlier in the week. In one section, we
came to a dense forest and undergrowth. It looked like we
could not possibly penetrate it, but we continued on with the
vines and branches rubbing the sides of the truck.

Birds of all sizes and descriptions surrounded us. Halfway
through the forest, we came to a breathtakingly beautiful green
valley in which a thousand or more cattle were grazing. The
Nuer tribes had temporary villages set up surrounded by high
lion guards made of thorny brush to protect their cattle camps.

Back in the forest the wild animals were numerous: oribi,
gazelles, and waterbuck. Suddenly one of the ladies cried,
"Look, a lion!" Sure enough, about a hundred yards from the
truck, lying under a tree, was a female lion. I stopped the truck,
got my .300 Savage gun, and climbed on top the cab. When I
stopped, the lioness jumped up, ran a few yards, halted, turned
sideways, then looked back.

That's when animals, as well as people, make their mistake. This was a chance for a perfect shot. I remembered what Dr. Heasty had told me about sizing up your animal and aiming. I fired. The lioness lunged into the air and was stunned as she came back to the ground. She walked a few steps toward us and dropped. My men informed me that the male had run back into the brush, but I knew to be careful of a wounded animal. Sometimes they charge when you get close.

We waited a few minutes and watched for the male to return, but nothing happened. We got down from the cab and walked forward. One of the men threw a clump of dirt at the lioness, but she didn't move. I had shot her in the shoulder, just behind the front leg. We still didn't want to take any chances, so I took two more shots. One hit the center of the head and the other went into the shoulder. We watched for the male to return. My three men and I dragged the female back to the truck, skinned, cleaned, and stretched the hide. The male never reappeared.

"I killed a lion!"—Jean Maxwell and Marian Farquhar

A little later we saw some waterbucks and I shot one to take to the school boys at Nasir to replenish their meat supply. I had greatly enjoyed my short visit with the folks at the Nasir Station and made the eight-hour uneventful trip back to Doleib Hill the next day. From that day forth, I was considered a great hunter in the eyes of the Shilluk and was made a Shilluk warrior. I had killed a lion!

This lion was only the third animal I had shot in my lifetime. I had no experience shooting guns prior to coming to Africa. The retelling of this story is sometimes unsettling to animal rights proponents, but it is an accurate description of survival for the people of Africa in the 1940s. Our work in these days was pioneering, with much of our time spent just surviving.

Some of the strangest things happened in this land of sunshine. One incident at Doleib Hill that was difficult for us to understand was the evacuation of our home due to the diminutive insect—the ant! It was around dusk one evening when these insects came in one by one, from different corners of the house, to check if there was anything appetizing to eat. Evidently they discovered what they were looking for because, a short time later, great hordes of crawling creatures covered one side of the veranda. First we got out the flit gun and then the DDT, but they crawled up our legs and over the flit gun and continued to invade.

The large fighters, sometimes a half inch long, had big heads with pincers. When they took hold, the head came off if you pulled too hard. (Army ants are notorious for eating any animal that gets in its way, including snakes and lizards, and even the lion has respect for this insect. The only exception is the anteater, which feeds upon them.)

We checked to be sure the ants hadn't taken up residence with the children on the sleeping porch and decided to put pans of water under the legs of their beds to prevent the ants from climbing up. While we were getting the water, Penny Sue cried out. In those few seconds, the ants had attacked from the other side of the house and crawled into the children's beds. It left us no alternative but to take the family to the neighbors. Dr. Al Roode and I got blow torches and burned the ants by the thousands, but they still kept coming, regiment after regiment.

By morning the ants had all cleared out without leaving a trace. Several nights later, when we were sound asleep and least expecting them, they returned. With the beds sitting in pans of water, we thought we were ready, but they outsmarted us. They cleverly connected their bodies to make bridges over the water which enabled their fellow comrades to march up onto the beds. When the army ants moved in, there was only one thing to do—move out!

The R.P.M. UnLtd. was busier than ever. I explained earlier that the R.P.M. referred to Rasmussen, Pollock, and McLaughlin. But what about the "Unlimited"? Since everything in English territory was labeled "Limited" instead of "Company," like in the United States, we three agreed the word "Unlimited" better described how we felt about our mission in Africa.

One job on the compound at Doleib Hill was tearing down a concrete blockhouse, the first permanent house built there in 1912. For some unknown reason, the ground had cracked wide open underneath the house, causing the walls to split and the house to be condemned. However, the building material was still usable so we decided to salvage it to build a new house. The blockhouse lived up to its name of snake villa until the very end. The day the last of the blocks were being removed, a large seven-foot Egyptian cobra stuck out an inquisitive head to see what the disruption was. Not only was the house a thing of the past, but when Dr. Heasty got his gun and shot the cobra, the snake was too.

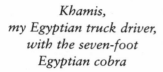

Khamis,
my Egyptian truck driver,
with the seven-foot
Egyptian cobra

About this same time there was another snake encounter. Dolly had gone to the garden to pick some eggplant, and as she lowered her hand to grab one of the purple-skinned vegetables, she was startled to see a viper. The viper, the most deadly poisonous snake of the Sudan, was known for being lazy and didn't move until some of the men came with a shotgun and made Dolly the proud owner of a souvenir hide.

On the same day as the snake encounters, natives appeared and asked us to come quickly with a gun. A hippopotamus had been harpooned and chained, but they were unable to kill it. (The hippos here weighed around three tons and the fat on them made wonderful shortening.) Although it snorted and fought and raced up and down the river, the hippo never reappeared long enough to get a good shot, so the natives continued the fight. After following the hippo all night, they finally shot it the following day about ten miles up the Nile. The snake and hippo excitement this particular day was more like most imagine life to be in Africa; however, much of the time life there was very peaceful.

By now, the R.P.M. UnLtd. had finished the second temporary house at Doleib Hill. Reverend Bill and Martha Adair moved in and eased the housing shortage a bit.

The R.P.M. named the two trucks used for the building program "the Jerk," a jerky old Ford, and the "Stubble Jumper," a Studebaker that seemed to jump over stubble left on the dura fields. This bit of humor, I'm afraid, was purely American, because the British folks never seemed to quite understand it, even when the titles were explained to them.

The R.P.M. was very busy with maintenance work on the original buildings and was preparing for a shop where doors and windows could be built for the teachers' training school the next dry season.

When the rains came, the Sudan was transformed into a place of great beauty. The corn was in tassel and every color and type of flower imaginable was in bloom. The rainy season continued into late August, but we remained just as busy as ever.

With the coming of the rains, the river rose steadily. And as the river rose, the steamers came. In July we saw our first Gambela steamer that went up the Sobat to Gambela, Ethiopia. It traveled once a month during high water. The flooded roads to Malakal had been closed for some time and we anxiously awaited a shipment of cement on the steamer. The steamers had no schedules and were just as likely to arrive at midnight as any other time. We had asked the native workmen to come help load and unload at the sound of the boat whistle.

When the first boat whistle sounded one evening, all the workmen came running. Some traveled for two to three miles. Unfortunately, it was not the Gambela steamer but the

Steamer at Doleib Hill that had no schedule

governor taking a group of Nuer chiefs up the river for a meeting. That same evening another steamer came into view, but, as we later found out, it wasn't the Gambela either. Just as we were leaving church on Sunday, a third steamer whistled. It was another boatload of Nuer chiefs and workmen. But each time our workmen heard the whistles they were "Johnny on the spot." When the fourth boat whistled, thinking surely this would be the Gambela, they all rushed to the boat landing to find it was a government steamer stopping to make a pickup. We were afraid that it was getting to be like the boy who hollered, "Wolf!" once too often.

The following day, just as we were getting ready for bed, a fifth boat arrived, and we were all greatly relieved that it was the Gambela. Yes, the workmen came out one more time, but the cement that they had come to unload had been delayed and was not on the steamer. So we gave a sigh of relief that the waiting game was over for another month. Life here was unscheduled and you quickly learned to be flexible.

We had completed the repairs on our workshop at Doleib Hill and had it in working condition. It was reminiscent of a workshop back in the early 1800s and collected just about as many sightseers and old chiefs from the villages as an old-time grocery store. Usually they sat around and marveled at the things that could be done here, gave advice, and just talked.

We had a forge in one corner of our shop and a large workbench in the center. All the work was done by hand, down to ripping the logs and sawing and planing the lumber. For several weeks we built desks and benches for the school and made an ox yoke for the pair of oxen broken to work. Doleib Hill was too muddy to use the trucks at this time, so I put a long reach on our car trailer and hitched up the oxen. Not only did we use the trailer to haul bricks, sand, gravel, and materials to the new site where we planned to build the women's boardinghouse at Doleib Hill, but the children had an enjoyable ride in the empty trailer on the return trips.

One day Penny Sue came in for lunch and asked very solemnly, "Daddy, would you like to have nine cows?"

"Where," I asked her, "would I get nine cows?"

"Well, there is a boy out here who said he wants to marry me and he said he would give you nine cows for me, but I don't want to live with them because all they have to eat is black dura, and I do not think I would like to eat just black dura all the time," she said, getting more excited by the minute for fear I would prefer the nine cows to her. The Shilluk social custom of purchasing their wives with cattle was being tested by one of the schoolboys and Penny took the teasing quite seriously.

Every once in a while we got a reminder that we were in Africa. On mornings when the ground was still damp, there were a large number of lion tracks. The lion tracks seldom came close to the buildings since most of the lions were across the river.

One evening after dark, Dolly, the children, and I were returning from the ladies' house carrying a lantern when we noticed a brown animal walking about twenty yards to the left of us. At first we paid little attention to it and thought perhaps it was a dog. Wrong! As we raised the lantern we soon realized that those husky shoulders strutting up and down in the dura field belonged to a female lion.

Immediately I remembered that a lion always attacks from behind and never to turn your back. Ed and Penny started running to the house, and a fear emerged in Dolly and me that the lion might attack the children from behind while they ran. We stopped to look, and the lioness paused and returned our stare. Thank goodness, the lioness turned and very slowly sauntered away. Dolly and the children's excitement soared to think they had seen a real live lion in the wilds of Africa!

One evening I wrote a newsletter home describing the nights on Doleib Hill:

NIGHT LIFE ON THE HILL

Life is somewhat different here. When your work for the day is through there are no movies or church socials to attend. You can't go to the drug store for a coke or some ice cream. We have no radio and we don't get an evening paper. However, after a day out in the hot sun you are usually ready for bed by 9:00 P.M. We sleep out on a screened veranda all year round. You can lay there and look at the stars, and the moon shines in on you through the Doleib palms while you listen to the drummers playing sophisticated rhythms on native drums in the village. . . . In the rainy season many of the boats stop at night and we get up and go to the landing to unload them, often being serenaded by the lions and hyenas across the river.

Mail day was an exciting time for the mission folks on Doleib Hill. Mail traveled very slowly but was always greatly appreciated no matter how long it took to arrive, often up to two months. Every two weeks a steamer brought mail from Khartoum to Malakal. From there a runner (a native man who walked about thirty-four miles round trip) delivered our mailbag to us. With the many circulars and packages included, these bags averaged around one hundred pounds. If the mail happened to arrive before we had eaten our supper, we waited until all of it was read. Who wanted to eat if there was news from home? During the dry season we were able to get a truck into Malakal to pick up our mail more often, but that lasted for only five to six months of the year.

Air service direct to Malakal was available and speedier, and, of course, more expensive. We had received some letters from the United States in only one week. New air letters that arrived on the scene about this time provided less space for writing but had speedier delivery. They were ideal for writing to the family, and only cost ten cents for stamp and letterform.

Before we left the United States for the Sudan some people asked, "But why do you want to go to that Godforsaken land?" At first glance it did look a little forsaken: the native people wore little clothing, had very little food, and lived in tiny mud huts. But after we were there just a short time and saw some of the most breath-taking sunsets over the river reflected in the water, and saw the beautiful and so plentiful colorful birds and animals, it struck me that it was not Godforsaken but rather "God's own country."

Many of the tribes' social customs and ways of living and dressing resembled the Old Testament stories in the Bible. For instance, when a man died, one of their social customs was that his wife automatically became the wife of her husband's brother, even if the brother was already married. Of course, Christians are changing the customs, but it was very difficult when you had to work against many old traditions.

Dolly's journal revealed her thoughts on God's forsaken land:

God had lavished as much beauty on the Sudan as he had on America with brilliance of tropical flowers, soft meandering rivers, millions of bright plumed birds, and unbelievable large fish.

Even the pagans of the Upper Nile were not Godforsaken; they had just never heard the story of salvation. Did you ever try to tell the story of God's saving love to someone who had never even heard the name of Jesus? Where can you begin and where do you end since it may be the only time he will ever hear it?

Our life in the Sudan was a lot like pioneering in the 1800s back in the States. We depended on our garden for most of our food. Since Dolly didn't know the language and couldn't do much teaching or preaching, she was put in charge of the garden. It consisted of five acres of fruits and vegetables. Communicating with the men who worked in the garden was a problem, but she learned a few words of Shilluk and they knew a few words of English. For the most part, they managed quite well.

We had a wonderful supply of fresh vegetables the year round. During the dry season, crops had to be irrigated and didn't do quite as well as during the rains. We were able to raise nearly everything except for Irish potatoes, and these we could often buy in Malakal—at a price. Sweet potatoes served us just as well. If we wanted peanut butter, all we had to do was go to the garden, dig the peanuts, shell them, roast them in the oven, and put them through the food chopper seven times to get them smooth. We added a little salt and then enjoyed a delicious peanut butter sandwich!

Of course, we had to bake our own bread, using ground whole wheat flour that had to have the bran sifted out—and the weevils (which were included when purchased). Weevils multiplied very quickly in the tropical climate so we had to sift the flour constantly. We bought our coffee beans, but they too had to be sorted, roasted, and ground. For cereals, we raised and ground our own corn and could buy wheat at certain times of the year that also had to be cleaned, roasted, and ground. Nothing was as good as fruit picked ripe from the tree: tangerines, oranges, grapefruit, papayas, limes, custard apples, mangoes, and bananas—all delicious. Most of the native folks cared little for the ordinary vegetables we grew in our garden since they raised dura.

The natives used a heavy-handled hoe with a wide blade on the front for digging. Except for this hoe, the ground was never plowed, but it did well in most places since it was very fertile. Although we had hoes in our mission garden, the locals preferred to use their short handled version so they could squat while hoeing. Amazingly, the natives could work all day in this squatting position. Little holes were punched into the soil with

Five-foot Nile perch

long poles called planting sticks, and seeds were planted in each hole. Extra vegetables were sent to a Greek merchant in town to sell, enabling us to earn enough money to buy a lathe and a water pump to irrigate the garden.

Our water system consisted of two big stone jars called zeers balanced over two buckets. Water was dipped directly from the river and poured into these large clay jars in order to filter out the mud and fish. Then it was boiled and cooled before drinking.

Some of the Sudanese were willing to sell us milk, but due to different customs, it wasn't as simple as it sounded. They couldn't understand why we gave them a perfectly clean container for our milk since they preferred to leave a bit of the old milk in the container to allow it to sour properly—like yogurt. And they could not understand why Dolly objected if they held the container over a dung fire to catch the smoke. I liked my sausages smoked, but not my milk! Often they would dilute the milk but then deny it, until one day I found a tadpole in the milk. Their answer, "Well, didn't the cow drink from the swamp?"

Our cooking was done over an open grate with charcoal. We had kerosene stoves for baking, but kerosene had to be imported and was very expensive. We needed a six-month supply of some of the imported goods like flour and sugar since the roads closed during the rainy season.

There were a few kerosene refrigerators on the compound at this time, but we weren't fortunate enough to have one. The other mission families took care of us, though, by keeping our meat refrigerated. It never had to be kept for long since game was so plentiful, and with nineteen folks on the station, we used it quickly. Besides, the R.P.M. boys shot a gazelle or tiang once or twice a week, and, what wasn't used, was given to the workmen and schoolboys. Their only means of getting meat was with their spears, and with the swiftness of these animals, it was a tricky maneuver.

Some of the natives tried to make money by catching and selling baby animals. Our children purchased two baby gazelles and an oribi and enjoyed feeding their pets with a bottle and nipple. One day the natives brought in two baby ostriches, but knowing they would grow to be six and seven feet tall, we were fearful they would eat us out of house and home and decided against them.

In September we were on the lazy Nile en route to Khartoum to get materials for the next building season. There was nothing to do but take life easy for a few days. We managed to get on the *Omdurman* again, a very slow going, wood-burning paddle wheel steamer that stopped two to three times a day to refuel. At each stop, men spent from two to four hours carrying wood piled on top their heads and shoulders that was needed for burning.

The *Omdurman* towed three passenger barges and one cargo barge, and I especially found it fascinating to watch the Arab or Sudanese passengers on these second- and third-class barges. Wrapped in two or three cloths of the brightest colors, they walked to the front of the barge and cooked their own food. The Arab ladies especially reminded me of roving gypsy bands in the way they killed and cooked their chickens and roasted their corn and other food over little charcoal fires built in old sofia (Shell oil) tins.

As the *Omdurman* pulled into a wood station one day, loading appeared to be going along well . . . at least until we got stuck on a sand bar at the bottom of the river. We spun, and spun, and churned the water with no success. After two long hours, we were still in the same spot and began to think that we would have to stay there until the next boat came along in two weeks. The engineer finally instructed some of the men to take a cable attached to a wench and swim out and hook it onto a stout tree. They turned the wench until it jarred us loose and allowed the back end of the boat to swing out into the middle of the river, enabling us to back up and be on our way again.

As part of the trip north, we decided to take a two-week vacation near the Red Sea, in what we thought would be a cooler climate. We got to Khartoum at its worse, with temperatures ranging from 110 to 115 degrees. Imagine, we came north looking for cooler weather! It wasn't long before we missed the "cool" weather back at Doleib Hill. At least there it sometimes dropped down to eighty degrees. Most folks took their vacation during the hot, dry season, but, that being the builder's busiest time, we had to take ours during the rainy season.

One advantage to vacation during the rainy season was to get away from the snakes that found a natural haven under our house. Except for the slight rise at Doleib Hill, the South Sudan is swamp lowland, and all the water drained down the hill and covered the land. The snakes preferred the dry existence under our home, at our front and back doors, and sometimes even on our veranda if the door had been left ajar. We killed an average of two to four snakes a day.

Close by in the town of Omdurman, we had the privilege of visiting our Boys' Boarding and Day School. It was interesting to see how self-sufficient small boys of nine and ten could be. They made their own beds and were proficient in doing their own laundry.

We also had the privilege to visit and meet all of our workers in the Girls' Boarding and Day School in Khartoum North. Here the girls often had to care for tiny babies and, at the time of our visit, they were caring for a two-year-old girl and a six-week-old orphan boy who had been abandoned on the street. The government hospital took in the boy and turned him over to the girls for care. The older girls in the school took turns caring for the babies, with supervision from the missionaries. (This Girls' Boarding and Day School later became just a day school when the Nile Theological College took over the use of their boarding facilities. Later, in 1994, we renovated a building into two offices and two classrooms here, and in 1996, we added a library to the Nile Theological College.)

After a few days back in Khartoum, we went by train to Erkowit, a Sudan railways rest camp up in the Red Sea hills. In America we would call it a hotel or resort. The vegetation around Erkowit resembled our desert states, with cactus trees and little else. We spent a couple of quiet weeks there, and then we returned to Khartoum where I purchased materials for the next building program in the south. After scouring Khartoum I managed to get everything I needed except for a few items. Screening, one of the most important items in the South Sudan, proved completely unavailable in a small mesh. Bathtubs were another could-not-get item, but showers could always be substituted.

One day someone mentioned an abandoned American airbase at Wadi Sedina, about fifteen miles outside of Khartoum. I was able to retrieve some used soil pipe (cast iron), commodes, and packing for pipes that were American articles the British had no use for. It was just what I wanted.

On our return trip up the Nile, we were more fortunate to get on an oil-burning steamer, the *Nasir*, enabling us to make the trip in four days. When we reached Malakal, we were informed that there wouldn't be a province steamer going up the Sobat to Doleib Hill for another month. That was a long time to wait since we were only fifteen miles from home. We called Doleib Hill to inquire, and Ken indicated they would be able to get only halfway by truck to pick us up because of an area where the water was several feet deep. Eventually we managed to hire an old Model A Ford—with no windshield— to take us the first half of the trip.

For most of the way the grass on the road was higher than the car, and the grass seeds were just ripe enough to blow off and hit us hard in the face when we drove over them. At least we could keep our eyes shut, but the poor driver had a terrible time. The only way we could see the direction of the road was to follow the footpath that the natives had worn down walking to and from town. We finally reached the water holes, waded knee-deep, and found our truck from Doleib Hill waiting on the other side. By the time we arrived home, it was dusk and we had many mosquito bites. The chloroquine we took to prevent malaria must have worked since none of us became ill.

After we returned to Doleib Hill, the materials that we bought in Khartoum started to arrive. One day we received word that the floor ballot (similar to tile in the States) that I had ordered for the houses at the teachers' training school had arrived. The twenty-six tons of floor ballot and two tons of lumber were being delivered to us by a government steamer on the Sobat River. Since natives were not to be rushed, I knew it would be a real challenge when the captain insisted that the materials be unloaded as quickly as possible. I told the workers the situation and challenged them to do their best.

Before long we heard what sounded like a celebration down by the boat—seventy men and women singing and laughing at the top of their voices. The women carried the bundles of tiles on their heads; the men carried a bundle in each hand. They moved at great speed up one gang plank and down the other and made the bundles appear to be featherweight. Dolly tried to lift one of these bundles from the ground and couldn't make it budge. And the interesting part of this event was that they sang—without knowing the meaning of the words—"Joshua Fought the Battle of Jericho!" In just forty-five minutes, they had the entire twenty-five tons of tile and two tons of lumber unloaded!

There was a reason these workers knew this tune. Apparently, one day Ken had sung "Joshua" and the men imitated the tune and copied the words as they sounded to them. From that day on Ken's name became "Ginnyco," the closest the natives came to saying Jericho. There was a time later when Ken was singing "Joshua" and the workers said, "That is the song we sing!" After that, every time they had an especially hard job, this was their theme song.

Ken and Robb had done a grand job on the ladies' house at Doleib Hill while we were on holiday. The house was nearly ready for the roof but couldn't be completed because we lacked cement and screening. We had received word that cement had been shipped from Khartoum, but screening was still a problem. Despite all the obstacles at Doleib Hill, several temporary houses had been built, the windmill repaired, thatch huts for a clinic set up, and work started on a three-room brick school building.

OBEL TEACHER'S TRAINING SCHOOL

Building the teachers' training school for the village teachers during the dry seasons of 1947 and 1948 meant so much to the people of the South Sudan. We worked directly with the Anglo-Egyptian government and they welcomed our work. In fact, they not only paid for three-quarters of the costs of our schools and our salary, but we traveled first class for one-fourth fare on all British railways and steamers. All our plans had to be inspected and approved by Anglo-Egyptian government officials.

It was decided that Three Trees, the original site for the school, was too small and another site had to be chosen. The new location, situated on some beautiful seventy-five acres, three miles from Doleib Hill, was known by the natives as Obel, after the old village that used to be located there. Not only were boats visible going up and down the Sobat River from this site, but we could also see steamers traveling the Nile about a mile away in the distance.

The completed school at Obel would consist of approximately forty-five buildings and two missionary residences. These buildings would be able to accommodate 180 teachers, teacher trainees, and blue boys (small boys who wore blue cloths—a piece of fabric thrown over the left shoulder—furnished by the government in Atar, on whom the teacher trainees would practice their teaching skills). Most of the buildings would be small compared to buildings in America, consisting of only one story and one or two rooms. Red, burnt brick would be used for the outside, with mud brick on the inside. The roofs would be constructed of sealag (a small, straight hardwood tree resistant to insect infestation) poles, bamboo, and grass thatch. (The mission residences were different in that they were red brick with metal roofs.)

The bricks were to be laid in mud mortar with cement pointing, since cement was expensive and almost impossible to obtain at this time. The insides of the buildings were to be plastered with a sand coat (the same as the natives used on their own home), using bare hands for trowels. The ends of the buildings would be circular, making them easier to thatch. The doors, window frames, and shutters would be the luxurious parts of our buildings—made of beautiful solid mahogany. It is the most common African lumber (just as yellow pine is in the States) and is valuable since mahogany is white ant-proof in this land of termites.

The buildings in this school would serve different purposes: two classrooms for the teacher trainees; a chapel; eight teacher trainees' dormitories, with room for four teachers in each; thirteen small boys' dormitories, each accommodating ten small boys; four married teachers' houses (the staff for teaching the trainees); and six practice schools of two rooms each that would be built of just mud. The remaining eleven buildings would be smaller for shops, storerooms, and a clinic.

A short worship service was held every morning before work and sometimes up to seven hundred locals came out in hopes of being hired to be one of our workers. I always told them, "I want good strong warriors. The work is hard." In order to be chosen as a worker you had to be able to pick up a ninety-eight pound anvil from the ground, set it on a bench, and put it on the ground again.

At the time, we had 227 men and women in our crew of workers and some walked as far as six and seven miles to get to work. They were allowed to ride on the trucks to and from Doleib Hill and, to them, this was a great treat since many had never ridden anything in their lives. At first it was complicated because all of them wanted to ride at the same time, and, unfortunately, a three-ton truck could not haul two hundred people. But they piled on, climbing over each other to claim their spot, covering every square inch of the hood, fenders, roof, and running board so that the truck was hardly visible. I had to persuade them that the truck couldn't possibly haul that many riders and that only those who lived the farthest could ride. We left Doleib Hill before sunrise and arrived at Obel just as the

Workers piled on the truck

sun rose over the river, making it a perfect setting for worship
and prayers held each morning before work began.

Each day as I arrived at Obel to begin work, I heard
singing, and it was always the same song. I soon discovered
that this was the workers' way of warning everyone that the
boss was coming and to get busy. Eventually it was disclosed
that the song was written by one of my thatchers about me, Jal
Dong OK, and my unusual haircut! Jal Dong was a title used
by the natives in respect for an elderly person. The name OK
was earned when one day the thatcher was trying to teach me
some Shilluk and, getting my tongue twisted around the
words, I would just say, "OK." After enough OKs, the name
stuck and has followed me through generations in the Sudan
and Ethiopia today.

Many of the workers lived far away and were unaccus-
tomed to eating their first meal until the day's work was
finished, around 2:00 P.M. Eventually we started to serve one
meal on the job to give the workers more energy. There were
four girls who cooked the food native style and by 9:00 A.M.
there was a wonderful aroma that wafted over the station. Out
in the open beneath a tree a fire was built under a large oil
drum set. Water and dura were cooked and stirred with a large
wooden paddle until the mixture was the consistency of a
sticky pudding. This was then dished into gourds for over two
hundred workers. Four or five gathered around each gourd,
and with their fingers, the workers rolled the mixture into a
ball about the size of an egg and gently slipped it into their
mouths. When we were fortunate enough to shoot a tiang,
meat was added to the mixture, plus simsim oil, onions, and
red hot peppers, making a special treat for the workers. The
cost of this meal was approximately three cents per person.

Since burnt bricks here were scarce and of very poor
quality, we were making our own mud bricks. In an experiment, I built a brick kiln and planned to burn some bricks

ourselves, but the biggest problem was the scarcity of wood. We needed about one million burnt bricks for the job that year and half a million mud bricks for the school. Most of the workers had never worked on construction before and had to be schooled in brick making, bricklaying, and carpentry while we were building the school.

One day we ferried across the river and looked for a forest where we might cut wood to use for burning bricks. A huge sleek leopard appeared in the tall grass. Dr. Heasty was on the back of the truck with only a twenty-two rifle and did not dare shoot. Being too small, the gun would have only wounded the animal. By the time I got the truck stopped and jumped out with my .300 Savage that Doc Johnston had given me, the leopard ran into the grass. I was disappointed since it would have made a beautiful coat. We did manage to shoot five guinea fowl which Dolly prepared for our first Thanksgiving in the South Sudan. It was a good dinner but, unlike the holiday in America, it was just another workday.

Sand normally was difficult to acquire, but again the Lord provided. There was a large sand pit right on the site that more than supplied for all our needs at Obel. Instead of dump trucks, we had our own group of native women who filled the sofias on their heads and neatly dumped the sand in a designated spot. By December 8 we had begun work on many of the school buildings there at Obel, had one completed, and planned to have them all finished for school to start by May 1.

There was some commotion one day when the men heard a sheep crying in distress. They ran down to the banks of the Sobat River with their spears and found a huge python, fourteen feet long and seventeen inches in circumference, wound around a sheep and crushing the life out of it. We were too late to save the sheep.

We had received many Christmas greetings, letters, and gifts and with the uncertain mail service, the holiday was strung out

Fourteen-foot python killed on the banks of the Sobat River

for several months. With the temperature remaining in the nineties, our first Christmas in the South Sudan in 1947 was very different from any we had spent in America. Reverend Lowrie Anderson from Atar and Dr. Trudinger from Abwong were with us for our big Christmas Eve dinner, plus all the folks from the Hill. Uncle Lowrie brought a turkey, which we combined with a couple of chickens and the trimmings. (All missionaries were referred to as aunts and uncles to our children and were thought of as bloodless relatives. They knew them better than their blood relatives.) We had a dinner fit for kings! We had no white potatoes, but mashed sweet potatoes were just as good, and no cranberries—but young beets gave the same color effect and did not taste bad either. Including children, there were nineteen at our celebration. We finished a perfect evening by having Uncle Ron and Uncle Lowrie read Dickens's *A Christmas Carol* and we all sang carols. We hurried home and put the children to bed so Santa could put the finishing touches on Penny's dollhouse and Eddie's desk.

With a good imagination, our thorn Christmas tree with its long green leaves looked a little like a long-needled pine. However, after it started to wilt, it took on the appearance of a weeping willow. Regardless, the children were thrilled with the tree and our native houseboys were excited about the prospect of making handsome necklaces out of the trimmings and tinsel.

It had long been a custom of the natives to spend their Christmas at a mission station. The special attraction at the Christmas church service at Doleib Hill this year was the attendance of the king of the Shilluks. He always attended a church service here when in the vicinity. I was honored to escort him to the church in my 1941 Plymouth from the native village where he was temporarily staying. How different—a white man chauffeuring a black man! In his best royal garb, the king attended the service in a bright red robe adorned with gold braid and was painted with brick dust and feathers. Instead of the usual spear, he wore a sword with a gold handle. He was accompanied by his bodyguards and a large group of warriors from the villages. As the bodyguards ran beside the car, they paid tribute to him with their dances and brandished their spears.

As a boy, the king had attended the first class of five students at the school on Doleib Hill. He currently had a multitude of wives and therefore was not a true Christian, but the fact that he was interested and not hostile to our work here helped with our acceptance from the natives. Although no count was made, there must have been a thousand people attending this church service on Christmas Day. The church was far too small to accommodate everyone, so the service was held outdoors. Dried dates were given as a treat to all the children in attendance, probably their only sweets for the whole year.

The following day I took the king to Obel and sat with him on a red carpet as a special guest. He gave the workers an ox, praised them for the work they were doing, and encouraged them to work hard.

On New Year's Eve, 1947, I got up in the wee hours of the morning and headed for Wanglel to arrange the layout of the mission station site there with the Heastys and Adairs. Here we planned two houses, a rest house, storeroom, garage, servant quarters, bookstore, and printing press building. First we would build a storeroom, and when the approval for the station came from Khartoum, we would start on the rest house.

After surveying the Wanglel station, we soon realized that the present buildings were all in bad shape and would have to be rebuilt. We planned to start building the three houses, a boys' school, a girls' school, and a clinic the next dry season. This was New Year's Eve, but no one saw the new year come in since we were all in bed early.

Ferry stuck in the sudd

In the beginning of the new year, 1948, I documented a typical African day in my diary:

"24 HOURS IN AFRICA"

At 3:06 P.M. I left with "the Jerk" and three men for Wanglel to deliver crates to the Gordons. At the Khor Filus ferry we were half way across the river when a large amount of sudd became tangled on the cable. Before we could get the cable loose, there was a lot more sudd. It took the ferrymen, our men, and some other helpers one and a half hours to cut the sudd loose. The men had to go down into the water with spears, machetes, and grass hooks and cut the tangled mess from the cable, and all this time they were taking a chance with crocodiles in the water.

After getting on the road again we went past Khor Atar and turned onto the Wanglel road. In the first forest we saw water bucks, shot a young one, and loaded it on the truck. By this time it was sunset. After driving for some time, I saw something running down the road in front of the truck. When I got closer, I saw it was a male lion. Before I could stop and get my gun, he was off into the grass. We also saw wild cats and gazelle, and the many trees trampled on the side of the road were evidence that elephants had been there. We reached Fangak at 8:10 P.M. and as I fixed my bed on top the truck, ate my supper, and went to bed, the men skinned the water buck and had a big feed. At 6:00 A.M. we crossed by ferry and were on our way again. It was 6:45 A.M. when we reached Wanglel. I had breakfast with the Gordons and went to the Nuer church service.

At 10:10 A.M. we were rolling on our way home again and things were going well. But sometime during the night the elephants returned and knocked down more trees, and a big one completely blocked the road. Some of the trees were

eight and ten inches in diameter making it necessary to cut
our way through with an ax. We looked for the elephants
but none were in sight. We arrived home at 3:06 P.M.,
twenty-four hours after we left.

As I had stated in the *Christian Union Herald* ("Meet
My Friends," July 1948: 16) there were several men who
had worked as my foremen and were instrumental in making
it possible for us to be able to complete the teachers' training
school at Obel. Okic Ding started working as my timekeeper
but eventually acted as interpreter, accountant, and person
in charge of morning worship. He kept track of materials
and tools that were used on each building, was first-aid
man, and oversaw the cooking and distribution of the food.

He also acted as personnel man, and since he knew Shilluk
law, could settle most minor problems. He was an orphan who
taught in the school at Doleib Hill for a while but didn't have
enough education to be approved as a teacher by the government. Besides his own Shilluk tongue, he spoke English quite
well and Arabic and Nuer. He was very valuable to take along
when I went out in strange country or when I had business
dealings with the Arab merchants. Before working for us, he
helped Dr. Heasty translate the Bible into Shilluk and also ran
the mimeograph machine. He said that he liked his present
position very much.

Okic Ding's personal life had been complicated by the fact
that he was an orphan and therefore didn't inherit cattle like
other boys with families. Cows meant everything in this land.
They could seldom be bought or sold but could only be inherited by the sons and paid out as dowry for a new wife. He also
happened to choose a girl whose father had died and, according
to Shilluk law, her father's brother should have inherited her
and her mother. Her mother happened to be a Christian and
since the uncle already had a wife, she refused to be inherited.

Things proceeded well until Okic and the girl decided to get married. He didn't have the eleven cows required for the dowry, but the mother had agreed to accept money instead. Okic paid her all he had earned for a number of years, and the daughter and he were duly married and had a child that they named Sabbath, being born on that day.

In the meantime the uncle said, "You cannot do this, the girl is still legally mine and I want the eleven cows. You are not married until you pay the dowry, and because you had a child before you were married you also owe a debt of three cows." So then Okic was fourteen cows in debt instead of eleven. I wondered at the time if he would somehow manage to get enough money to buy the required cows or, if like Jacob and Rachel in the Bible, he would have to work fourteen years before he could reclaim his wife and child. To this day, I don't know the ending to this tale.

Abwonyo, another invaluable foreman, was in charge of all bricklayers. He was very ambitious and set a good fast pace for his men. This was unusual for these people who never sensed a need to hurry. Working for the mission for ten years, he was one of the few Shilluks to own a set of false teeth. Because of this, his own people accused him of being a foreigner. As a tribal custom, nearly all Shilluks knocked out their lower front teeth, and the uppers weren't much use without the lowers. But Abwonyo had accidentally knocked out his own teeth while working against a rough piece of bamboo and had a set of false teeth made. Unfortunately, these were broken while he was learning to ride a bicycle. In a land with a terribly low wage scale, this was very unusual, and expensive, to own both a set of false teeth and a bicycle! Every morning Abwonyo rode his bike or walked the three miles to Doleib Hill before sunrise so he could ride on the truck the rest of the way to Obel and be at work on time. He had a grown family and one of his sons had learned bricklaying at our school and was working under his dad. Abwonyo was one of my most dependable men.

As an example of his reliability, one night I had come in from across the river after dark. All the men that worked the pontoon had gone home, and the pontoon was on the opposite side of the river. I blew my horn and sat there hopefully waiting but rather doubtful that anyone would respond. In a short while, Abwonyo came running from his village a half mile away with some men. He knew I was out and had recognized the horn. He was still wrapped in his red blanket, the only bedding he possessed. I could rely on Abwonyo.

Abanyawet, another veteran who had worked for the mission a long time, was my gang leader who put up framework for the thatch roofs and put down the concrete floors. He and Abwonyo were very good friends. The girls on his crew did the sand coating and plastering on the walls. They took damp sand and rubbed it smoothly on the walls with the palms of their hands.

Achebek was the foreman of the thatchers. Considered one of the best thatchers in the Sudan, he made almost unbelievable smooth roofs from grass. Achebek was also in charge of gathering grass for the roofs. One time a grass fire was accidentally started near a huge pile of cut grass that had not yet been hauled to the building site. When we arrived with the truck, Achebek and his men had built a backfire around our pile of grass with no thought of danger to themselves. In many places, the uncut burning grass was six to ten feet high, and with the wind blowing heartily, it made a really fierce-looking fire. End of story—they saved all the cut grass.

My quietest foreman, Ajading, was in charge of making mud brick, burning red brick, and putting up the mud buildings. This six-foot-tall man, with shoulders to put Joe Lewis to shame, spoke no English and communicated with signs. I liked to take Ajading along on trips, not just because he was husky, but because he always knew what needed to be done and did it without being told. Although they had never made bricks previously, he and his men knew the different types of clays, sands, and mixtures used in making good strong bricks. He somehow got his men to get the work done and made over a half million mud bricks that year.

Their method was different from the speedy, modern way that we use in the United States. First, they took the clay and sand and made a good mixture. The mixture was put in a hole in the ground, wetted, and left to soak overnight. Another pit was filled with water for washing the brick mold. In the morning they mixed the clay with their feet (if you ever walked in knee-deep mud, you know what that's like) and filled the molds by hand. The molds, holding two bricks at a time, were carried to a place where they were smoothed off with sand, emptied, and then returned for a refill.

I was very proud of my foremen at Obel, as well as of the 350 men and women who worked under them. They had no prior training as skilled laborers. The biggest reason for their success was that they took great pride in their work, mainly because it was to be an advanced training school for their *own* children, the first of its kind in this area, and would directly impact them. Most of the men worked from sunrise to sunset and their only time frame was completion before the first of May when school was scheduled to start.

April brought the birth of another son, William Kelly Pollock, named after Dolly's father. Dolly was having labor pains during the night, and early in the morning on April 29, went over to Mary Ewing's, a nurse at Doleib Hill. It looked like this was to be the big day. Mary had fixed up Dolly's room and she and Dr. Roode had everything ready. I went in every so often to check on Dolly's progress and at 5:00 P.M. I washed up since things started to happen. Just as the sun set on April 29, 1948, little Billy was born. Dr. Roode had to use a flashlight to see, but with the help of some friends, everything went well. Eddie and Penny were happy with their new brother who weighed in at nine pounds and measured twenty-one and a half inches long. Soon after birth, Billy's fists were hitting the sides of his basket, so my first job was to build him a bed. The following year Billy was baptized by Dr. Heasty.

Since we modernized our workshop, we had become more efficient. The electric generator allowed us to run a saw and jointer, metal turning lathe, and electric hand drill. If we ran out of materials and couldn't obtain more, we often made our own. Nails were unavailable for a while, so I showed our blacksmith how to make them out of number nine wire. We didn't have plaster for the women's boardinghouse so we made a mixture of lime, sand, and brick dust. It didn't compare with the plaster back home but it was better than mud, the only other alternative. Since we had no bathtub, we built one from brick and lined it with floor ballot which served the purpose surprisingly well.

A large barrel filled with river water supplied us with running water in the houses—that was until someone remembered the airplane that had crashed the prior year with a large gasoline tank that was still intact. We drove a truck out to salvage the tank and found that it had a few holes. After patching the holes and mounting, it made a fine water tank; in fact, one of the largest we had at Doleib Hill. It held 203 gallons!

One morning across the Sobat River from Obel, grass was being burned on a horseshoe-shaped piece of ground that encircled the river. A fire was started at the small end and left to burn toward the river. Several hundred natives with three spears apiece lined up behind the fire line and closed in. As animals became trapped, they were forced back from the river's edge through the fire and were speared. The ones that tried to swim across the river were speared by men in canoes or by men on the other bank. In this annual custom of supplying meat, the animals had no chance.

Believe it or not, I did get tired. Since the South Sudan was considered a hardship assignment due to isolation, vacations were a necessity. A one-month vacation within your assigned country was customary in the first and third years of your term, with a two-month vacation out of country in the second and fourth years. By the end of July 1948, we had plans for an out-of-country vacation south to the headwaters of the Nile, circle Lake Victoria, and on to Nairobi, Kenya. Our main hope was to come back refreshed, but we also wanted to have our teeth checked and do a little shopping.

By August of 1948, another building season had come to an end and, with materials slow coming in, we did not finish all we had set out to do. The forty buildings were ready for school to open in May, but the missionary residence wasn't completed in time for the missionary in charge. The small house we built at Obel was ready for the roof, but the large one lacked almost everything: lumber, cement, and roofing. For this large house, we dug the footers and stopped there. As we were leaving on our vacation, we received word that the lumber had finally arrived in Malakal and that the cement had been shipped from Khartoum and should arrive about the time of our return.

My men had worked extra hard that past year at Obel, something to which they weren't accustomed, so they were taking vacation at the same time we were. I shouldn't call it a vacation, since most of them were taking this opportunity to plant and cultivate their fields and a few were still working at Doleib Hill under Dr. Roode.

In August it was time to leave on our out-of-country vacation. After loading our luggage and the children onto two dugouts fastened together (with an outdoor motor to push them), we left Doleib Hill en route to Atar to catch the steamer. By late evening we left Atar on the steamer *Rejaf* and were on our way south. At first the land was flat and swampy. It was difficult to know what direction we were heading due to the way the river wound around the swamp, and we touched every point on the compass. After winding through the sudd where mostly papyrus grew, we docked at Adok. Adok, a river landing used for access to Ler mission station, was in the middle of mosquito-infested swamps and this was where I turned to Dolly and said, "I hope God never sends me here."

On August 21, Dolly and I celebrated our wedding anniversary on the steamer, six happy years together. On that trip I actually read and wrote letters, things I never took time for when I worked.

Eventually hills showed up in the distance. Rapids prevented us from traveling by boat, so after exchanging for East African money, we loaded our luggage onto a truck and traveled gravel roads for a hundred miles over hills and mountains. It was more tropical here in the most southern Sudan and we experienced some of the most beautiful scenery of the entire trip. We ate good lettuce, fresh sweet pineapple, and crackers with lots of butter for the first time since leaving the United States. How I appreciated it.

As we continued up the Nile River, we saw baboons and eventually entered Uganda where simsim grew (for oil) along the river. The many animals that dotted the lower bank included several different kinds of antelope and herds of elephants. We reached the part of the Nile called the Albert Nile River that began at Lake Albert and was sometimes quite rough. At one point our bus passed sawmills and large forests of mahogany and eucalyptus trees.

On the next leg of our trip we boarded an old train car that had two compartments with leather seats on each side. The leather looked like it had worn out years ago. Eventually the train crossed over the Nile at Rippon Falls and before long, we found ourselves back on a ship, crossing the equator to Lake Victoria in Uganda. Lake Victoria has an area of 26,000 square miles and is 3,724 feet above sea level. Swahili was the main language spoken here. The shore and surrounding area looked like Bar Harbor, Maine, with the rocky shoreline, short stretch of sandy beach, and rocky hills nearby. At various spots along the way, coffee, kapok (silky fibers used for insulation), cotton bales, sisal (a kind of hemp used in rope making), rice, shelled peanuts, and cottons were loaded onto the ships.

Boarding another train, we found ourselves climbing to an altitude of 8,321 feet before arriving at Nairobi. Here you could have most everything you wanted, but the prices were out of reach. Nairobi, the capital of Kenya, has an area of more than 32 square miles, and is 5,400 feet above sea level. It was here that the children saw their first picture show, *The Perils of Pauline* with Betty Hutton as Pearl White. In the main part of town, while we were walking back from the show to the hotel, a car stopped and a girl offered us a lift. We thanked her and said that we were only going a short distance. Before we had gone much farther, another car stopped and inquired if we were all right. Evidently, during the time of the uprising of the Mau Mau (a secret Kenyan movement during the 1940s opposing British rule), white people didn't go out after dark unless they were in a car.

The meals were good in Nairobi and one evening we had a very English, ten-course dinner plus dessert and coffee. The landscape change was similar to the southwestern part of the United States, with mountains and valleys, lots of grassy plains, and some cattle ranches. As we left Nairobi by bus, we enjoyed gazing out the windows at the giraffes, ostriches, and zebras.

We stayed in one hotel in the Rift Valley in Kenya that had a hill in front which actually was a peninsula between a small and large lake. One day after breakfast Dolly, the children, and I left the hotel and walked along the ridge between the two lakes. It was a beautiful site. We saw more than a thousand animals of different kinds: monkeys, some as large as Eddie and Penny; a herd of zebra; a herd of waterbucks; hundreds of Thompson gazelles; a few hundred pelican; and some larger animals, probably bushbuck or Grant gazelles. We walked six miles and saw two golden crested cranes that were larger than ones in the Sudan, and I saw my first African jackrabbit. I discovered the reason for this wonderful variety of animals—hunting was forbidden on this property. I took many pictures of this gorgeous valley before we boarded our train and headed for home. As we bid farewell to the Rift Valley, we saw many large apes and thousands of pink flamingoes that made a gorgeous pink fringe surrounding the lake.

Train, steamer, bus—our trip progressed from one town to the next, from one hotel to another. Large groves of rubber trees could be seen along the way and there were lots of paw-paw (papaya). Along the river there were hundreds of elephants and, for the first time, I saw brown ones among the gray. For more than two hours, the elephants were in view and we were delighted.

Often the steamers towed barges, one behind the other, and this was the case when crossing Lake Albert on our return trip. Our steamer towed four barges, and the one on the tail whipped back and forth.

There were many stops. At Packwach in Uganda, the women came down to the boat dressed very sparsely, many of them with nothing but a string around their waists with a bunch of leaves attached in the front and back. That was the extent of their wardrobe.

At Loropi, Uganda, the game warden brought in a truckload of eight elephant skulls and thirty lower jaws to be loaded on the boat. These were to be used for scientific studies. (The elephant's lower jaw continues to grow new teeth in the back and as the ones in front wear out, the new ones in back move forward.)

At Nimule, Sudan, there were eighty-two men lined up in a double row unloading sugar, passing sacks down the line to a storage shed fifty to sixty feet away where it was being stored. It was a slow process.

And while stopped at Mongalla, Sudan, the natives swam out to the boat with bananas and sugar cane to sell to those on board. All of these stops were interesting experiences.

On September 30, we reached Obel, Sudan, the end of our Kenya trip, and my mind started shifting to Wanglel.

In the Pollock newsletter dated November 8, 1948, Dolly asked:

How would you like to come and spend the day here with us at Doleib Hill? Around 5 A.M. or shortly after, we are awakened from a sound sleep by the beating of drums. The sun has not yet risen over the horizon. If I am lucky and Billy did not hear the drums, I can roll over and catch another forty winks. Ted rises and gets ready to go out for the day's work.

The drums are beaten to awaken the schoolboys who live in the dormitories on the compound. From sunrise until 9 A.M. they work cutting grass, hoeing the fields and gardens for the school, and have their craft classes. If we have managed to get back to sleep, we will be awakened shortly before six by the ringing of a bell, just as the sun rises over the horizon.

At this time Ted's men and all the workmen on the compound gather in the chapel for morning prayers. The bell is a large school bell and is mounted on the windmill that is about twenty-five feet from our house. Since we sleep outdoors on a screened porch, even if I do put my head under the pillow, I still hear it.

About the time we are getting up we will hear the clatter of a tin can and the splash of water. This is the water woman filling our water tank. She makes trip after trip to and from the river with a five-gallon tin full of water on her head. Our water tank is on a platform and runs into the house through a tap, but it is impure river water. Before drinking, our water is put into zeers (large clay filters) and then boiled and cooled. If you should like a drink you can get it from the goulas (porous clay bottles that keep the water cool by the process of evaporation).

Mynero and Octor, the two boys who help me with the housework, have just come in. Mynero helps in the kitchen, so he has gone to bring in some wood to start the fire. We have a little old wood-burning stove that has been discarded as useless several times before, but due to our need, was repaired one more time and is still serving the purpose nicely. If it is Monday, Octor will be putting the water into the tish (a shallow pan about five inches deep and thirty inches across) getting ready to do the washing. He will sit on the floor and swish water through the clothes with his hands. The clothes are not always clean, and they do not wear as long, but I am sure they are still better than if I did them myself by the same process. Should it be Tuesday morning you would find him building a fire in the charcoal iron getting ready for the ironing.

We do not eat breakfast until seven, so let us take a quick trip around the compound. The first house that you see on your way in from Malakal as you enter the compound is the new women's boardinghouse. It is on the riverbank, under a cluster of Doleib palms with their fan-shaped leaves. Then as we follow the path from the women's house we pass the native type, mud and grass roof cattle barns, then the concrete block workshop. This is where Ted now has his power saw, and where the carpenters and blacksmith work. To our left we see the schoolboys' dormitories and playground. The dormitories are also made of mud with grass roofs. To our right we have two temporary missionary residences (Theodore Roosevelt spent a night here while on a hunting trip in 1907), followed by the house we live in, then the red brick buildings with the grass roofs. On our left are the school and church.

Let's take a peek into the church. It is quite different from any church you have ever seen. There are no furnishings except the pulpit. The floor is concrete and everyone sits on the floor when they come to worship. Above the pulpit is a wooden cross, the only decoration. They have no musical instruments, but the birds are always welcome.

As we leave the church, we pass a two-room school building, another missionary residence, and the concrete block clinic building and clinic tukls (round mud huts with grass roofs) where the very ill patients stay. But unless they are desperately sick, they prefer to stay in the village and come just for treatment. Sometimes we marvel how a man with pneumonia can walk in under the burning sun for treatment and then walk home again. They certainly bear pain without complaining much better than we do.

The other tukls with culls (yards fenced in with grass matting) are the homes of the native teachers. We must not miss the garden on the riverbank with its tall bamboo thicket, the stately mango and kapok trees, the banana and papaya groves, citrus trees and vegetable garden, and of course our Doleib palms.

At 9 A.M. the school bell rings. Eddie comes in for his lessons. I try to balance Billy on one knee and quickly leaf through the teacher's guidebook, trying to stay a little ahead of him, while Penny Sue walks around saying, "Mother, what can I do?" We no sooner get nicely settled before someone comes to the door calling "tonguen," meaning that they have eggs to sell. Since this is my only means of getting eggs, I drop everything and go to buy the eggs which they bring in one, two, and three at a time. They either sell them or exchange them for needles, razor blades, tin cans, headbands, or fish hooks. Before I buy, I must test them to see if they are fresh. If they do not float when I put them in a pan of water I accept them, but still I never break more than one egg into a dish at a time. The hot sun spoils them mighty fast if they are allowed to lie in it for a short time.

Instead of a bell, the drums that you hear beating every half hour until two o'clock are used in the school as a signal for the boys to change classes. It must be nearing lunchtime since we can hear the boys singing at chapel. They have a service every school day at eleven thirty. I have been speaking of the pupils as boys, and all the boarders are boys, but there are a number of girls who come to school as day students.

Because of the heat, most folks like to take a short rest in the afternoon, and I attempt to have the children take a nap to which they greatly object. I no sooner have them down (or at least think I have them resting) when two o'clock rolls around and the boys start gathering at the door wanting to work. For pay they will accept nearly anything from money to pencils, fishhooks, and tin cans. For this they will sort grain, cut grass, and the job they like best of all—shell peanuts. But it always seems that there are more boys than there is work.

While you are here, you must not miss our beautiful birds of every size and description. There are pelicans, geese, stork, kite, vulture, and even ostrich occasionally for large birds, and then every kind and color imaginable among the small song birds. Let's just sit and rest awhile on our screened veranda. It is such a blessing to have a place where we can be outdoors where we can feel a bit of a breeze and still be away from the flies.

Of all the things we have here I think the flies are the most numerous and the most persistent. But one thing that nature has provided to combat the flies is the lizards that you see crawling all over the screening. They crawl along with their heads shaking like a leaf in the breeze in order to fool the insects, then jump and eat them. We have a lizard that patrols by day and night for the millers and mosquitoes.

It has been so much fun having you visit, but we have taken too much of your time already. Please do come again.

Sunday, November 21, 1948, was a most joyous day. Thirty-five Shilluk boys and two girls had accepted Christ as Savior and were baptized. We had so much to be thankful for in this pre-Thanksgiving season. The worship service at the church was packed, with most of the congregation consisting of young people. Following the service we went down to the river's edge and sat in the shade of a large wild fig tree. Nature had provided a beautiful setting by forming an arch of fig tree branches on one side and bamboo on the other.

Reverend and Mrs. Anderson came from the Atar school and brought eight Shilluk boys who wanted baptism. Reverend and Mrs. Anderson and Rev. and Mrs. Matthew Gilleland, who came from Malakal, assisted our Shilluk minister, Rev. Law Amoliker. (Reverend Amoliker was the first Shilluk to be ordained.) While singing songs of praise, the schoolboys wanting baptism marched down to the river between the Doleib palms. Since the riverbank was steep and slippery, an elder stood on the banks of the river to assist them as they entered and exited the water. Reverend Lowrie Anderson gave the address with Adwok as interpreter.

It was such a great joy to see so many young boys and girls accept Christ. These boys and girls had just finished a series of lessons in communicants' class. Some dropped out along the way and had not appeared before the elders, but on the day that the accepted ones were being baptized, they slipped in at the end of the line in hopes that they too would be called. We were happy to know that even if they weren't baptized this time, they still were interested. We prayed that in time they too would fully accept Christ.

Soon school would be out and the boys and girls who were new in Christ would return to their villages, many miles from any mission station. Only our prayers could keep them from the temptations and pitfalls that were before them.

It was a memorable Thanksgiving in 1948. Dolly had made a formal dress just for the affair—a dinner for all thirty-five missionaries and their families in the area. It was such a thrill to be among so many Americans at one time. The dinner was delicious. All the folks from Doleib Hill, Obel, Atar, and Malakal were there, along with Dr. Adair from Wanglel. Even though it was only Thanksgiving, we celebrated by singing Christmas carols while we were together. Since it would not be proper to celebrate an American Thanksgiving without a proclamation, the governor of the South Sudan issued one to the American mission.

In mid-December we traveled to Wanglel to review building problems with Dr. Adair, who was busy clearing ground for our work. On a hunting expedition while there, Robb and Ken shot three tiang and one waterbuck which Dr. Adair served to the natives for their Christmas dinner.

On our return trip, we sighted two lions. First I shot a seven-foot female, and then Ken shot an eight-foot male that was about fifty feet from the lioness. When the male was hit, the female started over to help him but never made it.

Some of the local natives worshiped lions as their gods. As proof, the next morning a Nuer woman came to place beads on one of the lions as a sacrifice. But killing the lions was necessary—the truth was that many people were killed each year by lions and leopards—just as the automobile kills many in the United States. I spent the morning skinning the lions. Today this skin hangs in my den in upstate New York.

One Friday afternoon in December, the four single ladies at Obel announced they were going on a picnic in the station wagon out into the "wild and wooly" places. They also made it clear that they were not taking any men along or revealing where they were going. Just before supper, a note arrived asking for help and said they were near the mouth of the Sobat River.

The R.P.M. took the car, the only vehicle running at the time, and went to Obel. We could see the spotlight about a mile away and tracks that went off into grass seven and eight feet tall. Most of the land was swampy and made it necessary for us to leave the car and start walking, all the while questioning why the girls would continue driving through the marsh.

Before long we found the girls—station wagon stuck in mud with water up to the bumpers. Leaving their station wagon in the mud, we R.P.M. walked the ladies to our car and delivered them back to Doleib Hill. It was no surprise that their shorts-clad legs revealed a multitude of mosquito bites.

Christmas 1948 was not far off and the children were excited. Billy had not experienced all the wonders of the holiday yet and Eddie and Penny Sue tried to explain it to him. "In Africa," they told him, "you do not have to write a letter to Santa Claus; you just tell him at the dinner table." The children and I found a Christmas tree and set it up. On Christmas Eve, Dolly and Mrs. Heasty helped the ladies cook a formal dinner. The rest of the packages from America came in the mail bag that evening. It was a big day for the children; they received many gifts that year. A Christmas church service held under the wild fig tree by the river had one thousand people in attendance, including the Shilluk king.

In January 1949, the American South Sudan Association was formed, separating it from the north. Since the North Sudan was predominately Muslim and the South Sudan was mainly populated by pagan tribes, it seemed wise to make the division. Each association would have its own meeting, and this year the South Sudan Association met from January 14 to 19 with approximately thirty participants. The builders at the meeting attempted to plan and organize all the Presbyterian mission projects in the South Sudan. Sometimes I felt that there were too many jobs over too wide an area.

Their first order of business was to draw up a constitution and elect committees. It was a good opportunity to put missionary names with faces and to hear of the successes and failures from the other mission stations. Some meetings continued well into the night, and the help and advice were invaluable.

One day there was a note from Rev. Don McClure saying he had an accident and had hit a piece of iron on the bridge at the first khor not far from Atar. He had wrecked the steering on the station wagon and had sent back a runner to Doleib Hill as messenger. After receiving word, we took a truck and went after the station wagon. Upon locating it, we decided to leave our mark. On one side of the truck we inscribed in chalk, "Odon (name given to Don McClure by the natives) Search and Research Expedition," and on the other side, "Wanglel or Bust." Below, we wrote, "They Busted." When I reached the khor, Don and his wife, Lyda, were sitting on the bridge and Don came over calling out, "Hello, Mr. Stanley."

I shouted back, "Hello, Dr. Livingstone." We picked up the front end of the station wagon and swung it onto an A-frame on the back of our truck. Since Don had been towing a trailer on the station wagon, we had to make two trips across on the ferry. It was just another late day returning to the Hill.

All was going well on the Obel big house until we ran into the nail problem. Since the short nails hadn't arrived, we had to use longer ones which, unfortunately, bent and broke in the hardwood. Driving the nails was difficult, and one day, in desperation, I stood on the roof and prayed. Things went fairly well for the rest of the afternoon, and we finished the job.

After two years we were almost finished at Obel. We received a letter from Dr. Reed indicating that the mission board expected us to continue with the building of the house and clinic at Wanglel, and would be taking a vote at the next meeting.

The rainy season made traveling very difficult. One day at the end of March, a five-inch rainfall left some roads below water. Often it was necessary to make new roads as we traveled and, frequently, we had to drive through fields. Fog was a rare occurrence, and I vividly remember the one time it was foggy all day. With no sun it was a funny sort of day, and since the locals didn't wear watches, it had people fooled. Not able to tell the time of day, some of the workers at Obel who normally quit at two in the afternoon, worked until four. It was described as the tail end of a *haboob*, a dust storm, one of the largest the Sudan had ever had. Khartoum and Port Sudan were badly fogged-in, and the planes, flying at four thousand feet to clear the dust, had to bypass those cities and land in Malakal.

It was important for Dolly and me to keep accurate financial records. Many hours were spent scrutinizing the books, making them balance as best we could. Most expense records were kept for labor, materials, food, and truck accounts and had to be done for each site. I can recall reviewing the numbers for eight hours straight one day and knew then and there that I could never do it for a living.

All was well going home from Wanglel one Sunday until our car hit the halfway bridge and tore off the oil plug. After driving a few miles further, the motor started to knock, and I stopped and discovered that all the oil had run out. I knew it was a bearing knock. Reverend Lowrie Anderson and two Nuer boys began walking to Atar and we sent a runner to Doleib Hill for help.

While waiting, I attempted to patch the hole, but with little success. I drove another five miles, but we were still fifteen miles from Atar. Not knowing how long I would be stuck, I thought of the little water and food I had and knew I would have to use them sparingly. Since it looked like rain, there was a chance I could catch some rain water for drinking.

A half mile ahead, I could see the huts of a Dinka village and was relieved when some Dinka found me shortly before sundown and offered to push the car to their village. Even though we couldn't communicate, we got along very well. In fact, the chief of the village instructed his boys to catch a red rooster and he offered it to me. One of the boys gathered dura stalks for the fire while another dipped some dirty water from a hole. We killed the chicken and they cooked it—not long enough though, for it was still quite rare as I ate. I boiled some water and strained it into my water bag and had a good night's sleep. Eventually I heard a car and looked out to see the headmistress of the girls' school at Obel coming with the station wagon to tow me home.

The name "new look tukls" was given to my new house plan at Wanglel referring to the two longer oval tukls joined by a veranda. With seven hundred feet more floor space, it cost less than the little house at Obel. When meeting with the committee, most were in favor of the new design, and Dr. Mary Smith liked the idea for her hospital at Nasir.

Hunting trips were often quite an adventure in the South Sudan. Leaving Doleib Hill one afternoon, Robb, Ken, Al Heasty, Bill Adair, Al Roode, Matt Gilliland, and I went across the river in the Jerk. Robb was driving and we realized that we were getting low on fuel. As we started back to the Hill to replenish, we ran out of gas about eight miles from our destination. Al, Ken, and Robb started to walk back. While they were gone, the rest of us ate supper, set up our beds, and went to sleep.

About 11:30 P.M. they returned in the station wagon bearing an oribi they had shot near the Hill. We folded up our bedrolls and started out again. Al, Robb, Ken, and I were on top of the truck with the spotlight and our big guns. We spotted a dead hyena stretched in the middle of the road a short ways

New look tukls

ahead and could see the eyes of another one off in the grass. We shot a jackal and by 2:30 A.M. we had a serval cat (a wild medium-sized cat with heavy black spots), a mongoose, a reed buck, and two more oribis.

Thorn branches that had been piled up around an old cattle camp to keep lions out served as our protection as we prepared for sleep again. Since I wanted to shoot some tiang at daylight and knew the sun would soon rise, I got up a little after 4:00 A.M. and awakened the others. Down the road a short distance, we saw eyes off to the side. They were tiang. Heasty, Al, Ken, and I spread out behind the trees near the small khor and waited for daylight. Heasty shot two, I got one hit, Al got one, and Ken hit one that got away—making four hits. We loaded up the tiang and started for home. It was quite a load!

As I sat on the veranda after supper one evening at Doleib Hill, I heard a clap and someone say "Jal Dong." I took a lantern and went out to investigate. A Shilluk was standing there with two spears in his hand and dressed in nothing but a string of beads around his neck. He wanted me to call Malakal and tell them that he had killed a man. I called the police and while we waited, he told his story.

His mother was dead, he had no sisters, and, since he wasn't married, he lived with his father and cooked for the two of them. In this country, cooking is considered strictly women's work. So, when his neighbor called him a woman, he picked up his spear and buried it in the left side of his neighbor's chest. This Shilluk then walked five miles from his village and asked me to call the police.

Some of the other Shilluks in the compound didn't think he should cook. Since he didn't have cattle to get a wife, they thought he should live with his relatives or friends and work to raise crops until he had enough money to buy cattle. The police came and took him off to jail.

———◆———

The parting of the R.P.M. came on May 26, 1949, when Ken Rasmussen and Robb McLaughlin headed back to the Pittsburgh Theological Seminary after their temporary mission assignment. (Later they both returned to the mission field in the Sudan: Ken as a medical doctor and Robb as an evangelist. Eventually their mission work would take them to Ethiopia, and the next time we were all together was at a missionary picnic in Addis Ababa, Ethiopia, in the late 1960s.)

One morning in July, I loaded up building supplies to be taken to Malakal and left at 9:30 A.M. When the canoe men who were to accompany me saw my load, they refused to go. I had twenty-three pieces of four-by-four lumber, most of it over twenty feet long, tied together to make a raft. Masonite was piled on top of the lumber. Two canoes, one lashed to each side of the raft, would help steer, and were loaded with glass, hardware, and some limes to be taken to market in Malakal. Eventually I found two other men who were willing to accompany me for a fee of twenty piasters (for a laborer, approximately two weeks' wages in Sudanese currency).

After a stop at Obel to pick up mail, we continued on. Top speed was floating with the current, and we traveled nonstop from 1:00 P.M. to 8:30 P.M. until we reached the Gillilands, missionaries in Malakal. The entire time I sat cramped in the canoe and could hardly straighten out my legs when I tried to stand. The trip by river from Doleib Hill to Malakal was twenty-five miles, and we were traveling a little over two miles an hour. At one point, where the river separated around an island, we started down the left side. To our surprise, the current caught us, turned us around, and had us heading down the right side—not exactly what we had in mind. The natives tried to persuade me to quit, but I convinced them to continue on, perhaps fulfilling a boyhood dream of playing out one of Tom Sawyer's adventures. Before we reached Malakal, the wind whipped up and we were drifting sideways, riding the waves for the last few miles.

In July 1949, I started working on the drawings for the Wanglel hospital and Wanglel house, both the new look tukl plan, and sent the drawings and the blueprints to the mission board in Philadelphia. Also, for several weeks, Dolly and I devoted twelve-hour days to bookkeeping. For a week at a time we didn't move from the desk except to eat and sleep. It was very tedious and time-consuming to keep accurate accounts, but it was absolutely necessary. We had to see that all the supplies used in building were charged to the right project.

By the middle of August, another building season came to an end. Without any idea of where we would be going the following season, we packed up and left the Sudan for a holiday at our mission stations in Ethiopia (Addis Ababa, Gore, and Dembi Dollo). Since the roads in the Sudan were closed due to rain, we were doubtful whether we could find a way to Malakal in time to catch our plane. Eventually two Shilluk boys agreed to row us down the Sobat River in a dugout canoe.

The Shilluk boys had never seen a plane on the ground before and were quite excited as they boarded with us and viewed the inside of the "big birds." The Ethiopian planes, used mostly for freight, were not very luxurious. They were old American DC–3s that had been used to haul troops and had only bucket seats along the sides. Usually the seats were folded up and animal hides were packed up to the ceiling. At the Nile we boarded the *Queen* (a small launch owned by the government), and continued on from Malakal by plane to Dembi Dollo.

Our first stop, Sayo Mission Station in Dembi Dollo, Ethiopia, was but a cleared strip on top of the mountain. Not even the grass was cut on the runway. Here we picked up some native passengers who proceeded to get airsick. Unfortunately, the smell affected the rest of us. If that wasn't bad enough, the odor from monkey skins loaded on at Gore added to the stench.

There is nothing quite like Christian fellowship. Upon our arrival at the American Mission in Addis Ababa, we were given a royal welcome. It gave us a wonderful feeling to be welcomed by our mission folk wherever we went and be taken into their homes as if we were family. There were no strangers in Christian fellowship.

It was strange to be cold again and wear woolen clothes. Although it seldom frosts in Addis Ababa, they have very chilly rains and hailstorms, and the children were tickled when they went out and gathered a dish full of hailstones. It was a new experience for our Billy to wear shoes, sweaters, long trousers, hat, and raincoat, since his usual attire in the Sudan was either a sun suit or just a diaper.

The mountainous countryside was beautiful with the steep hills, rocks, and spectacular views out over the valleys.

Especially interesting were the hot springs and baths. In general we found prices to be very high in Addis Ababa and the natives here to be more sophisticated than in the Sudan. Saturday was the big market day when vendors gathered outside the mission fence to sell everything from salt and lumber to mules and clothing. People moved in every direction to chase goats, hens, and donkeys, and gather up little piles of salt, beans, spices, and onions. Some of the donkeys carried crude-looking goatskins full of honey left in the shape of the animal with the head and feet openings tied shut. When we tasted the honey, it was delicious; so thick and light in color, it nearly looked like butter.

Our seven days in Addis Ababa passed all too quickly and soon we were heading back home with a stop in Gore. Our first taste of native Ethiopian food in Gore was a bit hot and spicy, but we soon learned to like it. It was a joy to visit the government school near the mission and find it run by Christian folks from India who had grown up in one of the American mission schools. In Gore, too, the week went quickly.

All too soon we were back at Dembi Dollo and met by our Sayo Mission folk. Piling into the Jeep, all eleven of us started over typical Ethiopian roads toward the Sayo Mission Station some eight miles away. The station (originally opened in 1920) was on top of the mountain and our first glimpse was of the hospital where they treated everything from tuberculosis and appendicitis to sewing up a cow's horn wound. One of the nurses here ran a baby clinic which treated far more babies than she and her staff could possibly handle. She had seen seventy-five babies that day.

While visiting the Sayo Mission Station in Ethiopia, Dolly developed a sore throat, and upon investigating, the doctor decided to remove her tonsils. Removal was difficult and she required a stitch on one side. Several days later, in the middle of the night, her throat started to hemorrhage. She was taken back to the hospital where the doctor put in another stitch and cut out more roots. She was very weak, put on a stretcher, and carried back to the house to recuperate.

During our first two weeks at Sayo (though we only planned to stay for one), we enjoyed the dedication service for the ladies' house at the Sayo Mission Station. On the first night the service was held for any foreigners in the vicinity, and, the next evening, it was held for the Ethiopians. On both nights, the house was packed. We had the privilege to meet Reverend Gidada, a blind pastor and evangelist who now shepherded sixteen churches and used muleback as his only means of transportation. Smallpox had blinded him as a young child, and the mission at Sayo found him as a blind beggar. He was the interpreter for the dedication of the young ladies' home since he spoke English as well as his native language.

Each time we planned to return to the Sudan from furlough, the plane developed engine trouble. So, instead of staying one week in Sayo, we spent four. Why would we ever complain when the climate was lovely and the mountain views breathtaking? Every station we visited had a job list that longed for attention and here, too, I helped with the building program.

While at Sayo I had the opportunity to do blacksmithing in a most primitive shop where stones were laid around a little hole in the ground. Here bellows were made of goatskin that had been carefully removed without cutting down the belly. A cow's horn was placed at the hole in the neck and a piece of pipe was stuck into the tip of the horn. Two sticks (each about a foot long) at the tail end of the skin opened and closed. A boy sat between two of these bellows and worked them up and down. As the stick came up, he opened it, and as it went down, he closed it, forcing the air into the fire.

One day we found ourselves in the middle of a field where an Ethiopian holiday celebration called a Muskil was in progress. The dejasmat, or governor, was there, and we were fortunate enough to sit near him. The men brought sticks with flowers on the end, stood them around a large pole, and burned them, commemorating the Coptic Church's belief that St. Helena found a piece of the true cross in Ethiopia.

Our final day at Sayo, we were awakened to a beautiful, but alarming, scene. The valley below was completely filled with big fluffy clouds the shape of huge snow drifts. Unfortunately our airport was under all those clouds and we wondered how the plane to take us home would be able to land.

Trying to be optimistic, we started out by Jeep for the airstrip. Every few minutes the big turkey gobbler bought for Thanksgiving dinner stuck his head out from his crate in an attempt to catch flies that landed on my head. I was concerned when, instead of the flies, the gobbler pulled out a beak full of hair. It was raining and it was only the four-wheel drive of the Jeep that kept us from sliding off the road. To our amazement, when we arrived at the airstrip, the clouds had lifted and the plane had landed. It was a beautiful clear day.

The Sudan felt much hotter when we returned from Ethiopia. It really wasn't, but the quick change made the heat more obvious. We spent the night in Malakal, then sailed on the *Queen* up the Nile to the mouth of the Sobat River. From there we walked through mud the last four miles to our home. We were all a bit hot, thirsty, and weary when we arrived—that was, except for Billy—he had a grand time riding on my shoulders the whole way.

Our main goal was to finish the financial records, complete the few jobs at Obel and Doleib Hill, and then go on to Akobo (the American Mission station with school and clinic on Akobo River) until the first of the new year. After that, Wanglel would be our next big project.

We looked forward to Christmas 1949. It would be the last one during our short term in the South Sudan. Some of the men and I worked in the afternoons building a server for Dolly and a table and four chairs for the children. As time

neared, the children and I looked for a tree and set it up for
the holiday. The children were happy. With friends back
home sending boxes, they received many gifts. Everyone was
so good to us. Dolly prepared dinner and invited the entire
station. We all had a joyous time together with a prayer
meeting and singing afterwards.

By the end of December we journeyed to Malakal and had
all the site plans for Wanglel approved. Next, we gathered up
all the tools left at Malakal that would be needed at Wanglel.
Arrangements were made and we could start anytime. On
January 1, 1950, we started our books with a clean slate for
the new year.

WANGLEL

A two-room school building with mud floor was to be our
living accommodations until our house was built at Wanglel.
The office would be our kitchen, and we drilled a hole and put
grass mats up for our toilet. At the bedroom end we were to put
in a shower and a place to wash clothes.

At one point we had five men clearing the sudd on the riverbank in front of the house to enable the sailboats to unload
bricks, bamboo, lumber, and sand that we desperately needed
to continue the construction. By the end of January we started
digging footers for a hospital.

You didn't dare leave anything on the floor in the South
Sudan. One night the white ants were so bad that they actually
ate a hole in my boots, ones handmade by the army harness
maker. Coming through a little hole in the aluminum, they got
into a cloth basket and ate sacks of dura flour. Besides the white
ants, we also had a problem with rats in the storeroom.

We had a variety of workmen at Wanglel: Nuers, Shilluks,
and Arabs, all working together as bricklayers, carpenters, and

roof thatchers. There was one common problem encountered by the Nuers who were tying up the roof grass—where to store their money when they got paid. These men wore no clothes and, thus, had no pockets; some carried it in their mouths and some behind their ears.

Work at Wanglel had been started years ago by the Church Missionary Society of England, and the chapel was a memorial to a woman doctor who had served there. For the uninitiated, church services here in the South Sudan's newest mission station were a real experience. Roy Grace, D.D., pastor of a Presbyterian church in Upper Darby, Pennsylvania, described his visit in "Addressing a Service in South Sudan's Newest Mission Station:"

No doubt it was a church. High up at the point of the conical grass-thatched roof was a cross, the universal symbol of the Christian faith. But all the rest of the building was strange. It had no wall; the steep thatching of the roof came down so low that even I, who am built rather close to the ground, had to stoop to enter. The tall Shilluks and Nuers had to double up to get in. Instead of walls, the roof was supported on bamboo poles. And inside, the seats were made of solid blocks of hard, dried mud, about eighteen inches high and a foot wide. There were no backs, of course. Running down the center was an aisle.

This morning the building was crowded. The bugler had assembled all the men for the service and they came, workmen, schoolboys, teachers, and evangelists—a mixed crowd from various South Sudan tribes. They spoke several languages. Some were Christians, but most were still pagans. We had two interpreters, one for the Shilluks and the other for the Nuers. The mission staff was there, including Dr. and Mrs. Adair, Dr. Gordon, and Mr. Ted Pollock, who is busily engaged in building a doctor's residence and a hospital.

We started with singing, led by a bright-faced evangelist, and
after prayer I was to give a message. Where would a pastor
from an American suburban congregation start with an audience like that? We chose John 3:16, what Luther called "The
Little Gospel."

God—but what did these men know about God? I thought I
would try to ask them questions and get their own answers.
Did they believe that there was one great God, only one, who
existed before all things, and who was the Creator?

Yes, they believed that; all of them.

"Are you sure you believe there is only one, not many gods?"

Even the pagans were certain. His name was Jwok.

"Was he good or evil?"

"He was good," they said.

"But do you worship this good God who created the world?"

No answer this time. So I went on to say, "Of course you do
not worship him. You know he exists (all African tribes admit
his existence), but you are afraid of the evil spirits around you
and try to keep in right with them by offering sacrifices to
placate them, by wearing charms, by consulting the witch
doctors, all to assure yourself a minimum of trouble from the
evil powers around."

Sheepish grins were the acknowledgment that this was the
truth.

Then another question, "Did they believe that this great God
had created them?"

"Oh, yes!"

Then in the sense that God had created them and given them life God was their Father and they were his children. Did not Paul say to the cultured Athenians, also pagans, "We are also his offspring" (Acts 17:28)?

"What about the life after death?"

"The body dies," they said, "but the spirit goes back to God."

"But if you do not worship or serve God what will happen when you meet him?"

No answer this time, so we take a different tack.

"Are you good men or bad men? Is there any man here who has never told a lie? Put up your hand so I can see you."

Not a hand was lifted. We went on down through the Commandments, which are written on the hearts of pagans (Rom. 2:14–15). Finally, I said, "Is there any man here who is not afraid to meet the great God when he dies, who thinks he is good enough to please God? Let him stand up so we can see him."

Dead silence. Finally, a black way in the back said something and everyone chuckled. The interpreter repeated, "He says none of us are good men."

"Then what will this God do to you, who knows you do not obey him, and do not worship him?"

They had the answer to that question; every man was a fundamentalist on that point at least.

Now we are ready for the gospel. Until now we were dealing with "natural religion," what every man can know from the light of nature and the light of conscience. They knew much truth already. What did they know? That "God so loved the world that he gave his only begotten Son."

"Can we be sure that God really loves us?"

"He made us and we are his, would he not have pity on us even though we are sinners against him?" A few yards away the Sobat River flowed, where crocodiles lurked in the tall grasses and reeds lined its bank. At night hippos come up and wander around the compound. We said, "Suppose you told your boy to stay away from the river because the crocodiles were there, but he disobeyed you and went down. Then one seized him and he shouted for help; what would you do?"

A man said something and everyone laughed out loud. The interpreter didn't want to repeat it, but finally said, "If a crocodile got him I would just have to let it have him."

That was distinctly not the answer I hoped for, so I tried again. "But remember, this is your own boy, and though he has disobeyed he is in danger of losing his life. In his great terror he calls your name and asks help. Even though you know it is practically hopeless, what will you do?"

Instantly the answer came from all quarters, "I'd run down and try to help."

"Certainly you would. And that is what God has done for us. He sent the Lord Jesus to rescue us at the cost of his own life. He will hear your cry and save you, 'for whosoever shall call on the name of the Lord shall be saved'" (Rom. 10:13).

I told them how our ancestors also were pagans once, offering blood sacrifices in dark groves, but the gospel came and changed their lives and it is still the power of God unto salvation. Someone asked me afterwards if I had American Indian blood! But I reminded them that the worship of Europe was cruel and bloody, but it was so long ago that we have forgotten the pit from whence we were lifted.

The pagans went out and the Christians stayed for a further word. What a difference Christ makes in the face as well as in the life! The Christians look different from their fellow-tribesmen. To them I had just a simple word from the Lord's own lips: "Ye are the salt of the earth . . . ye are the light of the world; let your light so shine."

So ended the service at Wanglel, our newest mission station in the South Sudan.[3]

By the end of February, the folks from the South Sudan Association Meeting returned and reported that we were to go back home after the job at Wanglel was completed. Our plans were to be on the post boat on June 22, 1950, en route to America by way of Egypt.

Clapping awakened me one morning in March. When I went outside, two of my men said that a hippopotamus was on the bank up the river and was bothering them. It seemed that

Wanglel church

the rogue hippo charged the men when they tried to retrieve their fishing lines and it had knocked down the fence they had surrounding their houses.

Putting on boots and getting my gun, I had doubts whether the hippopotamus would still be there when I arrived. I left the house in the dark and went to the village a half mile up stream from the mission. It was starting to get light when I arrived and I could make out the outline of a hippopotamus standing on the bank. When about sixty feet from it, I fired a silver-tipped bullet in the vicinity of the ear (since the best shot for a hippopotamus, according to Dr. Heasty, was behind the ear). It dropped to the ground and lay there a few seconds, then quivered a little and started to slide in the water. When I was about twenty feet from the hippo, I fired three more shots in its head and debilitated it so much that it slid under water with its feet in the air and disappeared.

I took one of the small anchored sailboats up stream to where the hippo was shot, but there was no sign of it. I knew it would take approximately four hours for the hippopotamus to surface so I left behind some men to watch for it and went to breakfast.

A short time later one of my carpenters announced that the hippopotamus was coming downstream. I sent word to the men to get the big boat and try to hook a rope onto it. When I got there one man had the boat coming upstream with the ropes tied around the hippo's leg. But suddenly the current changed, turned the hippo around, and it got away. Unfortunately, the boat was too big to turn quickly and go after him. Just when it looked like the rogue hippopotamus was on its way to Malakal, two men in palm tree canoes jumped in the water and started to paddle out to it. One of them reached the hippo, jumped on it, and was soon riding downstream on its back, steering it to the bank. The men maneuvered the hippo to shore and tied it with ropes until the big sailboat arrived with the hook.

It was a real challenge for more than one hundred men to drag the hippo to shore. Weighing in at over two tons, it measured twelve feet long and four feet high when lying on its side. Several of the men spent four hours cutting up the two-inch-thick hippo skin. People came from miles around to get a taste of the meat and all went home happy.

Because I had killed a hippo and previously had killed a lion, I was made an official Shilluk warrior! A hippopotamus hide shield (made by the Shilluks), a bat wing hat duplicating their hairstyle, and waterbuck hide shoes were all bestowed upon me to celebrate the occasion. The spear that the Shilluk king gave me completed the outfit.

———•◆•———

It took ten weeks from the laying of the first bricks to the completion of our new look tukl house at Wanglel. How good

Cutting up the hippo

it was to be out of the school and living in a house that had a veranda with lots of light and fresh air again and a bathroom with shower and toilets. The living veranda was on the bank of the river and not only did crocodiles come up in our yard at night and lay their eggs, but lions, hyenas, and antelope came to drink at the river's edge and walked past the house. Besides the sounds of hundreds of species of birds nesting across the river, we also could hear the noise of elephants trampling down trees.

It didn't take long to learn that we couldn't construct mud buildings in the rainy season. Most often the rain and mud this time of year determined our work schedule, whether we could travel the dirt roads that turned into mud pits, and whether we could continue to make the mud bricks that were often spoiled by too much rain. We were getting one good mud brick out of every five made.

The rain also wreaked havoc on construction; the inside of the classroom building was washed down and the partition wall was leaning. It would all have to be rebuilt. Rain washed out some of the mud mortar on the hospital and caused some arches to crack. The roof grass, wet and moldy, was awful to work with and was difficult to dry in between rains.

Many times our vehicles got stuck and spun out with mud flying everywhere. If no one came along to dig us out, we would have to wait a few hours until the sun dried up the mud.

Due to the early rains and the lack of labor, we were unable to complete our work by the beginning of May. The station had met with the executive committee of the South Sudan Association to ask if we could return to Wanglel after our trip to Egypt to finish up the work, but it was decided that we should return to America from Egypt. Somebody else would finish the hospital.

At the mission complex supplies were running very low—everything from food to cement—and would not be replenished

Sailboat docked at the landing with supplies

until the sailboat arrived. A man came and announced that our sailboat was only nine miles away down the Zeraf River, but because of lack of wind, a crew of six men would have to tow the boat. The crew walked beside the river pulling the sailboat by ropes that were slung over their shoulders. Occasionally they could follow a towpath, but more often they made their own path. Eventually the sailboat docked at the landing and my workmen were excited to have food again and gas for running the generator.

By the end of May the workmen were finishing the classrooms at Wanglel as I started to pack. It was fun having an auctioneer sell Eddie's tools and toolbox and our personal things. On June 21, I had everything packed to go. I checked in all my tools, paid off the workmen and turned them over to Dr. Adair, and left Wanglel. As short termers, we thought this was the end of our mission work in Africa.

True to form, boat problems developed. Before we got to Malakal, the flue developed a leak in the boiler and we had to stop for repairs. During this time I worked on tools and materials' reports and wrote letters to my head workmen. Before we had left Wanglel, Okic, Abwonyo, and Aba agreed to do some evangelical work the next year among our workmen since many of them seemed interested.

On June 22, many of the workmen from Malakal and Doleib Hill came to say good-bye as we departed from Malakal and traveled down the White Nile toward Khartoum for Egypt. In Khartoum I closed my bank account and completed the necessary paperwork at the post office. I also filled out forms with the game warden in order to export my gun, horns, and hides.

It was terribly windy in Khartoum and everything was covered with dust. One night we had a small haboob, and by morning, our beds had dust a quarter-inch thick, making it difficult to breathe. From Khartoum we flew to Cairo and took a train to our destination, the United Presbyterian Church mission station at Tanta, Egypt. We arrived on June 29, 1950, and planned to stay with Dr. Hutchinson, the head of Tanta hospital.

TANTA, EGYPT

A letter written by Dolly to friends back home at Chartiers Church in Pennsylvania expressed her sentiments well:

We wish we could be with you at this joyful time of celebrating 175 years of Christian fellowship and service. We find our trip home delayed because we found here in Tanta that they needed a little help in completing their new hospital. We consider it a great privilege to work in another of our mission fields, especially in getting acquainted with all the folks here and seeing the fine work they are doing. Their great need here at Tanta is for doctors and nurses to staff the new section of the hospital that is being built. . . .

*In Tanta, Egypt, women carried sixteen to twenty bricks on their heads—
with some walking up a ramp to the third floor.*

The mission in Tanta had a large hospital, about 120 beds
(with plans to double its size), and hundreds of day patients. It
didn't take long before I got involved with various jobs here and
also at the girls' school across the street. Customs were different
in Tanta; the people rode in horse-drawn carriages and on the
backs of donkeys. Horses and wagons were used to haul goods.
The two wheels in the front of the wagon were smaller than
those in the back, making the bed slope forward. Unfortunately
the horses were malnourished, and the drivers beat them
constantly. When the wagons were being loaded or unloaded,
the drivers put a basket of wheat straw and a little corn in front
of the horses. This was the only food they were offered and it
seemed so little for the work that was expected of them.

It wasn't long before Dr. Hutchinson requested that we
stay a few months and help equip the hospital when it was
finished. We delayed our return to America and assisted the
workers with the special installations. I had many jobs: I

moved light switches, coordinated the electricians' and the plumbers' plans so the equipment was placed properly, worked on a leg brace, repaired an old operating table, and generally managed things. I took on more jobs every day and eventually had more work than I could handle. Before long, new plans had to be drawn for the hospital because of all the changes that were being made while building it.

One day I traveled to Cairo to see the pyramids and the Great Sphinx. After stopping at the mission girls' college, I visited some of our churches in Cairo. I felt good about the work they were doing there.

Work at the new Tanta hospital was progressing well. I added more jobs: I built a garage at the girls' school, a sterilizer for the new operating room, and had an idea for flush toilets to clean out bed pans. Work came to a halt in the middle of July during the three-day feast following Ramadan (twenty-eight days of holy fasting in the Muslim year). Eventually work resumed and ground was being cleared for a chapel.

Most of the hospital buildings were reinforced concrete and bricks. Work crews dug holes, nine or ten feet deep, and filled them with concrete which had been mixed by hand in a wooden frame. The crews consisted of three men: one man working down in the hole and two on top who pulled the dirt out in small baskets called *guffas*. (Girls carried all the needed materials for the projects in guffas on their heads.) A tripod with a roller pulley was used to pull up the baskets.

On July 21, 1950, at 2:25 A.M. we welcomed a healthy son, Ronald James, to our family. Ronald was delivered by Dr. Hutchinson at Tanta and weighed in at nine and one-half pounds.

Shortly after Ronnie's birth, Penny and Eddie went on holiday at Sidi Bishr, a missionary camp along the Mediterranean shore where they played in the sand and swam in the ocean. Meanwhile we received word that they could attend Schutz School with the mission kids in Assiut during our stay in Egypt.

Cultural differences were always apparent. On the way to the station one day in late August, I passed a Muslim funeral. A large group of men were singing, followed by a cloth-covered coffin carried on the shoulders of six men. The front end of the coffin had a large mirror with a picture of the deceased in the center. The women followed behind the coffin screaming and wailing.

At the end of August, we received word that a plane had crashed near the village of Cafaseat and that doctors were needed. After gathering medical supplies, we traveled there. The plane had crashed seventeen miles west of Cafaseat in the desert and, since we couldn't get any closer by car, we took a train. We found the plane's wreckage scattered several hundred yards across the sand. The plane, TWA Constellation, the *Star of Maryland* flying from India to the United States, had left Cairo for Athens and all forty passengers and seven crew members were killed. The right motor was on fire in the air and the other one exploded when the plane hit the ground with great force. Bodies were badly mangled and burned. Another plane landed nearby and loaded the bodies to take to Cairo. Camilia, the Egyptian film star, was among the passengers.

At the beginning of September, Eddie and Penny packed up and we traveled south by train to Cairo en route to Schutz, the mission school in Assiut. (Schutz School, originally located in Alexandria, closed down during World War II and relocated to Assiut when reopened.)

The train was crowded and we stood in the aisle for part of the way. As we looked out the windows, there was nothing but sand and desert on either side. We rode through similar terrain for more than six hours until we arrived at Schutz School. After getting the children settled in the boarding school, we returned to Tanta.

An Egyptian's work was affected by the type of clothes he wore. The men wore a *galabea*, a gown that reached to the ground and made it difficult to work. The girls' dresses affected their work as well; their hems touched the floor and always seemed in the way. Their shoes had an open heel and came halfway back on the foot making them slide back and forth as they walked. From a workman's perspective, their clothing wasn't very practical.

Muslims believed that three trips to Tanta equaled one trip to Mecca, and during Muskil, their holiday celebration the last week of October, many of them made their annual pilgrimage to Tanta. A big parade packed the streets with thousands of people. In order to avoid the crowds, we traveled early on the back roads and positioned ourselves on a second-floor balcony to watch the parade. To clear space for the parade, two motorcycle policemen zigzagged in front of the crowds. Behind them were more police—these were on horseback and had whips to beat back the crowd if they didn't retreat. Drummers riding camelback played kettledrums and many Bedouin tribes (poor Arabs living in the desert) danced native dances and played music.

The kalif, a spiritual and civil Moslem leader, was dressed in a bright red galabea and a hat that looked like a large football helmet with two big round straps under his chin. He rode on a horse with his eyes closed, as four men held him up. Since the people believed they would be blessed if they touched him, it was difficult for the many bodyguards to keep the crowd at a distance. Floats of many kinds, advertising local shops and stores, followed the kalif.

On my thirty-eighth birthday, I felt good about the building progress in Tanta. Construction here included the new hospital building with its 3,500 square feet (150 rooms) and planning the kitchen, laundry room, nurses' station, and laboratory. I worked on making writing armchairs for the nurses' school, IV stands, a cart to hold patients' charts, dressers, bedside tables, blood bank furniture, an aluminum table for the operating room, and a bedpan washer. I also became the engineer for the generator, an important job since power was not dependable and was especially needed if the doctors were in the middle of an operation. Contractors and subcontractors inspected the project and informed us of mistakes that needed our attention.

Tea was the drink of the day and gallons were consumed on this job. A cook shack stood in one corner of the lot where the big Egyptian cook with his long handlebar mustache worked on the job all day with his container of tea. It made no difference where the men worked, he would bring them tea. If a man was in a ditch, he went there, or if the worker was on a scaffold or on the roof, he took them tea. Many of the workers had a glass of tea in their hand most of the time.

Many people in Egypt, including some of the men on the job, smoked and drank hashish. Sometimes the government confiscated boats that smuggled up to a half ton of hashish that would be sold for large amounts of money.

The government school was on both sides of the hospital and, since England had refused to remove her troops from the Suez Canal, there were many demonstrations by the schoolboys. Wanting to change their treaty with England, the schoolboys rioted and police had to wear steel helmets as they patrolled the area. Our hospital messenger was stopped, and the American Mission sign was taken from his bicycle. Police were also stationed at our mission gate.

In mid-December, Dolly and I left Tanta to visit with Eddie and Penny while they were on a several week holiday break at Schutz School. When they met us at the train, their clothes and shoes were in need of repair and they seemed a bit homesick, but basically they were well.

While at Schutz I drew floor plans for a new four-story nurses' home for the mission hospital at Assiut, visited the

Tresher Orphanage for eight hundred children, went to the Presbyterian Memorial Institute, and attended the children's Christmas program entitled "The Obliging Clock." Since we couldn't take the kids back to Tanta for Christmas, their gifts consisted mostly of clothes instead of the usual toys. Eddie got his first long pants suit, a gray tweed, and Penny, a green corduroy suit made by Dolly.

Even though our family was the only one to remain at the school, the cook prepared a good dinner with all the trimmings and we played games with the children. Before leaving to go back to Tanta, we traveled the Nile at Luxor for a couple of days, and then crossed the river to see the tombs at Valley of the Kings. It was amazing to realize they were thousands of years old.

At the beginning of the new year, most of the hospital staff attended the Egyptian Association Meeting (similar to the South Sudan Association). The weather turned very cool and it felt good to sit by the fire in the evening. Since there was no central heating in the houses, most of them had a stove or fireplace in one room. It was hard to keep the kids warm when the temperatures dropped to forty degrees at night.

Even though the outside of the chapel at Tanta wasn't completely finished, the inside was splendid and was dedicated on April 20, 1951. Ronnie was baptized in the new chapel.

As time grew short, I sent for reservations to return to America. We wanted to travel through Europe and sail on the *Queen Elizabeth* from England. We were to leave Cairo on May 14 to fly to Paris, then on to London by steamer, and sail from Southampton on the *Queen Elizabeth* on June 15 for America. After Eddie and Penny had a successful year at school, we went to Assiut by train to pick them up and bring them back to Tanta.

By the end of April, the work was still slow, and we wondered if we would complete the Tanta projects. I didn't anticipate seeing any of the new hospital in use before I left. The American mission personnel at Tanta, Egypt, had a big farewell turkey dinner for us in the beginning of May, and on May 12 I made my last visit to the hospital, answered any last questions, and prepared to leave. It was pleasing to see some of the buildings being used: the Assiut nurses' alumni tea was held in the dining room in the new building and prayers were said for the workers in the new chapel. We had dinner with the American staff of nurses and they all seemed sorry to see us go.

On May 13, 1951, we left Tanta behind and began our return trip to Butler, Pennsylvania. With no idea if we would ever return to the mission field again, we wanted our children (Eddie, nine; Penny, eight; Billy, three; and Ronnie not yet one year old) to see as much of Europe as possible. We toured Greece, Italy, France, the Netherlands, England, and Scotland. In Southampton we boarded the *Queen Elizabeth* and sailed for the United States. By June 20, thirty-five days later, we saw the lights of New York City from her top deck. It was great to be back in America!

Our train left Penn Station and headed for Pittsburgh where Father and Mother met us to travel by car to Butler. We felt blessed that our return trip was safe and we were all in good health.

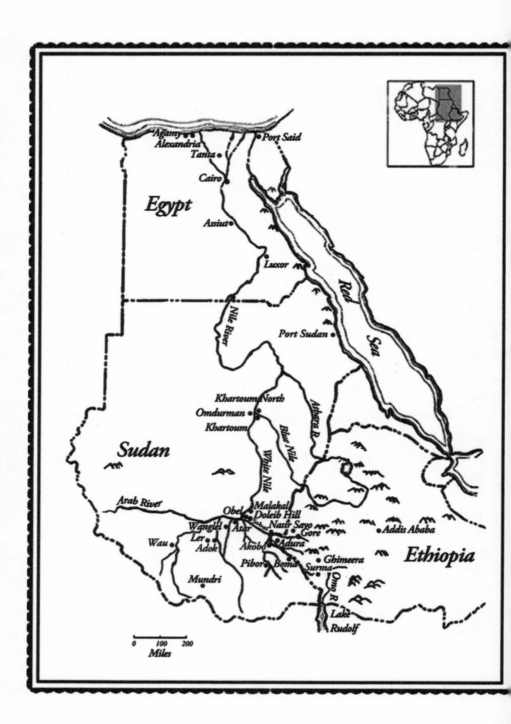

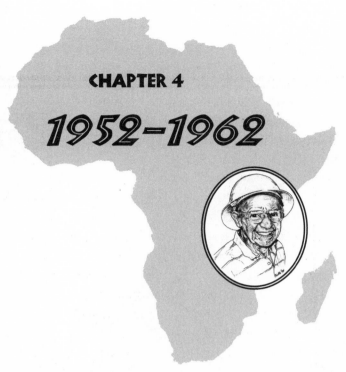

CHAPTER 4

1952-1962

"We make a living on what we get; we make a life on what we give."

—*Winston Churchill*

REENTRY UNITED STATES

It wasn't easy returning home. In fact sometimes we found readjusting to life in the U.S. (what I refer to as reverse culture shock) more difficult than adjusting to life in a third-world country. We stayed with my parents while trying to get reestablished—this time with two more children than when we left.

At home my first order of business was getting a learner's driving permit. In Pittsburgh I bought a new suit, and after recovering from the shock of high prices, continued by bus to Canonsburg, our old hometown, to see friends. Things hadn't changed much; the old shop looked about the same with only the machines and tools missing.

Houses were hard to find, but eventually we found one with six rooms and bath for sixty dollars a month on Smithfield Street in Canonsburg. As we set up housekeeping again, our needs were great. Major purchases included a used 1946 Chrysler that cost eight hundred dollars, a projector for showing our African slides, and a refrigerator. Our washing and sewing machines that we had loaned out were returned. Chartiers Church held a reception in our honor and gave us an ironing board, electric clock, toaster, and check for fifty dollars. Dolly's Sunday school class (Daughters of the King Class) and mission circle at Chartiers had a shower for her and gave us many items we needed to get reestablished. This mission circle eventually changed its name to the Pollock Circle in honor of Dolly and her mission work.[1]

We enjoyed seeing old friends again and revisiting projects I had built years ago. Our experiences on the mission field meant so much more when shared with others—and that we did. Many hours were filled with speaking engagements for groups within the local churches and various organizations: Rotary, Kiwanis, the Daughters of the American Republic, and the Women's Christian Temperance Union. Sometimes Dolly and I would give the presentations together, other times on our own. Besides our African slides, we enjoyed sharing more than one thousand photos taken during our short term in the Sudan.

By the beginning of July, all our crates had arrived from the South Sudan and were being stored in the old shop. We borrowed a trailer and began to haul things, dirty and generally in bad shape, from the shop to our rental home where we proceeded to clean and fix them up. On the Fourth of July 1951, we took a break from unpacking and traveled to Hickory, Pennsylvania, to a reunion of descendants of my Grandfather Pollock where we met many new nieces and nephews.

The Forty-sixth New Wilmington Missionary Conference (NWMC) took place the end of July with 625 enrolled and 700 to 800 more that came on the weekend. After the three Sunday morning church services, the missionaries had their mission displays in the church basement and, of course, I had to show off my mementos that I had brought back from

Africa: hippo hide shield, spears, and the lion skin that I had tanned and made into a rug.

On August 21 we attended the YPCU conference at Lake Geneva and, while there, Dolly and I celebrated our tenth anniversary. How ironic that we were at this same spot ten years ago on our honeymoon!

My time was divided between sorting the hundreds of black and white pictures and slides of our short-term mission work and making box springs, a mattress, and double-deck beds for the children's and guest's rooms. Besides, I was doing some work for Dr. Johnston. Thirty-five years had passed since I first washed windows for him. Back then he paid me 30¢ an hour. Now he was paying me $2.25.

One Sunday in September we attended church in Butler and went out to my dad's farm. For the first time since Easter of 1946, all of my family were together—five brothers and five sisters— eleven of us, and we had an enjoyable time. Of the eleven, six of us were married and together had fourteen children.

Nearing my thirty-ninth birthday, life was pretty low-key compared to the wilds of Africa. That was until one morning in mid-December when I went into the basement of Dr. Johnston's building. Another problem, or should I say, opportunity, presented itself.

Water was flowing from the boiler and as it got hotter and hotter, steam poured out of the bottom. I didn't have a wrench to shut off the gas at the meter, so I had to approach the boiler. With the fire burning full force, I knew it might blow at any minute. Fear presented itself—even greater than meeting a lion in the dark forests of Africa! But I had no choice, I had to shut off the gas, and that I did. With great relief I said a small prayer, "Thank You, Lord." I then repaired the boiler and got it back in operating order.

Christmas was fast approaching and I was trying to finish gifts for the children. Penny, who had just turned eight, received a doll; Eddie got a bicycle; Billy, a tricycle; and Ronnie, a duck swing. On December 31, Eddie and Penny ushered in the new year with Eddie ringing the Egyptian gong on the porch.

In retrospect, 1952 was a busy year. I was elected to the board of trustees at church and got the job to clean, sand, repair, and refinish the church pews for a salary of fifteen hundred dollars. At the same time I was trying to get a Cub pack started, Dolly was elected president of the mission circle she was attempting to reorganize. In May I was informed that I would be work boss at the 1952 Youth Fellowship Work Camp for two weeks that summer in a rural community near Salineville, Ohio, renovating Grant Hill Presbyterian Church and Glade Run Presbyterian Church. The camp, sponsored by the youth department of the United Presbyterian Church in Pittsburgh, was a volunteer staff of men and women in their late teens.

WORK CAMPS

I made a car rack, packed our things, and on June 20 we were on our way to Grant Hill Presbyterian Church in Ohio. Upon arrival we were shown our accommodations—beds set up on the stage at the Grange Hall. Boys were to bunk on the first floor while the girls made their home in the basement with a kitchen. The rest of the work crew, twenty young people in all, arrived the following day and I put them to work nailing and scraping immediately. At the evening meeting each one was given two minutes to give a personal history and, from this, I learned enough to determine which job best suited each crew member.

The list of completed jobs at Grant Hill was long: we wood-planked the walls, wood-tiled the ceiling, enlarged two small storage closets into classrooms, sanded and refinished the floors, tiled the floor in the vestibule, and replaced coal stoves with two automatic oil floor furnaces. (These furnaces were purchased with money that the church had given to the campers as a token of their appreciation. The campers refused to accept the generous gift, so the board of missions put enough money with it to buy the two floor furnaces. Church members were very touched by the campers' generosity.)

The leaders of the congregation planned a picnic for all of the campers. Young people from nearby churches joined us to help clean, sand, and refinish the pews. In addition, we received help from the community and several neighboring ministers joined in working on the project. We repaired and painted the outside of the building, erected a new chimney, put new doors on the entrance, and repaired windows. After eating and working together we formed a close bond with the locals.

The rededication of the Grant Hill Presbyterian Church, in appreciation of the 1952 Youth Fellowship Work Camp, was held on July 6, two weeks after we started. I was asked to read Scripture (1 Kings 8:10–23), and I felt uncomfortable among the important men—reverends and doctors—but I did it. The church was full, it was a good service, and the renovations were presented and accepted.

That evening, after our candlelight rededication of life service, each of the campers was asked to write about his or her work camp experience. Most of them benefited tremendously from their volunteer work and they were thankful that they had learned to be "doers, and not only hearers, of the Word." The group was quite diverse; some came from mining towns and farms while others were from wealthy families with servants. But at camp they were all the same, dressed in overalls and working with their hands. Only one boy had ever done similar work. They were all willing workers and when night came, you couldn't get them to stop. In order to have the walls completed for the rededication, they worked twelve- to sixteen-hour days, with time out only to eat.

Glade Run Presbyterian Church, ten miles west of Grant
Hill, was equally challenging: we replaced the double entrance
with a new center entrance, repaired the sills and windows, put
in two Sunday school rooms and vestibule, gave the buildings
two coats of paint, and repainted the name on the outside.

Since there was more work on the Glade Run Church than
we expected, we held a post camp with some campers staying
over to finish up. By the middle of July we completed the work
we had set out to do, closed up post camp, loaded all our
things, and left for home.

In the beginning of August 1952, all the children stayed
with Grandma while Dolly and I went to the New Wilmington
Missionary Conference. It was the first time in ten years (since
Eddie was born) that we had gone out without at least one of
them. Large crowds, good meetings, and seeing old friends all
contributed to another enjoyable gathering. Conference had
grown since my first one in 1934.

Returning home, I began to plan the material I needed to
paint our ninety-foot-high church belfry. But before we knew it,
we were back on the road to visit a few young peoples' camps:
Camp Fairfield in western Pennsylvania, Camp Putnam in New
York, and Camp Topsham in Vermont. We stopped to see a
Presbyterian church at Ryegate Corners in Vermont (with the
possibility of having a work camp there the following year).
The steeple at Ryegate had been hit by lightning, not once but
twice in five years, and after the minister was told I was a
steeplejack, he wanted me to come back and do repairs. The
insurance company offered five hundred dollars to do the
work, and I accepted the job.

By the middle of September I was heading back to Ryegate
to do the steeple repairs. I started to build the scaffolding from

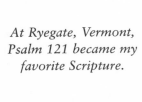

At Ryegate, Vermont, Psalm 121 became my favorite Scripture.

the ground, realizing it was the only way I would be able to handle the work by myself. Psalm 121:1–2 came into my mind, "I lift up my eyes to the hills. From whence does my help come? My help comes from the Lord, who made heaven and earth" (RSV). Fog, wind, and rain slowed my progress but, by the end of September, I had the work completed. From that time on, Psalm 121 became my favorite Scripture.

I also was asked to complete the repair work of the belfry at Topsham in Vermont. Because of bad weather, this job took a week longer than I had expected, and I actually had to finish up by flashlight.

While working in Ryegate, Vermont, I received a telegram from Rev. Lowrie Anderson, the general secretary of the American Mission Upper Nile, and Allan Webb, headmaster of the Obel teachers' training school in the Sudan. It stated that the Executive Committee of the South Sudan Mission voted unanimously to ask the Board of Foreign Missions in Philadelphia for Dolly and my appointments as career missionaries to the South Sudan.

Since Dolly and I had "earned our spurs" on our short-term trip, the thought of becoming career missionaries was exciting.

In a short time, I had another letter from Dr. Glenn Reed acknowledging our acceptance and stating that he was delighted we were willing to return to the Sudan. I was always ready for whatever God wanted me to do. By the middle of October, Dr. Reed visited and told us we had been appointed to the South Sudan as full-time missionaries! I hoped to be ready to leave sometime in January 1953, and once again we had to arrange for chest X rays, shots, and passport photos.

"Life begins at 40" and as I hit that stage in my life, I was involved in drawing up plans for the Canonsburg house that I had started building for our family on the lot I had bought from Uncle Jim. Eddie was actually old enough that his help made a difference.

Digging the foundation, pouring footers, and laying blocks were jobs squeezed in between other work I had scheduled. Next came the I beams, floor joists, roof rafters, and laying of the bricks. By the middle of January, the outside of the house was finished.

As the work on the house progressed, we organized things to be shipped to the Sudan. Our eight crates and two barrels weighed in at 2,620 pounds. A farewell party held for us at the church was a wonderful evening with many good friends. Besides canvas overnight bags for the children, they gave Dolly and me a camera with telephoto lens and a generous cash gift.

CAREER MISSIONARIES—BUILDING THE UPPER NILE

"What you do speaks so loud, I cannot hear what you are saying."
                                                —*Ralph Waldo Emerson*

In January 1953, we finished packing, put things in storage, and sold the Plymouth. My brother, Jack, took us to

Butler on the first leg of our journey to the South Sudan as full-time career missionaries. We left Canonsburg like a thief in the night, too late to bid a final good-bye to our neighbors. After a stop in Philadelphia, we headed to New York City.

While touring the RCA building in the city, we were surprised to be chosen to go downstage for the radio show *Break the Bank*. Unfortunately we never had an opportunity to get on the radio since we had to leave to meet our ship. How disappointing since the bank that day was over two thousand dollars! We could have put the money to good use on our African adventure. We also went to see the TV show *Chance of a Lifetime* while in the city.

On January 23, we sailed past the Statue of Liberty and headed out to the north Atlantic where rough sea storms were predicted. The turbulence never bothered us, so either the sea was much calmer than expected or we were better sailors than we had thought. In Halifax, Nova Scotia, we quickly had our passports stamped, received shore passes, dashed ashore, and entered the first church we came to—five minutes late but just in time to hear "My Faith Looks Up to Thee." Rare for this time of year, an iceberg came into view not far from Halifax.

By February 1, we saw the coastline of southern Ireland and soon docked at Liverpool. Here you were fortunate if you liked cabbage since it was served for every meal.

On a side trip to Stratford-on-Avon, we visited Shakespeare's birthplace, a half-timbered building of the early sixteenth century. Our accommodations were at the picturesque Shakespeare Hotel. All the hotel apartments were named after Shakespeare's plays, had huge high-ceiling rooms, crooked walls, narrow halls, little stairways, and were cold. Small gas heaters in a corner of each room required that a shilling be deposited every few hours.

Back in Liverpool we boarded the ship the S.S. *Prome*. The manifest included forty-five passengers, two horses going to Burma, two airplanes for Rangoon, and some large tanks, all headed for Port Sudan. The wind was with us all the way and our little ship sailed along without even a dip. After Port Lisbon it wasn't long before we saw the coast of Spain and followed it into the Strait of Gibraltar. As we passed the Rock, just after sundown, we thought of Paul of long ago and how rough the sea can be if it so wills.

By February 19, occasionally we could see the coast of Africa to the south of us. Eventually we passed the island of Malta and arrived at Port Said, Egypt, on February 23. Here one of the boilers developed a crack and there was a twenty-four-hour layover. This was a perfect opportunity for us to visit our friends and the hospital in Tanta.

Dr. Harry Hutcheson met us and gave us a quick tour of the hospital. It was a good feeling to see the complex in use, knowing we played a part in its construction. Many missionaries came in for the evening to visit and, needless to say, I couldn't get away without doing at least one job. This time it was fixing a record player. It felt familiar to stay in the same room in our third-floor apartment where we had stayed in 1950. How happy Billy was to play in his sand pile once again and to see Hasson, our friendly Egyptian cook.

Continuing on our trip to the Sudan, we started through the 104-mile-long Suez Canal where 50,000 English troops were stationed. The fee for our ship to pass through the canal was almost six thousand dollars. Coming out of the Gulf of Suez and into the Red Sea, we passed by Mt. Sinai off in the distance. As the temperature increased, the crew changed into their whites and shorts, and so did I. It wasn't long before we could see land and, after dark, we could see the lighthouses along the shore. On February 28, the lights of Port Sudan were in view.

An abundance of coral made for slow going and it was critical to follow the channel in the harbor. Finally we docked and the ship was tied up, but unloading was delayed until 6:00 the next morning. We finally disembarked at 10:00 A.M. and, after going through customs, we arrived at the Hotel Red Sea. Port Sudan had grown since we were there last in January 1947. All the wood buildings were being replaced with stone and looked more modern. The preacher from the Presbyterian church in Port Sudan took Dolly and me to Sunday school in his home, and in the evening we attended a Church of England service.

From Port Sudan we traveled over desert by train until we reached the train station at Khartoum North. Here we were met and transported to our accommodations at the Girls' Boarding and Day School. According to the booklet "Africa and the United Presbyterians," this school was established in 1908, and was the oldest continuing girls' school in the Sudan.[2] Classes from kindergarten to post high school prepared girls for university examinations.

During afternoon prayer meeting at the girls' school, we became reacquainted with many old friends, met some new ones, and reunited with some of the South Sudanese there on leave. Due to a strike, our train for the South had left earlier in the day and we were informed that we would have to stay in Khartoum another seventeen days. All of a sudden we had lots of spare time.

Besides doing odd jobs around the school, most of my time was spent buying building materials for our first work projects as career missionaries and figuring out how to have them shipped. It was the beginning of the rainy season and the river would be rising. Often, at this time of year, the towpath that ran beside the river was flooded and made it impossible for sailboats to be towed when there was a slack in the wind. Unable to find a boat that would sail to Malakal during the rainy season, I had to rely on Sudan railways and steamers.

On March 21, we left Khartoum North by train and headed south for Kosti where we met up with our freight from Port Sudan. We loaded our freight onto the boat, the *Annak,* and discovered that things were different on boats from what we remembered. In order to cut expenses, there was not only less food being offered, but they had cut back to one sheet on the beds. Regardless, we were thankful that we could drink the water without using purifying pills.

MALAKAL, DOLEIB HILL, AND LER

We were back in the land of the Nilotic peoples with their grass-thatched roof mud homes and their shining black faces. Our first assignment as career missionaries was in Malakal, with plans to go on to Ler the next dry season to build a doctor's house and hospital.

It was four days until we docked at Malakal on March 25 and saw familiar faces on the bank, including Robb McLaughlin and Ken Rasmussen who had traveled with us on our first trip to the South Sudan in 1947. Seeing friendly faces helped ease the hollow feeling caused by leaving dear friends in the United States. Ken was in the process of digging footers on a house and I would be helping him.

Initially we were taken to a government rest house where I would be staying. Since there was no other place available, I took the family to Doleib Hill to stay in the same house we had lived during our short term. It was like going back home. Mary Ewing, the nurse, had added a table and some chairs and had fixed up some beds.

Things looked about the same at Doleib Hill. As we unpacked, we discovered some of our freight had been damaged. By the beginning of April, however, we had things in fair shape, and living accommodations for the family were comfortable.

Until Ken's departure, I was to be in charge of carpentry at Malakal. After he left, I would take over the entire house building project. When the word got out that I was back, some of the carpenters returned who had worked for me during our short term and wanted to work for me again. But about mid-morning, their contractor came over with a letter from the Public Works Department accusing me of stealing his workmen. Ken answered the letter and instructed the workers to return to the PWD. Since they weren't happy with their contractor, I knew the carpenters would be back. As it worked out, they went to the district commissioner and were told they had to work for the contractor another two weeks before they could work for us.

Toward the end of April, I still didn't have any carpenters so I started making veranda framing myself, and, up to that point, I was able to keep up with the bricklayers. By the end of the month, thank goodness, all of my carpenters were back and moving full steam ahead.

So back and forth from Malakal to Doleib Hill I went—from job to family and family to job. (One day I made the sixteen-mile trip from Doleib Hill to Malakal on Eddie's little bike in two hours and five minutes.) I was not looking forward to taking over the house building project at Malakal since things were not in good shape.

After one month I brought the family from Doleib Hill over to Malakal and temporarily moved us into the bookstore building. Eventually we built a house and moved into two of the rooms while workmen continued working on it. Here we were located directly behind the community church and, beginning at 7:00 A.M. and continuing until 7:00 P.M., we could hear Sunday services in all different languages from our porch. We felt especially blessed that we could attend a service in English and have our good friend, Rev. Lowrie Anderson, as pastor.

Malakal, a town of thirteen thousand people, was mostly black. In fact, there were exactly nine white children and four of those were ours. Seldom did you meet a white person at the market since many folks sent their hired help to do the shopping.

We liked Malakal with its touch of civilization yet still retaining that which was the heart of Africa. We had no taxis, streetcars, or buses, so we relied on the few government trucks and one or two privately owned cars that were available. Bicycle use had greatly increased since the last time we were in Malakal in 1950.

A telegraph, post office, two general stores, an airport, the mosque, a hospital, and the native market were all part of the town of Malakal. Most of the little town shops, with beads of every color hung on their doorways, had wares piled out front on the sidewalks: onions in little mounds, handfuls of rock salt, a sack of grain, and peanuts and lentils. The pungent odor from hot peppers and spices was evident. The little tailor shops with sewing machines out front had gone modern and displayed at least one dress form on which a finished creation was hung. The butcher shop, an open building with only a roof on poles and a fenced off area around it, used a hatchet as a carving knife.

The Muslim holiday of Ramadan fell during the ninth month of the Mohammedan year and lasted twenty-eight days. This month commemorated the time that the Quran, the Muslim holy book, was revealed to the Prophet Mohammed about fourteen hundred years ago.

The Prophet Mohammed fasted one day of this ninth month, but not knowing which day, the Muslims fasted the entire month from sunrise to sunset. A siren blew at the big mosque in the center of Malakal at 5:00 A.M. for the faithful Muslims to get up and eat before sunrise. Observant Muslims abstained from eating, drinking, smoking, and sexual intercourse during this time in order to spiritually renew themselves. Men worked from 7:00 A.M. to 1:00 P.M. without eating or drinking and on a hot day, with the temperature up close to one hundred degrees, the sun took its toll. Everyone welcomed the last three days of Ramadan, which were reserved for celebrating and feasting. Even though I am tolerant of Islam and all other religions, I praised the Lord that I was born in a Christian land and brought up in a Christian home.

At Malakal, just like on short term, I had workmen who couldn't speak to me or to each other. Five different languages were spoken without an interpreter. Usually I used sign language plus a little Arabic and Shilluk that I had picked up along the way.

Eventually I formed my posse of six fine Christian leaders—a Nuer, a Shilluk, a Dinka, an Anuak, a Murle, and an Arabian—to accompany me on my travels. All of my interpreting needs were covered from then on. These leaders demonstrated how Christians should work, act, and treat their fellow man. Most of my laborers were illiterate and were not able to read a Bible even if translated for them, but we felt our greatest witness to them was in our daily living.

One day while at Malakal, an invitation arrived from the governor of the Upper Nile Province inviting us to join him for tea. Our acceptance enabled us to become better acquainted with the governor and gave our children an opportunity to play together. Later on, the governor held a formal open house for the coronation of Queen Elizabeth and it was then that I was introduced to the idea of wearing my first cummerbund.

After I finished making six dining room chairs from old crating wood, Dolly's paint job thoroughly covered up all the flaws. As the Fourth of July 1953, rolled around, Dolly invited everyone at the station for a holiday picnic.

As we were finishing up our first house at Malakal, money was slow coming from the States and I had to reduce my crew. The executive committee met to discuss building plans and decided we were to finish up at Malakal, go to Doleib Hill and repair the ladies' house, and when that was finished, go to Ler and build a doctor's house and hospital. Jumping from one site to another was typical for me but lends itself to confusion when trying to describe our projects in the South Sudan. To this day I say I was so confused I spelled confusion with a "k"!

When we started work on a second house at Malakal, the rains came and filled the footers with water. The house footers, six feet deep, were full to the top and between eight to ten thousand gallons of water had to be taken out at one point. Each time we had the foundation dug out, it rained and filled up again. Even though we were bailing, there still was a lot of mud and some cave-ins.

One time we had seventy-five men in the hole to remove the water and mud. After taking off the few clothes they had on, the men slipped down into the mud up to their knees and threw handfuls of mud up onto the bank. With the average yearly rainfall at 321 inches, over 200 inches fell in less than two months. Eventually we cut a ditch through to the town drainage in order to remove the water from the foundation.

At the beginning of August, Dr. Jim West, his wife, four-month-old son, and I left Malakal by post boat for a three-day trip to survey Ler (354 miles), our new mission station in the Western Nuer District. The Wests were a British family from the Church Missionary Society, and, due to a lack of doctors at Ler, were scheduled to work with our mission. There was nothing to see but sudd and papyrus on the way, so our time was used to work on plans for the Ler hospital.

Our first stop, Adok, was nothing more than a landing on the Nile—but it happened to be in the middle of one of the largest swamps in the world. A little Arab shop and storehouse were all that was here.

Ler was situated seventeen miles west of Adok on the Nile and those last seventeen miles could only be traveled by foot. We got off the post boat at sundown and set up tents and cots to prepare for a rest under an open-sided grassed-roof hut. The ground was wet and muddy and the mosquitoes were bad. It rained hard for several hours during the night, and with the leaky roof, my bed became wet.

After eating a little bully beef and bread for breakfast, I packed up, strapped on my knapsack containing food, camera, and a bag of water, and started walking the seventeen-mile trip from Adok to Ler with briefcase in hand. I left behind the bed roll and cot to be picked up on my return trip. Dr. West put bamboo poles under the baby's carriage and found one native boy to help carry it.

The first five miles were downright torture. Covered with more mosquitoes than imaginable, our arms, legs, and faces became indistinguishable and I hardly had a free hand to swat them. When I managed to squash some, the blood smeared on my arms and face and attracted flies. I about went crazy! Dr. West said it was no exaggeration that he had one thousand bites.

The mud was slippery and, since our feet kept sliding, we couldn't make time. Covered in mud, we were quite a sight. I walked faster and got ahead of the others and stopped to eat some crackers and cheese. All the way from Adok to Ler there were native homes and barns in every direction, as far as the eye could see. Thankfully, about five miles from Ler, a chief of one of the villages sent some of his men to help us carry our load. By the time we arrived at Ler, my feet were sore and my legs were stiff and I wondered why anyone would want to work there. It was the first time in three years that I had walked seventeen miles in one day and I wouldn't have been able to go on much further.

It was back in 1948, the first time we traveled past Adok, that I said to Dolly, "I hope God never sends me here." But God had other plans. Here we were, going back again, this time to look over the station and make plans for the doctor's house and hospital we would build.

When we got to the mission station, Ler's reason for exis-tence became obvious. It was situated on a sandy ridge and named by the Nuers for a tree that was very prevalent there. The district commissioner estimated that fifty thousand people lived in a radius of twenty miles, a place with lots of potential for evangelizing—but a bad place to travel during the rains. Even though it was one of the most heavily populated areas in the South Sudan, there was no church or mission station other than Ler.

Thank goodness the road dried up for our return trip to the post boat and the boat took us back to Malakal.

After taking Penny and Eddie back to Schutz School in Assiut, Egypt, I worked on two missionary homes in Malakal and continued with the estimates and plans for the Ler hospital. The minor changes I made were sent off to the building board for their approval, and it wasn't long before I received word that the plans were passed.

Sometimes construction work had its hazards—and there at Malakal, snakes were one of them. In mid-October, I killed a six-foot three-inch cobra in the storehouse and a few weeks later I killed two more snakes, a hooded cobra and a viper.

We received an invitation to the Mahdi, the Prophet Mohammed's birthday, with the governor and all the officials in attendance at Malakal. The evening was spent going from tent to tent, eating candy and crackers, and drinking coffee and lemonade.

Eventually our supply of cement ran out and held up our progress on the houses in Malakal. As we waited for a new shipment, we started hauling material to Doleib Hill to get ready for our next project. The approval was given for the Doleib Hill school buildings, and I could build as many as time permitted. By December both houses in the Malakal project were completed, Dolly started packing, and we all made the move to Doleib Hill.

Work began immediately with laying out two dorms and an office/storeroom at the girls' boarding school at Doleib Hill. Having ample supplies of cement and roof grass was always a challenge. My biggest week I had over two hundred workers, a little larger work camp than what I was accustomed to in the States. Sometimes I longed for a few fellow work campers from the United States to help supervise. In one month at Doleib Hill we completed four mud and thatch-roofed dormitories and a classroom, one brick office/store building, and helped start four more mud huts for dorms.

In December, I made the presentation of certificates to the teachers who were finishing at Obel Teachers' Training School. It was a big day at Obel as the first graduating class of fifteen boys became teachers. I was proud to be invited back to hand out the diplomas. The celebration included sports in the early part of the day and a presentation service by Mr. Webb, the headmaster, later in the afternoon.

It was traditional in December at Doleib Hill for the Shilluks to gather for a church service on the riverbank under the wild fig tree. There must have been close to one thousand folks there—each in his brightest and newest cloth, with brilliant red, green, and yellow colors ruling the day.

Our Christmas was quieter than usual, no frost in the air or smell of pine (although we did bring an artificial tree from America this time). It was a day to think of loved ones back home and reflect on the magic of the birth of Christ. Eddie and Penny remained in Egypt over the holiday and vacationed in Tanta, a second home to them since they had lived there for one year.

In seven short weeks at Doleib Hill, on January 30, we finished the last work on my five school buildings. A farewell picnic, with all the ice cream we could eat, was held for us in the garden. As we moved our personal things back to Malakal, I was planning an airfield at Ler, our next assignment. The airfield would make it possible for the Mission Aviation Fellowship (MAF) plane to land and take us to the February association meeting at Nasir, another American Mission station on the Sobat River.

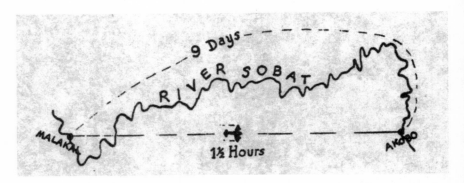

Nine days versus one-and-a-half hours

In August of 1950, Mission Aviation Fellowship arrived in the Sudan. MAF, a vision of World War II airmen, was first started in England. At first there wasn't much request for its use, but as missionaries became educated to its purpose and airstrips were built on mission stations, business increased. MAF made it possible to reach the farthest corners of the Sudan. These Christian pilots were paid no salary but trusted God to supply their needs through donations. According to Winburn and Fairman, missionaries using the planes paid for the fuel, oil, and running costs.[3] The planes carried missionaries, mail, and supplies enabling mission work to be done much more efficiently and saving days of difficult travel. A trip east from Malakal to Akobo, nine days by riverboat, now could be made in ninety minutes by plane.[4]

Medical aid and lifesaving drugs could be transported quickly by MAF, and the sick could be airlifted instead of having to walk or travel by mule for days to the nearest medical facility. Malakal was chosen as the base of MAF's operations due to its central location, communications, availability of help, and accessibility to other means of linking transportation. I helped layout and build some of MAF's first airstrips in the early fifties. These airstrips were few and far between and without control beacons or safety systems.

I viewed every problem as an opportunity. After being told that the road to Ler was closed for driving and that I couldn't get our truck on the post boat, another opportunity presented itself. I didn't know what I should do. Down to the post boat I went with crates, tool boxes, benches, and other building materials—ninety-two pieces in all. There was no problem finding room for all of our goods on the boat, but finding room for the truck was a challenge.

Suddenly I noticed some lumber being unloaded from the barge and was relieved when I managed to convince the crew to let me put the truck in its place. But upon seeing the truck, the crew said the space wasn't big enough. Checking out the

MAF plane with pontoons for the wet season.
That's the pilot, Captain Marshall, and his family.

situation I saw two big boxes full of iron that, if moved, would open up more room for the truck. But when the watchman on the barge informed me we would need a crane to move them, the challenge was too much for me to resist. I called on my crew of six men. We moved the boxes, took the outside back tires off the truck, put the truck on the post boat, and left Malakal for Ler.

On our way to Ler I rested and worked on the books as we moved up the river toward Adok. Chuck Jordan met us at Adok and transported Dolly and the kids by Jeep the seventeen miles into Ler. I loaded six workmen, household goods, tools, supplies, and their families on my truck and headed for the same destination. Due to the dry season, the mosquitoes weren't as bad as the first time we visited Ler. Now it was the flies that were annoying.

Son Tom and the "long fellow"

A mud, grass-roofed house, consisting of three large and two small rooms (without plumbing), was to be our home for the next six months at Ler. It needed a lot of work. All the water had to be drawn from a well and carried into the house and out again. There was no screening on the verandas and part of the floor was mud. The windows had no glass but were merely openings with screening. Our goal was to make the home more comfortable for the next family that came to live here.

At Ler we would be working with the Nuers, a Nilotic tribe with their own language. A young Nuer came to me looking for work and upon asking him his name, he rattled off a string of them a yard long. When I demanded that I needed a shorter name by which to call him and to write in my time book, he retorted that he was a long fellow and needed a long name. He was well over six feet tall, a common trait of the tribe.

Because of the high maintenance required on thatched mud huts, we decided to use Arcon kits for construction of the Shrader Memorial Hospital and the doctor's house at Ler. These kits, steel frames with aluminum roofs (a disappointment to the millions of termites, I'm sure), had to be ordered one year in advance from England. The walls were constructed of cement blocks which we made right on the site. Sand, dug from pits, was plentiful but gravel wasn't so easy to acquire as it had to be picked up one piece at a time in the swamps. The mahogany for the shelves and cabinets was to be hauled over very bad roads from a mill near Wau, a town 214 miles from Ler. Water was our greatest problem since we were seventeen miles inland and most of the wells were dry. A cup of water given in His name really meant something here.

At the end of February, an MAF plane came to Ler to take us to Nasir for the ten-day South Sudan Association meeting where I would be working on the building and finance committees. MAF was a blessing. When we traveled by steamer to Malakal and then by road to Nasir, it took sixty hours, but flying with

MAF took only one hour and twenty minutes. There was only one drawback—the post boat ran its route only once every two weeks and it was our only means of contacting MAF. We longed for the day when our outstations would have two-way radios.

Plans for the missionary children's school in Malakal were passed, and, if all were approved by the board, we would finish Ler and then go back to Malakal to build the school. We were invited to go to a work camp in Egypt the summer of 1955 where I would be work boss building a conference center for young people there. Before going back to America from Egypt, we planned to go to Nasir to build a hospital and then on to Pibor Mission Station to work on finishing a hospital. It *almost* seemed like a mission impossible.

Work progressed on the Ler Arcon house, and with the temperatures getting hot in to March, we began laying out part of the first hospital tukl. April rolled around and with a lot of fuss from the Nuers about their pay, most of them quit. Only five or six workmen remained out of forty-three. Even the higher paid men wanted more money, and, although we hired six new workers, the work was dragging. Eventually some of the men returned and wanted to be rehired, but they didn't want to work in the hot afternoon sun. When they saw me working, a few of the men were inspired and came to help.

In the beginning of April, I left in the Ford truck for the mill at Wau to get the last load of mahogany I needed for the Ler hospital. En route my attention focused on herds of animals— some large herds with four or five hundred heads and other smaller herds with forty to one hundred. After ten hours and 214 miles, I arrived at Wau, shot a male Reed buck, bought some benzene, and loaded the mahogany at the mill.

At first our return trip back was smooth sailing. I stopped and shot a male bushbuck and told the four Sudanese with me to take the buck to the truck and pick me up down the road a ways where I had seen some tiang. I started walking and after three miles wondered why the truck was delayed. Going back to investigate, I discovered that the clutch had gone out on the truck. We were about fifty miles from Ler and our water supply was very low. The men cooked some of the meat and ate; I had an orange and mango for my supper and drank a little water before setting up my cot to spend the night atop the lumber.

It was cold and damp and my joints ached. Early next morning I sent one of my men to Ler by bicycle to ask Chuck Jordan for help. I recalled there was a stream eight miles away and left, with no water and little food, to investigate. After ten miles my legs were tired. By eleven miles I saw tiang and thought water was near. After twelve miles I stopped for a fifteen-minute rest and thought I could hear cattle in the distance, but there was no water. In a little over three hours I had walked thirteen miles and, finally ahead, I could see the khor. I walked faster and upon reaching the water, I filled my water bag and put in the purifying pills. It was a terribly long half hour as I waited for the pills to take effect. There was no sign of the boy on bicycle and if he didn't return soon, I would reach Ler before him. As I took off my clothes and bathed for the first time in several days, the water was refreshing. I shaved, brushed my teeth, and had breakfast with all the water I wanted to drink. I felt a lot better.

I was tired and wanted to rest, but there was no shade. I continued on for two miles before I found a small tree and laid down for a nap. But the shade moved and the ants found me, so I had to move on. That afternoon I walked eleven more miles in several hours. I picked up a quart of water from a mud hole before coming to another khor. It was nearly sunset and there was no word from Ler. What was I to do—walk or wait? I had already walked twenty-five miles that day. The mosquitoes were biting and I knew if I stopped to rest I would be eaten alive, so I decided to walk.

It was a tough five miles in the dark. By 9:30 P.M. I arrived at a merchant's shop and savored every last drop of hot tea he shared with me—especially since the water out of the last khor was kind of thick. Still there was no word from the man on the bicycle. The merchant put up a net and laid a mat on the ground for my bed. Since the merchant's shop was only a couple of hundred yards from the road, I made a sign using grass, pointing to my location. It wasn't until 12:30 that night that Chuck Jordan came along and found me.

In the middle of the night, Chuck and I arrived back at the broken-down truck and found my men on top trying to protect themselves from hyenas. Not only had they depleted all their water supplies, but they had drunk the water from the radiator as well. It wasn't long before we had a fire going, and the men were drinking tea. Towing the truck home was a slow process, and I managed to shoot a female cob, a male tiang, and a bustard on the way. It was good to have a clean bed back at Ler.

Work was progressing at Ler: water pipes were being installed at our house, the footers were being dug, concrete was being poured for the columns on the hospital, and we were working on the hospital aluminum roof. By the middle of May, there were fewer and fewer laborers since all the workmen left to plant their gardens.

Dr. West filled our great need for a doctor at Ler. Our only hope was that his "hospital," a small grassed-roof mud building set on poles, would stay standing until I had time to put up a new one and make his life easier. At this time there were approximately sixty thousand western Nuers in the area, and this was the first and only medical facility within three hundred miles.

Dr. West's operating table looked like it might have come out of the ark, but still he continued. A day's work might include draining a lung abscess, performing an eye operation, or tending to a skull fracture. No job was too big or too small. Dr. West never knew what to expect. Several Nuers who had been clawed by lions were brought to him as well as a boy gored by a bull. Some natives had sewn this boy's stomach shut with the hair of a cow's tail before bringing him to Dr. West several days later.

One day a Nuer man arrived at the Ler clinic carrying his son in a basket. His story was that his son got bit on the leg by a puff adder (a large, deadly snake), and they had traveled downriver in a canoe for four days to get medical treatment. With rotted flesh on the boy's leg exposing bare bone, Dr. West had no choice but to amputate the leg. After the amputation, the boy remained at the mission, and as far as I know, he would stay there for the rest of his life. What good would it be for him to return to his village if he couldn't herd cattle or hunt?

At the beginning of June, Eddie and Penny returned from school by post boat and immediately started putting up swings and building tree houses. For a challenge, I added a twenty-foot-long pipe as an entry to the tree house and a twenty-foot sliding board to exit. They had grown a lot and were able to help with various jobs at the house and the hospital. Eddie, Penny, and I started reading about the Old World at nights to try to help them prepare for their history the following year.

Meat was getting low at Ler and often a lot of effort was spent getting even small amounts. One day toward the end of June, I left Ler to go hunting with Eddie and Penny and took along Mynero (one of our houseboys) and a schoolboy who knew the location of some tiang. Five miles south, we passed the last village and located tiang in large herds in the forest. While the others walked ahead to keep the animals' attention, I left the party to work my way behind some bushes. I took a shot at one buck standing on an ant hill but hit him a little too far back in the shoulder. I followed the buck and worked around to head him back toward Ler, taking shot now and then on the run. I was doing some bad shooting. I had five shots in him before he went down permanently.

By the time the others caught up to me and we skinned and cut up the meat, it was 5:30 P.M. I tried to persuade some Nuers

*Dr. West and Nuer boy
with bone exposed from
snake bite*

to carry the carcass back to the mission, but they refused; they all wanted the meat but no one wanted to work for it. In fact, some of the women and boys started to fight over the stomach.

I sent the schoolboy to Ler with one of the tiang legs and told him to bring men back to retrieve the rest of the meat. At 6:30 P.M. it was time to get Eddie and Penny back home. Mynero stayed with the meat and built a fire to keep the lions and hyenas away and as a light to guide the men back to the site. By 7:00 P.M. it was pitch dark and the sky was cloudy. For a while we could see one star in the east. Then after the clouds covered it, we spotted a light to the north.

The boy after amputation

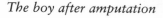

The country was rough and walking was hard. It seemed like Eddie, Penny, and I would never reach the crossroad. After passing a native cattle barn and campfire, we could see the lights in the house at Ler—but we were still a half mile away. Suddenly a bright light flashed through the sky and I could tell it was someone using my five cell flashlight. It wasn't long before we met ten workmen on their way to retrieve the meat. It was 8:00 P.M. when we reached home and learned that the schoolboy didn't know the way back to the carcass, so, Mynero, after waiting by the fire until 9:00 P.M., returned to Ler.

Ronnie was diagnosed with malaria just about the time Dolly was due to deliver Pollock baby number five. His fever was elevated for several days before the local dresser (nursing assistant) diagnosed it as malaria from blood tests taken. Since the malaria medicine that was available was not effective, we had to get some new medicine from a Greek merchant at another mission station. On June 15, 1954, a healthy nine-and-a-half-pound baby girl, Leah Ann, was born and dedicated to the Lord. Termite Tenement was the name given to her first home at Ler: a mud-walled house with leaky grass roof full of termites that we determined would have fallen down if the termites had not been holding hands!

Both the nurse from Nasir and my sister Martha, who worked in the Malakal office as a short-term bookkeeper, came to assist in the delivery. After patiently waiting for two weeks, and with no sign that the new baby was going to make its entry into the world, both the nurse and Martha packed up, left for the river, and waited for their steamer to return back to their stations. While they were sitting on the riverbank, little Leah Ann decided it was time to make her entry into the world. Thank goodness, Dr. Jim West was there to assist. Because the bed was low and the doctor was tall, Dr. Jim made the delivery on his knees. Penny Sue was overjoyed to finally have a little sister and diligently took over the housework while Mom recuperated.

July rolled around and the children celebrated the Fourth. About this time our house was being sprayed for bugs and scorpions, and they were falling everywhere. At one point we counted ninety-six scorpions. When moving the box springs that I was making, I got stung by one of the scorpions on my right little finger and the sting made that hand useless for the rest of the day. The shot from Dr. Jim made me sick in my stomach, so I spent the day at home with heat applied to the wound.

We remained busy at Ler as we laid out and dug footers for a house, put up ceiling mats, dug a well, and worked on a veranda for the hospital. It was the rainy season and raining every day now. Everything was soaking wet with lots of mud. In some of my spare time I was tanning a skin to make a pair of slippers, reading Homer's *Iliad*, and working on a chuck wagon tea cart for Dolly. We even went to a Nuer dance one evening after work, and sometimes Dolly and I would walk to look for birds. Saturday nights were game nights when we had lots of fun with the children.

Using the floor blocks from the old building, we finished the operating room in the new hospital at Ler, painted the windows and doors silver gray, lime coated the walls, and put native mats on the ceiling. It made a good-looking room. This was quite a change from Dr. Jim's old mud building.

On August 10, 1954, it had been one year since we came to Ler to make plans and choose the site for the hospital. By the end of August, the airstrip was almost finished and I worked on plans for the school buildings. Since the areas of the Upper Nile were considered hardship stations, we were required to take vacation every year. I turned all my men over to Dr. West to continue with the construction of the school buildings while the family and I went on holiday to Uganda and the Congo. Our trip, lasting forty-one days, wasn't exactly restful, but it was a change of pace and a time needed to release the cares pressed on us in everyday life in the Sudan.

While I was away on vacation, building materials continued to arrive. Dr. West worked my men hard, and progress on the school building was obvious when I returned. I immediately started on plans and estimates for the school for missionary kids in Malakal, and, as I finished them, I started on the Malakal house plans. I spent sixty hours one week at my desk; I accomplished a lot, but sitting was my least favorite thing to do. Until the early 1960s, I drew up my own blue-prints by using tracing paper and ink to transfer my drawings onto blueprint paper. I put the blueprint paper in the sun, then washed and hung it to dry.

Shortly after my return to Ler, I traveled to Malakal and reviewed the school site, worked on the books, and then went on to Doleib Hill to make an estimate to finish the girls' house repairs. From there I went to Obel to see what repairs were needed on the two houses there. As I hopped from one site to another, I took care of the most urgent request.

When I returned to Ler, work progressed on the hospital walls and floors and, with the return of all my masons, I went full speed ahead on the well to increase the hospital water supply. Cleaning out the well was quite an ordeal. Men working waist deep, in an attempt to extract mud, removed more than four hundred gallons of water in an hour.

When we had first arrived at Ler, the well contained no more than a couple of feet of water which was pulled out with a five-gallon can on the end of a rope. The challenge was to make the well deeper in order to collect more water and keep out the sand.

I had an idea to make concrete rings, one meter in diam-eter and two feet high, which were placed in the well to hold back the sand and mud. Also, by standing inside the rings, the workmen were able to stay dry while bailing out water and mud. As we dug into the sand to make the well deeper, we inserted a concrete ring and let it settle before placing another ring on top, until there were four rings placed. A twelve-foot wall of cement blocks was built on top of the rings allowing the well to contain nine feet of water and never go dry.

As 1954 came to a close, I helped Dr. Jim West put up the trusses for the new classroom building and started wiring the hospital at Ler. After putting the water tank on the stand and hooking up the waterline, we painted them aluminum and lettered "American Mission" in black. It looked quite snappy.

Even though many pieces of the windmill were stolen while we were away, I attempted to set it up. To replace the stolen steel, I took apart an old Rugby car (British make like our Ford model-Ts) that I found in the storehouse at Ler.

One day a woman came selling wood and some of the men saw she wore bracelets made from rods of the windmill. We knew they were made from our stolen windmill rod since the end had a right and left thread. The police were notified and they discovered that one of the workmen was involved in the theft. One morning we went out to investigate where the stolen iron was supposedly being worked but couldn't find it. Eventually there was a hearing about the iron and a Nuer admitted he took three pieces and that he had lied about it. He was fined and given six months in jail.

At the beginning of February 1955, I packed up and left for the South Sudan Association meeting at Akobo, an American mission station near the Ethiopian border. Most of my time was spent in finance and building committee meetings or working on their reports, and I tried to get a layout of the station. The meeting lasted ten days and afterwards I took the first plane to Nasir, one of our older mission stations where work was being done with the Nuers near the Ethiopian border. At Nasir, like I had done at all our other mission stations, I made a plan of the compound in order to know exactly what was on the site. I also made a design to remodel the old house and went over plans for the new hospital building at Nasir.

Back at Ler, the weather was hot and reached 106 degrees on the veranda. In the sun it peaked at 135 degrees. I started to pack our things to be shipped back to Malakal.

As we constructed the windmill, we put the gear box (the heaviest piece to go up) on top and put the shaft in the gear box. Once again we painted our name "American Mission Ler" across the tail and built a scaffold on one side to put the tail in place.

Toward the end of April, we completed our work at Ler and paid the workmen. We continued to pack and took one last load to the river to be shipped to Malakal. At the river we got the bad news. Due to overcrowding, the boats refused to take the workmen and our truck. This meant that we would have to travel some 364 miles over unused and unmarked roads in a truck with no brakes. Knowing that the rains could close the roads any day made the trip even more suspenseful.

Even though Ronnie had malaria when we started, Dolly's newsletter back home described our two-and-a-half-day trip to Malakal as fun and with the Lord beside us all the way. We had stayed longer than we expected at Ler, and our food supplies were very low. Like the quails and the manna, the animals would appear near a camp spot and seem to wait until I shot just the amount we needed for the family and the five workmen with us, according to Dolly. We always came to a well or other source of water just when all the cans were dry. Although sometimes the road was only a trail, it always led directly on to Malakal, with never once having to retrace our steps. Ronnie's fever remained low the entire trip and in Malakal, we finally found a new drug that brought him back to normal. Two days after our arrival, we had a heavy storm and the road was closed for the rest of the year.

After a month in Malakal, we were on the move again—this time a ten-day trip to Cairo, Egypt, by train and post boat to meet up with Eddie (thirteen) and Penny (twelve) at Schutz

School. We didn't mind the long, dusty train trip the length of Egypt mainly because we hadn't seen our children for a year and had a son and daughter with whom to renew acquaintances. They both had grown over three inches since we had last seen them, and I wasn't used to having a son to look up to. So, with the whole family together again, we took off in a crowded second-class train car to Alexandria to prepare for the work camp to be held at Agamy. Penny spent her time trying to get acquainted with her long-awaited little sister, but Leah was just at the stage that she would have nothing to do with strangers.

"You must earn your spurs before you wear them."

—E. O. Pollock

AGAMY WORK CAMP—EGYPT

In Alexandria we were met by Rev. and Mrs. Ed Fairman and son, Tim, and went directly to Agamy. Agamy, fifteen miles west of Alexandria, was on the shores of the Mediterranean where the wind blew constantly and the sand covered everything. It was here that we were to have the Egyptian work camp to build the first youth center for the Coptic Evangelical Church in Egypt. A building, ninety-seven feet long by thirty-two feet wide, would eventually house a kitchen, storeroom, and dining hall (seating two hundred) for the church conference grounds in Agamy, Egypt.

According to A. C. Forrest in an article titled "Egyptian Evangelicals: A New Life Stirs," the Coptic Evangelical Church, a tiny denomination, was established and nurtured by the former United Presbyterian Church of North America (UPCNA) as a daughter church in the United Arab Republic. A minority church, started at the arrival of the first American Presbyterian workers in 1854, was hard-won among an

Egyptian community where Islam claimed the loyalties of more than nine-tenths of the populace.[5]

The six-week work camp was comprised of eleven American volunteers from the United States under the direction of the Presbyterian Board of Foreign Missions plus thirty Egyptian workers. The thirty Egyptian workers were divided into two work groups, fifteen members each, for three-week sessions. Knowing that Egyptian campers were all educated young folk who thought it a disgrace to work with their hands, we were apprehensive.

Reverend Ed Fairman, in his article, "The Miracle of Agamy," stated that the Egyptian mission thought it impossible because the work camp "proposed to cut across Egypt's most cherished social belief—which boys and girls of marriageable age must never be in the company of one another."[6] In the pamphlet "The Nile Project," Rev. Ed Fairman found it fascinating that there were no duplicates of talents in the American contingent:

> We just had one apiece of everything. We thought to ourselves, now this is a matter of selection and choice the likes of which we have never seen. And then something about this choice became increasingly clear. . . . Of those eleven who were sent out, each one of whom filled a desperate need from the American angle, there was none who was chosen over anyone else by any committee in the United States. We took everyone who applied, who could afford to make the trip, but God did the choosing.[7]

At first sight Agamy was rough, rocky, sandy desert, with white, white sand and blue sea. There was nothing but fig trees in the distance, sailboats with either blue or green sails on the sea, and huge spider crabs everywhere. We all lived in the beach cottage which was rented to serve as a dining hall and kitchen, storage center for personal effects and valuables, and sick bay.

Our eight tents were pitched a couple of hundred yards from the actual work site.

My job was to be work boss with Reverends Ayyad Zakhary and Ed Fairman as codirectors. A tarpaulin-covered "shed" was erected as a kind of workbench for carpentering and ironwork. Everything had to be made from scratch, including the dining tables and benches.

We sawed and hammered to build tables and benches, collected pots and pans and everything necessary for forty people to live. Marion, Ed Fairman's wife, and Dolly spent most of their time convincing the Primus (a pressure kerosene stove) to work. Mostly it would not. Ed and I drew plans, ordered materials, and pushed hard to get things ready before the campers arrived. Our children sawed and hammered too, went swimming every day, and were very tanned from chasing the crabs through the sand.

Carloads of mission folk from the area came out to help level off the desert and set up tents and beds. Then the bricklayer came, since the building was to be made of blocks and reinforced concrete. I had to be directing a dozen places at once, and I loved the challenge.

When the campers arrived, we didn't know one face from another, but this was to be an experiment in Christian living. It didn't take long to break down the barriers when you shared a pan to wash dirty socks and jeans, so stiff with sweat and mortar that they could stand alone. We were grateful for the blessings received in the privilege of sharing this experience. It wasn't just the building that went up, although we were proud of that too, but the fellowship and the love made visible.

Reverend Willis A. McGill described the daily schedule in his pamphlet "Work Camping in Egypt":

> The work was hard, the glare of the sun and the blowing of the wind perpetual, and the days long. Ted Pollock had

everybody rise at 5:30 A.M. so as to be ready for an hour's labor before breakfast. That was from 6 to 7 A.M. At 7:30 breakfast was served over at the villa, and by 8:30 everyone was back at work again—always leaving a group on kitchen duty, helping to prepare mid-morning lemonade and popcorn, paring vegetables for lunch, cleaning up the toilets, and other chores. Work stopped at 12:30, leaving a half-hour in which to clean up before one o'clock lunch. Then there was rest until 3 P.M., an hour's freedom for bathing in the sea until 4, and then another work period until 6:30, with supper served at 7. After breakfast and again after supper there were worship, Bible Study, and discussion periods. . . . Saturday afternoons and all of Sundays were rest times which were appreciated by all. As Reverend Fairman described in his address to the National Youth Fellowship Convention in Lake Geneva, Wisconsin, "some things took dogged endurance. We worked in 110 degree sun for eight hours a day. Any time you try to work for Ted Pollock, our work boss, less than eight hours and get away with it, I'd like to meet you. If we took off a half-hour here, we put it on there."[8]

Ed Fairman described the closing as follows:

The last Sabbath we were there, we got up at 5:30 A.M., and filed quietly into the new building we had built. We looked out a window toward the lovely Mediterranean Sea . . . this was a closing Communion service. It was my privilege to conduct the service. . . . There was something that happened in thirty days that I cannot tell you about. You would have had to see us that morning. . . . But they had learned to bear their share of the world's pain; they had learned to labor long and well, and they had learned to find for both East and West that Jesus Christ is everything we say he is and more. He had bound us together in an indissoluble union which I dare anything to break. . . .[9]

When all the volunteers left, it was as if some very dear ones had departed from us. Then we had an opportunity to relax and realize how very, very tired we were. Much was accomplished when the forty young people worked shoulder to shoulder for thirty days. Two languages and two nationalities ceased to be barriers when united in Christ. We came, and there was nothing. When we left, there were six toilets and showers, a well, and a water system in addition to the big youth center—all of it represented twenty-five thousand blocks laid and almost twenty ton of cement mixed and poured.

Many memories were relived in May 1958, at a reunion of the 1955 Egyptian Agamy work campers held at the home of Jack Rogers, one of the original eleven campers. (It is interesting to note that five of the original Agamy volunteers became ordained ministers.)

Today the Coptic Evangelical Church has grown into thousands of members and bears little resemblance to those earlier days. The site is a first-rate conference ground in affluent suburbia west of Alexandria. Agamy Conference Center continues to welcome young people who come to study, play volleyball, swim in the Mediterranean, and worship together in the chapel overlooking the sea. Ministers, laymen, and over fifteen hundred youth book Agamy solidly from April through October each year for Christian instruction and inspiration.[10]

In the summer of 1998, I was surprised to receive a letter from Gordon Kunde, one of the original American campers who had constructed the first building in the 1950s. The letter stated that Mr. Kunde had an opportunity to return to the campsite while on a business trip to Cairo that past spring. He wrote:

For several years the place had little done to it, and I gather was not too well utilized. Then sometime in the 1980s one of the leaders in the Christian community, who had been affected by the center, became troubled about the condition of the facilities and the lukewarm condition of the churches.

So he left his law practice and dedicated himself to rebuilding the place, forming a board that would take leadership, and developing a program that would be effective in presenting the personal challenge of the Gospel and promoting serious fellowship. About four years ago the present director, through the influence of the previous gentleman who has since passed away, also sensed a leading to leave his corporate job and assume the position of director.

It was a very moving experience to listen to him describe his vision for the resort (I cannot call it a camp anymore), and for the several thousand people from the churches who come there each year and catch some of the force and passion of the Gospel. There is a constant stream of young people who give a week or two as volunteers doing the cleaning and serving for the groups that come—a very unusual thing in a Muslim country.

The place is not recognizable; I had to have the original building pointed out to me—which was the first floor dining hall underneath the chapel. That our original motive had survived, grown, and continues to bear fruit after all these years made me feel that I was a part of something much bigger than any eager and green nineteen year old could have known at the time.

A letter sent out to the original volunteers by Jack Rogers, moderator of the 213th General Assembly stated that in 2002, twelve thousand people participated in its programs and five thousand made decisions for Christ at Agamy. At the time of this writing, a fiftieth Egypt work camp reunion is being planned for the original American Agamy volunteers.

We had a month of vacation due us and again the Lord provided. After a couple of days of sleep at Schutz School, we sailed from Alexandria, Egypt, on third-class passage for Beirut, Lebanon; Damascus, Syria; and Amman, Jordan. We felt that this might be Eddie and Penny's last opportunity to see the Holy Land before returning to the United States permanently. Of course, only because we were in Egypt and near the Holy Land could we afford the trip.

How we enjoyed relaxing in the hills of Lebanon with the cedars all about us. We had our fill of apples and peaches—significant since we had not seen any of these fruits since we left the United States. We felt very much at home in Damascus with an ex-United Presbyterian missionary from Egypt. Then in Bethlehem, we walked the little winding covered streets that Jesus walked, washed in the pool of Siloam, and the children waded the length of Hezekiah's tunnel. We visited the Garden of Gethsemane and climbed the Mount of Olives to see the sunrise on the city of Jerusalem. Again we felt richly blessed in the fact that we remained in perfect health through all our travels. (With water that sister Penny got from the Jordan River on this vacation, Leah was baptized on the hospital lawn at Assiut in 1955.)

Back to Egypt, this time "home" to Tanta. At least we felt that it was one of our homes, where old friends greeted us. I had a great time going over every inch of the hospital and helped to solve a variety of problems.

Finally it was on to Assiut to leave the children at school and head homeward toward the Sudan. But in Cairo, between trains, we received a telegram saying, "Advise Pollocks remain Egypt until further notice. Emergency in South Sudan, do not return." Even though we felt concerned, it was still a blessing since it meant that we could stay with Eddie and Penny for the remainder of their vacation until school began. And so we stayed on long enough to be houseparents at their school for two weeks. This gave us an opportunity to see how our children lived for nine months of the year and get acquainted with the school staff. They were all first-rate, and we were pleased to have our children in such good hands.

The emergency was a mutiny of the Sudanese army. On the fourth of October, because our Sudan reentry permit was about to expire, and because I had much unfinished business, we decided to go as far south as Khartoum. Even though we had been told that it might be six months or more before we would be allowed to continue home to the South Sudan, we again said, "Praise the Lord," when our permission to return to the South Sudan arrived in Khartoum the same day we did.

Back in Malakal, I had our treasurer's new Arcon house almost half completed. During this time, we were always under suspicion and restricted with an evening curfew since we missionaries were foreigners and had a different faith. With our closed district permit, we weren't allowed to travel from one station to another, nor anywhere without written permission from the governor.

On Sunday, December 18, we received word that the emergency in the South Sudan was over and we were free to travel where and when we wanted. On January 1, 1956, we were invited to the government office in Malakal for the flag raising. The Sudan was no longer the Anglo-Egyptian Sudan but was now the independent Republic of Sudan.

Bill, Ron, and I had a front seat, and orange drinks were served. The band, army, and police lined the street while the governor made a speech. During special ceremonies, the British and the Egyptian flags were lowered; the new Sudan flag, with its three stripes, was raised on a new pole that was a little higher than the old one. A blue stripe on the top represented the

Nile River, the middle yellow stripe, the desert, and the bottom stripe was green for agriculture. With all the horns blowing, it was a great day for the Sudan now that it had declared its independence. Most important, the new constitution guaranteed religious liberty.

At the end of January 1956, we attended another association meeting—this one held in Akobo. In the beginning of February, MAF flew Monte Parr (a builder to replace me when I went on furlough) and me to Pibor Mission Post to do an estimate for the completion of the hospital there. This hospital had been started by a builder and volunteers from the Reformed Church, but was left unfinished.

After returning to Malakal, I started to purchase materials for the Pibor project. When we mentioned that Pibor Mission Post was to be our new home, many said, "Bura el Dunia" (the end of the world)! This was home to the Murle tribe of Southeastern Sudan, a nomadic cattle herding people, who, until recently, had continued to follow their traditional life.

> *"Every problem is one of God's opportunities."*
> —E. O. Pollock

PIBOR, DOLEIB HILL, AND NASIR

We arrived at Pibor Mission Post on March 1, 1956, and I immediately began to work on the completion of its hospital. In the middle of March, Rev. Bob Swart and I left Pibor and traveled more than one hundred miles east over dirt roads on our first survey trip to the Boma Plateau and the mountains of the Sudan-Ethiopian border. Here we were looking for a site that the Pibor mission could use as an outpost for evangelistic and medical work.

At the Boma Plateau we loaded 175 poles to be used for roof trusses at Pibor then started our return trip. I was amazed at the thousands of animals I encountered and stopped to shoot an eland, bushbuck, and a zebra. We also saw white ear cob, tiang, several kinds of gazelle, hartebeest, waterbuck, giraffe, buffalo, jackal, ostrich, oribi, roan antelope, and two big lions. The skin from my eland would be used for the station drum at Pibor, and I thought my zebra skin would make a nice rug. (Today this skin hangs from the loft banister above my study in my home in New York.)

It was on this trip where we met up with women from a local tribe who cut their lips in order to stretch them. By inserting progressively bigger wooden plates, they slowly made the lip larger and larger. Some were stretched to the size of saucers.

At the beginning of April, we left Pibor Post once again for Boma Plateau, but this time on a sight-seeing expedition. I wanted to share the myriad animals and beautiful countryside of the plateau area with the Pibor mission group and also wanted to meet up with the Swarts.

We started out a party of seventeen: the two mission families (my family and the Andersons), Chuck Jordan, Dr. Mary Smith, and seven of my workmen and two houseboys. We were greeted by large herds of tiang and occasionally a beautiful roan antelope. Thompson gazelle nibbling at the tender grass and a smaller antelope, the oribi, bolted upon spotting our truck. Many giraffe (with their long necks stretching eighteen feet into the trees) and herds of zebra roamed the plains. Even though they are night prowlers, sometimes lions and leopards were spotted in the daytime, so we kept close watch. How could you not fall in love with this countryside and its bounteous gifts of nature and wild beasts!

Initially the country was almost level with large grassy plains and some stretches of forest and shady streams. With dry roads, we planned to be back at Pibor Post in twenty-four hours and had everything necessary for an overnight stop. But all did not go as planned.

At day's end we stopped and set up camp by a small stream and dined on a meal of hartebeest and small birds supplied by two of the workmen. I took my big flashlight and investigated the area. Eyes were everywhere peering back at me. Next morning we ate breakfast and left camp.

It had rained hard ahead of us, and after we had gone a few miles, the road was muddy. We crept along and plowed through, and in the middle of nowhere, not even a village or a decent shade tree, the old Ford truck stopped and refused to budge. Upon examination I found that some teeth had broken from a gear on the end of the distributor shaft—one of the spare parts I did not have with me. Khartoum, five hundred miles away, was the closest place to get a new part. A Jeep and a short wave radio were our only means of communication, but they were located about eighty-seven miles from us back at Pibor Post. There was no alternative than for me to walk back to the post and return with the Jeep to rescue everyone.

I asked for volunteers to go with me and two of my faithful workmen immediately stepped up. I carried a blanket, mosquito net, rifle, knapsack, water bag, hunting knife, and shell belt—in all weighing about forty pounds—and took very little food: a package of dates, two tangerines, a tin of cheese, some melba toast, a can of pineapple juice, and a tin of smac (canned ham loaf) in order to leave as much food as possible for those left behind. The two workers that accompanied me took only a water bag and bed roll, planning to eat wild plants and nuts they found along the way. I figured it would take three days. Dolly wrote in her journal:

> *It was a dreary feeling to watch him go. But, praise the Lord, there was work to be done. The truck had to be unloaded of our gear and shelter put up quickly to protect*

*the children from the terrific midday sun. We cut saplings
to make a framework for the top of the truck and tied it
to the tarp for a lean-to along the side. But by the time we
were finished we were well burnt.*

*Some of the African men started off to see how far to
the nearest water, Khor Rubarub. We had fifteen gallons
along but that does not last long under the tropical sun
with so many drinking and even a baby's formula to fix.
They brought back water so full of mud and vegetation
that under ordinary circumstances we would have hesitated to wash in it. But now we boiled it and drank it,
sometimes hot and sometimes cold, pretending that it was
tea or coffee to stretch our meager rations.*

*That night the women and children bedded down on the
back of our five-ton truck, with the men under the lean-to
along the side. We were not in bed long before the lions
began to roar. It was a bit of comfort to know that Bill
Anderson had his gun, but what could he see in the dark?*

*Then it began to rain, and what a rain! We did not expect
it at all because it was not our regular rainy season. It
blew so hard that it broke the strings that tied our canvas
covering and we had to hang onto the corners by hand.
Eventually the canvas filled with pockets of water and
there was no choice but to push up and empty it, or have
all the water in our beds. As we pushed, gallons of water
spilled between the truck and the lean-to, soaking the men
sleeping there. I expected curses or worse, but instead one
of the workmen, our Nuer Christian, Chop, said with a
laugh, "I'm wet. Couldn't you have saved some of that for
tomorrow so we wouldn't have to carry it so far when we
want a drink!" It cleared the air. We were all tense with
worry, I, with visions of my husband soaking wet with no
protection from rain, mosquitoes, or animals, and out of*

food. I knew for certain that even when he walked the distance to the station, the little truck there could never make the long trip back. We had food enough for a few days but with the roads wet we would probably be there a week or more.

Rations that were already scant we cut in half again, even doubling the water in the baby's formula. But the children seemed to understand and never whimpered. The only way we knew they were hungry was when Ronnie, who hated papaya, said, "Wouldn't it be fun to have some of the papaws from our garden here."

We would walk to the river about two and a half miles away to cool off and try to wash some of the mud from our clothing. One evening Billy ran ahead and met a lion just at the lion's customary feeding time. But the Lord was looking after him, and the lion continued after larger prey.

Sabbath day dawned clear and bright. We sat down, African and American alike, and read a portion of Scripture and each led in prayer. Just as we were finishing, a couple of Nuer men who had been crocodile hunting came walking down the road to see why we were there. They wondered if all the white people were of one family. "Yes," we said, one family in Christ. That led to the question of who is Christ and an opening to tell the story of salvation.

They sat and listened a half hour, then said, "Well that is a good story. The white man must have a good God." Then Chop, our Nuer Christian workman, spoke up and said, "But my flesh and blood is the same color and I know that story to be true, and I know that God personally, and know that He can save us from all of our fears and is much greater than any Nuer god."

The first afternoon of our walk back to Pibor Post, my two workmen and I covered fifteen miles. When the sun set, we set up nets and crawled in for the night. None of us slept much that night due to the hungry mosquitoes and the howling of the hyenas. In the middle of the night it rained hard for several hours, so we rolled up our blankets and nets and walked on. It was dark and we had to feel the way by digging our feet in the ruts in the road. Many times we got off the road into the thorns and for awhile a lion walked along beside, keeping us company. When the rain slacked a bit we dropped on the road to rest knowing there would be no traffic.

After an hour's rest, it began raining hard again, so we moved on. Shortly we came upon some tumbled-down mud huts. We felt for a dry place inside the huts (hoping that no snakes were seeking the same refuge), chased out the bats, and eventually went to sleep. It rained hard the remainder of the night.

Sloshing through the muddy road the next morning was a struggle. Our muscles got stiff and sore and the pack seemed heavier with the mud sticking like glue to our boots. Realizing that the roads would be too muddy to drive over for at least several days, I started making plans to call MAF when I arrived back at Pibor. I needed them to drop food and medicine to our stranded travelers back at the disabled truck.

By afternoon we had walked out of the rainy area and the road was getting drier—but so were our water bags. Thankfully, we came to a small Anuak village and were able to refill our bags from a nearby swamp. It was here that we met an old woman who wanted me to visit her hut and attend to her sick daughter. The hut was only five feet high and was made of sticks covered with grasses. I had to stoop to get through the hole that was used as a door. It was dark inside and at first I couldn't see anything. The smell was terrible. As my eyes got used to the dark, I saw a woman lying on a skin on the ground, her arm raw, swollen, and badly infected. I had no drugs or bandages along to give her to relieve the pain. All I could do was promise to return later to take her to the doctor and hospital. So we tramped on.

It was evening and dark and we dropped on the road. My food was gone and we were almost out of swamp water. I had a bad ankle that had been sprained several times and was sore and swollen. My back and shoulders ached from the weight of my pack and water bag. I figured we had walked over fifty miles in two days and that we still had more than thirty to go. As I lay on the ground praying for strength to go on, I was thinking of home back in America. I wondered why I had ever come to Africa.

Then I remembered it was Sunday, a little after 11:00 A.M. in the States, and the people would be in church. Chartiers United Presbyterian Church had prayers every Sunday morning during the service and every Wednesday night at prayer meeting. I had a feeling they were praying for us right then.

Suddenly one of our men jumped up and shouted. Headlights were approaching on the road, a road that was never traveled. It was an Arab merchant coming to pick up Nuer crocodile hunters and their kill of crocodile skins at Khor Rubarub. (These hunters worked at night by canoes, shining a flashlight into the crocodile's eyes and harpooning them.) We talked with the driver and he agreed to take us back to the stranded truck. He also agreed to allow our entire party to ride from the truck back to Pibor on top of the load of crocodile skins.

The Arab merchant, the crocodile hunters, and my crew spent the rest of the night fighting our way back to the stranded truck through the mud. When the crocodile hunters' vehicle stuck in the mud, they used gourds and their hands to dip water from the ruts and put down dry grass and weeds. Fifty Nuer warriors then pushed the truck to get it moving. This process continued all night long, as we moved about one mile per hour.

It was noon on Monday before we got back to our truck and family. Dolly's journal described the scene. "When we who were with the truck looked out the next day at the road, still covered with six inches of water in spots and mud as deep beneath it, we were sure no vehicle could travel over the road. When we saw the shape of a truck in the distance, we thought it must be a mirage!"

Everyone survived at the truck, but the food was in short supply except for the meat. The formula for the baby was all gone.

On the way back to Pibor, with one hundred crocodile skins plus some of our supplies, the truck was holding more than it should. Seven of us got into the wide front seat, with thirty-five people on top of the load in the back. Once again the men dipped water out of the ruts and filled in with dry grass, and with everyone pushing, we moved only a car length before having to repeat the whole process.

Amazingly, by early Tuesday morning, we reached Pibor. Later that afternoon I took the Jeep truck and returned to the village where the woman with the sore arm lived. It seemed that she had been to see a witch doctor and, although she was no better, she feared his curses and refused to come with me to the clinic at Pibor. That was until the chief of the village insisted she go. Eventually she did go to the clinic, was treated with antibiotics, and was healed.

Trucks constantly broke down and finding replacement parts was always a challenge. It was eleven days before the repair parts for the truck arrived and Bob Swart and I were able to travel to the stranded truck. After the repairs were made we progressed only a few miles before the rain forced us to stop overnight again. We saw ducks near a small stream and took the gun and followed them. Eventually we found a village, sixty miles from Pibor and back off the Boma Road, that we had never seen before. They were the Murle tribe.

The Murle, numbering approximately fifty thousand, were a very unlovely people, as primitive as you could find. They pulled out their lower teeth, cut a hole in their chin, and stuck in a piece of bone against which to bite. They didn't shave their heads like some of the other tribes, but had long, shaggy hair. Since many did not live along the river and didn't have access to water in order to bathe, they lacked cleanliness. They never buried their dead, but left them in the bush for the birds and the beasts of prey. Their clothing (if any) was a raw animal skin that had a design made by strategically removing some of the hair. The skin was worn from the time it left the animal until it disintegrated.

Murle homes, built by the wife, resembled a haystack. Twigs were stuck into the ground in a circle, bent into a basket shape, and then woven in and out with other twigs to hold its shape. A small hole was left for the door. She threw a handful of grass over the top and that became home for her family, the

Murle girls

goats, sheep, and dogs as well. When it rained it was hard to find a dry spot.

For food the Murle lived on a diet largely consisting of milk, meat, and blood. They raised a little grain, hunted for animals, and had an interesting custom of fishing. After damming up the khor, the women entered the water with cone-shaped baskets. The men, also in the water and walking toward the women, pulled short sticks with hooks attached on the ends, swishing them back and forth. Either the fish were forced into the baskets or caught on the hooks. Whoever caught a fish first claimed it.

The Murle men had no desire to work since they were just learning about money and how to use it. Their language had never before been written and at that time we had two missionaries who were writing the language and translating the Bible for them.

It was a drum village, one of only four in the Murle tribe. Here in the drum village one could find refuge until granted a fair trial. (Perhaps similar to the cities of refuge in the Bible, Num. 35:9–34.) Over and over again, as Bob Swart talked, he told them why we had come to their country. I could decipher enough words to know he was telling about Jesus and how He had died for them.

I took some pictures of the Murle and discovered that never before had they been photographed. Most likely, neither white man nor missionary had ever been here. Bob knew the language and talked to some of the women and to one young man who was sick. They had never heard of the mission station at Pibor that was first opened up by Dr. Al Roode and Bob Swart in the early fifties and weren't aware that there was a hospital or doctor at Pibor Post.

It was raining again and at the last place we stopped in the drum village, a young girl could be seen through the door hole of a twig house. We heard someone inside and the girl said it was her sick grandfather. As we entered the house we could see an old man on the floor huddled up in the only dry place on the far side of the room. There were goats inside also trying to stay dry. After Bob told him the story of salvation, we headed for the truck. As we returned to Pibor, I could see another good reason why God had brought the rain and kept us out another day.

<hr>

Several years ago there was great rejoicing. In a booklet titled "Presbyterians Praying through the Window 111," more recent Murle happenings were described:

> In November 1996, seven hundred Murle in Nairobi, Kenya, celebrated the first Murle New Testament. Eight choirs from different tribes sang songs created especially to honor the new translation. Dancing in the aisles, singing, shouting, and spontaneous cries of joy from the women charged the atmosphere.
>
> Before they fled the war in southern Sudan, these Murle were nomadic cattle-herders like the rest of their people. Their sojourn in Kenya has enabled them to work with Wycliffe Bible translators . . . to translate the Scriptures into the Murle language. . . .
>
> Although the Presbyterian Church (U.S.A.) has worked with the Murle since 1952, the Murle church did not grow until the 1980s. The first small church was closed when the first Murle Christians were killed in the Sudanese civil war. In 1981 work began on the New Testament translation. In 1983 the government of Sudan ejected all foreign church workers, but the translation continued. The younger Murle people longed to learn to read. Bible translation and literacy projects met this hunger, and Murle churches began in the

cities and in the countryside. In 1992 mission workers went back into the Murle homeland and found a growing Jesus movement, thoroughly Murle in its language, its music and its style. . . . There are now more than forty Murle congregations in Sudan, mostly Presbyterian, and some twenty-five percent of the Murle follow Jesus Christ.[11]

In 1999, according to an article titled "Old Testament Translation Effort Launched for the Murle People of Sudan," a formal request had been made that the Old Testament also be translated for the Murle.[12]

By the end of April 1956, the Pibor hospital was completed. How amazing it was that our doctor showed love and compassion while caring for patients who had a strong stench of rotted flesh and odors from unclean bodies and raw animal skins that the patients wore as clothing. Obviously a doctor wouldn't stay long if it were only to practice medicine, nor would it be of much avail if the love of Jesus did not shine through.

Reverend Bob Swart told of a Murle woman who came to the Pibor clinic with the traditional bone removed from her chin. In its place was a padlock that was hooked through the hole and locked. Unfortunately the woman had lost the key and wanted Bob to open it. Bob cut the padlock with a hacksaw and as the woman started to pull the lock out of her chin hole, she jumped and let out a scream. She didn't realize it would be hot from the friction of the saw.

After finishing up at Pibor, our thoughts shifted to constructing a clinic at Doleib Hill. Doleib Hill wasn't really much of a hill. Its higher elevation was explained by the fact that it was built upon old Dinka villages. As we started digging footers for the clinic, we dug into clay bowls and shells. One day we found many bones buried together, more than nine feet deep. This indicated there had been a battle with mass burial or an epidemic, since, as a rule, the Dinka had separate graves. One of the skeletons had a string of beads that was made from the shell of an ostrich egg.

As we tore down the last old house shown on the Doleib Hill survey map of 1909, we couldn't help but wonder if perhaps this was the house where Theodore Roosevelt spent a night in 1907, when on a big game hunting expedition.

At 1:15 A.M. on July 21, 1956, baby Pollock number six arrived at Doleib Hill. Our big (almost ten-pound) son, Tommy, decided to announce his presence on the very same day that brother Ronnie was born six years prior! Since there was no doctor present, nurse Mary Ewing delivered Tommy in her bedroom in the middle of the night.

The other children were growing fast: Leah, two years old; Ronnie, six; Billy, eight; Penny, thirteen; and Eddie, fourteen. Eddie, being the oldest, helped finish the furniture that was needed for the house at Doleib Hill and learned to cook and hunt.

With the children back in school at Schutz, we received a telegram from the Malakal office the beginning of November saying that the school was closing and the American children were being evacuated from Egypt. During the Suez crisis on October 29, 1956, Egypt was invaded by Israel, and on October 31 was attacked by Great Britain and France in an effort to restore international control of the canal. Originally we planned to fly Ed and Penny back to the Sudan, but when word got out that the Cairo airport was bombed, Dr. Reed agreed to transport the children across the desert in a mission Jeep at the earliest opportunity.

On November 8, 1956, we finished the clinic at Doleib Hill just as I turned forty-four years old. By the beginning of 1957, we were settled at Nasir, a mission station on the Sobat River inhabited with Nuers. Here, just like all mission stations, there was a lot of maintenance work demanding our attention, and also, I planned to put up an Arcon house.

Much of our time at Nasir was spent dredging for sand. The sand, sharp and clean, was mixed with cement to make hard, good-looking blocks which were better and cheaper than using burnt brick.

One night at Nasir, I was listening to the British Broadcasting Company when my carpenter came to the door to inform me that the cookhouse was full of merrisa (strong beer). After I investigated the house I asked for Dr. Gordon's assistance. I discovered clay pots, gourds, and sofias full of the alcoholic beverage and proceeded to empty them—all forty gallons. Mynero, our cook, was the guilty party, and knew full well that we did not allow brewing on the compound. Sometimes after a good pay the workmen got drunk and would be absent from work the next day. Their excuse was they were sick, but we all knew they had consumed too much beer.

Scorpions were prevalent at Nasir. While asleep in our old house one night, a scorpion dropped from the grass roof onto my bed and stung me on the third finger of each hand and on top my head. Dolly got the doctor and he gave me an injection to numb the stings and pills that put me to sleep. When the bell rang announcing the arrival of the workmen next morning, I awoke to start the day, but not for long. A feeling of drunkenness permeated my body and I could muster up only enough energy to get the men started on their jobs before going back to bed. Several times during the day I checked on their progress, but most of the day I remained in a supine position.

Life often was unpredictable at Nasir. I was standing at the workbench when a tall Shilluk who was in charge of the health department came and asked if I had seen a dead man going that way. He pointed down the river. I said, "Yes, about ten minutes ago." He inquired if the police and prisoners were following it and I replied that they were. They had caught up with the body below the mission and it apparently had a hole in the back of the shoulder where the man had been shot. Both hands had been cut off, most likely making it possible to steal his ivory bracelets.

Besides working on the Arcon house at Nasir, we took down an old windmill and put up a new one. The new windmill enabled us to have water for cement for the new house without carrying it from the river.

Toward the end of May 1957, we started packing for furlough in the United States. With stops in Rome, Naples, Genoa, and Cannes, France, we did as much sightseeing as possible and covered a total of over forty-four hundred miles before arriving at New York City.

———◆◆◆———

After returning to our hometown of Canonsburg, Pennsylvania, we sold our 1946 Chrysler at a junkyard for $48.10 and resumed building the new house that we had started back in 1952. A rented house down the street from where we were building served as home until we had the water, gas, and electric systems installed in the new house. Initially we moved into the basement of the new house, and as we progressed and made the house habitable, we spread out onto the first and second floors. Career mission work didn't seem to lend itself to a permanent residence, and little did we know that this would be the last time we would live in the house. Eventually, my brother, Jack, moved into our house for a short time and later my parents made it their home for many years. During these years Grandma and Grandpa's house became our children's home away from home where they returned on school breaks and holidays.

I had attended many New Wilmington Missionary Conferences at Westminster College in Pennsylvania since my first one in 1934. According to the brochure, "Good News for the New Wilmington Conference" (Anderson Auditorium Fund, 1957), it was in the mid-1950s when the board of managers of the conference made a request to the Board of Trustees of Westminster College to set aside a piece of land on the campus to build a much-needed auditorium/amphitheater as the meeting place for the conference.

From the time of its inception in 1905, the conference was held in a large tent and was vulnerable to wind and rain. Also, since the beginning, crowds increased beyond the capacity of the tent and a new auditorium was needed to provide shelter and seating for congregations up to seventeen hundred people. The trustees responded by designating a beautiful parcel of land for the amphitheater on the south end of campus over-looking Brittain Lake. This reinforced the strong bond between the college and the conference.

At the July 1957, New Wilmington Missionary Conference, when all the missionaries were on the platform, I dressed and reenacted the role of a Shilluk warrior with cloth, shield, and spears. Also, at this conference I was presented with the plans for the new amphitheater at Westminster College and was asked to be the builder. I met with the leaders of the conference to review the building site and on August 3, we had the groundbreaking for the new building. Twenty boys remained after the conference for a work camp and started to dig footers and put in the concrete base.

With the conference behind us, our schedule rapidly filled with speaking and slide-showing engagements at churches,

Kiwanis, and various organizations. Sometimes Eddie dressed in costume and played the role of a Shilluk as I asked him questions. It was always well received.

Christmas was approaching and my diary entry revealed: "We had two nice services at the church today. This is what I like about being home at Christmas." It was a big day with Mom and Dad, lots of presents, big turkey dinner, and our fifty-cent Christmas tree.

Spring 1958 arrived and so did our new daughter. Virginia (Ginny) Louise Pollock, weighing in at over nine pounds, was delivered on April 8 by Doc Johnston's son at Canonsburg Hospital. Ginny and Tommy were both baptized by Dr. Brownlee, our pastor at Chartiers United Presbyterian Church in Canonsburg.

It was an honor to receive a request to be a guest lecturer at Pittsburgh-Xenia Seminary (now Pittsburgh Theological Seminary) the end of January to speak to a senior mission's class. My hope was to make a spark that would one day ignite the students' desire to pursue mission work. Also, from May 20 to June 3, 1958, at the seminary, I participated in the new chapter of church history: the celebration of the merger of the Presbyterian Church in the U.S.A. and the United Presbyterian Church of North America, forming the United Presbyterian Church in the United States of America. I had a mission display of all my "trophies" at the seminary for the occasion.

ANDERSON AUDITORIUM

Construction of the amphitheater for the New Wilmington Missionary Conference began on June 7, 1958, under the direction of Rev. Richard Goodhart. Dr. Robert Woods (chairman of the physics department at Westminster College) and I were the work supervisors. Since my family and I were scheduled to fly out of Pittsburgh on June 14 to return to the Sudan, I had only one week to get the project started. Work camps that were formed included Presbyterian volunteers from all over the Youngstown, Cleveland, and Pittsburgh areas. It was described as an old country barn raising atmosphere, down to the community bringing in food for the eighteen campers who worked dawn to dusk (including Ed and Penny).

The frame of the amphitheater was shipped from the state of Washington on three flat rail cars into a siding in New Wilmington, Pennsylvania. The two-pieced arch, weighing thirty-eight hundred pounds, had a plate at the center to bolt the pieces together. In order to insert the bolts, thirty-five feet of scaffolding had to be erected. The heavy roof deck required using three quarters of a ton of eight-inch spikes. At the end of the week, we had three fourths of the roof in place.

Unfortunately, I had to leave at this point. Our furlough was ending and the family was returning to the Sudan and had to be

Setting up arches for amphitheater at New Wilmington

in New York City the following Monday. Or so I thought. God, in His mysterious way, had other plans for us. As it worked out, that Friday Leah and Tommy became ill. Dolly took them to the doctors, got medicine, and woke up the next morning staring at two kids covered with red dots. Two cases of measles quickly changed our schedule. With the family at home in Canonsburg, I left Sunday for New York City and delivered our trunks and footlockers to be shipped to the Sudan. Then I went to the mission office to change our flight plans to fly out of Pittsburgh on June 24. By Tuesday I was back in New Wilmington to continue my job as work boss.

Perhaps some of the work campers were disappointed in my return, since immediately I put the campers to work driving eight-inch spikes into the roof timbers on the arched roof until after dark.

We were held up by rain, but progress was made. By the end of the week, with the help of some volunteer carpenters from a local construction company, one side of the roof was completed. That left twelve rows of deck on the opposite side to be finished, but it had to be done without me. This time, with no turning back, I had to be ready to depart for the Sudan in a few days. Would the workers be able to complete the amphitheater in time for conference in August? Yes. In a total of six short weeks and with twenty-three hundred volunteer man-hours, the construction was completed. Director Ed Fairman gave the keynote speech at the first meeting in Anderson Auditorium on August 1, 1958.

A book compiled by Marion Fairman titled *Remember What You Have Received* (to mark the seventy-fifth anniversary of the New Wilmington Missionary Conference), stated that the cost of the amphitheater totaled seventy thousand dollars (over one hundred thousand if factoring in the value of work by volunteers) and that fund-raising had begun more than two years before beginning construction.[13] The "Good News for the New Wilmington Conference" brochure publicized the new

W. B. Anderson Auditorium and stated that it was named by the conference board of managers in honor of William Brennan Anderson, a spiritual leader who graduated from Westminster College in 1894 with D.D. and LL.D. degrees. Anderson served four decades in missions: sixteen years in Pakistan-India; twenty-three years as corresponding secretary of the Board of Foreign Missions in America; and chairman of the conference from 1917 to 1925. This brochure described W. B. Anderson as being "'Well Beloved' among men and 'Well Beloved' of God, as W. B. came to signify—it is fitting that a conference institution, which has an out-and-out commitment of life to Christ as its main motive, should be housed in a building that bears the Anderson name."[14]

Our return from furlough to the Upper Nile Mission region of the Sudan coincided with the rainy season. This time we were going to Nasir to build an Arcon house. Besides Nasir, my attention was focused on making estimates and drawing plans for projects at Ler and Akobo.

Somehow another year slipped by and Dolly and I were celebrating our seventeenth wedding anniversary. Summer vacations were ending for Eddie, Penny, and Billy, and it was time for the children to return to school in Egypt. This involved flying from Malakal to Khartoum, and then from Khartoum on to Cairo—not your typical school bus ride across town. Normally the children received good school reports and they all seemed to be thriving on the rough lifestyle we exposed them to on the mission field. One of my letters to the children revealed my sentiments about work on the mission field: ". . . I feel that every Christian should be a missionary wherever he is, and can be a missionary without serving on the foreign field."

My journal entry on November 16, 1958, revealed a coup: "The Sudan government was taken over by the army today. It was done peacefully. All is quiet here." General Ibrahim Abboud led the military takeover of the government and abolished all political parties and put many politicians in jail. Southern leaders were still objecting to being dominated by the northern Arab Muslims and wanted increased self-government. This takeover meant new stricter rules for the missionaries since the army became responsible for running the government in the Sudan and every person had to adhere to their instructions.[15]

In June 1959, we took leave when our youngest son, Tommy, required minor surgery. MAF transported the family to Kampala, the capital of Uganda, where he was to have his operation. After successful surgery, we spent six lazy days waiting for the removal of his stitches before heading out for a little rest and relaxation on one of our annual mandatory leaves. We traveled southeast over Lake Victoria to Nairobi, Kenya, and on to Mombasa on the Indian Ocean, a total of 869 miles.

MOUNT KILIMANJARO

While in Kenya, Mount Kilimanjaro just across the border in Tanzania beckoned to us. How could we ignore the challenge? Africa's tallest mountain is an extinct East African volcano with two peaks about ten miles apart. Kibo, the tallest peak at 19,341 feet, is always covered with snow and ice and is about two hundred feet deep with a crater in the center. Several large glaciers cover the slopes of the peak. Mawenzi, the other peak of Kilimanjaro, does not have glaciers but is harder to climb due to loose rocks. African farmers grow coffee on the lower slopes of the volcano.[16]

After shopping for supplies and borrowing bedrolls, blankets, boots, mittens, balaclava (knit cap covering ears, chin, and neck), scarf, and anorak pack from our hotel, Eddie and I began our adventure at 10:00 A.M. on June 25, 1959. To save money we decided to carry our own packs, each weighing approximately thirty pounds. We had a guide and two porters; one porter carried Eddie's and my food and the other porter managed the guide's and porter's supplies.

We stopped twice to rest before we had lunch at 1:00 P.M. About 2:30 my legs were getting tired, and I was thinking that I might have to admit that age was taking its toll. At 2:50 we reached Bismark Hut and I was glad. After we covered twelve miles and ascended forty-five hundred feet, Eddie was still going strong and was elected to prepare the dinner consisting of rice, stew, and bananas. The heavy fog allowed us to see only a few feet and there was a chill in the air.

After a good rainy night's rest, we finished breakfast and started day number two. The first part of the trail was steep. Mid-morning we rested by a small stream and shocked our insides when we drank the icy cold water. Our feet were wet and we rung the water from our socks and massaged the blisters we were developing from the borrowed boots. We were above the timber line where only small shrubs managed to survive. Gazelle tracks and signs of some kind of leopard or wildcat were visible but hardly any birds.

Our guide tired, so we rested, and Eddie took the lead until we reached Peter's Hut at 12,800 feet. From here we had a good view of Mawenzi Peak while Kibo remained cloud covered. The hut, made of sheet iron on the outside and lined with wood, had six bunks, a small stove in the corner, and a table and benches. As the temperature outside dropped down around forty degrees, the porters brought in wood for the stove and we cooked dinner. Several hundred feet below us, the clouds gathered to form a beautiful soft white blanket while the clouds above had cleared to expose a good view of Kibo Peak.

Probably exhaustion induced our good night's sleep and we awakened to colder temperatures. Regardless of my stiffened knee joint, we had a steady climb all morning until we came upon the saddle, the tree barren area dipping between the two peaks. We descended for a ways before we started our climb again out of the saddle to the last hut. The strong wind blew against our shorts-clad legs and we felt the brunt of the cold. We had walked ten miles by early afternoon and reached the hut at 16,000 feet. We all went to bed early, but sleep didn't come easy at this hut with only a set of box springs upon which to sleep.

I put on all the clothes I had brought along (T-shirt, two sweatshirts, three shirts, a parka, three pairs of socks, a pair of rolled leggings, a balaclava on my head, cap, a scarf, and mittens), and started up the peak at 3:00 A.M. There was moonlight, the stars were bright, and the air was cold. We were grateful for the layers of clothing, but our fingers and toes were still cold.

The climb was steep and it was difficult to breathe the thin air, so unlike the air of the lowlands in the Sudan. Every time we took a step forward we slid back, making it difficult to progress. After two hours I was ready to give up and go back, but, with the encouragement of the guide, I continued. Every five or six steps I wanted to sit down, so by daylight I instructed Eddie and the guide to go on without me. They followed my instructions and in a short time made it to the top of Gillman's Point at 19,341 feet.

After sunrise, my toes and fingers warmed and I was ready to continue. Thirty-five minutes later and with the help of those Everlasting Arms, I was standing next to Eddie at the highest point in Africa! Within a sealed metal case anchored to a stone at the top was a book for the brave souls to sign who survived the trek. We were proud to sign. How could you not feel good about a challenge you met head on?

We took a few pictures of Kibo with its ice-covered dome and ice-filled crater. Our descent consisted mostly of slipping and sliding and I especially enjoyed the trip back across the saddle. As we left Kibo Hut the vegetation was sparse, but as we descended a few miles, the rocks were blanketed with different-colored mosses. Further down, patches of multi-colored straw flowers had sprouted, growing flat on the ground. The grass eventually got thicker and small bushes came into view. Soon we came to big meadows with small streams of water trickling down through the rocks and we stopped at a water hole to drink.

We reached Peter's Hut (covering ten miles in two and a quarter hours at the rate of thirteen and a half minutes per mile) and were hungry. Again Eddie cooked, this time a big celebratory meal of soup, Kraft macaroni dinner, meat, corn, and pudding. After dinner we crawled into our sleeping bags contented and bunked down for the night.

The last day of our journey, the landscape changed to twisted trees covered with hanging moss. Nearing Bismark Hut, we walked down steps of roots through a real jungle of vines and large ferns. As we left the hut, the trees were larger and there were signs of elephants. The surroundings became almost tropical for the duration of the trip. As a token of our accomplishment, our porters placed floral victory wreaths on our heads. We reached our hotel feeling relief and pride and happy to join the family after being gone for four days. *(See photo section.)*

In the middle of July, we arrived back to the mission station at Malakal where projects were waiting: working on an Arcon house and building a workshop trailer that could be moved from site to site.

How could it be that Penny was turning sixteen and Ron would be joining Eddie, Penny, and Bill this year returning to Schutz? It had been a wonderful summer and I hated to see the kids leave. Sunday nights were reserved for letter writing to help ease the separation, and Dolly and I wrote religiously. We dared not let ourselves worry and were happy that we could trust God to look after them. Later in one of my letters to Eddie and Penny I mused, ". . . I cannot quite figure out how you get along without your very own Daddy all these years, but I guess you just get used to it. We really appreciate you two managing to be away from us all this time as well as you do, and, of course, Bill and Ron, too. I guess children are really missionaries, too, in letting their parents be away from them so much."

BACK TO LER

On the road again—this time leaving Malakal and returning to Ler, where Leah had been born in 1954, and where we had built a new house and hospital. Our plans at Ler were to construct two ward buildings for the hospital, a home for the nurse, and a home for the evangelist. For years Ler had been a very isolated station with outside contact only once every two weeks when the post boat passed by seventeen miles away. But now we had a weekly post service and more important, we had a radio telephone run by a small generator. Each morning at 7:30 we all listened and relayed any messages run through our Mission Aviation Fellowship. It was critical to have in an emergency. Sometimes we had trouble with Russia blocking the radio programs. Was it just coincidence that the transmission was fuzzy for shows like *Voice of America* and Billy Graham— but suddenly became clear for any music that followed?

I wish I could say our move from Malakal to Ler (364 miles, twenty driving hours) went smoothly that February in 1960. We had loaded our five-ton truck and the two-wheel trailer with tools and building materials and had all the necessary equipment for spending several nights on the road:

bedrolls, mosquito nets, food, plenty of drinking water, and a barrel of gas for the trip. The trailer held the fifteen-hundred-pound welder. The trails we had to travel could hardly be called roads. There would be no hotels or service stations, and very few villages along the way.

We left Malakal and crossed the Nile by ferry. By sunset we had driven far enough to consume all the gas in our tank. When we were ready to resume the next morning, we were confronted with another opportunity—a dead battery. The "new, modern trucks" had no crank, so what to do? Three of us spent the whole next day trying to start the truck, but to no avail. Even though the ground was flat, the five-ton truck was too heavy to be pushed fast enough to start. There were a few ant hills near the road and, with the use of rope blocks, we pulled the back wheels onto the hills. Then we released the rope block and gave the truck a push, but with no luck. There was not enough speed for the engine to catch.

By late afternoon we were still stumped as to how to resolve our dilemma. Not knowing how long we would be here, I took the bike we had brought along and went to find water. About two miles away, I found a small stream that would suffice for drinking water after purifying with our pills.

At the end of the day we made camp, cooked our supper, and went to sleep. During our second night under the stars, in answer to my prayers, I had another idea. Robb and I jacked up a back wheel and wrapped a rope between the duel tires. Two of the natives grabbed the rope and ran down the road, while I stayed in the cab. After the wheel was spinning well, I let out the clutch. On the second try the engine caught!

We continued on our way to Ler. I had a system that seemed to work. Each night before retiring I prayed, and then I slept soundly. In the morning, I listened for the Lord's answer. I always thought you need to find God in the morning if you need Him through the day. Psalms 121 informs us that God neither slumbers nor sleeps, so I saw no reason for both of us to stay awake.

Our home at Ler would have been more enjoyable if it weren't for the mud and the mosquitoes. But the three-unit ladies' house that we lived in while finishing it was the best home we ever had in the Upper Nile. With the different angles, and window and door openings on all sides, it caught most of the breezes. It was almost like three little individual houses connected with a wide U-shaped veranda. Here Dolly had a vegetable and flower garden which everyone said they had never seen the likes of before.

It wasn't long after our arrival at Ler in 1960 that we were again en route to Malakal for another meeting of the American Mission Upper Nile Association (the name changed from the American South Sudan Association). The minutes from the meeting stated that I was to interrupt my work at Ler and proceed to Mundri (over four hundred miles to the south) sometime in November 1960, to install an electric power plant at Bishop Gwynne College. I went to Mundri to make a sketch of each building on the college compound and noted that it was a good size layout and would take a big electric plant to supply it all.

At the end of March, we were back at Ler working on servants' houses; patients' houses, including ten tuberculosis (TB) houses; and two hospital ward buildings. As soon as we finished up the badly needed postoperative ward, the patients could recuperate here instead of out under the trees.

It was so hot at Ler that the workers' feet were burning on the sand and we felt weary by the end of the day. We were putting more water into the workers than we were putting into the concrete for the blocks we made. At the beginning of April, our thermometer reached one hundred fifteen degrees on our veranda every day, with the humidity below 10 percent. It would get worse though. In June the humidity would rise with the beginning of the rainy season.

Gravel was a necessity since something other than sand was needed as an aggregate in making the concrete for the floors and reinforcing bands. Before being used, dirt and grass had to be removed from the gravel. One day I purchased 142 sofias full of gravel and the means by which it was transported into the mission was surprising. Hundreds of people, from young children up to the elderly, traveling as far as six to eight miles, used every kind of container imaginable (baskets, sofias, sacks, cans, pans, bags, goat skins, old wash basins, and gourds) to carry the gravel. Schoolboys even carried it in their shirts.

Another time I purchased gravel from a lady down the road who had a good size pile. My purchase entailed having my five-gallon tin filled, paying for it, and then men loading it onto the truck. This process was repeated until I had the amount I needed. The woman, not having any pockets in her grass skirt, popped each payment in her mouth. Eventually her cheeks were bulging with a mouthful of coins!

In April we left Ler for Alexandria, Egypt, to attend Eddie and Penny Sue's graduation. It was a big day at the school since the 1960 class was the first to finish high school at Schutz. Penny and Eddie were half of the commencement class, indicative of the small class size. As a side trip, we took a train to Cairo and visited the zoo, museums, and the Pyramids. Then in May it was time for Eddie and Penny to fly from Cairo to the United States where they both would attend Westminster College in Pennsylvania the next fall. It gave me a warm feeling to see two wonderful kids going off to college to find their place in the world. Still, I felt lonely as I viewed the Caravelle jet take off from the Cairo airport. We watched it ascend and turn into a silver streak, then disappear into the clouds. As it circled it came out into the blue sky again, only to move out of sight.

Our train trip back to Ler was slow going, like most traveling in the South Sudan. It was a hot trip over desert. Since there were one-way tracks between Wadi Halfa to Khartoum, we spent time waiting on sidings until trains passed going in the opposite direction. Our steamer, with nine barges attached, fought its way through the water hyacinths that covered a substantial amount of the river. In some places, the hyacinths spread the full width of the river and at night it was hard to distinguish where the bank began. We had to move along slowly.

It was dark the night we arrived at Adok, and the rain soaked through my raincoat. How delighted we were to see the Ler Jeep waiting for us. Still, it took one hour to load our things into the Jeep, and for the first five miles we were in four wheel drive creeping along through mud at five miles an hour. After two hours and seventeen miles, we were at Ler. It was good to be home, even though the house was a mess. Some of the grass had blown off the roof, water had washed some of the mud from the walls onto the floors, and the white ants were working overtime. The next day I went on a business trip from Ler to Malakal with MAF. I made the startling realization that this fifty-minute flight had taken fifty hours traveling by steamer.

Welding was an integral part of construction, and many jobs would have been impossible without it. Because of its importance, I introduced Bill and Ron to this fine art. Besides welding, they both were becoming handy with tools. Ron made Leah a blackboard with ABCs painted on it for her sixth birthday and Bill made his little sister a shovel, rake, and hoe. Also, I wanted Ron and Bill to know the proper use and handling of guns, so I took them out for target practice.

To avoid errors at Ler, I checked my workmen's every move. As we began laying out the hospital, they had trouble lining up the columns. To add to the challenge, beer was being made at two different locations on the compound. I delighted in pouring out seventy gallons of the strong brew.

In November, my forty-eighth birthday felt more like I had turned one hundred. The long work days were taking their toll. Also a lab test revealed that the fever I had developed was due to malaria and caused me to have weakness and cramping, but I continued to work. It wasn't long before malaria hit Dolly too, for the second time.

There were so many patients coming to Doc Jim that the patient houses were filling as soon as I had them completed. It wasn't long before the numbers were overwhelming and Doc got discouraged with his inability to treat them all. One week after the dedication, the ward building was already filled with patients.

BISHOP GWYNNE COLLEGE

Our work was interrupted at Ler in late May 1961 in order to start the generator house project and the wiring of Bishop Gywnne College in Mundri, South Sudan. Like most of the others, it was not an easy trip. Our five-ton Ford truck and two-wheeled trailer carried a heavy load of trusses, windows, electric line poles, and a door that we made in advance at Ler. On the road across the swamp, ants had built large anthills, one to two feet high, that looked like toadstools with large rounded tops—reminiscent of a fairy village. Sometimes you could go around the hills, but often you had to drive in the swamp below the road to avoid them.

Bishop Gwynne, the first theological college in the Sudan, was founded in Yei in 1945, and moved to Mundri in 1948. Here students from many different tribes were trained to serve the Episcopal Church in the Sudan, the Church of Christ in the Upper Nile, and other Evangelical churches as ordained pastors, layworkers, and volunteers. After passing examinations, diplomas were awarded by London University for the two- to three-year course. Sudanese Christians insisted that the college be named for their beloved and trusted friend, Bishop Gwynne, a deeply committed Christian pioneer.

According to Dr. J. L. Anderson, editor of *Light*, it was 1898 when Bishop Gwynne traveled mainly by foot to the Sudan. In his early days he trekked throughout the entire country by every means of transportation available: train, steamer, sailboat, camel, donkey, and by foot. He founded two mission stations, and, when he was over seventy years old, he flew in open airplanes with the British Air Force pilots in Khartoum as a means of reaching every corner of his big diocese. Bishop Gwynne was a man of God and a man who loved men of every race and religion and was loved by them in return. He was just as welcomed in the governor-general's palace as in a simple Sudanese hut.[17]

Upon arrival at Bishop Gwynne, I hired sixteen laborers and started to clear the site for the generator house. After hauling in sand and stone, I laid out the plans and started to dig the footers. Obstacle number one was stone. Every place we dug, we hit stone, and most places we had to dig through stone for three feet.

Some of the men were learning to cut stone for the generator house walls, but since it was new to them, it was a slow process. How ironic it was that the five men cutting stone could barely

Generator house at Bishop Gwynne College in Mundri

keep up with the one man laying them. Only sixty-five stones were cut and laid in one week's time.

All the children were excited to see Ed when he arrived at Mundri in June. I was relieved to have Ed's help setting up the electric plant since I didn't have one single man who was qualified. Immediately he and Bill got busy wiring up the dorms and pushed things ahead. Unlike the mission doctor's and evangelist's children, the mission builder's kids could get hands-on experience working on the sites. "I am sure glad that the three boys are here to help with the wiring. I do not know what I would have done without them," I entered in my diary.

By mid-July our work on the generator house was completed. After testing out the small and large generator, I checked all thirty-four buildings. It was a good feeling that we had to make only minor adjustments to balance the load. One Sunday evening everyone met at the church and marched to the generator house singing for the dedication of the electric plant. After a short service, I started up the machine. Before everyone returned to the church for the duration of the service, I handed over the key to the director of Bishop Gwynne.

In 1960, there was growth of new buildings on the campus of Bishop Gwynne College, but, in 1961, there was just that one new addition: the generator house for the electric lighting plant which my family and I installed. Since it served the whole college with lighting, the electric generator was considered a generous gift from the American Mission and was greatly appreciated by the staff and students.

———————

Back at Ler, it was a miracle that the rainy season held off until June—one day after we had the roof finished on the third unit of the ladies' house.

Dolly and children in front of our three-unit house

Every rain-free day was a blessing. But when the heavens opened up the very day after completion, the Nuers were amazed and dubbed me the witch doctor that controlled the rains! Asked why they weren't planting their gardens, the Nuers responded, "It will not rain until Mr. Pollock gets his roof on." So, as the boys and I put the last roof sheets on the ladies' house, we looked out over the countryside. There they were, busily planting their gardens with their planting sticks. That night two inches of rain fell. How could I live down my title? Once the rain did come, it came with a vengeance and everything was standing in water. Five inches in three days meant that construction progress was deterred with time spent cleaning up mud and water. We would have the rains to contend with until September.

It was about this time we received word that the U.S. ambassador to the Sudan and his wife were coming to Ler on an elephant hunting expedition and would be staying in our three-unit house. It was an honor to share dinner with the ambassador and his wife and enjoy the evening with them. Unfortunately after a day of walking through the swamp, the ambassador didn't spot a single elephant.

Ron and Bill headed off to Schutz the end of August 1961—this time going to school without big brother and sister, Ed and Penny. Ed traveled as far as Cairo with his brothers before continuing back to the United States. They were all a big help over the summer and once again we would have to rely on letters to keep current with their lives. Besides the four pictures on my writing table, anticipating their mail and their next vacation kept us going.

By the end of September 1961, we had completed the work at Ler that we had set out to do. At the October association meeting, a change was made in our next assignment: instead of Akobo we would be working on the church at Malakal. But first we would take leave at the beginning of November for a vacation in Kenya. How strange not to have Ed, Penny, Bill, or Ron with us this time.

Usually I described our vacations as "nobody has more fun than we do." This one started out the same but unfortunately it turned into an adventure, or as Ed Fairman describes it, "hardship viewed from a distance." During our Kenyan vacation, we were stuck in mud holes and tolerated many delays due to major flooding that washed out bridges and closed roads and railways. We returned from our adventure a month later. It still was an enjoyable time from Dolly's perspective since we were beyond the baby stage and she had no diapers to wash while en route.

Describing our furlough in a letter from Mombasa to our children I wrote, "God sure takes care of us much better than we ever ask or even expect. And He does that for each one of you, too. We are not always sure the things that happen are what we want, but in the end we find they are much nicer than if we had planned it all ourselves. Don't forget this when you have disappointments or changed plans."

During our last days at Ler we held auctions to get rid of things we no longer needed, including clothes that we felt had very little wear left in them. One Sunday morning in church, Dolly commented that it looked like Pollock Day since every third person in attendance had on a piece of our old clothing.

The first order of business upon our return to Malakal that December 1961, was the church roof repair. Discouragement set in when supplies were unavailable to do the job. As I sat there looking at the rough wall, steel trusses, and corrugated roof, I was thinking of the Christmas vesper service we used to have at Chartiers United Presbyterian Church with all the Christmas trees, wreathes, and flowers. I wondered if they were having their service this year. But even without all the decorations, the meaning was the same and I enjoyed the Christmas service at Malakal just as much.

By January 1962, we were working on plans for Operation Roundup—named after my efforts to round up all my equipment and supplies from Malakal, Doleib Hill, Nasir, and Pibor and get them to Akobo. Akobo, a mission station 292 miles southeast of Malakal, was opened by Don McClure in the late 1940s and our job would be to repair some houses and demolish others. Besides locating my equipment, there was also the great gathering of boxes which included things that Dolly had managed to live without for sometime. It was Christmas all over again when the children's toy box arrived. Prior to this time they had only a few small toys to play with. But now Dolly was back to saying, "Pick up your toys," and felt they were all happier without them. As I opened a box that had just come in from Juba, I questioned Dolly as to what to do with it: pack to send to Akobo by air, pack to take to Akobo by truck, pack to store, pack to take to the States, or sell?

When my work schedule was printed up in the minutes of the 1961 American Mission Upper Nile Association Meeting, I had to remind myself that I was just one person: Malakal church repair, six weeks; Nasir Girls' School, one week; Pibor office, four weeks; Pibor well, two weeks; Akobo repair and demolishing houses, four weeks; Akobo Girls' School, five weeks; and Akobo storehouse, six weeks. I thanked God for all my work and the ability and strength to complete it. But as you will see, some of these projects never came to fruition.

AKOBO

Akobo, on the Pibor River, had its challenges. Because of a yellow fever scare along the Ethiopian border close to the post, it was critical that we get our shots. Families of bats, rats, fleas, and white ants were exposed when we cleaned and moved the materials for the Arcon house to be constructed here. Flooding was a serious problem, and with many roads closed, it was impossible for me to get my equipment shipped in. The land was flat and when the waters rose high enough to overflow, it spread ever so slowly over thousands of square miles, including the roads and airstrips. And when the waters receded just as slowly, mosquitoes became prevalent and malaria was worse than usual.

Another challenge was the massive sudd blocks. Sudd delayed the supplies being shipped by steamer and it had to be cleared by cutters. Sometimes the steamers sat for a couple of weeks before being freed from the entangling plants to continue on their journeys. This created a tremendous backlog with everything overbooked on government boats, rails, and planes.

I love challenges and one was moving our twenty tons of goods by steamer from Malakal to Akobo. Bob Swart and I had to figure out how to float the Arcon from Nasir to Akobo and how to build a bridge to get trucks across at Pibor. Dolly described my feelings to the children in a letter, "He thinks it is fun, so I guess I will too," and "Dad loves it, so I guess I'll survive."

But surviving wasn't easy in our old thatched-roof house in Akobo. Since there was no drainage, at one point we felt like we were on a boat surrounded by water. Mud—black, sticky, and gooey—was eventually unavoidable. The frogs made so much noise at night that it was hard to hear someone talking across the room. Mosquitoes were so thick, they ate us to bits at night. Thankfully Dolly and I had what was called a mosquito house, a dome that fit over our double bed to protect us while we slept.

When we put mosquito nets over the children's beds, they complained it was too hot for them to sleep. They had to decide which was worse, the heat or the mosquitoes.

There were no big fish at Akobo like there were at Omo or Doleib Hill, but the little ones still tasted good. Since the grasshoppers devoured most of Dolly's garden, we ate canned goods plus the native mangoes and bananas.

Often it was a problem having enough sand for construction at the mission stations and likewise at Akobo. To ease the shortage I used scrap metal at Ler to design what I called a clamshell bucket for dredging up sand underwater. With two legs of its metal frame in one canoe and the other two legs in a second canoe, the big bucket in between could lower its "claws" into the water, up to twenty feet deep, and scoop up a load of sand into a third canoe. The clamshell bucket was portable and could be taken apart in thirty minutes for use at other projects.

Dredging sand using the clamshell bucket

By the end of June we had finished up the storehouse and the Arcon house at Akobo and paid off our men. Soon afterwards we left on furlough for the United States with a tour stop in Vienna, Austria. Twenty-year-old Ed met us in New York City where we spent a few days before flying on to Pittsburgh to meet Mom and Dad. Canonsburg was our destination before heading for the mission house in New Wilmington where we would stay over furlough.

With Penny and Ed on their summer jobs near New Wilmington, Penny as a nanny and Ed as caretaker at a Girl Scout camp, we managed to squeeze in a family supper with everyone in attendance for the first time in years. While attending Sunday school and church, I fully appreciated hearing the message in English once again. Of course, summer wouldn't be summer without attending New Wilmington Missionary Conference, and it was a wonderful week seeing so many friends that I wouldn't have seen otherwise.

Most times furloughs were just as busy as being on the mission field—but in different ways. I bought myself a new slide projector and put it to use immediately. Often I drove long distances to the myriad speaking engagements that were requested by surrounding churches. The '56 Buick station wagon, available to missionaries on furlough, was put to good use.

Besides showing slides, we displayed many of our "trophies" at these speaking engagements. Our audiences especially enjoyed when I dressed up and played the part of a Shilluk. Due to my shyness, when we returned from our first mission trip in 1951, Dolly did most of the speaking. But with the encouragement of close friends, I eventually learned to be comfortable talking about life on the mission field and even came to enjoy it.

A lot of furlough time was spent at family gatherings: a fiftieth wedding anniversary open house for my parents at the beginning of September and cross-country meets that Ed and Bill participated in.

Once again I had to make the rounds of appointments required for shots, a physical, chest X ray, and dental checkup. As birthday time rolled around and I hit the half century mark, I rejoiced in not having to wear bifocals.

EXPELLED FROM SUDAN

Life is uncertain and even more so for missionaries. On December 8, 1962, we received word that our friends, the Hoekstras, had gotten orders to leave the Sudan. The next day, while Dolly and I were involved with a church speaking engagement, our children notified us that a cable from the Sudan arrived at the mission house. It listed the names of five more United Presbyterian missionary families ordered to leave the Sudan, and ours was one of them. Others expelled were Rev. and Mrs. William Adair and Rev. and Mrs. Robb McLaughlin.

We were due to sail from New York on January 4, on our return trip to the Sudan and had already gotten our reentry permit to the closed district where we had been working. Projects had already been planned, including the Arcon house and a girls' school at Akobo, a girls' school at Nasir-Pibor office, and a well to be drilled at Pibor.

How could this be happening? I had been building schools and clinics in the South Sudan since 1947. Now the army had taken over and put an end to education in the south. With the door closed, I wondered what God had planned for us. My thoughts went to scripture: Matthew 10:22–23, "All men will hate you because of me. But he who stands firm to the end will be saved. When you are persecuted in one place, flee to another" (NIV).

The Sudan government was no longer interested in Christian missions. Eventually a statement was issued by the Sudanese government and gave no reason for the sudden expulsion of seventeen United Presbyterian and Reformed missionaries. All seventeen, who had shared an average of twelve years at their posts, had to quit by January 19, 1963, and at the time of the statement, six had already left the country. Also, two other missionaries who planned to return to the Sudan were refused reentry visas without explanation. More than thirty Roman Catholic missioners were also evicted.

According to an article titled, "Missionaries Told to Vacate Sudan," a new Missionary Societies Act was enacted and required mission organizations in the Sudan to obtain an annual license which would permit "limited and localized forms of activity." Everyone performing a mission act had to have a license and anything connected with Christianity was considered a mission act. In part, the new act limited social contact between Christian clergymen and the people, and restricted education by Christian instructors. Americans had complied with the new law and made application with the hope of continuing their service to the Sudan.[18]

There were sixteen remaining missionaries scattered among nine stations who tried to regroup and carry on their programs as best they could. Previously there had been similar evictions in the adjoining provinces of the South Sudan that had practically eliminated other Christian missions.

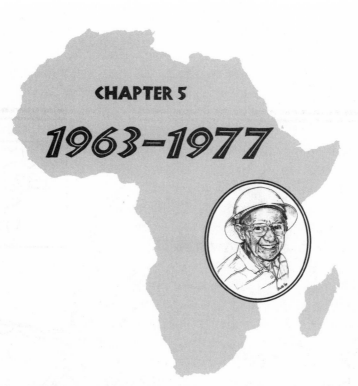

CHAPTER 5

1963-1977

Ah, land of whirring wings which is beyond the rivers of Ethiopia; which sends ambassadors by the Nile, in vessels of papyrus upon the waters!

—*Isaiah 18:1–2 (RSV)*

I. K. PROJECTS—ETHIOPIA

Expulsion papers—not everyone gets such a unique Christmas present like we got that year in 1962. What next? This was the thought that was going through my mind. The Lord had opened the doors again, so it was time to move on. Perhaps this was God's way of getting his Sudanese children to stand on their own two feet and look to Him as Father.

With our reentry permit in hand we were to set sail from New York City on January 4, 1963, to return to the South Sudan. But new orders stated we were being expelled and had to be out of the Sudan by January 19. What would happen to all our goods and tools that remained in the Sudan? We had started over before, but where would God lead us this time?

Letters written by missionaries in 1962 concerning the eviction described the Sudanese government as very suspicious, with mail being carefully censored. In the minds of the Sudanese authorities, our expulsion from the South Sudan was not viewed as religious discrimination, these letters explained, but rather a matter of "political significance." Evidently action was taken to reduce and/or eliminate what they believed to be the source of resistance to "Sudanization" of the people in the southern provinces.

Their hope was to remove any obstacles to a more rapid integration of those peoples into the Arabic-Moslem culture. There had been a policy building up for years insisting that Islam must unify the country. The biggest stumbling block to uniting the people behind their prophet, they thought, was the missionary. Once they had us removed they figured the people would flock to the mosque.

The Sunday before Christmas, 1962, Dolly and I left our mission home in New Wilmington, Pennsylvania, for New York City and headed to 475 Riverside Drive. Here the Program Agency of the Mission Office of the United Presbyterian Church (USA) informed me there were three places that were in need of a mission builder: Iran, Cameroon, and Ethiopia. My question to them was, "Where is the greatest need?"

Back at New Wilmington, several days before Christmas, I received word that my sister, Maye, had been killed in a train accident. I made arrangements to fly to Los Angeles for the funeral. I regretted not having Christmas with my family, especially because it was the first time since Ginny was born in 1958 that all seven children were home for the holiday.

Pennsylvania had a lot of snow the beginning of the new year 1963 and our boys took advantage of it. Using a dishpan to shape the blocks, the boys built an elaborate igloo with circular tower and spiral staircase in our yard. The igloo received a lot of attention. Not only did our local newspaper send out photographers to capture the creation, but curious school teachers paraded their classes pass the masterpiece.

January 4, 1963, the day we had been set to sail from New York City, came and went. We hadn't heard from the mission office in New York City concerning our next assignment, so I visited them to find out what I could. Coincidently, while there, I took the 1962 Ethiopian General Assembly Minutes back to my hotel to read and made a discovery. A request had been made the prior year by the Ethiopian mission for me to head up the building of their Illubabur-Kaffa Project (I. K. Project)—even before they knew we were put out of the Sudan. Perhaps this could be our next opportunity!

The I. K. Project in Ethiopia was a plan to allow foreign missionaries to combine their skills with trained Ethiopian workers. The provinces, four hundred miles wide and bordering the Sudan and Kenya, were a triangular area that remained of the old tribal empire of Ethiopia. Each community spoke its tribal language and had its own unique way of life, and much of the area was unmapped territory.

That same day I met with Dr. Earl, secretary for International Affairs of the Presbyterian Church, and he assured me he would try to get me a six-week visitor's visa through the United Nations. Because of the Sudan expulsion, there was to be an intake of personnel to Ethiopia from the Upper Nile Mission in the Sudan, and the Ethiopia mission stood in great need of my services as a builder. Fortunately, our experience in the Sudan would help us qualify since the Ethiopian project was related to tribes that were akin to the Murle, Nuer, and Anuak tribes back in the Sudan.

My family and I had already spent fifteen years of pioneer mission building in the South Sudan, plus a year at the large hospital in Tanta, Egypt. When I accepted a mission assignment, it was a given that where I went, Dolly wouldn't be far behind. We went everywhere and did everything together. In a mission evaluation profile, it described her as giving our neighbors a demonstration of Christian family living. Also, our seven children were always an integral part of our team. After all, four of the children had been born in Africa and they all grew up and lived a life of a mission builder—moving from one country and tribe to another and being exposed to many different languages. And as for me, I liked a challenge. If it was an easy job, let someone else do it. I am a dreamer who loves to work with his hands. I wanted the impossible jobs. Often I would end up asking, "Well, now, Lord, how are we going to do this one?"

According to a book titled, *Ethiopia, General Information*, except for five years of Italian occupation in the mid-1930s, Ethiopia was a country that had three thousand years of independence. It was the oldest self-governing country in Africa. With Christianity present for sixteen centuries, Ethiopia was one of the oldest Christian countries in existence. In a country of twenty million, 90 percent were illiterate and only seven thousand Ethiopians were high school graduates. In 1964, there were only five Ethiopian doctors. A large percentage of the five thousand Americans living in Ethiopia at this time were teachers.

Ethiopia did not follow the western change to the Gregorian calendar in the eighteenth century, so in our year 1963 the Ethiopians were celebrating their new year—1956, approximately seven years and eight months behind us. The Ethiopian calendar has thirteen months—twelve with thirty days and one month with five days. Unlike our twenty-four hour day divided by noon and midnight, Ethiopia's day is divided at sunrise and sunset.

Although Ethiopia is mentioned many times in the Bible, probably the best loved and most significant story historically to the Ethiopians is the visit of the Queen of Sheba to King Solomon

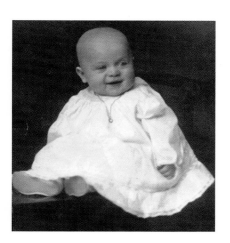

Ted as a baby (1912)

Ted and Dolly on their wedding day,
August 21, 1941

Ted and seven children
(1999)

*Ted killed his first lion
(1947)*

*"Jal Dong OK"
—dressed as a Shilluk warrior
at a New Wilmington Missionary
Conference (early 1950s)*

Murle tribe (circa 1956)

*At the top of Mount Kilimanjaro,
19,341 feet (1959)*

Mesengo tribe, Ethiopia (1964)

Erecting Polycon buildings for I. K. project (early 1960s)
—first building at Omo, Ethiopia

Jeep stuck in mud on way to Omo
to start work on I. K. projects (1964)

Abandoning the Jeep after getting stuck in mud on way to Omo

Polomo windmills in Omo (1960s)

Polydome at Omo, Ethiopia (1960s)

Surma lip plates (1970s)

Grace Memorial Hospital in Wagner, Brazil (1992)

Work at refugee camps (1994)

Glen Nora Church in Harare, Zimbabwe (1997)

New Wilmington Missionary Conference in Anderson Auditorium (1998)

Haile Selassie (taken by Dolly Pollock at a celebration in 1964)

of Israel in 1 Kings 10. Tradition has it that although the queen at first refused to become his wife, she later bore him a son who became Menelik I, first emperor of Ethiopia. His imperial majesty, Haile Selassie I, who was emperor of Ethiopia for forty-nine years, is the 225th monarch of that line and is called the Lion of Judah.

The high plateau of Ethiopia, almost split in the middle by the Great Rift Valley, had a chain of many fascinating lakes. The rugged terrain that protected the high plains from invaders for so many centuries kept out progress as well. Only in recent decades, particularly since World War II, had the country begun to develop as a modern state, largely through the efforts of Haile Selassie. Emperor Selassie, recognized as the architect of modern Ethiopia, compared Ethiopia to Sleeping Beauty, in that time had stood still for two thousand years in his country. He instructed to take great care and not overwhelm her with change now that she was beginning to awaken from her long sleep.

It wasn't until 1918 that missionaries were allowed into the interior of Ethiopia. During the great influenza epidemic in western Ethiopia at Dembi Dollo (Sayo), a Macedonian-like call was sent out: "Come to Ethiopia and help us." At that time Dr. Tom Lambie from Pittsburgh, Pennsylvania, was working at Nasir in the South Sudan, and responded to the call. He trekked two hundred miles to Sayo where scores were dying from influenza. The following year Dr. Lambie returned to Sayo with his wife and opened the first mission station of the United Presbyterian Church in Ethiopia. Dr. Lambie later helped start the W. S. George Hospital in Addis Ababa, which was taken over by the government after the Italian War in 1935. This hospital is now the Pasteur Institute, home of vaccine research and testing.[1]

----•◆•----

According to a brochure titled *Mission through Medicine*, in the 1920s, Emperor Selassie solicited the United Presbyterian Church for medical help, specifically for a contract between the mission and his government for the staffing of a hospital in the town of Gore. He requested that missionaries come and bring "the Bible in the language our people can understand." Within the next five years, work was opened at Gore and a hospital started at Addis Ababa.[2]

During the early days at Sayo, beggars cried out pitifully to the missionaries for a handout of a bit of bread or piece of cloth to cover their bodies. Eventually the missionaries planned a weekly meeting to give the beggars gifts and share Bible stories. They couldn't help but notice one young man who was faithful in attendance and listened intently. Although blind from smallpox, he was soon able to attend school and eventually learn English Braille. He accepted Christ as his Savior and "blind Gidada" became our first evangelist in Western Ethiopia.

The missionaries were forced to withdraw during the Italian occupation, 1936 to 1941, but during this time, Gidada traveled by mule or on foot from one remote village to the next, teaching and preaching about his new friend and Savior. (I first made mention of "blind Gidada" in chapter 3, at the dedication of the girls' school at Sayo in 1949.)

When the missionaries returned after the Italian hostilities, Gidada had organized fourteen churches in the Sayo area. Gidada spent several years helping to start a church at one of our new mission stations and returned to Sayo in 1964. He was then a frail old man but still spent full days working with the church, the hospital patients, and the students in the school there at Sayo.

After World War II, the United Presbyterian mission expanded with work in Maji, Ghimeera, and Pokwo, other villages in Ethiopia. For over fifty years, it had been a dream of our mission to reach the many scattered tribes in Ethiopia with the gospel of Jesus Christ. Our missionaries at Nasir in the South Sudan had lifted up their eyes to the purple mountains of Ethiopia and prayed that, if it were the Lord's will, they might be permitted to go into that country and preach the gospel. According to a report of the Evangelistic Committee, "His Imperial Majesty, Emperor Haile Selassie, in private audience with a member of our mission, expressed specific interest in the possibility of our mission serving the interests of his land and people by Christian witness and social assistance in this undeveloped area of the empire." Our assignment from the emperor was "to help extend Christianity—together with improved health, education, and living conditions—to thousands of tribesmen in two interior provinces," Carl Karsch stated in "An African Adventure."[3]

Since the United Presbyterian mission workers from the Sudan were entering Ethiopia from the southwest, this was the area to be opened up for our mission work. After the joining of the Presbyterian Church in the U.S.A. and the United

Presbyterian Church of North America, an offering called the Fifty Million Fund was set aside to finance mission outreach projects. In the early 1960s it was voted upon to open up work for seven backward, illiterate, unreached tribes in southwestern Ethiopia. These included the Mesengo, the Teshenna, the Geleb, the Surma, and the Nuer tribes. At this time there were eighty-six tribes throughout Ethiopia.

Now that the government was opening up these backward areas, it gave outside forces an opportunity to move in. As these changes took place, the Nilotic people were more vulnerable to having their old superstitions and witchcraft replaced. New religions, including Islam that stretched over northern Africa and Asia, would compete with the old paganism for their loyalty.

Foremost in my mind was the question of whether we would be permitted to return to the Sudan with a visitor's visa to retrieve our goods and equipment worth thousands of dollars. The most disheartening task before all the remaining missionaries was the disposal of unused materials and equipment at the various mission sites. It was a terrific job finishing out a station with little notice.

Related to this problem was the question of transporting equipment into Ethiopia for the displaced missionaries who could get residence there to do service. The equipment consisted mainly of shop machines and tools used in building operations, including my welder and generator, and some translation equipment. Also, there were my family's personal belongings, plus goods of five other families who did not have visas and were moving out of the South Sudan into Ethiopia. If these things were to be moved, it would have to be done in April or early May before the rainy season set in.

It was February 1963 that my diary first mentioned the idea of writing a book of my missionary adventures. Dr. Marion Fairman, wife of Dr. Ed Fairman, suggested putting the book in chronological order using the journals I had started writing back in 1947. When on furlough in 1962 at the Furlough Mission Conference in Chicago, I decided to take a writing course being offered specifically for missionaries. But when I got my assignment to Ethiopia, the book was put on hold. Since that time there have been many more adventures about which to write.

Faith, I insisted, was like walking up to an electric eye door. Just as you get there, it opens. It was at this time I learned that God expected me to trust Him completely. At the United Presbyterian Church (USA) Mission Office in New York City, the travel director questioned whether I should continue with my plans since we had neither the Sudan visitor's visa we needed to retrieve our supplies, nor a visa to enter Ethiopia. "Who makes that decision?" I inquired.

He said, "You do."

It was a critical moment for me and I had to make my decision on faith. I said, "We will go!" Little did I know we would be going so soon. We received a call at twelve noon saying to be at the airport for the six o'clock flight that evening. That gave us six hours to pack and drive the two-hour trip from New Wilmington to Pittsburgh, Pennsylvania.

We flew from Pittsburgh to New York City and left the Big Apple on March 27 with no Sudan visitor's visas or promise of them, especially since we were on the blacklist. Nor did we have visas for our new land of Ethiopia. We sailed smooth seas on the *Queen Elizabeth*, a time of rest and relaxation, not thinking about what lay ahead and trusting that the Sudan visas would be granted by the time we arrived in Cairo. But the visas were not granted, so we continued on to Alexandria to leave Ron and Bill at the American school at Schutz. After two days in Alexandria, we received a call from Khartoum saying that our temporary Sudanese visas were granted. Was it a miracle or was God testing my faith? Many times in the coming weeks the doors opened, but never until that last second. If I had faith to walk up to the door, it would open.

Because of our six-week visas, our time was limited in the Sudan. I had a tendency to name all my projects and this one was called Operation Exodus. It was put into motion in Akobo as our family got busy preparing to move our personal things, welder, generator, scaffold frame, ladders, and builder's tools across the border into Ethiopia. The trucks, boats, and outboard motors would have to be left behind. The exodus was in full swing.

There was one major hang-up during Operation Exodus. It so happened that the clerk at Nasir copied the numbers incorrectly on our export permits, and when we tried to get our goods into Ethiopia, the sergeant refused to let us move anything until they were corrected. Because of this, Robb McLaughlin traveled the seventy-seven mile trip from Jokau back to Nasir and spent a day at the police post attempting to get the numbers corrected.

While there, the police brought in a runner who had been picked up at the border. The runner was carrying some bread rolls sent to us from the mission post at Adura, Ethiopia, about twenty miles from where we were crossing the Jokau River. Evidently the missionaries at Adura had heard of our export trials on the Radio Telephone (RT) and in a kind gesture they decided to send us some rolls with a note stating that they were "Praying for Operation Frustration." When the sergeant saw the name "Operation Frustration," he became suspicious, arrested the runner, and put him in prison. Due to Robb's threats, the sergeant eventually changed the permit numbers and let Robb go. It wasn't long before we were all cleared and could proceed with the crossing. To this day I don't know what happened to the runner.

Our next problem, or should I say opportunity, was fording the river into Ethiopia before it rose too high. At this time of

year the Jokau River was low, about waist deep and twenty-five
feet across. We used my steel scaffold framing to build a bridge
across the river and hired eight Nuers to help carry the load.
The bridge was slippery and there were times when we fell into
the water. Leeches in the river stuck to my skin and sucked my
blood. My bare feet stepped on thorn branches, but I had to
keep going. Sometimes my feet became infected and I would
have to soak them in hot water back at the campsite. Instead of
using the bridge, some of the natives preferred to wade through
the water with loads of our goods on their shoulders.

Almost instantly the rains began to fall, the floods came,
and our bridge was out of sight. Then our boxes and trunks
had to be moved by a small aluminum canoe. When the river
rose to nine feet deep and seventy-five feet wide, it was a real
challenge getting the welder across. The canoe could haul
fifteen hundred pounds and the welder weighed just that. It was
a full load. We had to build up the inside of the canoe by
putting two aluminum ladders across with four empty barrels
at the end for outrigger. Amazingly—just as the water was
lapping over the top—and with a prayer, we made it.

The next stage of our operation involved waiting for a truck
and fifteen workmen to arrive and load our heavy pieces,
including the welder, and take them to an empty rented warehouse in Gambela. Gambela, in western Ethiopia close to the
Sudan border, had a customs' agency and an airstrip. Everything
there was tomorrow, tomorrow, so patience was critical.

Throughout Operation Exodus, I camped a total of ten
days on the bank of the Jokau River. Amazingly, I made it back
to Malakal with the truck just before the rains closed the road.

In a letter to our children on April 10, 1963, Dolly wrote,
"We were not sure when we would get here but we made
it pretty quickly after all. Dad says that God must be operating
his doors with the new electric eye. . . . Everything is working out just as it should." She also informed the children

that, "Daddy's letters will be late in coming this week again, but you can be assured that when you do get one, it will be exciting."

In May I traveled back to Doleib Hill in the Sudan to get a load of Arcon building supplies from the storehouse. The storehouse was the same old bee-infested house as I remembered but with one addition—a nine-foot, thirty-inch-wide beehive at one end. I waited until after dark to retrieve the Arcon hoping that the bees would be settled for the night and there would be less chance of getting stung.

In those few hours I let my memories carry me to the past. On many occasions the bees had been troublesome, but I especially remembered the one harrowing experience when I was stung hundreds of times here. Sons Bill and Tom were born here, and it was where we made the gates for the cemetery where friend Dr. J. Alfred Heasty was buried right beside Marion Adair (daughter of Bill Adair, former missionary at Doleib Hill). Twelve years ago I had walked around the Hill and said my good-byes, expecting never to return.

Without a visa, our family was not allowed to enter Ethiopia via its back door the same way our twenty tons of equipment had entered that spring of 1963. My family's entry would be much more complicated. Because we had no visa, we had to first return to Malakal in the Sudan.

We made quite a sight going through the airport and boarding the plane for our trip from Malakal to Khartoum and eventually on to Addis Ababa, the capital of Ethiopia. We all had our hands and arms full of various small items. I carried the typewriter, camera bag, and briefcase, besides my two rifles. This was the only way I could get these guns out of the Sudan without an export permit. The white safety helmet on my head did not complement my good suit and seemed to attract attention in its oddity, but it was the only way I could transport it since there was no space in my luggage.

We arrived in Khartoum on a Monday and, in faith that our visas would arrive, we purchased tickets on the next plane to Addis Ababa for that Thursday. Tuesday passed by with no sign of our visas, but on Wednesday we received a phone call from the Ethiopian Embassy. Again the door opened and, miracle of miracles, the visas were granted before the time of our flight.

On May 23, 1963, we were greeted at the airport in Addis Ababa by the general secretary of mission in Ethiopia, Don McClure, and his wife, Lyda. We had arrived and established a beachhead, the first of the Sudan-expelled missionaries. With my Ethiopian driver's license and ID cards, I qualified to become a permanent Ethiopian resident.

From Addis Ababa it was west on to Gambela on the Sudan border to clear our goods being stored in the rented warehouse. It was here that things got rather screwy and I dubbed the whole Gambela inspection process Operation Screwball. The custom officers instructed us to open every piece of goods, all 133, and unpack at least half of every barrel. Instead of using our lists of goods, the custom officials used their own list. Since there were no names in their native Amharic for many of our items, this took way too much time. With all eight thousand kilos of freight finally cleared, we separated, weighed, and marked it all in preparation for a charter flight from Gambela to its final destinations.

We were to remain at the mission station in Addis Ababa for the first two months before going on to the I. K. projects. Our arrival at Addis Ababa was very similar to our arrival in the Sudan back in 1947: many new people, not enough accommodations, and everyone having different ideas about how things should be done. The house we were staying in was also occupied by two other families and with no refrigeration, it was hard keeping enough food on hand for everyone.

The mission station in Addis Ababa was a hectic place with people coming and going continually. Because of the high altitude, the weather was delightfully cool and most evenings a fire felt good. Their rainy season ran from July to September (with an average rainfall of fifty inches) and, because it had precipitated most days since our arrival, we named it the Rainy City. (So much for the flyers describing it as "13 months of sunshine!") In compensation, beautiful flowers were abundant and vegetables plentiful.

Other than attending orientation courses for new Ethiopian missionaries, we started tackling the one-month Amharic language lessons required by the government. I must admit Dolly's enthusiasm and devotion outweighed mine, as I had never found language study easy. Although I had no trouble memorizing numbers, learning time presented another scenario. That was until I realized Ethiopians started counting their hours from 6:00 A.M., just as in Bible times. I was most intent on learning the Amharic words for the names of my tools in order to communicate with my workers. All in all, I never made much progress in language use—mostly due to our many moves, each requiring a new language.

Driving in Ethiopia was tricky: not only did they drive on the left, but there was an absence of road signs. Half of the population lived at least ten miles from any road, and due to flooding, only one third of the roads could be used all year long. Not knowing the language, we couldn't stop and seek directions. We were always getting lost or, at the least, not finding where we wanted to go.

Even though agriculture supported 90 percent of the population here, it was subsistence farming and inefficient. Half of the produce was carried by mule or donkey. Big American cars drove right beside the herds of goats and donkeys and made driving challenging. The herds had the right of way so we could only sit and wait for these beasts of burden to pass. Besides the herds, the two-wheeled horse carts that served as taxies slowed down traffic.

Native Ethiopian houses were poorly built of mud, grass walls, and metal roofs on eucalyptus poles. They were not built as well as the Shilluk or Nuer houses in the Sudan. Women did the cooking and laundry on the doorsteps and often you would see abject poverty right beside big villas of the well-to-do. Unlike the Sudan, the people here in Addis Ababa all wore clothes—ragged as they were. To make it affordable, the people shopped at the market where there was a big block of used clothing. Nearly all the men wore suits to work that came through CARE or some other agency in the United States.

———————

In July 1963, I left Addis Ababa to make my first survey trip to Ghimeera—our home base for the I. K. projects. There was no one to meet me at the airstrip and since the mission was seven miles from the airfield, I hired a donkey for two dollars and rode to the mission through the mud. The donkey boy who led the animal took me on a shortcut up a crooked trail that wound through the mountains and crossed many streams.

Upon arrival I noted that the mission was a beautiful spot on a rolling plateau. To the south was a high range of mountains. The water from the north side flowed down to the Nile and water from the south went into the Omo River. Before returning to Addis Ababa, I made a few notes and took a look around the station, thinking this would make the best I. K. base from which to work.

From the beginning of August to the end of November 1963, most of our time in Addis Ababa was consumed with building a stone retaining wall along the east side of the mission property. A road laid along the back of the mission was cut too close to the cyclone fence and caused the bank to slip. My job was to build a stone wall and drainage ditch to hold up the bank and then put the fence back on top of the wall. Moving dirt, getting large stone in from the quarry, cutting the stone, and keeping the masons busy laying it was challenging—especially in the mud. In order to hold the bank from cave-ins, it was necessary to shore up some spots.

The work area in the vicinity of the wall was very limited and, with no place for storage, could only hold one truckload of stone or sand at a time. At the end of each day the supply had to be replenished to start the next morning. Trucks were arriving throughout the night to make their deliveries. Due to heavy rains and the mud, it really wasn't until the beginning of October that we started to lay stone. I had ten men carrying dirt in round pans similar to those we had used in the Sudan. Each pan held three shovels full and, with the amount we had to move, it meant approximately forty thousand trips. At this rate I figured it would take about a year and a half. I had to figure out how to speed things up.

I compared my stone retaining wall at the mission in Addis Ababa to the one in the Bible built around Jerusalem by Nehemiah (Neh. 4:16). Half of Nehemiah's crew worked on construction while the other half stood on guard with swords, spears, and bows. Similar to Nehemiah, half of my men were productive workers, including sons, Bill and Ron. Unfortunately, the other half of my workers stood idle. When things were moving at their peak, my work crew numbered seventy-four: fifty laborers, fourteen cutters, nine masons laying stone, and one timekeeper.

But when comparing my wall to the Great Wall of China, there was quite a difference. Even though the Great Wall was 1500 miles long and mine only 466 feet, I used 414 sacks of cement (50 kilos each), 134 sacks of lime (100 kilos each), 91 cubic meters of sand, and 600 tons of stone to build it. There were 5,833 stones cut for the wall and each cutter got paid by the piece. I had to check for size and if they didn't fit, I threw them back. I had to approve all 5,833 stones before the cutters

Stone wall at Addis Ababa

were paid. This attractive wall with two iron gates was finished on November 30, 1963, and I felt sure it would never blow away. (When I returned in the 1990s, how rewarding to find but one crack in my wall.)

In addition to the stone wall, there was a long list of projects for me to do in Addis Ababa before going on to the I. K. projects. Besides the endless maintenance needs on the compound, I was working on plans and estimates with the doctors to renovate and expand the Sayo hospital buildings at Dembi Dollo. Also, the mission was planning to start a secondary school at Dembi Dollo and I was to draw up the plans and make estimates of those buildings, too.

In July all Americans in Addis Ababa were invited to the country club to meet the visiting Chief Justice and Mrs. Earl Warren. He was introduced to us by the American ambassador. We received gold-engraved invitations to a lecture given by Chief Justice Warren at the Haile Selassie Theater.

In the fall of 1963, our children appeared to be well and happy, even though most of them were far away. Ed and

Penny were in New Wilmington, Pennsylvania, completing their last year at Westminster College, and Bill, Ronnie, and Leah were at Schutz, the American mission school in Egypt. Leah, just nine years old and away from home for the first time, helped cheer us when she remarked in a letter, "School is so much fun." Ginny and Tommy, the only two at home at this time, enjoyed the cool mountain air in Addis Ababa but were anticipating our move into a tent home to work among the untouched tribes of the Illubabur and Kaffa Provinces.

In a letter written to the children dated September 1, 1963, Dolly exclaims, "Dad is tickled to get the new tribes work . . . and, if he is happy, so am I. . . . And joy, joy! We are to get a new house all our own, too. At Ghimeera too, if we ever find time to build it. . . . But it sounds heavenly, and we will always get to call it home." Dolly's joy was obvious since our life in the Sudan never lent itself to having a home or garden of her own.

On November 24, 1963, I first heard of President Kennedy's death by way of the RT. Flags of all countries were flown at half mast, schools closed, and a memorial service was held at church. I could see that the world was taking it hard. I went to the American Embassy for a memorial service in Addis Ababa where I was rubbing elbows with leaders from many countries. I wrote in my diary, "As they addressed us, 'Your Honors' and 'Your Excellencies' . . . I signed the condolences book, too, right along with the Honors and the Excellencies."

After Addis Ababa, we planned to spend a month at Dembi Dollo before going on to the permanent base for our new I. K. project at Ghimeera.

My project at Dembi Dollo in February 1964 was installing a water filter storage system to increase the water supply at the mission station during the dry season. Here I learned that it isn't necessarily how much you know but rather how much you get done that counts. In order to dig ditches in the muck, I battled my way down into the bog. The ditches eventually filled up with water and had to be dipped out. Since the locals didn't like working in the mud, some Anuaks came along, were interested in working, and removed their clothes and crawled in.

Gravel was our main holdup at Dembi Dollo. Like in the Sudan, I bought gravel by the sofias full, with schoolboys hauling it. It was a challenge to have enough gravel and sand on hand for the project. We encountered some tough rock while installing the filter bed and, as incentive, I told my workmen I would give forty cents to the man who could split the rock in two. There was one particularly big rock that the men had trouble breaking and they insisted that if we built a fire to heat it, and poured salt water over it, it would crack. The water experiment was not successful but the fire expanded the stone enough to make it easier to crack with a sledgehammer.

Many times our actions looked strange to the natives. An old Gulla woman gathering fuel in the swamp came by to observe our filter bed project at Dembi Dollo one afternoon. She had a piece of rope wrapped around her wrist and a bush knife in her hand. I wondered what she wanted when she rattled off something undistinguishable. First, she looked at the men digging ditches while standing in water up to their knees, and then at me filling the ditch with gravel. All she wanted to know was, "What does this crazy foreigner think he is doing?"

Besides the wall in Addis Ababa and the water system in Dembi Dollo, my time was focused on making surveys and on designing and erecting the buildings for the new I. K. posts. Was it a daunting task? Not really. I knew that besides being the master builder for the Ethiopian mission posts, I was working for Jesus the Master Carpenter. He was always willing to answer my questions and I knew anything was possible.

After one month I finished the water storage job at Dembi Dollo. Everything was working well so I erected a fence around the filter bed to keep cattle from walking on it, paid off my men, and packed my tools to move on.

As it turned out, from 1962 to 1977, our job in Ethiopia consisted of helping to pick sites and erect the physical plants for five of the seven new I. K. posts in order that the regularly assigned ministers, doctors, and teachers would have the facilities to carry out their work. My duties included the designing of metal-framed buildings small enough to be transported to the sites and supervising their construction. With the medical and educational work proposed to follow, it would open a vast new area of Ethiopia to the world, giving its primitive people a better life. I prided myself on setting work goals and carrying them through to completion.

Instead of "station," the term "post" was used to name the I. K. projects in order to denote a simple, more modest type of construction with less expense. "By its very nature," the Evangelistic Committee Report stated, "this new work among primitive tribes whose language, manner of life, and social and religious cultures are largely unknown, necessitates the employment of at least a limited but well qualified staff of American personnel. We mean by this an evangelistic missionary with special training in linguistics and anthropology for each tribal area, supported by Ethiopian dressers (medical assistants) and teachers."

The I. K. Report of January 1964 stated that:

> we would remind the builders and the new I. K. missionaries that the first impressions made upon the population of a new area during the building program by such things as make-up of work crew, attitudes of missionaries and foremen, and salary scales, all make very lasting impressions on the local populace, and we must keep in mind that these impressions should, as far as possible, further the Gospel.

Since our expulsion, matters continued to get worse in the Sudan. Because of the troubled news we received, we were happy to be in Ethiopia. In order to keep us informed, Rev. Lowrie Anderson, the general secretary of the Upper Nile Mission, sent out copies of missionary letters to all the former Sudan missionaries who had been expelled. Lillian Huisken was a nurse with the Dutch Reformed Church and managed the hospital in Akobo. After being expelled from Akobo in the Sudan, Lil departed for Ethiopia. Her letter described the happenings at Akobo.

Apparently, many Anuak and Nuer young men crossed over the border into Ethiopia during the first exodus. The area was under curfew regulations from 6:00 P.M. to 6:00 A.M., patrolled by police, besides being loaded with secret service men. They felt constantly watched.

On the second exodus, most of the mission personnel left. There were no houseboys, the foreman was gone, most all the teachers were gone, and they had to start over with new replacements in the school and train new boys in the clinic. Roads and the river were being patrolled and rebels would come onto the compound with guns, vandalize, and assault those in their way. People were exiting across the river with few possessions, petrified with all the shooting.

But by February, enrollment in the girls' school was gradually rising, and they were again having more patients in the clinic. This fluctuated, Lil explained, depending on the local situation: army maneuvers, visits from the raiders across the border, imprisonments—all had their effect on the lives of the villagers.

By the end of February, they received notice of expulsion and given, in some cases, only twenty-four hours to leave. They were asked to make a list of all mission property and asked to put some reliable person in charge of the compound. Their patients were very disturbed and felt that all the people would die with the clinic closed. But the commandant said that now, with the clinic closed, they would get an Arab doctor from the north and everyone would be happy. They had to turn the school over to the headmaster and say good-bye to the Christians. Their response was, "It would be easier to leave than having to stay." "How well we knew this to be true," Lil exclaimed. "With the missionaries gone, who could tell what would happen and there would be no way of news getting out."

For a week and a half, the tension had risen considerably. Soldiers were flown into Akobo by air and by the truckloads. "Were we really at Akobo?" Lil wondered. In the end, a police car came to pick up the missionaries and they were escorted to the airstrip by the army. Baggage would come later by army truck, they were told.

"As you can see," wrote Lillian on March 9, 1964, in a letter written from Eritrea, Ethiopia, to loved ones back home in the States, "the missionary has become the scapegoat for the Sudan's own internal troubles, the conflict between the north and the south." Her letter continued, giving an excerpt from the *Sudan Daily*, dated February 28, 1964:

> The government of the Sudan has on several occasions affirmed its expressed genuine policy of providing all conditions necessary for the free exercise by all citizens indiscriminately of any faith or religion they may choose to adopt. They can freely practice their ritual or any form of religious activity without fear, influence or coercion. Certain subversive elements and saboteurs, however, have deliberately misdirected or misused that sacred freedom to serve purposes other than the normal missionary work, and the propagation of ordinary religious tenets. Contrarily, such freedom as was extended has been exploited to the detriment of the country's unity and the defamation of its reputation by spreading sedition, hate, discontent, and animosity amongst the people in certain backward areas in the country, through exploiting their simplicity and primitiveness. Though the government has never been oblivious to the subversive activities of the foreign missionary, it has generously conceded them

the privilege of staying in the country without any restrictions on their movements. Experience has proved, however beyond any doubt that such tolerance has bred lack of discipline, arrogance, and order. The government has consequently resolved the repatriation of all foreign missionaries who are presently engaged in the southern provinces because it has proved beyond any doubt, and through legal proof, that their continuing to function in that region is detrimental to the country's unity and will seriously endanger its internal peace and security. Let it be known to all fellow countrymen living in those regions that the repatriation of such foreign elements would in no way jeopardize their freedom to practice their religion without any fear of influence in its widest context. The government will, however, undertake to assist those religious posts previously occupied by foreigners. Furthermore the government has deemed it expedient as a protective measure to resolve also the confinement of trading activities by foreign merchants to district and province headquarters in the south. They are completely prohibited from infiltration into the village and the bush as has been the case previously.[4]

"This kind of slander has continued in the papers," Lil expressed fervently, "and the Sudan is objecting very strongly to the adverse criticism it is receiving from the foreign press."

On March 14, 1964, Mary Smith, a doctor at Nasir, Sudan, also sent a letter from Eritrea, this one describing the trouble at Nasir. Mary said their letters were censored and double censored and there was an undercurrent of tension and unrest everywhere. The government was making a huge airstrip and army trucks and personnel were on the move constantly. There was no shooting like at Akobo but in February the RT was taken away and, because of the big campaign, there was an order "not to go anywhere out of Nasir till further notice." An all-out offensive against the insurgents by the army was being planned and they were told that there would be as many as three thousand troops in the area between Nasir and Akobo.

(Both Akobo and Nasir first heard about the eviction of three hundred missionaries from the South Sudan on the radio through the British Broadcasting Company and mentally prepared themselves for news to come.)

At least at Nasir they were able to have a last clinic and not just lock up doors with no explanation. This meant that Ler and Pibor, two other mission stations where I worked, would have to be closed up, too, because they were not able to turn them over properly. Dr. Bob Gordon and his family, and Marian (in charge of the school at Nasir) and Mary left with an armed guard ("whether to see that there was no foul play from these dangerous exportees or to protect us from the dangers of the way, we will never know"). Mary's letter expressed gladness in being able to leave the station by road and seeing the country for the last time. It looked perfectly peaceful to her. She was made to feel like they were being rushed out, probably, she thought, so the maneuvers could begin without spectators.

Natives questioned whether their church services could continue and Mary told them she thought they would be allowed and that "even if they couldn't meet formally in the church they should never forsake the meeting of a few together wherever they could." A young pastor trainee was left in charge of the church. Mary explained to the natives that they would not be able to write because anyone getting letters from the mission folk would immediately be under suspicion.

Mary's letter tried to describe to her friends that even before they left Nasir, they could sense a change of feeling towards them and coolness in friendships, but indicated she did not know until she got to Malakal, and even more so when she got to Khartoum, of the great hate campaign against all missionaries going on in the Sudan press and over the Sudan radio.

Their time in Malakal was full and busy and was a series of seeing each other off. That Sunday evening, they gathered for a last little prayer meeting as a mission and also to talk over a few matters of urgent business. "MAF, too, was being evicted and had seven days to get out," she continued. "Even being sent out of the country did not mean that we could get our exit visas with great ease, for Sudan red-tape must always be difficult it seems. But in the end we all have nice big 'finals' underlined in red ink in our passports." Her letter ended as she "went off to be a refugee for a while."

A letter from Rev. Glenn Reed, corresponding secretary of the Board of Foreign Missions, July 24, 1964, to me and Robb McLaughlin had an attached list of "medical" buildings belonging to the former American Mission. After visiting our buildings with the Sudanese public minister of health, Glenn stated that "the Ministry of Health is definitely interested in the purchase of the buildings, some which, I believe, the Ministry wanted to put to use at the earliest possible opportunity." Consequently my job was to send back information on the floor plans of the major buildings, their cost, and their age, to help the Ministry of Health arrive at a proper appraisal. Many of these buildings I had constructed. The three-page list included Ler, Nasir, Akobo, and Pibor. As far as I know, we were never paid for our buildings.

A letter written to former Sudan missionaries by Robert Meloy, a United Presbyterian pastor from the American Mission in Khartoum, Sudan, was informative:

> The "October Revolution" caught almost everyone by surprise and unprepared. When things began to get out of control, a hastily formed Popular Front representing all political factions stepped into the picture with a representation to the President to end the military regime. It seems that the President was overwhelmed by the popular uprising all over the country showing the unpopularity of the military government, so he "bowed to the will of the people" dissolving the Supreme Council and the Council of Ministers. With this announcement the silence of the evening curfew was broken

by distant rumblings of moving and shouting hordes of people. Soon automobiles began pouring down Kasr Avenue towards the palace. . . . For an hour the street was filled with marchers, shouting and waving tree branches in joy over the news. This was Monday night the 26th. Then came the long wait for the announcement of the new government. More demonstrations on Wednesday were broken up with rifle and machine gun fire in front of the palace where scores were killed or wounded. Rumors filled the towns and the general strike called on Monday continued full apace. Of course, we kept inside with our heads down, so to speak. Wednesday it was announced that the country was returning to the constitution of 1956 and that the Popular Front would form a government to take control. . . . The new government was announced on Friday morning with Abboud as President and in control of the army and the various political factions represented among the different ministries. Four are purported to be Communists, one of whom was released from prison to fill his minister's chair. . . . The Southerners have been encouraged by the change in government and promise of more freedom.

Correspondence written by Jerry Nichols, a teacher at the mission school, from Omdurman, Sudan, to friends in Ethiopia on December 20, 1964, and another letter written by Rev. Bob Meloy and his wife, Dorthea, American Mission, Khartoum, Sudan, December 24, 1964, described an awful night in Khartoum with rioting in the streets against the Southerners. A large number of Southerners destroyed the airport, stoned cars, beat people, and burned buildings. There was looting and mob attacks, and they overran the mission in Khartoum during a Sunday evening service and burned it. With no time to retrieve things, they all rushed out into a waiting police truck. The Communists were using most of the opportunities to their advantage.

Dorthea and Bob Meloy responded to concerns of their families:

. . . the feeling of this wonderful peace has made this awful experience most profitable in the face of worldly loss. Long ago when coming first to the field we covenanted with the Lord that all the things we had would be entirely dispensable and that we would never care if we ever had to lose any or all. And now having escaped with only the clothes on our backs, we praise His Name that our concern was more for your (those back home) anxiety than for anything that we left behind!

The Meloys were housed temporarily in an empty embassy flat and were much better off than many of their Sudanese friends who were seriously injured and who lost all their possessions. "We have published a statement that we will remain here only so long as we can contribute constructively to the building of the country and for the glory of God," the Meloys wrote.

GHIMEERA

Ghimeera Mission Station was chosen as the base for our I. K. operation. It was a beautiful spot in a rain forest with a high range of mountains to the south and a river winding its way through the valley 350 feet below. A hydroelectric plant was located here that supplied all the electricity needed twenty-four hours a day at very little cost.

A family-size tent was called home while we built our first real house on the mission field. A concrete mixing platform made by the children the prior summer in Addis served as a floor in our tent. With four beds and a dresser in the tent, there was hardly room to walk. To alleviate the crowdedness, I set up scaffold framing beside the tent to use as our kitchen/dining room, but we still had to sit two to a chair.

Boxes were everywhere: some from the States, some from the Sudan, and the rest from Addis Ababa, and it was difficult to find what we needed.

Dolly did a good job of managing the family, especially challenging since our gang was like an army and moved on its stomach. She was adaptable, energetic, and a hard worker, plus she supported me in all my activities. Besides "keeping house" (or tent) and managing all the building accounts, she homeschooled Ginny and Tommy until third grade when they were able to go to boarding school. Gardening helped to maintain her sanity; mangoes, guavas, papayas, and a banana/pineapple patch all grew around the tent. In a letter written to the children in February 1964, I informed them that "the work around here is easier. Mother even cuts the grass with an electric lawn mower. What we need is men with brains, not brawn. We will be able to use the power tools on this house just like we did in the States."

Son Ed joined us in Ethiopia in April 1964, after completing his bachelor's degree at Westminster College in New Wilmington, Pennsylvania, and put his master's degree on hold. He got approval to draw up plans for the hospital at Dembi Dollo and was waiting for authorization from the board of missions to stay in Ethiopia one year as a special term builder. He was also doing work on the secondary school plans there at Dembi Dollo. Eventually he would be a tremendous help with the building of portable houses at some of the new I. K. sites.

In May 1964, we received Penny's commencement announcement from Westminster College. "It would be a thrill to watch you get your diploma," I expressed to Penny in a letter. But I couldn't attend and wondered if it would ever work out that I would be at the right place to see any of my children graduate. This was the toughest part of the job—you see so little of your children. There was still work to be done and I believed God wanted me to be putting in the stations for the unreached tribes. My response to questions Penny had concerning her abilities when pursuing a job was, "You're a Pollock and we can do anything. That is, with God's help." All of the children, except for Penny, were home the summer of 1964 and I wrote, "I wish that I had the money to bring you out for the summer so we could all be together once more."

Work had stopped one rainy afternoon in Ghimeera and the family met in our tent and started to brainstorm. We pictured in our minds mission building designs, small and light enough that could be transported in MAF's single-engine Cessna 180. It was May 1964 when Ed and I first came up with the idea for our Polycon building designs.

The Polycon, a portable kit consisting of a metal truss and purlin roof frame supported by steel columns, was to be fabricated (cut, welded, and prepared) in the workshop at Ghimeera. These big erector sets, similar to the Arcon buildings we used in the Sudan, had standardized components that could be taken apart and fit into a Cessna. These kits could be flown from Ghimeera by MAF and reassembled on the new mission posts to be used for schools, clinics, staff houses, and workshops. Local materials such as stone, cement blocks, or burned brick would be used for the walls. There were five Polycons planned for each post—all of them to be made in our base shop at Ghimeera. *(See photo section.)*

Since my local unskilled labor had never seen construction like this before, I would have to train them to use the unfamiliar tools and materials needed to erect them.

In July 1964, my sons finished a domed steel-framed tent that we called the Polyvillion, and all the station gathered to watch us erect this strange structure. I stitched the tent canvas together with an old foot treadle sewing machine that we had brought along from the States. (Later we would use this steel-framed tent for living quarters at two of the I. K. projects.)

Back in January 1964, in a letter to Ed, I first mentioned the idea of another Pollock original—the Polydome (a pun on our name Pollock—Poly, as well as the term for a structure which is made up of many parts—dome). In a letter to the children I wrote, "If I get time I want to try making a dome. They would be light and easy to transport and could be used for building at the new posts. I haven't sold anyone here on the idea yet. What do you think? Is it possible?" I knew with God's help nothing was impossible.

In September 1964, I presented Ed's and my Polydome plans to the building committee—a round six-sided geodesic dome made of 216 triangular sections (six different sizes color-coded for ease of assembling by national laborers) with a lightweight roof. There were two big considerations: that it be lightweight considering the high shipping costs, and that it stand up to tropical storms. The dome structure was the strongest type of construction for little weight, and I felt it would blend with the local architecture of Ethiopia. Two domes connected by a breezeway could form one three-bedroom home or a three-room school building. I was aware that Buckminster Fuller had used two computers and eleven thousand dollars to figure out the specifications for the Henry Kaiser geodesic dome in Hawaii, but all we had were pencils, paper, and enthusiasm.

We desperately needed a workshop since, no matter what project we started, some machine needed to be fixed. All the furnishings for the clinics and schools on the I. K. posts would be prefabricated in the workshop at our home base in Ghimeera. After I had my tools and materials assembled I organized a very efficient shop. In order to make all the parts needed for the domes, I set up assembly-type procedures for each machine. Penny remembered, "It was exciting to assemble the drill press, build a stand for the grinder, and set up a table for the lathe." Often, when a part was missing, I improvised with local materials and relied on myself for repairs.

There were plenty of large trees in the rain forest and, since we needed timber for our house and shop, we set up a logging camp fourteen miles from Ghimeera. The beautiful tropical jungle valley was thick with wanza trees and vines commonly seen in Tarzan movies. (The wanza, three feet in diameter with some towering 150 feet tall, had good tough wood with straight grain and was easy to work with.) Baboons and hundreds of black and white Colobus monkeys swung through the trees in this valley, and elephants trudged by our camp at night.

From Ghimeera we transported our sawmill (with table and track) to the logging camp in the rain forest and ran it by power takeoff from the back of the Jeep. It used a forty-inch diameter circular blade that could handle a sixteen-foot-length log and cut a sixteen-inch-wide board. After cutting the trees, we hauled small loads to the top of the hill by truck, and then trucked the big loads to Ghimeera. This whole operation was a major undertaking. We agreed to pay the village chief five dollars for each tree we cut, knowing that each one would supply approximately five hundred feet of timber. Son Ed was a tremendous help in the operation of the logging camp.

When our boys decided to move their beds out of the tent and under the roof of the new shop, some of the crowding eased at Ghimeera. To stay dryer, it wasn't long before we all made the shop our home. The narrow passageways between the tent and the storeroom, and the curtains hanging over the doors of the girls' and boys' rooms in the shop, reminded us of a ship. The children soon dubbed the shop the S.S. *Necessity*. It was quite cozy.

As work continued on our new home, we put in a drain ditch. Since it was too wet and muddy for the truck to get through, my men carried stone on their heads from the river to the new house location in preparation for the stone foundation. According to our house plans, the view from the living room picture window included the valley below with a winding river. We anticipated the roar of the river after a heavy rain and watching the sun set over the mountains in late afternoon. In front of the house a stone patio was planned with planters around the edge, but I wondered if I would ever have time to sit and enjoy it.

Because of the lack of unskilled labor, the children were put to work. I called it "summer school with Dad," and even Tommy was driving spikes into the floor joists for our new home. According to Penny, having seven children has always been an asset for me. She remembers me training them to use hammers from the time they were preschoolers and, if they weren't participating, they were observing and absorbing. With the I. K. projects this was most obvious.

Using rock and sand from the local river, Ed worked on the foundation of our house along with the local masons. He and brother Bill not only instructed some of the workmen, but helped build a stone wall that enclosed the flower bed around the patio. Ron mostly worked with me, sharpened saws, did roof caulking, and built roof trusses for our house. Leah kept busy nailing lathe to the house. One week they each had put in over sixty hours. It was unusual for mission kids to work alongside their parents for entire days. We not only were in the process of building our house, but the Pollock team lived, cooked, cleaned, studied, and worshiped together there in Ghimeera in 1964.

Ed also was working on the figures for a dome home at Omo (location of one of our I. K. projects) to make sure all the angles fit properly. We constructed a paper model at one-quarter scale before making our first geodesic dome. The I. K. Committee gave approval for building Polydomes at two of the I. K. posts and we started getting set up for mass production. The metal angles and other construction materials were flown into the government mud and grass airstrip at Mizan Tefari, seven miles from Ghimeera. It was then hauled by truck through five rivers and up a dirt road to Ghimeera, almost an impossible feat. But that was only in the dry season. In the rainy season the dome materials had to be cut up in small pieces to fly in the small Cessnas. (We planned to build three of these homes at the posts—each with two domes connected by a breezeway.) I recorded in my diary, "I cut the 840 sides for the Omo domes. That is all the side pieces for one home. If all the angles were laid out in a long line it would make 105 linear feet of 4 mm. iron. What I cut today would make an average of one cut every thirty seconds." Besides the cuts, a total of 7,788 holes had to be drilled in the triangles.

Not only did the heavy rains in the rain forest slow down construction there in Ghimeera, but at times the rain and mud got me down. One week in August we were deluged with 6.2 inches of rain and, for the month, we had over one foot. The average annual rainfall was seven to eight feet. If it was raining when it was time to start work for the day, we sent the local workers home since it was too expensive to have them sit around the shop getting in the way. One letter to Penny said it all, "Greetings from your wet and muddy family . . . I am trying to write with the water dripping into a can on my desk and splashing in my face." Rainy weather wasn't building weather, but my depressed moods were almost always elevated with the youth and enthusiasm of my children.

From the time the roof was put up until the domes were in place, the locals were inquisitive and came from miles around to observe. Everything was new to them—from the loud chain saws and the magical liquid cement that hardened, to the tractor and trailer that saved hours of physical hauling.

Often names were used interchangeably for the same area or town and can be confusing for the reader. For example, Mizan Tefari was the name of the government town and airstrip where Ethiopian Airlines was located, Ghimeera was the name of our mission station, and Gatcheb was the name of the local river. However, all three of these names were used to make reference to the same area. Also, there was often more

than one way to spell the same name. To this day I like using
Andrew Jackson's quote, "It's a poor mind that can't figure out
more than one way to spell a word." Andrew and I have something in common.

The only means of transportation to the Mizan Tifari
airstrip in heavy rains was by mule, and this meant having the
mules swim across five streams. So, needless to say, the first
landing of MAF on our new airstrip at the mission compound
in Ghimeera was a historical day in June 1964. I'm sure the dirt
airstrip built into the side of a hill was one of MAF's most
unusual landing strips. Its oddity was due to its being high in
the center and lower at the ends. The starting point at takeoff
was so low that, standing at the center of the strip, you were
unable to see the plane. This necessitated someone standing on
a platform in a tree holding brightly colored paddles to signal
the pilot that all was clear.

At the other end, where the plane left the strip, it proceeded
out over a valley. The mountains straight ahead were so high
that the pilot had to immediately bank either right or left to
make the climb in order to clear them. Eventually more work
had to be done to make the airstrip safer. Mail service was often
restricted due to the heavy rains, but we were blessed with
MAF's arrival at this landing strip several times a month to
bring us mail, supplies, and building materials.

MAF's services would be critical at our new posts since
roads were either nonexistent or very difficult and time-
consuming to travel. With each post to be manned by only one
missionary couple (in addition to some Ethiopian medical
dressers and teachers), it would be imperative to have outside
contact with others or "missionary maintenance," as Ann
Rowe referred to it in an article called "Circuit Rider with
Wings": "Each couple is trying to become immersed in the
surrounding culture, learn a difficult, unwritten language, and
understand a people far removed from them in development

and concept. . . . Frequent visits for consultation, coordination, and decision-making are important. . . . The plane has made this possible."[5] MAF would be a vital link in connecting the new I. K. posts.

When we were ready to open work with a new tribe, we had a plan. First, we flew low over the country to locate villages, and then looked for trails that we could use to find our way into the village. Also we would look for any rivers that had to be crossed. Usually we could tell from the air where one tribe ended and another began by the difference in the type of huts.

Next a team of four went in overland with pack mules. Natives transported our trek supplies which had been packed in manageable sizes and shapes for mule and carrier. Most likely, I would be one of this team of four since I was the builder. After picking a site where we could best work with a tribe, a family was assigned to live there in order to study the language and the culture. Supplies would be air-dropped from the plane until an airstrip was built.

Due to the heavy vegetation in this mountainous area, choosing locations for these posts was an arduous task. The tribes were spread out and located in different climates, and it didn't help that the local building supplies were very limited and that not one of these peoples had ever seen a white man.

I wondered how we were to reach these new tribes without roads. It would be almost impossible to get materials or supplies into the posts without the help of MAF, which meant that most of our building component pieces had to be small enough to fit into a Cessna 180.

Also, how could we build mission posts with no trained or skilled labor? At each one of these new posts, we planned to build a school and a clinic that would be staffed by Ethiopians trained at our other schools and hospitals. Gradually young missionary families would be recruited, trained in linguistics, anthropology, mission methods, and Amharic (the national language of Ethiopia). But this was only the preliminary reason for reaching these tribes. Our goal was to prepare their hearts and minds to receive God's message of salvation and to train leadership in each tribe as quickly as possible so we could move on to open other areas.

After we completed the surveys, I continued to wonder how I was going to get building materials to the first three new posts. With one site in the mountains (Chebera), one in the forest (Godore), and the other in the desert (Omo), and no roads or rivers that were navigable, we had to rely on MAF and its Cessna 180-185 to do our hauling. That meant we would be restricted to hauling nothing longer than six feet in length, and I didn't know of any prefabricated buildings to buy on the world market that would fit this dimension. I had to rely upon my ingenuity and my own designs.

In 1964, which I called the year of exploration, our family moved six times: into our tent, the workshop, the Haspels's home, Dr. Miller's home, and finally into our new house. Some of these moves were for as little as six weeks, but just the same, they were moves. We moved mainly to acquire additional conveniences. That same year, I traveled ten thousand miles in Ethiopia by plane, Jeep, boat, mule, foot, and on occasion, air, and slept 156 nights in a tent. I wrote home to the children, "There is never a dull moment here; you never know when you get up in the morning what you will be doing before night."

With the myriad jobs required in finishing our home at Ghimeera, it was taking many months to complete. By July, the outside wall framing and the roof trusses were up. By August, two months after starting construction, the house was ready for the metal roof. All 209 roofing sheets were installed and caulking was completed by the end of summer, just at the time the children prepared to return to school. They had all contributed many hours toward the completion of their home.

Besides the time spent on construction, there were many other jobs that were competing for my attention—so many that I felt like I needed at least two of myself. First, time was spent on the survey trips looking for the best locations for our new mission posts. At the same time, Ed and I were working on the shop buildings for the new posts at Godore, Omo, and Chebera. Some days Ed worked late into the night. Also, Ed was preparing an electrical wiring code designed to improve the service and increase the safety of the electrical systems used on the Ethiopian mission stations. Unlike the United States, Ethiopia had no electrical codes.

The year flew by, and in no time, it was another summer. In June 1965, Penny had landed in Addis Ababa and I wrote in my diary, "It sure is nice to be blessed with children who know how to work and like to work. . . . We all took the day off and as Ginny said, 'It's a fun day.' We all piled into the Jeep and plowed through the mud to the airstrip to meet Penny. It's the first time we have all been together as a family since March 1963."

It wasn't long before the family was back to work. Besides pushing to complete our house, the entire family worked in the shop constructing prefab parts for our Polycon buildings at the new posts. Ed did welding, Penny drilled iron, and Ron sawed T-iron, while Bill filed the ends.

We pushed hard on the prefabrication work for the posts, and in three months' time we had the frames for ten buildings finished. On July 21, about the time that Tom and Ron celebrated their mutual birthdays (Tom, nine and Ron, fifteen), the last of the fifteen buildings were delivered to the three I. K. posts. All of the roofs and fifteen buildings at the three posts that were begun at the end of March were completed by the end of July. We had used 1¾ miles of ¾-inch pipe, ¾ mile of 1½-inch T-iron, covered 8,220 square feet of floor space, used 9,000 hook bolts (with 7,700 of them made in the shop), and made and used 18,000 felt washers.

By mid-August 1965, we enjoyed the balmy evening and cooked corn and meat on the patio of our new home in Ghimeera before Ed and Penny returned to college in the States. The rest of the group worked hard to get as much completed as possible before they, too, would have to leave to go back to school. "Bill, Ron, Leah, and Tom flew off to Addis Ababa on their way to Schutz School in Alexandria. They are a great bunch of kids and I am going to miss them," my diary revealed. "They have been a big help with the work here this summer and have learned a lot at our 'summer school,' much of which they will be able to use later in life." As soon as they departed, Ginny immediately tried to fill the shoes of all the missing children.

Early morn on September 11, there were approximately fifty children dancing and singing in our yard and on the front porch in celebration of the Ethiopian New Year, 1958. (The Ethiopian year has thirteen months, so in our year 1965 it was 1958 in Ethiopia.) We treated them with candy and they in turn gave us flowers. None of my men were working.

As November 1965 and my fifty-third birthday rolled around, Dolly planned a celebration and invited the entire mission station to supper, ice cream, and cake on our new patio. Work progressed: floors, doors, cabinets, electrical, and plumbing until March 1966, when we moved the last of our things into our new home.

Minutes of the Ethiopia Mission Executive Committee meeting in Addis Ababa in October 1965, stated:

> We are sorry to ask the Pollocks to stay over but there are so many critical situations which await Ted, and only Ted can work them out, that we have little choice but to ask them to stay. After we get our I. K. missionaries out of the weather and a roof over their heads we can take a breather and respite from the tremendous push and pressures the Pollocks have been working under.

In view of the critical needs of the I. K. building program, we were requested to delay our furlough until May 1967.

Often there were language difficulties, Dolly stated in an article titled, "Pollocks Originate a New Dome Building for Remote Mission Posts." She described how we had worked with fourteen different languages in our twenty-three years in Africa and had developed our own brand of sign language to communicate with the nationals. Since we never stayed long enough in any one area, we regretted that we didn't have time to learn some of the languages for practical use on the building projects. Our tools were foreign to the tribal peoples and many had never seen most of them or our building materials before. Therefore, it was no surprise that they had no words in their language for them. We had to teach them the name of the tool as well as how to use it and for what purpose. It was genuine on-the-job training.[6]

"Wages mean little or nothing to local villagers who have no shops,"[7] Dolly added. Perhaps salt or grain might have interested the workers more as pay, and brightly colored shirts might have appealed to those who wore clothes. We realized that we had to discover what it was that the people wanted or needed to use as wages for the workers on the new posts.

In the same article Dolly stated:

When we go into a new place, the women and children usually appear first and want to help. The men come to see what is going on, sitting in any available shady spot and moving on when the sun reaches them. They enjoy watching their women work!

But the men are curious and interested in everything. Some day they will make good craftsmen when they learn the dignity of work. Occasionally a man will work for an hour or two, mainly because he wants to try the strange tools we use. . . . And handling a wheelbarrow is great sport, since at first they cannot coordinate both hands at the same time. . . .[8]

During the rainy season mud was a constant irritant and delayed our building progress. Also, there was no trained labor to help me with the I. K. work. Since there was little chance of training one man to manage all of the jobs, I had to take some time to train men for each of the jobs of carpenter, mason, electrician, welder, and mechanic. Often I found it was quicker to do it myself and I so much appreciated the help of my sons and daughters when they were available. I was only a few months at each post at a time (besides working at Ghimeera, the base) and was allowed by the I. K. Committee to take two of my men to move with me.

At first it was unknown whether the tribesmen, who could be warlike, would prove friendly. But most of the tribes welcomed us. If anything, I think they feared us more than we feared them. Usually they would be off in the bush hiding before we even got near them. We found their lives full of fear and superstitions and every village had its own witch doctor. Everywhere we went we found sickness and a willingness to accept our medicine and let us treat their wounds.

I named 1965 the year of construction when I supervised the prefabrication and construction of five metal framed and roofed buildings in each of three locations. An article titled, "An African Adventure" written by Carl Karsch described the setting:

> The logistics of this feat are impressive. In six flights to the base camp, an Ethiopian airline cargo plane delivered nearly two miles of steel pipe and three fourths of a mile of iron braces. . . . A light mission plane, making sometimes a half-dozen trips a day, airlifted the completed braces, bolts, pipe collars, and other gear in forty flights to new outposts. . . . He made jigs to speed production; even so, he, his seven children, and eight Ethiopian workers often went without sleep to make an early morning shipping deadline. . . . The Ethiopian government, pleased with Mr. Pollock's simplified designs

which encourage the use of unskilled labor, will use his plans for buildings of their own in isolated locations.[9]

"And challenge it was!—for there are many problems concerned with building in Ethiopia," Dolly described in the 1971 *Ethio-Echo* article:

There's the planning and fabricating of the structures, collecting local materials, encouraging and training people as workers (most of whom have never seen a brace or bit, saw or even a hammer before!), struggling with language and culture differences, and waiting months for supplies when some air fields are closed during the heavy rains and trucks cannot always travel over the muddy roads. And then there's the bookkeeping and the budget—not to mention the nomadic life we live at times, camping in tents while the buildings are begun in a new place.[10]

Some of the workers were very sloppy and it bothered me to have to work with them. Some days they were no help and only held me back. We came up with the saying, "Give them the job and they will finish the tools."

Since Dolly was a member of the Schutz School board, the end of 1965 we traveled to Alexandria, Egypt, for the board meeting. What a treat it was to watch Leah and Tom in the school's Christmas program, to see Bill win a cup in one of his cross country races, and to have Christmas dinner in the school dining room. After laying out plans for the new building and swimming pool at the school, we toured the Valley of the Kings where pharaohs of ancient Egypt were buried.

Back at Ghimeera, the locals desired to have me help them with the construction of several bridges, and I went to inspect three locations. I built a model of a bridge for a crossing nearby and worked out a design for a cable swinging bridge. At first the whole community was enthusiastic about the project. By

April the locals started to pile up stone for the bridge and it wasn't long before I welded up the bridge iron. The men dug the holes and I set one of the steel frames in place and built stone up one third of the way. Frequently women and children stopped on their way to market to help carry a few stones or some chicka, the mud mortar.

Eventually problems between the Christians and non-Christians developed among the bridge workers, and the numbers of workers dwindled. In May I continued with the bridge work and set up the other steel frame. Some of the villagers started to return but I had to mark, check, and recheck each piece. We finished our part of the bridge in the next couple months and left the completion of the bridge floor for the locals. I felt the bridge left a lot to be desired.

With Dottie Rankin in charge of the I. K. province schools, I agreed to give some classes in woodworking at Ghimeera. I had a class of twenty-six village teachers (including six females) and gave them a choice of three items that they could make. They all decided upon a three-legged stool, but I soon discovered that twenty-six students were too many to have working in the shop at one time. Besides, there were not enough tools. After cutting out the stool tops and drilling holes for the legs, the entire class had a stool to take home in a week.

How much easier it would be to tell my tale of the I. K. projects if I had focused on one project at a time. Instead, there were many days when I hopped from one project to another. For ease of reading, I have separated each of the projects and written them up chronologically.

CHEBERA—TESHENNA

The Teshenna Tribe, my first I. K. post for the unreached tribes, was located at Chebera in the hill country of southwest

Ethiopia in some of the most remote country in the entire world. It was surveyed and opened up by Rev. William Muldrow. An article written by the reverend titled "Work Begins with Teshenna People," stated:

> Thus, on the 4th of February, work was begun on the airstrip and the construction of a mission post among the Teshenna people was underway. This day was the climax of some three years preparation and training for the Muldrow's and an additional year spent surveying the tribe and negotiating for the particular site.[11]

Reverend Muldrow's initial trip, some sixty miles into the heart of the Teshenna territory, took three weeks and involved the tribe's people helping to build roads in virgin territory.

First, there were three aerial surveys during April, July, and August of 1964 which covered most of the Teshenna country. Next were the preliminary ground and air survey, followed by two ten-day final surveys. One of these final surveys included three pack mules, a small horse, two native men to handle the mules, and a native guide. Since there were only enough mules hired to carry our packs, we four missionaries (myself, Harold Kurtz, Malcolm Vandevort, and Bill Muldrow) had five hard days of trekking over the mountains through mud and brush—and sometimes in the rain.

The beautiful mountain country had high grass and brush so thick that it had to be cut to get the mules through with their packs. Rather than being concentrated in communities or villages, Teshenna were a lowland people, primarily farmers, scattered in small groups in a huge area throughout the valleys and plateaus between the mountain peaks. Water was abundant, not only from the main rivers but also from the many smaller streams. Besides, there were numerous waterfalls where the streams dropped off the plateau.

We set up camp and before long, a large crowd of curious natives gathered around to watch us. They were friendly and brought us wood. In return we gave them our empty tin cans, of which the young fellows cut out the ends and wore as earrings. Men wore cloths around their waists and shaved their heads—except for the three long tufts of hair in front that they twisted in different directions. Women wore a grass panel in front with a piece of cloth around the back. A few wore a complete grass skirt but the smaller girls' attire was only a chain hanging in the center of the front. It was custom for them to pull out some of their lower teeth; the women pulled out four and the men two. Their houses were poorly constructed of stick walls with grass roofs and they owned very few cattle. Corn, their main food, they traded for our empty tin cans.

For two reasons, it was decided that our outpost would be located in the village of Chebera. First, it was close to the tribe's center of population density and was accessible to the most populated areas, with good, all-weather trails. Second, it was somewhat of a crossroads and already had a well-established flow of traffic into the area. Our goal was to find airstrips with water nearby and we noted several places at Chebera that could easily be put into shape for an MAF airstrip. There was even one that could possibly land a DC-3.

Chebera was situated on a high ridge overlooking the Rift Valley. The people were cordial and anxious for us to locate here, and as mission builder, I looked forward to building this post.

Much had been accomplished that first year with the Teshenna, all in the name of "hard, dirty work," Bill Muldrow stated in an article titled "Reflections on a Year with the Teshenna Tribe." An elderly Teshenna man confided in Bill:

> That land was my father's father's, and for all I know his father's father's. Those trees cover the graves of my ancestors. Now I've given you this land. You are my neighbor and we

drink the water of this river together. My sons take their children to your clinic and your medicine is good. No longer are we afraid of the evil spirit that lived in the rocks where your children play. You tell us that God, who made this country and gives us life, is Jesus Christ and that we must follow Him.[12]

Bill Muldrow delighted in the way the people received them as friends and neighbors from the very start. Prior to his arrival, their only contact with the outside world was the unwelcome visits of the tax collectors. Out of curiosity, the tribespeople often stopped by Bill's home to see all the "strange" things the foreigner had brought, Bill described in the newsletter. His backyard was frequently used "as a sort of court room where the chiefs sit on a big log to settle disputes among their people. . . ."[13]

"The I. K. Project had been envisioned from the outset as a 'partnership in mission' with Ethiopian workers heading up the medical and educational work from the beginning."[14] Bill felt especially blessed to have some dedicated young Ethiopian men who came with him from the "mother" station in Maji.

Solomon, a young man who had twelve years' service with the mission, was the teacher-evangelist. With an eighth-grade education, not only did he start up and supervise the school and lay plans for formal education throughout the tribe there at Chebera, but he tramped into the surrounding villages each Sunday to explain to the people the purpose for our being there and give them a Christian message.

Wendimu, a tribesman from Maji, was trained by the mission at our hospital in Dembi Dollo as the dresser (medical assistant) and was the Teshenna's first touch of modern medicine in the little grass hut that was used for the clinic. His penicillin treatment for tropical yaws, a severely disfiguring disease, was a spectacular overnight cure. When the clinic was first established, it was determined that 55 percent of the patients treated daily were infected with this disease. After approximately one year, statistics showed a drop to 10 percent. Wendimu also preached in the villages like Solomon.

Besides Solomon and Wendimu, there were two students from Maji who tutored the children in the school. It wasn't unusual for parents to pull their child from school since they needed help to keep the birds out of the grain fields. The children were taught early the motto, "No work, no eat."

As far as the language barrier, Bill explained, "Though it has been somewhat frustrating to have to communicate mostly through an interpreter, their interest in the gospel message has been a real incentive for us to work hard on our language studies, for we feel that their understanding is limited mainly by our ability to communicate." Bill continued in the article, reflecting on Teshenna thought and customs:

> Typical of many African peoples, they have a concept of God as the creator of the world, who gave them life and who protects them on their journeys. They have elaborate rites of prayer, which involve painting themselves with the ashes of a special fire made by laboriously rubbing two sticks together, and of purification by bathing in the blood of a freshly slain goat. But largely their lives are controlled by the evil spirits who threaten them on every hand and over whom God seems to have little active control. The concept of God as a loving Father, who sent His Son to be the Savior of the world, and the Friend and Companion of man, is a new and welcome thought and many have come from long distances to invite us to teach at their village.[15]

At the beginning of 1967, my time was spent sorting and color coding triangles for the Chebera Polydome. Materials purchased in Addis Ababa had to be trucked to Jimma before being flown to Mizan Tefari and on to its final destination at Chebera. I asked for MAF's assistance one day a week, from

Roof of Polydome

the end of March until September, to fly these building parts into Chebera and warned that it would take at least seventy trips. My hands were getting stiff and sore from cutting and bending of edges of triangles, and eventually were swollen, and I was having trouble cutting. We began work on the tower that was needed to erect the dome.

The Polydome was erected in the following way: First, a foundation was dug out and the concrete floor poured. Then a twenty-five-foot tower, made in sections possible to transport, was bolted together. Next, the first six triangles were bolted around the tower making a circle or hexagon. As the hexagon took shape, U bolts were installed to the six triangles. Wire lines (hooked to a hand ratchet puller) were attached to the U bolts, making it possible to lift the triangles. As each row was bolted into place, it was raised to its proper height allowing for work to begin on the next row. After all 216 triangles were bolted into place, they were put on six four-inch pipe columns as supports. An eave, bolted at right angles to the dome, also acted as a rain gutter. After all joints were caulked, the Polydome stood ready for use.

While some Teshenna men carried stone up to the site, the women carried sand—some as much as two sofias (five-gallon tins) in a sack on their backs. In an attempt to hire workers I gave out ten sand sacks, one per person, in hopes of having them returned filled. But the women were using all kinds of containers (baskets, bark cloth, skin bags, tied up bundles of leaves and grass) and it was difficult to keep track of the amount of sand being hauled. Because of this I developed a system of metal tags with numbers. Throughout the day I used my five-gallon tin to measure the sand brought to me, and for every full tin the workers got a tag. At the end of the day they turned in the tags for money. Everyone wanted in on the "big money." My diary entry of May 11, 1967, stated, "They cleaned up the sand from the river. We have 747 tins or 18¾ meters." By May the people had already paid their taxes, didn't need the money, and weren't as interested in working.

One day in the middle of May, Dolly and I walked three miles from the mission station up to the village of Chebera. The market was just closing when we arrived but I had an opportunity to observe some of the customs of this tribe: men greeted each other with several kisses on the lips, two drank at the same time from a can or a gourd (sometimes two fellows and other times a fellow and a girl), and if you asked directions they pointed with their lower lip.

With all the children away at school in 1967, we felt lonely. But the blessing was that Dolly was now free to travel with me on the many trips over the rugged and beautiful mountains to the I. K. posts. At the end of May, MAF arrived with our four children from Schutz. They had all grown; Leah looked taller and Ron's haircut (or lack of one) was a shock.

By the beginning of June, I was pleased with the way the dome looked at Chebera. At the end of the month the men had put the last triangles on the first dome and, thank goodness, it all fit together. We started work on the second dome. It took three men three days to bolt up the 216 triangles and one day to plumb up and pour the concrete.

Eventually I saw Chebera as my Waterloo. After building plans were approved, materials ordered, and buildings partly erected, the plans were changed not once, not twice, but four times—encouraging me to rename the project "Konfusion." Original plans were changed: the house now would be used as the school, the clinic used as the house, the school used as the clinic, and the staff house as the office, and my patience was getting very thin. I didn't agree that the changes were needed and felt it a waste of time and money. As I finished the second dome, I had sore legs, the sun's glare on the roof was hitting me from all angles, and I got badly sunburned with a swollen lower lip.

As my patience got thinner and thinner, I thought of a saying by Will Rogers, "A difference of opinion makes horse racing and missionaries." I just wanted to complete the assignment to the best of my ability. A selection from *The Living Bible* saying to take courage and work, for God is with you, encouraged me to continue on with the project. According to Edythe Draper in the *Living Light*, the Lord of Hosts says, "Get on with the job and finish it. You have been listening long enough!"[16]

The staff seemed surprised that the Polydome wasn't more expensive to build than the square metal-framed Polycon, and by the end of October 1967, the building committee gave the go-ahead for a Polydome at our next I. K. project at Omo.

That July 1968, we had a farewell supper for Ron, the fourth of our children to leave the nest and go out to make his way in the world. We would miss his help and good humor.

An old man who lived across the valley on the hill at Chebera died and we went over to the village one afternoon.

There were five sons who had all worked for us at Chebera the prior summer. Since the oldest son was away, they waited to bury the old fellow until the whole family was present. While there, we enjoyed watching dancers carrying spears and dressed in leather leggings with bells around the top. Others carried long branches with tassels on the top made of curls of monkey tails, hair, or cow tails. Some had black cloths around their shoulders and they chanted and at times used drums.

Cattle played a big part in the life and death of the Teshenna people, and at this old man's death, cows were being brought in from different people and villages. The land had been cleared near the house, poles stuck in for a fence, and a path cut for the entry to the opening in the fence. The man's body had been dead for two days before they removed the bracelets and gave them to the oldest son. Due to superstition, instead of bringing the body out through a door, it was brought out through a hole cut in the side of the house. After several days ten cows had been hit on the head with a sharpened stone and killed, and the man's body was sewn in an uncured cow skin. With time and shrinkage, the skin left the body encased like a mummy. The cow's intestines were tied and worn around the mourners' necks, and the head, heart, and liver were all hung on the fence post.

The grave, a round hole over six feet deep, had a ledge dug into the hillside at the bottom where the body was placed. The hole was refilled with large stones that were packed in tight. A tree was planted on top and the grave was guarded day and night for three months, so they said, to keep the cannibals away.

While in Addis Ababa for several days, I bought and shipped five tons of materials, most of what I needed to finish Chebera. We were still at Chebera in October, and I knew that a job that dragged out was expensive. There was Konfusion and more Konfusion and I thought of the saying by Thomas

Jefferson, "When you reach the end of your rope, tie a knot and hang on." As I turned fifty-six that November, I was feeling like we'd never get out of Chebera. As the Ethiopian Christmas, January 4, came and went, and February made its appearance, I felt like it would never end. My spirits were lowered even more with the news that my good friend, Charlie Haspels, had a heart attack at Ghimeera and died.

A little old woman came to the Ghimeera clinic one day and it was closed. Her remark was, "Well, I started early but the road just wouldn't end." That is the way it was back in the sixties when we were looking for a stopping place but the Chebera work just wouldn't end.

With the clinic finally completed, inspection of the buildings took place the end of March 1969, and everything was approved. On April Fools', no fooling, we packed up our trek things and were finally leaving for the last time. It sure was good to be finished and moving out at last. In my opinion, all the changes were not worth the extra hard work and expense. This was the only mission project where we didn't accomplish what we set out to do. Besides, I felt it was a waste of time and mission dollars since the Chebera mission project never reached the people. Shortly, MAF hauled the last of our trek things from Chebera into Ghimeera, we cleaned them up, and put them back in the attic. It felt so good to have a chance to relax.

OMO—GELEBS

The Geleb tribe, the third of the I. K. projects, was located on the muddy Omo River (just north of Lake Rudolph) on the Kenyan border in southwest Ethiopia. Unlike the Teshenna in rainy Chebera, the Gelebs resided in semi-desert country, mostly grassland with some low scattered brush and small trees. With an annual rainfall of four inches, most of the year was dry, but during April (the wet season) sizable areas were flooded by the Omo River. The mountains of Ethiopia, Kenya, and the Sudan could clearly be seen on the horizon.

The Gelebs built their villages on the sandy high ridges on the river throughout this area. Building sand and gravel were plentiful and close, and there were quantities of volcanic stone that would be useful for concrete aggregate in the nearby bluffs. Trees to be used for roof poles were located three hours upriver by truck.

The Gelebs' wealth was in their cattle and, as nomadic people, they were in constant search for water and grass. It was unusual for cattle to be killed for meat. Their herds included cows, sheep, goats, donkeys, and camels but they never used them in agriculture. Camels and goat provided milk and sometimes goats were used for meat. There was evidence of abandoned cattle *kaals* (shelters made of light thornbushes) since some of the Gelebs moved around with their stock during the dry season.

In May 1964, we completed our first aerial survey of the Geleb tribe and both the officer in charge of the post and the people of the tribe gave us a wonderful welcome. It was unfortunate that we could not speak their language since they were "very friendly and natural, yet reserved and soft spoken," according to the write-up in the Geleb Area I. K. Survey Report in May 1964. They appeared to be neither "afraid nor proud and haughty."

Members of this very primitive seminomadic tribe lived in igloo-style (beehive-shaped) homes consisting of little stick frames, about four feet high and eight feet across, which were covered with skins. One could not stand erect in these homes, nor did they keep out rain, dust, or mosquitoes. The igloo-style homes were similar to those of the Murle tribe who used grass instead of skins for the roofs. Sand was blown up around the sides.

The mother and children had skins for their beds, and the men slept in a thorn corral with the cattle. Traditionally men were warriors, raiding neighboring tribes for cattle, and devoting their time to tending their cattle. Women tended the gardens. Not a book, radio, TV, telephone, car, train, plane, shop, doctor, school, or church could be found here, and certainly no knowledge of Christ. This was truly a "virgin opportunity," the survey described.

Medically, there was evidence of tuberculosis and the usual tropical ulcers and sore eyes. Men wore cloths of a coarse weave, or no clothes at all, while women wore animal skins. Both men and women had an affinity for beads and all the women and girls wore several metal rings around their ankles and often on their upper arms which were removed upon marriage. "Their need for a Savior was exemplified by the pounds and pounds of iron bracelets the young unmarried girls wear on their legs and arms—we know they are a shackled people until He sets them free and they become His bride, the Church, pure and spotless, presentable for the Father," stated the Final Geleb Site Survey Report. The chief of all the Geleb elders was the big witch doctor, or spiritual head of the tribe.

Age dictated hairdos and accessories for the Geleb men. Teens had unique headdresses which appeared to be made of manure and mud: three strips of clay across the head with a space between where the hair had been scraped off. Young men had a different plastered style, often with ostrich feathers added as the final touch. As a gesture of friendship, I handed out many of the combs that I had brought along and one old fellow, probably the chief, combed his whiskers with his. Besides carrying wooden walking sticks, many men carried a curved piece of wood on a base that served a dual purpose: a pillow to protect their hairstyle when lying down and also a portable stool.

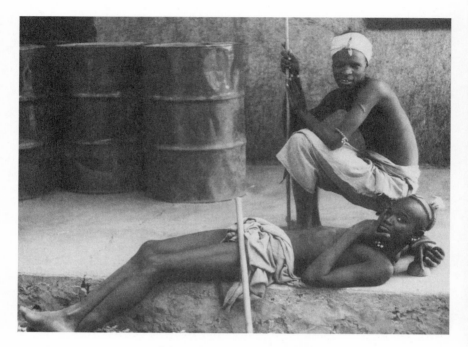

Geleb portable stool and pillow

This was the way we found these lean and wiry Gelebs when we first went into Omo. It wasn't until missionaries arrived and cut landing fields for the small MAF plane that even the local authorities in Ethiopia knew how very needy and primitive some of their own people were. An airstrip there at Omo could easily be made and maintained. Also, this brought attention to the world, particularly welfare agencies, of the severe droughts in Africa. Bringing in food would be a big help but it would not last forever. Neither would it preserve their dignity as people. There was great need for community development and I agreed with George W. Carver's philosophy, "Start where you are with what you have and make something of it. . . ." It was necessary to find alternatives for many things and I had to rely on the saying, "Wisdom is the ability to discover an alternative."

It reminded me of a story about a preacher who was staying with a very poor family which had not been blessed with a great deal of worldly goods. The little boy of the house looked up at the nicely dressed preacher and said, "Mister, if you want anything that you don't see around here, please tell us, and we will show you how to get along without it."

When I first arrived in this part of the Omo Valley and looked around, I saw only barren plain. After taking a better look I realized that there was sunshine almost every day with a lot of wind blowing in from Lake Rudolph close by (later the name was changed to Lake Turkana). Hundreds of colorful red and blue bee-eater birds built their nests in the mud riverbanks. Along the riverbank, we were pleased to have a generous supply of sand and a thick layer of silt and plenty of water in the muddy Omo River. The river was full of huge fish that weighed in at fifty to sixty pounds.

The Omo was a large river fed by the highland streams and, after heavy rains in the mountains, the river flooded its banks before emptying into Lake Rudolf. As the water receded, the Gelebs planted crops of corn and beans on the riverbanks, usually having one crop a year. Often there was a long span of hunger, usually six months, before the next planting. During this span, they depended almost entirely on the blood and milk of scrub cattle for their diets, supplemented with fish from the river and lake. (The cow's neck was pierced with a bow and arrow and blood was collected in a gourd.) Due to the closing of the Sudan border, pastureland for their cattle was limited, causing traditional cattle-herding activities to be reduced. Malnutrition was rampant. Cattle raiding from neighbors' herds was common. As the grass sprung up after the wet season, herds of cows grazing along the riverside were guided across the river for fresh pasture on the opposite side. The mobility of the Gelebs appeared to be effortless since they packed up skins, sticks, and grass mats from their huts onto their donkeys, slung babies on their backs, carried skins of grain on their heads, and took off.

With our Omo air survey completed, Harold Kurtz, Bob Swart, James Keefer, and myself were regalled by buffaloes, zebra, elands, tiang, hartebeest, and gazelles on our return flight. At first I thought I was seeing giraffe necks towering above the trees; then I realized they were giant anthills. Resembling a tall stovepipe chimney, the anthills marked the boundary of one side of the mission site at Omo. These hollow-centered anthills, made by white ants or termites, were impressive above-ground nests that rose up to thirty feet. Made of red clay particles cemented together with saliva, the termite mounds dotted the African savanna.[17]

After grain threshing was completed in the villages, it was stored in round bins on platforms and covered with grass. Some of the local natives took on the job of bird chasers, stationed on tall platforms every few hundred feet to prevent birds from devouring their grain. The grain would eventually be stone ground by the women, cooked into a thick porridge, and served in gourds.

Tall ant hill marking one boundary of the mission site (photo by Bob Swart for the Ethio-Echo)

Who would ever imagine that there was an English-speaking Geleb in all the world? By the grace of God, a twenty-year-old Geleb who had been studying in Addis Ababa for ten years and who had a fair knowledge of our language, helped to make tapes of Bible stories available to his people in the Geleb language—the first introduction to Jesus Christ in this pagan tribe.

In an article titled "Medical Clinic and Bible Teaching Begin for the Gelebs at the Omo Post," Morrie Swart states that change was inevitable for the Gelebs with the arrival of the missionaries, but there were two pagan rites performed each year by the elders that they resisted having changed. First, the fathers who had daughters reaching puberty had to be circumcised and, secondly, the puberty rites for the daughters dictated that they be laden with heavy, noisy, iron anklets around each leg, making it difficult for them to walk.[18]

In mid-September 1964, I flew from Ghimeera to Washa Waha to meet up with Bob Swart and Harold Kurtz. It was our first ground survey trip to Omo to discover the people, find a site to build, and make plans for building a mission post. Initially we planned to go by canoe, but the tributary to get the canoe to the Omo River was too low, forcing us to scrap our plans and travel by Jeep.

We took off for German Wuha and camped for the night. It was a pleasant spot and was delightful bathing in the river. Next day we reached some hot springs, right in the middle of the plain, where the water temperature was 190 degrees. The thin shell on top of the ground made it risky to walk. Bones from buffalo that had been trapped and left to die were scattered about.

The tangled thornbushes got thicker and thicker as we pushed through the plains, and all the Jeep could manage was low gear four-wheel drive. We plowed through and camped near the river on the Sudan border. Since the river was dry this time of year, we dug a hole in the sand of the river bottom in order to get some water. We saw some villages on the Sudan side and heard voices, but when we went across the border to examine, the people ran when they saw us coming. It was good to be in the Sudan again—even if only for a half hour. Back on the Ethiopian side, we saw three people strolling along the road and called out to them. They ran and hid behind some trees so quickly that one of them carrying a sheep left it tied and laying on the road.

Ten days into the survey trip, the chief of the district came to call upon us. He was a Geleb and had long fingers with wire bracelets up his arms to the elbow. As he spoke, his hand gestures revealed sleeves that were too short on his old army overcoat. After coffee the chief directed us to the police post and gave us a guide. A good road across a vast plain led us to the police station at Kalam, where we had to report our arrival.

As we reached higher speeds, the thorns from the prior day worked their way into the tire tubes. We put three patches on one tube, and when we ran low on patches, we had to cut them up into smaller pieces in order to have some for our spare. As we arrived at the Omo site and set up camp, men and boys gathered around to see what was happening. One boy knew a little Amharic, so it wasn't long before we learned a few Geleb words.

The best site for the mission, we decided, was a high ridge on the river in the center of the main part of the tribe where Ethiopia, the Sudan, and Kenya all joined. After serving the governor and the Geleb chiefs cookies and tea, we participated in the final inspection of the Geleb site. The Gelebs questioned having to concede one hundred yards of riverbank that their people cultivated after the water receded, since it was premium tillable land in this semiarid area. After inspection of the area, according to the Final Geleb Site Survey Report, the chief who had his home on this area spread his arms wide and said, "I gladly give it all to you—for you are coming to give us medicine, a school, and God's word." Their eagerness and need for our medical help was apparent and it was critical that we uphold our side of the covenant in promises made when asking for their land.

Our survey team recommended to the I. K. Committee that regular monthly medical visits be made by a mission doctor to the Geleb site, that a resident medical dresser be made available to the area as soon as possible (since their only current medical service, government or mission, was miles away), and that educational work begin.

With hope of finding a better way through the thorns on our return trip, we hired two guides to show us the location of the old trail. But due to fear that the people living in this area might kill them, the guides backed out.

On the last day of September, we worked our way across the valley where zebra, buffaloes, elands, and gazelles came into view. We trekked the fifty kilometers on rough road up the six-thousand-foot climb to the village of Maji. Through the thorns we went, making stops all day long to patch our tires—twenty-nine patches in all. Some of the patches had to be cut in two and three pieces and when we ran out, we used plastic tape to hold in the air. Much to our chagrin, we discovered that our return route through the thorn bushes was twenty-three kilometers farther than the trip out.

Upon our return from the Omo, a comment was made that I didn't look as tired as the other two travelers. Even though I was older, someone made the statement, "Oh, they don't make them like they used to."

In mid-November 1964, the Swarts and I, along with Dolly, Ginny, and Tom, left Addis Ababa by Jeep on a trip to Massawa, Eritrea. Our goal was to pick up Bob Swart's new four-wheel drive Scout so we could take it back to Omo. It was a beautiful drive up through the mountains with its tunnels, curves, and switchbacks built by the Italians in the 1930s. There were approximately two hundred curves before getting to the top. At one spot on the mountainside, an unusual curve was built up with old barrels to prevent the road from sliding. During a war with Ethiopia in 1935, the Italians had blown up the road behind them in order to prevent the British from entering, only to have the British rebuild it under fire and go through.

It was the dry season, and, as we continued through the mountains on our way to Eritrea, we noted that some of the hillside towns rolled their water in heavy galvanized barrels, fitted with two bicycle tires, uphill from the streams below. This method prevented the women from having to transport five-gallon containers of water on their heads.

After five days, we arrived in Massawa and claimed the Scout. Our return trip was slow through fog and rain. With no canvas top or windshield wipers for the Scout, we had to improvise. Bob Swart's wife, Morrie, standing and reaching over the top of the windshield, kept the glass clear by swiping it with her husband's handkerchief. We returned to Addis Ababa through the Blue Nile Gorge, covering a total of 2,917 kilometers, and having seen a lot of Ethiopia during our ten-day trip. *(See photo section.)*

Christmas 1964 was spent in a most untraditional way. The majority of our new posts in Ethiopia had no usable roads, so besides Bob Swart's Scout, we relied on my four-wheel drive Jeep that the mission had purchased for hauling materials and equipment. On December 20 we left Addis Ababa with the two vehicles and a small trailer, a borrowed tent, and food for the road. We were on our way to the Omo! We hoped to be to our final destination by Christmas. It was the first time we were traveling to the Omo with our families since all our other trips had been to make surveys.

The first two days of our trip went well, moving along at normal speed on dusty country roads. Eventually we reached the point where road maintenance ended, where bridges were missing, and where mud holes were sometimes over three feet deep. We were averaging only about ten miles a day. Then there was our first mishap—the trailer upset and broke the hitch, with our Jeep settling into mud up to the axles. Mud seeped into our suitcases and eventually caused a horrid moldy mess of our clothing. Digging out of one mud hole, we sank into another. How thankful we were that we had two cars along so that one could help pull the other out.

As we traveled through the rain forest and crossed a ridge of mountains, we battled mud all the way. We came to a curve in a narrow mountain trail with a wide, deep mud hole. We knew if we stopped to look, we would be stuck for sure, so it was best to keep moving. A path alongside the hole looked like it had a bit of solid ground where one wheel might catch, so we attempted to go around. It was slippery, apparently from the many bare feet that had walked along its way. As our Jeep touched the path, the traction gave out, and we started sliding over the side of the mountain. But, praise the Lord for the strong vines growing on the mountainside that stopped the roll of the Jeep!

We managed to extricate ourselves and ran back to warn Bob Swart about the slippery path. Our new challenge was how to get Bob's car through the mud hole. Hours were spent draining and cutting palm branches to place over the hole to prevent the Scout from sinking into the mud. But it was all for naught. There we were—December 23, with our Jeep over the side of the mountain and the Swarts's Scout and trailer so deep in mud that we could not even unfasten the trailer hitch.

The rest of that day we spent gingerly unloading our Jeep and trying to jack up the Scout to get more logs and timber under the wheels. The palm branches that we had put into the mud kept jagging into our hands and through our boots. We finally got the Scout out of the hole and were able to pull the trailer on through—but all our efforts at towing, due to the bend in the road, only put our Jeep in a more precarious position. At sundown we searched for a clearing to set up our tents and get the children to bed. We fastened cables to the Jeep and tied them to trees across the road to keep it from rolling down the mountain while we slept.

Since there was no stream close by, we had to use our water very sparingly. We fixed supper and crawled into our tents, tired, discouraged, and dirty, but sleep did not come easily. Most of us had dropped into a fitful slumber when there was a startling shout, causing us to sit up on our air mattresses. My first thought was that someone got hurt on the cables that we had strung across the road. But how wonderfully the Lord did provide. It was a letter delivered by a runner from a young couple who owned a coffee plantation some eight miles away. They had heard of our plight and sent food and a promise to send tools and men the next day. The letter ended "Sleep well and plan to spend Christmas with us."

True to their word, the next day a young man arrived with some tools (including two hand pullers) and some men and made it a minor matter getting the Jeep back on the road. This young man, who lived in the isolated part of Ethiopia, was the grandson of King Gustav of Sweden. He and his wife took us into their lovely, modest homestead that looked like one out of pioneer days in the old West in the United States and treated us like family. By candlelight, their only means of light, they served us a delightful smorgasbord Christmas Eve dinner. The ladies were furnished with shawls, the men with sweaters, and they even sent four hot water bottles to warm the children. They asked that we share the Christmas story from the Bible and enjoyed listening to a tape we had brought along of our children's Christmas music at their Schutz School. Few gifts were exchanged—but the several apples we shared from our food supply were greatly appreciated by the couple. It had been a long time since they last experienced that familiar taste.

It was a Christmas to long remember. We were all safe, our cars were running, and we were blessed by that lovely, gracious couple who shared all they had with us.

After a good breakfast on Christmas morning, we left the couple and continued our trip to Ghimeera on our way to Omo. One river had a log bridge that was in bad shape and it took three hours to dig down the banks and put in brush and stone before we could cross. One day was titled our "Rock and Roll Day" since never before had I driven a car over such rough country. It was a rocky wash down the side of the mountain with big boulders and it was amazing the cars held up. Sometimes we had to unhitch the trailer, pull it up with a cable, and then carry the supplies on our backs. At one place the bank caved in, and Bob turned the Scout on its side with all four wheels off the ground.

But eventually, from the top of a mountain, we saw the mission at Ghimeera. It gave us a good feeling to know that we were nearing home base. We had traveled 642 kilometers in nine days on the first leg of our trip to the Omo.

We remained at our home base, Ghimeera, for a couple of months in order to make further plans for our trip to the new Omo Post. It was during this time, February 1965, that the R.P.M. (Rassmusen, Pollock, and McLaughlin) were reunited in Addis Ababa—the first time in twelve years. It was a pleasant coincidental meeting and we all enjoyed a picnic together. (At this time Ken was a medical doctor at Dembi Dollo and Robb was working with the Nuer tribe on the Sudan/Ethiopian border.)

On March 13, 1965, we started out from Ghimeera on the second leg of our journey to Omo—a safari to take the Swarts to their new assignment at Omo. We flew from Ghimeera to Washa Waha, Maji's Ethiopian Airlines strip, and met up with Bob Swart and Harold Kurtz. Our caravan consisted of two Jeeps, Swarts's Scout (two pulling trailers), and food and water for fourteen persons, including four children. With a couple of us perched on top of the truck holding a large umbrella for protection from the sun, we were quite a sight.

The river was low but the large water holes served both as our bathtubs and as water holes for the buffalo to drink from at night. With the mountains behind us, we were facing vast, hot, grassy plains, flat but extremely rough. One big obstacle ahead was a valley choked with thornbushes. An attempt to "snake" our way through the bushes failed with "dead ends and doubling back on the trail,"[19] according to Morrie Swart. It was an awesome task.

Our stop at German Wuha for four days enabled some of the men to reconnoiter a path through the thorn tree forest, and prevented us from having to hack a road through. But there were many problems. Not only did the two broken shackles on the back springs of the Jeep have to be repaired, but the coil on the starter went bad making it necessary to lift the hood and short across every time I wanted to start. Also there was a flat tire on the trailer. As we ate our bustard soup for supper, how we dreaded the thought of the dusty, arid country that lay before us.

Six days later, we reached the police post at Kalam and the country became almost desert-like with rock of petrified bone and fossils projecting from the ground. "We heard lions during the night," I wrote in my journal. Continuing on, one day we twisted and turned, and fought the thorns, going round and round in circles—hitting every possible point on the compass. That beautiful moonlit night, we set up camp along the Omo River, but it was too dark to know where we were.

The next morning I went to the river to wash and shot one of the Egyptian ducks along the bank. As it plunged into the

Safari to Omo

water, I was shocked to see someone jump in to retrieve it. Right then I knew we had arrived. It was a Geleb boy from the Omo! On March 20, we set up the RT to share the news of our arrival with home base and revel in the fact that we had arrived at our destination. I led the way to the new site and set up camp on the lowland along the river.

About this time, my mind flashed back to August of the prior year when I first met Mr. Sunde. An English frontier hunter from East Africa, he was planning a trek into the rain forest to hunt for black leopard, red fox, and black bushbuck. After our first survey trip through this thorn belt in 1964, we had received word that Mr. Sunde was missing on a trip from Kenya into Ethiopia. MAF had flown down the valley but saw no sign of him. Later Mr. Sunde's Land Rover was discovered—four flat tires buried under the thorns with him dead inside. On our trip to Omo we passed by the site where the Englishman met his fate.

Our safari members remained a week at the Geleb village to help the Swarts with the daunting task of setting up housekeeping at their new mission post at Omo. It wasn't long after our arrival that Gelebs appeared and welcomed us with their lively, clamorous dancing and song. They were friendly and continued to greet us the entire day with expectations that we would host a reception as payment for their performance. After serving coffee to the entire village, including the governor of the district and head of police, we realized we had depleted our entire coffee supply. Becoming friends with the Gelebs took top priority, so the only chore we accomplished that first day was digging a latrine and surrounding it with privacy mats.

"Everyday we are feeling a little more at home here, although we are keenly aware that we are still very much in the initial period of 'establishing a relationship' with the Geleb people,"[20] Morrie Swart stated in the *Ethio-Echo*. To start, the Swarts pitched their tent on the stone floor that they had built and constructed a stick-framed kitchen-dining room next to it. The Swarts would live under canvas until the completion of their house. For cooking they made an outdoor stone fireplace and dug a plot of ground for a garden. Debris and bleached bones that littered the area were cleared for the MAF airstrip, driftwood was dragged in for firewood, and manure was hauled. On March 25, it was time for Dolly and me to bid farewell to the Swarts and head back to our home base at Ghimeera.

Morrie Swart described the Gelebs:

> Since the local women were the home builders, they came to get ideas by watching us work. Unfinished work didn't seem to bother the men and they frequently laid on the ground in the shade by the building and slept as workers either moved them or stepped over them. We are the first foreigners to settle in their country, and their curiosity about us is boundless. We live under almost constant observance, with groups of people clustered along the fence to watch our peculiar

ways. We give them much to talk about and laugh over just because it's their first glimpse of an entirely different way of life. We knew the unfamiliar sounds of their language would be hard for us to master.[21]

May 1966 was a monumental time. Bob Swart and I took a boat across to the eastern side of the Omo River and for the first time, used our tape players to play tapes of Geleb Bible stories. What excitement for the people to listen to the "talking box" in their native tongue! During the rainy season the river was high and some of the people who came to church had to swim across the river.

Also that May, Bill graduated from Schutz School. Our thoughts quickly turned to our upcoming furlough in June, although we had to get jobs completed at Omo and Godare before leaving. It would be our first furlough from Ethiopia.

Ed and Penny were at the pier to greet us as we arrived in New York City on June 14. In a few weeks, we took off from New Wilmington on a tour to see America. Traveling played a major role in our children's education, and since they had already seen much of Africa, they wanted to see the good ole' U.S.A. Our first stop was Chicago, then Wisconsin, and on to Minnesota to see the Badlands and Mt. Rushmore. In Wyoming, we visited Old Faithful and Yellowstone National Park before going on to the Grand Tetons, the Grand Canyon, and Bryce Canyon in Utah. We traveled to New Mexico, Texas, Arkansas, Tennessee, Kentucky, and Ohio before circling back to New Wilmington. We had purchased a Golden Passport which gave us access to all national parks.

In September 1966, Dolly and I took son Bill to college at Rensselaer Polytechnic Institute in Troy, New York. Our furlough continued until the end of December when all seven of our children gathered together for Christmas and filled up an entire pew at church. I was so proud.

The October 1966 Chartiers United Presbyterian Church newsletter stated:

> They are laboring in one of the most primitive pioneer mission fields remaining in the world and Ted's job of selecting and cleaning sites for new stations, traveling almost trackless terrain into the untouched tribes, putting up buildings, providing water and other essential needs, surely must tax to the utmost his strength, ingenuity, and dedication.

————◆◆◆————

At this point, the Omo story jumps from 1966 to 1968. In the interim we devoted our attention to one of the other I. K. projects, Teshanna Tribe at Chebera.

————◆◆◆————

Back at Omo, one Sunday in February 1968, Bob Swart and I took our tape recorder and went to a village up the Omo River to attend church. The Gelebs were inquisitive and had to touch me and run their fingers through the hair on my arms. They had remembered Ed and called me "the father of Eddie."

Five volunteers from Michigan arrived to help erect the dome homes at Omo. With the clinic, staff houses, and the dome for the Swarts completed, the buildings were inspected. In the beginning of March, Bob bought a sheep and had a big feed for the workmen before MAF came to take us to our base at Ghimeera.

It was about this time, while returning to Omo from vacation in Kenya, that we landed right in the middle of riots in Addis Ababa. Supposedly they were started by college students and all the secondary schools had to be closed. Car windows

were broken, as well as the front windows of all six floors of
the U.S. government building. We had just finished our shopping and, while leaving the market area, found ourselves in a
real dilemma. The shops closed down and large crowds lined
the streets. At one place I couldn't get through the mobs and
had to resort to using the backstreets, but even here the car
was surrounded if I slowed down. I was thankful to be able to
plow my way through without any serious trouble. Word came
from the U.S. Embassy for us to stay off the streets for the next
couple of days. School closed down for a week, allowing the
kids to come home until after Easter.

Back at Omo, Bob Swart gave out banana plants and
various seeds that we had brought to the locals. Eventually
one of them had three big bunches of bananas and some
tomatoes ready to eat. The same local had also started mango
and lime trees and was waiting for the papayas to ripen.
Gardening was popular and Dolly's garden at the mission
school was the envy of all the locals. Also for food, our boys
were catching catfish and humpback and schooling small
crocodiles. We ate the young crocodile tail and also enjoyed
cat and Nile fish.

A May 1970, journal entry described attending an
unusual church service at Omo:

*This morning after breakfast Bob and I went up the Omo
River with the outboard. It was a typical bright morning
with the sun shining on the muddy water. We saw a few
crocs, in fact one old granddaddy looked to be as long as
our boat. After a fifteen minute ride we tied up the
outboard and walked along a dusty path to the village.
Some of the women and children walked with us and
chatted while carrying gourds of water on their heads. In
the village we were invited into one of the larger houses,
eight feet in diameter and a little over four feet high. When*

the skin was dropped over the door, the only light remaining besides the sun shining through the holes in the covered dome, was the flames of the fire heating a boiling pot. Here a church service was held with a weak coffee served before and during the service. It was served in a large gourd and shaken until cooled. If by chance your mouthful was too hot, it was sprayed out through the teeth. With eleven of us in there, somebody was sure to get hit. When they had their fill, they would take a big mouthful and spray it out onto their hands and arms to wash them. Of course, this went onto the skins we were sitting on. The gourd was then filled by the women of the house for the next guest.

After they had sung a few songs, Bob played the tape message and led the discussion that followed. When the man of this house and his family expressed their desire to be baptized, it was difficult for Bob to find words in their language to explain the Holy Spirit. One of the songs Bob played had the word "hallelujah" in it. The five year old girl who sat beside me yelled out with a "hallelujah" every now and then as she played with my shoe laces and ran her fingers through the hair on my arms. Not only were the members of this family the first Gelebs to become Christians, but it was the first introduction of Christianity to this unreached tribe at Omo.

Ron, Ed, Bill, and his new wife, Carolyn, were all at the airport to greet us as we arrived in New York City from Ethiopia for the start of our furlough at the end of June 1970. It was a good Fourth of July weekend with all the children and their spouses. Penny had married John and Ed had married Dorothy by this time. We all worked on an old burnt-out house in rural Maryland that the kids were repairing to resell and, they hoped, make a profit. It was good to be working and all worshipping together.

That summer, while the New Wilmington Missionary Conference was winding down, we received a surprising phone call from the mission office informing us there was a cutback in funding and that we wouldn't be returning to Ethiopia. News spread fast at the conference and many of those present felt strongly that we should return.

Eventually it was decided that we would return to Ethiopia for eighteen months and attempt to complete our assigned work. If we could not complete the work in that amount of time, there was no objection to us staying on as volunteers, but this time we would have to furnish our own support. After much discussion, those interested in helping me formed the Pollock's Unfinished Tribal Training committee (P.U.T.T.) The Washington Presbytery in Pennsylvania guaranteed our full support if we went back as full-time missionaries. Our home church in Canonsburg offered to take care of our account and worked out the details for us to raise money to stay on as volunteers.

That summer we traveled to the Chicago conference, the Smithsonian, Shenandoah National Park, Monticello, Williamsburg, and Mt. Vernon. But like most of our furloughs, our time was mainly consumed with speaking and showing slides at the various churches and organizations that extended an invitation. In the fall I was invited to speak at my old hometown church of Chartiers with the headlines, "Local boy comes home." I found it especially difficult to speak in front of friends we had known forever, folks very dear to us. It was their prayers, letters, and interest that had lifted us over many a rough spot.

After we returned to Ethiopia from furlough, it was suggested by the Presbyterian mission office that the commission's consulting architect pay a visit to Ethiopia to review the I. K. buildings and to acquaint him with my skills for possible recommendation on reassignment. Due to the tight budget, there was some concern that the posts were being "overbuilt" and that they weren't completed in the allotted time. After the architect returned home from his trip, we received a complemintary letter. "As I told you then, there is no question in my mind but that you have done a most remarkable piece of work. To be able to build a house on the plains of Omo and in the hills of Ghimeera for only nine thousand dollars is a remarkable accomplishment in any language. You have taken native materials and used them to their fullest extent." In reviewing the I. K. projects, the architect found that the posts weren't overbuilt (meaning, they didn't exceed what was needed) and that they were very well constructed. It was the architect's visit and relaying of information back to the commission that helped to ensure that we would continue on with I. K. work from 1971 to 1972.

About that same time, I built a ten-foot water tower at Omo that held a one-thousand-gallon water tank to supply water for Bob's house and for the clinic. A three-room staff house with six-foot veranda was started in 1971, and in the months of June, September, and October of 1972, I continued finishing up staff house work at Omo. Son Bill and his wife, Carolyn, took a break from teaching at Schutz School and came to help me.

I'm not sure that I had any particular interest in windmills as a teenager, but I penned Henry Longfellow's verse, "The Windmill," in my seventh grade composition book: "Behold! A giant am I! Aloft here in my tower, With granite jaws I devour / The maize and the wheat and the rye, And grind them into flour." I can trace my first interest in windmills back to 1946 to our first mission assignment at Doleib Hill, Sudan. When we arrived at the Hill, there was an inoperable Dempster windmill from the States on the site. It was a challenge for me to get it operable in order to irrigate our garden. My interest in this windmill carried over to Omo where I saw great potential for the windmill's use.

In June 1973, work continued at Omo and I looked over possible sites for windmills. To become a prospective windmill owner, it was necessary to have land rights to a suitable site along the riverbank or have permission from someone who owned a suitable site. This in itself was very restricting since ownership of riverbank sites rested mainly with the seniors of a tribe and remained within families.

Along with the windmill idea, it was necessary to teach the Gelebs the idea of crop rotation to prevent soil depletion and the concept of multiple annual harvests. Besides fruit trees, soy beans were introduced as a suitable crop for rotation and as a good source of protein. Eventually the natives learned to grind the soybeans to make a coffee-type drink.

Due to the flooding of the Omo River, typically it was possible for the Gelebs to plant only one small crop of sorghum, maize, and beans each year. In an article titled, "Food from Wind," Bob and Morrie Swart described the spirit of the Gelebs after their harvest in the spring: "This is the time of year when the people sing and dance in the moonlight. Well-fed, they are exuberant. The Gelebs are masters at enjoying the present; they neither provide for, nor worry about the future."[22] But for the rest of the year, there was no way for them to harness the abundant water that was flowing by and, thus, the time came when they had to endure empty grain stores and empty stomachs. That was until a windmill scheme, called Food from Wind, was originated by Bob Swart, a plan to pump water from the Omo River to irrigate small garden plots and fruit trees. *(See photo section.)*

The fertility of the Omo riverbank became apparent when a small farm windmill-driven water pump, commercially produced in the United States, was given as a gift to the Omo mission school and installed to irrigate the school garden. Normally expensive diesel fuel was used for the mission's water pumping system, but due to the high cost, its use in third-world countries was prohibitive. Alternative sources of power had to be found. The locals' interest was peaked when they saw the effect of irrigation on the school garden. Eventually a simple training program in gardening was offered to the community for free, with the American Mission providing the seed. Three other Dempster wind-powered water pumps from America were donated and, as an experiment, two of these windmills were set up on a plot of Geleb land to allow them to cultivate a larger area. From this the Food from Wind program had its roots.

It was quite a surprise that the Gelebs so enthusiastically accepted the windmill idea, seeing that they had no prior mechanical knowledge. Recognizing that this machine could lessen their food shortage and alleviate the annual hunger problem was enough to sell them on the idea. But we knew we had to keep it simple and something that they themselves could eventually manufacture and maintain.

Due to the high cost of the windmills (approximately one thousand dollars), the mission realized that it was not feasible to consider importing these factory-made windmills from the United States, so Bob Swart and I decided to research building our own. I had seen a picture of numerous windmills operating on the Isle of Crete in a *Reader's Digest* and one day in October 1973, Dolly and I traveled to Athens to investigate. While at the Lassithi Plateau on the Isle of Crete I discovered ten thousand simple-sail windmills irrigating small plots of land. (Here the Greeks had their own style of native windmills made out of a variety of common products.) We talked to mill owners and took a lot of photographs and notes. We discovered that most everyone here owned a cow, a goat, and some chickens, and lived in the village. Since the streets were narrow and the houses built close together, the windmills and fields were located on the outskirts of town. One hundred twenty years ago this was barren land, but today crops were growing everywhere.

Bob Swart also had an opportunity to visit Crete and, with thoughts fresh in our minds, Bob and I drew up a design incorporating what we thought were the best features of the Crete windmills. Steel and other materials were ordered and sent by truck from Addis Ababa and the first "Ethio-Cretan" sail-windmill was designed and built. The first windmill to be used by a Geleb was commissioned in 1974 (the same Geleb who became the first Christian).

For the next year, we tried and evaluated many new windmill designs, including one that used small trees for the tower and grass mat sails made from reeds that were woven by the women. This attempt to use all local materials failed when the sails fell apart and termites ate the lower tower. We also experimented with an all-metal vertical-axis type known as Savonius rotors or "S" rotors but found it to be less efficient than ones with sails. After experimenting, we settled on a standardized design using steel frames with cloth sails, since steel sections were compact enough to bring in by truck and would last many decades in the arid climate. I was planning to construct more than one hundred of my Polomo windmills over the next several years and had agreed to make the heads of these Crete-type windmills at the shop in Ghimeera. (The name Polomo originated from a combination of the beginning of my last name, Pollock, and from the name of the river where the windmills were being built, the Omo.) The towers and wheels were to be made at a small workshop set up at the Omo mission. (Thirty-five of these were completed before the missionaries were expelled from Ethiopia.)

Very few standard woven cloths proved strong enough for sail making. To avoid frequent sail replacement, we needed something that was heavy, relatively inflexible, run-resistant, and ultraviolet resistant. I purchased Dacron, a type of synthetic material formulated specifically for yacht sails, from a chemical company in the United States.

Considering the possibility of the supply of Dacron sail-cloth drying up, we continued looking for alternative sail fabric to consider. For a possible substitute for the Dacron, we beat a pair of detachable, clip-on aluminum sails out of corrugated roof cappings. These we found to be cheaper and much more durable than any local textile materials. But lack of time prevented further experimentation with the aluminum sails.

The number of sails used at any one time was determined by wind conditions; extra sails could be manually added for light wind or removed when there was excessive wind. This required individualized attention. Rubber loops cut from motorcycle inner tubes stretched the fabric on the frames. The windmill towers had to be rather low to enable the owner to climb them and change the sails. Manually controlling the windmills allowed the design to remain simple and costs lower. Besides, sails could be removed every evening to prevent risk of being damaged by unexpected wind increases and to prevent pilferage overnight since cloth was a valuable commodity.

Our newly designed windmill pulled water from the river through a flexible plastic pipe attached to a simple piston pump. It raised water to a height of about three meters which was sufficient to irrigate about half an acre of the land that did not benefit from the river floodwater. The windmills lifted several liters of water an hour and their efficiency depended upon the size of the sails, the pump, and the wind velocity.

At the end of 1973 and the beginning of 1974, we were working on the Polyball, a name we gave to our copy of the Buckminster Fuller geodesic design. The Polyball was an experiment in low-cost housing. This Buckminster Fuller design was a dome made of triangular galvanized sheets put together with pop rivets and Kaiser vents, but no windows. One day a Geleb came with his daughter, watched me work, and offered to trade me his daughter for one of the Polyballs. She just smiled and didn't object. Since I already had a wife, I informed this Geleb that we would teach him how to build a Polyball. The Geleb tribe liked this style because it looked similar to their own dome-type home made from skins and mats. However, this Polyball, fifteen feet in diameter, would stand up to a lot more weather. We built one at Omo for patient housing.

Often times the Gelebs would leave home to find greener pastures in the city where they ended up destitute. In order to prevent this, we had to teach the Gelebs how to use their God-given gifts so they could have a better way of life both physically and spiritually. Since they had small herds of donkeys, I taught the men to make a donkey cart out of scrap lumber and old tires. It was the first vehicle with wheels in their culture and was greatly appreciated since most loads were transported on the backs of women. They marveled that it took only one man to

Polyball at Omo

pull the cart and were even more surprised to see that another man could ride inside it. And to think that when a second man got in the cart, the one pulling didn't even notice the difference! I also helped to improve their system of grinding grain by introducing the idea of a grinding stone and made a better harpoon for spearing crocodiles. I continued experimenting with the solar oven and made a reflector. The oven reached two hundred degrees—not quite hot enough to boil water because too much heat was escaping through its thin insulation.

From a book I purchased titled *China at Work* by Rudolf P. Hommel, I learned to make a cotton gin. After instructing the Gelebs to plant cotton, I taught them how to remove seeds from the raw cotton with this machine. The gin had two rollers, one of steel and the other of wood, which revolved in opposite directions. The raw cotton was fed between the two rollers and the seeds remained behind. Leah made a simple loom and instructed the Gelebs how to make thread and weave cloth.

Often we received a big welcome from the Gelebs when we walked into the village. "Bob Swart baptized seventy-five Gelebs by immersion at the khor this morning," I wrote in my diary. "It was a nice service." One Sunday we taped the singing at church and I had a gang of natives follow me all the way home while I played it back. Also, I wrote that we attended a dance across the river given by a wealthy man for his daughter. There was a feast with two cows and a camel.

It was February 1974, during an association meeting at the mission station of Bishofton that we encountered more riots. Normally this was a good retreat area, a place to escape from it all at the lake cottages. The schools were not in session because of a government change in programs and the taxies were down due to gas price hikes. The cost of living had jumped 50 percent, and all the people were upset. Glen Noble, a missionary in Addis Ababa doing illiteracy work, was driving his car through town with me as a passenger. We had to duck as stones were thrown through his open window. I reached for the wheel and did the steering as stones left their marks on the body of the car. Many other cars had broken windows and the mission truck following us had its canvas cover badly torn. The American Embassy warned us to stay off the streets.

In the beginning of 1974, it was not uncommon for me to feel dragged down by recurring amoeba and infrequent urinary tract infections. Some days I had to push myself while working on the windmills.

Not all of my experiments were successful. It was about this time that I had an idea for a dome constructed of bamboo. I covered the bamboo with grass mats and then plastered over the mats. Upon inspection, Geleb women gave their approval and some of the men wanted one, but they were not sturdy enough. Dolly called them my Polyboo-boos.

Windmill construction continued, and in August, Leah, Tom, and I delivered four windmill heads from Ghimeera to Omo and took photos of the windmill site. It was good to see that they were having a second crop as a result of the first windmill.

My March 17, 1974, journal entry stated, "We walked out to a Geleb village this afternoon. It is sad to see the skinny little children only skin and bones, the poor houses, and shortage of food. Our time here is up and there is still so much I could do to help them. If only I could have gotten more done."

I was putting in twelve-hour days working on Polyports, bridges, and windmills and was feeling a little worn down. I was glad I only had a week before we were to leave. As Dolly and I celebrated our thirty-third wedding anniversary at the end of August, we were cleaning up the shop and putting tools away, packing, and storing things in the attic. We had a farewell dinner for the mission gang and left on August 19, 1974, for furlough in the United States. It was the first time we flew in a 747. I wrote in my diary, "They sure are a big plane. It was much nicer than I had expected."

The executive committee voted to reappoint Dolly and me for a three-year (1974–1977) assignment to Ethiopia—and I would have a change of hats. No longer would I be called a mission builder but would now be involved in community development. This would be a major change for me. I would be answering to the local people instead of to the mission. I was to remain in Ethiopia until either sixty-two or sixty-five years of age and do technical work for the villages through the church at Ghimeera.

Upon arrival in the United States, we first connected with Mom and Dad and all the kids. Since I needed a car and most of them were too expensive to rent, I found myself a 1969 Mercury Monterey for one thousand dollars. My first trip was to Pittsburgh to meet with the P.U.T.T. committee to make plans for our future support. P.U.T.T., the committee of five started back in 1970 when we were laid off, met at the Pittsburgh National Bank. In 1970, it seemed as if our work as builders was ending, but due to P.U.T.T. contributions, we were able to continue our work in Ethiopia in community development as volunteers. All checks for our support came through this committee and were sent on to the program agency of the mission office in New York City for our projects. I learned that God's work done in God's way never lacks funds. If the money wasn't coming in, it was a sign to me that it wasn't God's will and I had to make a change.

The Presbyterian Board of Foreign Mission's Personal Interest Program, originating in 1958, stimulated the interest and support of local congregations to sponsor missionaries. In 1965, there were between thirty-seven to thirty-eight hundred United Presbyterian congregations participating. During our furloughs, it was our responsibility to visit churches with whom we were affiliated within a defined geographical area. Word was sent out to each of the congregations announcing our arrival to the States in the hope that we would be invited to visit the church and share our stories. Like Moses said to God in

Exodus 4:10–17, we felt we could not speak before a large American congregation; certainly we had no eloquence to do so.

Our 1974 furlough was a whirlwind of speaking engagements, slide shows, and church suppers from coast to coast—121 times (17 states and Washington, D.C.) in six months. Our furloughs were a time to meet our supporters back home, and I never turned down an opportunity to speak.

At Silver Dollar City in Branson, Missouri, I talked to craftsmen and got ideas from blacksmiths and from the foundry shop and learned about broom making, corn husking, and soap making. At Williamsburg I collected information from the blacksmith, the harness maker, the cooper, the miller, the cabinetmaker, and the basket maker for my community development programs back in Africa. Before the end of our furlough, I ordered a pump and some sailcloth and had them shipped back to Addis Ababa.

In October, while on furlough, we traveled to Tarkio College in Tarkio, Missouri. We spoke in the classrooms and showed slides to various groups at this Presbyterian-affiliated college, but my main purpose for going there was to meet with the Seekers. The Seekers, a group of college students (whose name originated from Matthew 6:33) visited us in Ghimeera while touring in Africa and invited us to visit them when back in the States. Some of them showed a sincere interest in the mission field.

In November I met with the Political Awareness Group at Westminster College in New Wilmington, Pennsylvania, in preparation for a talk I was to present at a town meeting concerning the world food crisis. The day of the talk, Eyewitness News was present to interview me about world hunger. I was certain that there was a way to feed the world. My windmills came to mind.

The holidays approached in 1974, and I went to see Santa—this one a female. It was my first experience with women's lib. Our children had begun presenting us with grandchildren, and I babysat for four grandkids while the rest of the family went to midnight service on Christmas Eve; I felt that they were all a blessing. This was our second Christmas morning together around the tree since Ginny's birth in 1958, and everyone was knee-deep in presents and gift wrap. What fun to have the little ones and watch their faces light up. Leah took charge of the big turkey dinner with all the trimmings. "It was a great day, one of a lifetime that will never be repeated. Thank-you God," I wrote in my diary.

As we continued our whirlwind trip cross-country, we stopped at Estes Park, Colorado, at the end of December. Dolly and I made sure we went to the spot where we had met some thirty-five years ago. We stopped to see our daughter, Penny, on our trip through Florida and spoke at the morning service at her family's church, Orange Park Presbyterian. At the family night supper we showed slides, talked, and answered many questions to an overflow crowd and ended the evening to a standing ovation. Our cross-country trip came to an end on February 2, 1975.

In early March, we left New Wilmington for New York City and stayed in a visitor's apartment at the mission office. After a day of touring, we headed off to Philadelphia where we plan-ned to attend services at the United Presbyterian Church in Upper Darby, Pennsylvania, where Dr. Roy Grace was pastor. (Dr. Grace was previously mentioned in chapter 3 when he came to visit us at Wanglel.) When I met up with Dr. Grace in the church hall, he was surprised to see me and said, "You will have to preach today. My sermon doesn't have anything in it so fresh that it won't keep." Before arriving, little did I know that I would be giving the morning service. So I talked to the men's class at Sunday school and had the service at church. What a day it was, and by the time we got back to the apartment in New York City, I fell into a deep sleep as my head hit the pillow.

By March 10, our furlough had come to an end and we were crossing the ocean one more time. We stopped at Schutz School in Alexandria to see Ginny, the students, and staff before continuing on to Ghimeera where everything was overgrown.

In July 1975, back at Omo, Bob Swart had a meeting of the farmers group for the men who owned windmills or for those who wanted one. When the locals were asked what they desired, they replied, "Dempster windmills, sugar, and shirts." The Gelebs didn't own much, but they were willing "to assume a percentage of the cost [of the windmill] commensurate to their means," Bob stated.[23]

The cost of my Polomo eleven-foot sail windmill was approximately seven hundred dollars and this included transporting all materials by air. In order to insure their commitment, the windmills were sold to interested farmers for two hundred dollars, with the American Mission paying the difference. The American Mission made a plea for financial aid to Oxfam in England, an organization active in famine-stricken Ethiopia for agricultural assistance and expansion of their windmill project.

For sometime, I had been working on improving my windmills together with the London-based Intermediate Technology Development Group (ITDG). ITDG, an organization launched in 1966, strived to introduce an intermediate technology in third-world countries—something between their primitive methods and those methods used in the more sophisticated west. Oxfam sought technical support from ITDG and wanted them to evaluate my project. One condition of the Oxfam grant was that an engineer visit my project to evaluate, advise, and report.

In July 1975, ITDG sent Peter Frankel as project officer to Omo for one month to evaluate our windmill project and make tests on the Polomo mill. Together we were working on ways to improve the Polomo mill: to extend the arms from twelve to sixteen feet for more power, to use four oblong sails instead of triangular ones (which we discovered worked quite well), and to use a wheel that would feather and have a stop if the wind got too strong. Actually, the Polomo mill pumped better when there was little wind, even only five miles per hour. In the event that there was no wind, we were working on a spring pole for pumping by hand.

Also, we were making up a beam so we could use two pumps on the same mill and get twice the water—the two pump mill. In a ten-mile-per-hour wind, the two pump mill pumped at the rate of twelve hundred gallons per hour, which was better than some of the high priced mills on the market. At times, when there was insufficient wind, the Gelebs climbed the towers and turned the wind wheel by hand.

ITDG had asked my permission to publish an article on windmill plans and make it available to anyone who needed them or was interested. Two men with Appropriate Technology Unit from Addis Ababa requested that they come to Omo in order to see the project in action and perhaps use the idea in the famine area of Ethiopia. I hoped to get someone in Addis Ababa to begin making the windmill heads so I could put my attention on other projects. It was a special privilege to meet with the mill owners and prospective owners while at the Omo: to see the progress they had made since we were last at the river; to worship with them; to listen to their problems; to hear their hopes for the future; and to see them at work in their gardens. At one stretch along the banks of the Omo, there were ten mills in a row. Previously the locals were only interested in growing corn and grain sorghum, but with the mills, they raised such things as peanuts, tomatoes, soybeans, and sweet potatoes.

Peter Frankel (with ITDG) and I experimented with many types of mills, but eventually decided that the Polomo mill was the best. I was pleased to get a good report from Peter on my windmill project. When Peter tried making all the windmill parts himself, he found it difficult, saying it was much easier to just draw them. But I felt it was good for the "desk men" to periodically get out on the field and have some hands-on experience.

Peter Frankel's book, *Food from Windmills*, reported on the windmill irrigation project initiated by the American Presbyterian Mission at Omo and gave particular thanks to "Rev. and Mrs. J. R. Swart who conceived this project . . . and to Mr. E. O. Pollock, the inventor of the original Polomo mills and the source of much inspiration."[24] It was all a matter of sharing ideas and working together to better mankind. Besides offering technical expertise, the cultural and social aspects of our building windmills at Omo played a major role in its success.

Bob and Morrie Swart described the project in the 1974 *Ethio-Echo*:

> . . . an unusual solution to their problems may have been found . . . the sight of a long row of windmills with different colored sails swishing rhythmically in the breeze which regularly blows off the lake and spewing river water into hand-dug channels to sustain crops previously unheard of in this inhospitable place. . . . This is a unique experiment in self-help irrigation which represents quite an international effort. Started and set up by American missionaries, it has recently gained British financial and technical support in adopting sail windmills traditionally used by Greeks in Crete for use in a remote corner of Ethiopia. For the first time the Gelebs were eating papayas, bananas and mangoes . . . since when the missing ingredient—water, is added to the combination of rich river silt and desert sunshine . . . fruit trees flourish and as many as three harvests a year of maize, sweet potatoes and soya beans in addition to their hardier traditional staple of millet become possible.[25]

With the windmill came a role change. Traditionally the women and children tended to the cultivation of the yearly crops, but with the advent of the windmill, it had been firmly adopted as the man's responsibility. In an interview with the Gelebs, one of the men indicated their concern of having to look after both windmills and cattle. Another Geleb, upon being interviewed, stated that his family had not been hungry since he had worked with the windmill—especially at critical times of the year. According to Peter Frankel, another claimed that "a man with a windmill that works well need never be hungry."

In October 1975, an instructional manual titled "Polomo Windmills—Omo River," was published by the Appropriate Technology Unit using information supplied by Bob Swart, Peter Frankel of the ITDG of London, and myself. The manual stressed that the simplicity of these windmills allowed them to be built on-site and demonstrated that they could be made of almost anything. The Omo Food from Wind project was a demonstration of technology being adapted from its place of origin to the needs and conditions of the new users.

At the end of October, Dolly and I had just returned to Ghimeera from a trip to Addis Ababa and discovered there was no electric power at the station. I hurried down to check the generator and when I returned, I found Dolly on the floor of the storeroom. She appeared to be very bruised, but at the time I wasn't aware what had happened. She was in a state of shock. I got her to the bed and sent for Dr. Mary.

Evidently Dolly had been in the storeroom and heard the transformer making noise on the second floor and saw fire shooting out. She raced up the steep foldaway stairs, moved the boxes, and pulled the wire loose from the transformer. Still there were flames. She needed my help and, knowing I was attending to the generator, started for the stairs. As she descended, she fell headfirst. There Dolly laid on the floor for fifteen minutes until I found her. She hit the right side of her forehead and blackened her left eye, bruised her left cheek and her back, and hurt her right wrist and both knees. Dr. Mary used the RT to get through for medical advice at Dembi Dollo.

Not only was Dolly completely helpless from the fall, but she was in a great deal of pain and had many restless nights. From then on, most of my days were spent the same: I took care of Dolly, washed dishes, did the laundry, ironed, cooked, and cleaned. I even tried my hand at making bread and bottling grapefruit juice.

In the middle of November, I took Dolly to Dembi Dollo for X rays and found that she had two fractures: one of the radius of the right wrist and another of the facial bone below her left eye. This was in addition to the fact that she had never regained complete use of her left hand from her brain tumor (discussed later on page 315).

About this time at Ghimeera I came up with the idea for Operation Pied Piper. Rats were a real menace and it angered

*Boy holding rat tail
at Ghimeera*

me to see undernourished children and sleek, fat rats in the same community. After killing a paltry number with poison and rat traps, I had an idea. I sent out word that I was willing to buy rat tails (at least three inches or longer) from the locals for two cents American (five cents Ethiopian). Upon hearing this, I'm sure they thought I had lost my mind. My goal was to make the Ghimeera people conscious that, not only did the rats eat their cultivated grain, eggs, and young chickens, but they also caused disease. At one time we had fifty patients receiving treatment for rabies prevention at Ghimeera and something had to be done. Many of the natives had leprosy, and with their numb fingers and toes, could not feel the bite of the rabid rats.

At first the rat tails just trickled in with only 299 the first month. But the project soon picked up momentum. By the end of the second month, over four thousand rats had been killed. This was only a fraction of the rats in the community, but when you considered that every pair of rats could produce 860 descendants in a year, that meant 1,720,000 fewer rats. And that in turn would mean an additional 137,600,000 pounds of food for the people! Many of the school children used the five cents I paid them to purchase a bread roll. A bun

Rat posters

made of wheat flour (white bread) was a delicacy to them—
better than a candy bar. After I stopped purchasing rat tails, I
used posters and cassette tapes to reinforce the importance of
rat eradication.

In March I designed and built a ferro-cement dome house for
the local people. Compared to the more complicated Polydome
that had to be shipped in, the ferro dome was simple to build.
These houses were made of one-quarter-inch reinforcing rod
covered with galvanized chicken wire, plastered with cement,
and then sprayed with water to prevent them from drying out
too quickly and cracking. Each step had to be monitored closely.
It was slow teaching the locals how to do the plastering, especially since the wind was strong, the dust bad, and the sun hot.
Sometimes the temperatures reached 110 degrees and the sweat
just poured off me. It was a fight all the way.

Eventually I received word that these ferro-cement homes
were successful, and that the locals liked them. They made a
good house and, with no windows and just one door, they
stayed cooler with just top and bottom vents. These ferro-
cement houses were stronger, lasted longer than the Polydome,
and were in keeping with the native style of homes. I originally
had planned to make ten of these houses but was expelled from
the country before they were completed.

In May 1976, we began a one-month vacation. On the way
to the United States, we stopped in London to meet with Peter
Frankel at the ITDG and bought ten windmill books. From
London it was on to Washington, D.C., to see son Ed, and then
head south to Parris Island, South Carolina, to visit son Tom in
boot camp in the marines. Returning north, we stopped at
Indiana University of Pennsylvania for Leah's rainy graduation
on May 16.

At a P.U.T.T. meeting in Pittsburgh, I discovered that our
support funds were coming in and that approval was granted
for me to work as a volunteer part-time after retirement if need

be. Also, it was agreed that part of the travel expenses for volunteers would be paid. (After we retired in 1977, funds collected by P.U.T.T. no longer went through the New York mission office but directly to us.)

At the end of May, on our return trip to Ethiopia, we attended Ginny's graduation from Schutz School. When the diplomas were handed out, there was special recognition given to the fact that Ginny was the end of an era; the Pollocks had children attending the school for the past twenty-five years and Ginny was the last of them.

Back at Omo, in July 1976, I listened to America's two hundredth birthday celebration on the radio. About this time we noticed planes were flying low over Omo, way below radar. Eventually we realized it was related to the raid on Entebbe, Uganda, that we had heard about on our transistor radio through the British Broadcasting Company and Voice of America. Palestinian terrorists had hijacked a French airplane and forced the pilot to land at Entebbe. More than one hundred passengers—chiefly Israeli citizens—were being held hostage. A week later, Israeli commandos staged a raid at the airport and freed almost all the hostages.

At Omo I taught my first class in simple blacksmithing to the windmill workmen in the village. At Ghimeera I introduced the village teachers to seven basic tools in hopes that by the time a boy completed sixth grade, he would have made a set of tools for himself and learned to use them. The set included a frame saw, plane, and a bow drill.

Leah was busy making sails, but by mid-August 1976, the day I dreaded arrived. Leah and Ginny left on MAF for Egypt and the States respectively. It was a good summer and fun to work with them. "Like all the rest of our children they are tops," I wrote in my diary. But before their departure they were secretly planning some little surprises for our thirty-fifth wedding anniversary. On my desk was an envelope that said,

Plastering ferro-cement dome house

"To be opened the morning of August 21." It instructed me to go to the attic and get some root beer and put it on ice for later. In the basket with the bottle of root beer were a tape and a note that said to go out and pick some flowers, bake a cake, and make ice cream for a party later. They instructed us to wait to play the tape until we were ready for "things to begin tonight." We had a lot of fun following their instructions and finding all the gifts they had made and hidden in various places.

Often I was using old-time technology in modern times. At Ghimeera I began experimenting with a stove that used very little fuel and one that the locals could make mostly from native materials. The chicka stove, made from a solid block of mud nine inches thick and a thirty-inch square, had three burners and a four-inch smoke pipe. Unfortunately we left the country before executing the plan. Also, I was experimenting with octahedron towers for windmills, clay pots for irrigation, and a food dehydration system that used a light bulb for heat.

I placed no restrictions on my ideas and there were no patents. Anyone was free to use them.

Ripples from our windmill project spread out and we were getting calls and letters from people in other parts of the world wanting information. Several groups from Kenya were interested but were unable to obtain the proper Ethiopian visas for them to come visit. Instead, in February 1977, Dolly and I made a trip to Nairobi on the invitation of a branch of English Oxfam and spent two weeks conferring with them about windmills. We, too, had all kinds of problems getting the necessary paperwork to travel but one thing we discovered—when God says, "GO!" you do as He says. He will take care of all our needs. While there I visited Nairobi University and discussed windmills with a professor of mechanical engineering and shared ideas on ferro-cement with a civil engineering professor.

In Nairobi we were taken to see a cattle dip used to control fleas, terrace gardens to prevent erosion, and a dam that enabled the locals to have multiple plantings. When it rained, water was caught in the dam, and in the dry season it could be pumped up to the garden by a windmill. Outside Nairobi in the town of Karen, we viewed ideas on display at the UNICEF village technology unit and also visited the National Christian Council of Kenya (NCCK) office.

GODARE—MESENGO

Another of the I. K. projects was with the Mesengo Tribe. During the first aerial survey with MAF in 1963, Harvey Hoekstra and I saw many Mesengo villages—some fairly large. The Hoekstras, of the Reformed Church of America and the parents of six children, were experienced missionaries in the Sudan. The time was ripe for work to begin. The Mesengo Tribe, near the Godare River, was widely scattered and separated from the last fringes of civilization by a vast screen of tangled rain forest and mountain terrain covered with heavy timber. They had no connection with the outside world except for a few footpaths. This forest-dwelling tribe was located northwest of Ghimeera and covered an area of about seven hundred square miles.

On October 9, 1964, a team of four missionaries— Dr. Campbell Millar, Ralph Borgeson, Harvey Hoekstra, and I—embarked on our first ground survey trip to find the best mission site for the Mesengos. Our entourage consisted of fourteen carriers to haul our tents and food, two pack mules, one donkey, and one riding mule. A more direct route was used in the past, but due to heavy undergrowth, we followed the only trail opened at the time.

Local officials expressed their approval of our interest in developing their land by supplying us with valuable information about the area and the people. The chief sent Mesengos ahead to widen the trail and cut the low-hanging vines and branches. This marvelous country had a crater lake approximately a half mile wide, some of the thickest jungle I had ever seen with monkey-laden large trees, and dozens of the loveliest rivers and waterfalls (some dropping over one hundred feet).

Villages were scattered along the way but many of the Mesengo houses were empty. The Mesengo were very mobile and were either out hunting or looking for pastures for their cattle in the dry season.

At the first Mesengo village, outlines of bodies disappeared into the bush when they saw us on the trail. Strangely enough, upon our arrival there was an empty village with fires burning—both indications that they ran in fear from us strange white men. Eventually a leaf fluttered and a little old man peeped out from behind a bush. Little by little the whole village returned and welcomed us with dancing. I handed out some of the thousand colored combs and packs of matches that I had brought. We soon made friends and they let me take their pictures. We set up camp in the middle of their village and had the Godare River close by supplying plenty of water and power.

The Mesengos dwelled in simple grass and stick houses in scattered clearings that they made in the rain forest. These intelligent, seminomadic people appeared to be musical and, for their dances, played tube-like instruments unlike any I had seen. These tube instruments were cut from varying diameters and lengths of wood, which when blown, created different tones. Brightly colored beads, predominantly neck yokes, decorated their bodies. Men dressed in leaves and loin cloths, while the women's "clothing" consisted of grass, skins, and bark.

The primitive bridge at the river crossing had poles for its base and grass mats for the deck. At one end of the bridge, where the mats didn't reach the bank, we had to unload and haul all our goods by hand. On the second day of our survey trip, as we attempted to lead the mules across the bridge, their legs slipped between the poles.

The trail through the low swamp was rough, and mud nearly reached the top of my boots. As we crossed one of the rivers, a mule fell into a hole and had to be freed from the straps holding his load. Even with all these problems we were making good time, and at the end of two days we had covered what we had planned to do in three.

On the third day of our Mesengo ground survey trip, we continued to cut our way through the jungle. Food for the mules was scarce and they moved slowly. Even after much persuading, one of the mules refused to move and had to be abandoned. We crossed several more rivers and came upon some beautiful country similar to the Florida Everglades. The Godare River, the biggest river we encountered on the trip, was deep but manageable, since it wasn't too swift. Half of the Mesengo tribe resided on the other side of the river.

Four days into the survey we left the mules and part of our gear, and took the carriers on to Balti, the center of the tribe.

We asked the old chief if this was Balti and he responded, "I am Balti." We quickly learned that the villages were named for the chiefs, making it very difficult to keep maps current.

Needs were great at Balti, with many sick and hungry. Improvements in agriculture methods were needed to help better overall health. Adding to their misery, crops were bad this year because of too much rain.

Several days after our arrival, we discovered that one of the village women knew Anuak and this changed everything. When Harvey talked through her, it was thrilling to see their faces brighten, indicating they understood.

According to the Mesengo Report, "the Mesengos appeared to be an industrious agricultural people, who raise chickens and who live mostly on honey, corn, and dura. . . . Each man had one hundred beehives (made from hollowed logs) placed in the trees up to one hundred feet high." These hives were carved from three-foot lengths of log and hoisted into the trees with vine ropes. Harvey Hoekstra in an article titled, "Missionary Family to Live Among the Mesengo People," states that "The Mesengo make extensive use of honey from the wild bees in the forest. It is their one 'cash crop.'"[26]

It was important to ask the local chiefs and elders for help in determining the best site for our mission site. Topography, building sites, airstrip sites, water supply, and sources of local building materials all had to be considered.

On the last day of our survey trip, we found an old clearing that looked like a good possibility for an airstrip. It was not readily apparent, though, due to the extent of the underbrush there at Godare. "The Chief had his expert bush cutters slash a swath down the center of a proposed site for the airstrip" wide enough for us to see and we paced it off, stated the Mesengo Report. It was good and long enough for a DC–3 plane. I was impressed by the skill with which the Mesengos cut their way through the brush using a curved knife sharpened on both edges.

In the same *Ethio-Echo* article, Harvey Hoekstra was impressed with their resourcefulness: "They have learned how to slash their way through the jungle in an efficient manner which will always be beyond the ability of their foreign guest."[27] We found a good source of water to supply a future mission house and, with all these considerations, we decided the site at Godare would be our recommendation for the location of the Mesengo mission post.

After finishing up our survey and starting back to Ghimeera, we returned to where we had left our mules and spent the night. We would have to push hard for the next several days in order to make our flight in Teppi for our trip home. The first day we walked eight hours and noted that, due to heavy rains, the rivers were higher. Harvey and I continued full speed ahead and, not knowing how far behind Campbell and Ralph (the other two survey team members) were, decided to stop for the night. Eventually some of our carriers and a pack mule came in with a note to inform us that Campbell and Ralph, because of hard rain, were bedding down on the other side of the forest for the night.

The next morning Harvey and I packed up and went to the river to wait for Campbell and Ralph. We weren't there long before a runner arrived with a note saying that Dr. Millar (Campbell) had an infection in his leg where he had skinned it on a stone in the river. We sent the riding mule back to retrieve him, and he looked bad. As they bathed the leg with hot water, I took off on foot for the government clinic at Teppi to see if I could locate a medical dresser to send back to Campbell with penicillin and tetanus shots. One Mesengo accompanied me to help carry my knapsack, poncho, and canteen. Taking a shortcut, we managed to make the twenty miles to Teppi in five and a quarter hours and instructed a dresser and some men to go help Dr. Millar. By midnight the dresser returned to Teppi with Dr. Millar, exhausted—carrying him on a stretcher for part of the way and then by mule. The next day Dr. Millar flew to the hospital in Addis Ababa.

On our return trip from Godare to Ghimeera, we had covered a total of one hundred fifty miles, mostly on foot. I had been gone a total of twenty-four days on the trail, and it was good to be back home to Ghimeera. To celebrate, I, along with everyone at the station, enjoyed ice cream and cake in honor of Dolly's birthday.

The Mesengo Report expressed our feelings precisely: "The team wishes to record its appreciation to the mission for the privilege we had in making this survey of this unique rain forest area and its people who live in it. The considerable physical difficulties encountered in the survey were more than compensated for in the enriched experience of all the team members." With the survey completed, the Hoekstra family (Harvey, Lavina, and three-year-old son, Paul) would be moving into the site at the new mission post near the Godare River.

After the surveys were completed, it was time to bring in the family to open up the post. Harvey Hoekstra's tale of the ten-day journey with his wife, Lavina, and his three-year-old son, Paul, to begin the new Godare River Post, read like a novel. It was during the beginning of this trip that Harvey asked my eldest son, Ed Jr., to help open up the station at Godare. In an article titled, "Hoekstra's Journey to Begin Godare River Post," Harvey described his trip: an entourage of six mules, two horses, rabbits, and chickens; food rationing alleviated only by the dropped bundles of supplies from MAF; stubborn mules; and soakings in the tropical rains. To add to the many difficulties, the carriers he had hired to help transport supplies went on strike and left them stranded in the middle of the forest. A shack was built and giant trees twisted with vines were cleared for an airfield during those first few austere weeks at Godare and the Hoekstras were exhilarated with the "unspeakable privilege of making Christ and the fullness of His love known among the Mesengo."[28]

I wasn't living permanently at the Godare site with the Hoekstras. At first, supplies had to be air-dropped. But after the airstrip was finished, I made many flights back and forth for a day or two at a time to advise on the construction. On a return trip from Godare one day the MAF pilot asked if I had ever flown a plane. "No," I replied. He instructed me to take over and, unless I got tired, I could stay at the helm until we landed. It was the fastest fifteen minutes I had ever spent in the air. Need I mention that there were dual controls?

At the beginning of February 1966, we used the chain saw to cut timber and make a table for the sawmill at Godare. After working beside the saw all day, I found that by nightfall I had lost my hearing—even with cotton in my ears.

Our plan was to start the workers making pressed mud blocks for the staff houses and clinic at Godare. Blocks varied at each post according to the type of materials available. Most times I had to include additives to make the right consistency, but at Godare, I had perfect soil to make blocks and therefore only had to add 5 percent cement.

At our mission base in Ghimeera, son Ed and I had the cutting and welding for the Godare buildings in full swing. MAF was making frequent trips from our Ghimeera workshop to deliver loads of finished components to Godare. One day in May, they delivered two thousand pounds of building materials.

Things sure looked different at Godare than when I saw it on our first ground survey. The Hoekstras had done a fine job—everything from cutting an airstrip right out of the jungle to building pole houses with grass roofs.

"But, alas, to establish a post takes many months, even years, of valuable missionary time—time one longs to have for language study, visiting in villages, and preaching," Harvey explained in an article titled, "Volunteers Build Mission Post in the Forest." "In the beginning a tremendous amount of exhausting physical work has to be done. A reasonably adequate residence and a modest plant, with buildings in which one can offer a ministry of education and medical care, need to be built," Harvey continued. "And in a new post, almost everything has to be done the hard way!"[29]

There were many volunteers from the States who lent a hand those first two years in Godare. By then I had partly completed the first two rooms and veranda of the Hoekstras' permanent residence, and for the first time, they could enjoy the "luxuries" of a metal roof over their heads and a level cement floor under their feet. Besides the Hoekstras' home and the clinic, houses for the Ethiopian medical dresser and teacher were almost completed, with the school building well on its way.

"Frequently, the work stops, and for a brief moment the missionary sits in the circle with his new friends and tells them of Jesus. Who can predict the eventual harvest of the seed being sown?"[30] Lois Anderson wrote in the 1967 *Ethio-Echo* newsletter. Besides unscheduled casual gatherings, regular worship services were being held twice daily.

During April and May of 1970 at Godare, we completed the first staff house and started work on the second, finished

Working the chain saw at the sawmill in Godare

the clinic, and started work on the school. Besides Godare, in 1972, Harvey Hoekstra requested buildings at other posts to start evangelistic work. Before being expelled from Ethiopia due to the Communist takeover in May 1977, Harvey Hoekstra had a clinic and school up and running, and the beginnings of a church at Godare.

———•◆•———

Before going out to the mission field, the Hoekstras were trained in Bible translation by Wycliffe Bible Translators. During thirty years in Africa, their translation work included the idea of making tapes of simple Bible stories and sharing them with the Mesengos using solar cassette players made and sent from California. They instructed native evangelists how to operate the players and encouraged them to take these tapes from village to village. It was thrilling to watch the faces of the local people light up when the little box talked in their native tongue. It wasn't long before they started asking, "Who is this Jesus?" Scripture tapes in their language and cassette players were left behind for the Mesengos when the Hoekstras were put out of Ethiopia in 1977.

After being expelled in 1977, Harvey and Lavina Hoekstra were led into full-time cassette ministry and began to establish overseas regional centers where they could train and equip nationals to record the New Testament for people who were unable to read. From Ethiopia, their cassette ministry went with them into other parts of Africa, into Asia, and eventually into the United States where Dr. Hoekstra founded Audio Scriptures International, or ASI, in 1989.

In 1987, ten years since our departure, much had happened with the Mesengos. Life was hard with the new Communist government. One of our native evangelist friends shared how he was locked in a dark mud-floor room in prison for seven months.

Food was shoved through a hole in the door, he slept on the floor, and he had no toilet facilities. Another evangelist was imprisoned for entering the village with his solar cassette player. Many Mesengos had given up witchcraft and accepted Christ. It was amazing how much they were willing to suffer for Him.

An article titled, "Tie a Knot on Your String for Me," states that in 1991, there was a report from the rain forest in which neighboring tribes were questioning what had happened to the warring, rebel-rousing Mesengos. The report said that 90 percent of them had proclaimed to be followers of Jesus— all because missionaries shared cassettes with the Mesengos in their own language.

Harvey and Lavina's son, Mark Hoekstra, was referring to his parents in this same article when he wrote:

> Some thirty-two years ago a middle-aged man and his wife went deep into the rain forest of Southwest Ethiopia to reach the Mesengos for Jesus. . . . It was very difficult for a missionary to bring the good news to those living in these small villages, but God had a marvelous plan for the Mesengos. He gave the missionary a vision to use the simple cassette player and the feet of the Mesengos themselves to cross the mountains and rivers and reach deep into the jungle for His Name's sake. God wanted the Mesengos to hear His precious saving Word in the language they understood best.
>
> Mesengos took the tape players into their villages and everyone gathered to hear the box that talked in their language. Listening carefully, they wanted it played again and again until the batteries were drained.
>
> One of the Mesengos who went out into the villages with the tape player returned saying, "Then one by one they would ask me to make a string and tie a knot on it for them. 'Tell the missionary I want to become a child of this Jesus, they

would say.'" As the missionary listened each knot was
pointed to and the name recited.[31]

In the late 1990s, after seventeen years of civil war, Denny
Hoekstra, an MAF pilot and another son of Harvey and
Lavina, made the first flight back into the remote area where
his parents had pioneered many years before. After seventeen
years of isolation, Denny was surprised to learn that the two
hundred locals who had accepted Christ during the twelve
years his parents were in Ethiopia had mushroomed into five
thousand Christians and thirty-five churches.[32] Today there are
more than twenty thousand believers!

———————◆———————

Plans for mission posts, other than Godare, had to be
changed due to a shortage of funds. In place of building new
mission posts, the idea of outposts was instituted. Evangelists
and clinic dressers were sent out to tribes north of Godare for
several days at a time to make contact with unreached tribes.

After Harvey Hoekstra's time in Godare with the
Mesengos, he focused on setting up a taping studio and bookstore in the village of Teppi, a small marketing town on the
edge of the rain forest. Here numerous tribal groups gathered
and could be reached effectively for Christ by using the cassette
players. Many people came past the bookstore on their way to
market and stopped to listen to gospel tapes. Originally tape
players were of the hand crank variety, but eventually solar
panels were used to power the recorders there at Teppi.

Teppi, because of its central location, became the base for
mass producing cassettes with gospel messages in native
languages. Village chiefs, ordinary villagers, evangelists, schoolboys and girls, and many others took the cassette messages out
to the people in distant villages to introduce them to Jesus.

Polyport

Harvey continued at Godare but used Teppi as his home base. I met with Harvey to review a site for the new Teppi base. It was here that I first used my Polyvillion, the dome tent. Later I put up four water tanks to supply running water and flush toilets in the houses at Teppi. The water system was comprised of two water tanks on the ground and two in the air on posts, all made on the site. My work at Teppi not only involved making a pre-fab soundproof taping studio for the Teppi Tapes Ministry but also a library in Teppi for school and community use.

Another of the outreach posts was the village of Sulli, sixty miles northwest of Ghimeera. We were the first ones to arrive at Sulli and started erecting our first Polyport, the ten-by-sixteen-foot pre-fab building that could be flown in a small plane and set up in one day.

Sulli was home to the Mocha Tribe, where we had plans to station a full-time missionary and send in a medical dresser a week at a time. This was originally going to be the sixth of the

I. K. posts, but due to a shortage in personnel, the mission decided to attempt to reach them through the Teppi Tapes Ministry instead.

As we landed at the very edge of the rain forest at Sulli, crowds of people surrounded the plane and helped carry the building pieces to the construction site. Because of the mist from the rain forest and occasional showers, building components, sleeping bags, food, and suitcases had to be covered with tarpaulins.

The second flight brought Rev. John Haspels to help with the erection of the Polyport. The Mocha people's first question to us was, "Did you bring medicine?" We were sorry that we had to say "no." But we had plans to build a small house where a medicine man or dresser could live when he made his regular visits. They were a friendly, gracious people and brought us gifts of milk and honey water. After watching Dolly struggle to light a fire in the rain with damp charcoal, one lady went home and returned with a shovel full of glowing coals.

The second day dawned bright and clear with no sign of rain anywhere. It gave John and me twelve hours of sunshine to complete the roof on the Polyport. A real sign of God's blessing upon our work was a double rainbow as the sun went down over the lush green forest. The next day MAF returned us to Ghimeera and we couldn't help but praise the Lord for His goodness.

Because we were expelled from Ethiopia, this post was never completed.

SURMA

Don McClure Jr. and his wife, Ginny, were missionaries assigned to open up work at Surma, the fifth I. K. post. After four I. K. posts had been completed (Adura, the fourth I. K.

project was built by Monty Parr for the Nuer Tribe), work on the Surma Post in the Tirma tribal area in southwestern Ethiopia was just beginning in October 1969. This mountainous region had little rainfall with streams running only a few months a year. There were no fish available. The people here lived in numerous scattered villages and a chief, who inherited his power by birth, ruled each village. Agricultural development was difficult, tree growth was scrubby, and there were only footpaths into the area. Our goals were to provide food, medical, and educational services, but, most important, to invite the Surma people to accept God's proposal of forgiveness through Jesus Christ.

Once upon a time the Surma people were a pastoral tribe. That was until an unknown disease killed most of their wild and domestic animals, forcing them to become hunters and gatherers. The unfamiliarity of this way of life resulted in the entire tribe facing starvation. Their "religion" centered around their fear of evil spirits in trees, fire, lightning, and other natural things. The witch doctor, who charged exorbitant prices, played the role of medical advisor and spiritual counselor. The Surma people could not speak Amharic, the national language, or English. In fact, they could not read or write their own language. Therefore, in order for Don to learn their language, words had to be associated with observed action.

The Surma site and airstrip was south of Ghimeera in rolling countryside that was void of high hills and sparsely covered with small thorn trees. Our camp was set up one quarter mile from the airstrip near one of the higher hills. In September, several of us climbed up more than one thousand feet above the camp and studied the lay of the land, including where to put our house and buildings. The soil looked like it would make good blocks, but unfortunately there was no sand to be found.

The people here crowded around to see us, not only touching the hair on our arms, but looking up our sleeves and down our collars to determine if we were white all over. Custom required girls of the tribe to be adorned with a six-inch clay plate suspended from the lower jaw. As teenagers, a slit was made in the lower lip and the lip was stretched around the rim of the plate. The custom was to start with a small-sized plate and increase the plate size until the desired lip size was attained. The bigger the lip, the more valuable was the bride-to-be. The custom had originated years ago as a disfigurement to discourage being sold into slavery.

About this time I had an opportunity to hear Dr. Earl Stanley Jones, the great missionary from India, speak at a prayer meeting in Addis Ababa. Dr. Jones, then eighty-five years old, was still traveling around the world preaching. He spent three days at our guest house in Addis Ababa, and on one of those mornings, I talked with him after breakfast. He felt that a generation gap existed and that adults needed to spend more time listening and sharing with the young. "Instead of spending all our time praying," he said, "we should spend sometime listening for God's answers." He told me about "listening time." Pray about your problems at night, he instructed, then get a good night's sleep, and listen for God's answers in the morning. To this day I follow his advice. I feel that one needs to find God in the morning if he needs

Surma lip plate in (left) and Surma lip plate out (right)

Him throughout the day. "It has been wonderful to have a chance to visit and talk to E. Stanley Jones," I wrote in my journal. Often I incorporated this idea of Dr. Jones's when speaking on furlough.

As discussed earlier, toward the end of 1969, it looked like there was a possibility we wouldn't be returning to Ethiopia after our furlough in 1970 due to lack of money. At my personal interview before furlough, I didn't fulfill the requirements. But then I never did. Typically, missionaries were educated doctors, teachers, and preachers. I was self-taught with no degrees. As Glenn Reed, the field secretary of the board of foreign mission said, everything with me was an exception. Christ didn't always take the Pauls and the educated, but He took the fishermen and the poor. There were many highly educated men, but I felt strongly that one must earn his spurs before he wore them.

We waited to hear the decision of the mission as to our future plans in Ethiopia. In November 1969, the personnel committee voted that, due to cutbacks, we would not be returning after furlough. At the time, money wasn't coming in and the church had used up their reserve funds. Thirty missionaries would be laid off in Ethiopia (seventy in all of Africa) so it didn't make much sense to send us back for eighteen months. The story in Acts, chapter 5, came to mind where a teacher of the law named Gamaliel said to the Pharisee, ". . . for if this plan or this undertaking is of men, it will fail; . . ." (NRSV). We had been scheduled to go on furlough in July 1970, and, even though the board voted that missionaries wouldn't return, the chairman of the personnel committee felt that, at all costs, I should return and finish the I. K. projects.

We really didn't mind a change but I did inform the commission that after furlough, it would take two years to finish what I had started and been assigned to do at all four I. K. posts. In my mind, if we moved before the work was finished, it would be a loss, not a savings. Much of the iron had already been cut, and there was no time to assemble it or show anyone else how.

Since we worked all day, Christmas this year at Surma came and went like any other day. It was the first time in over twenty-five years that none of the children were home for the holiday. We were alone with no Christmas music, no snow, no turkey, and no other human with whom we could share the wonders of Christ's birth. Up to this time we could not converse with the Surma people so none of them had heard of Jesus Christ. Regardless, the Christ Child was there and it was His birthday.

In February 1970, I walked up to a Surma tribal village hoping to find the chief. Neither he nor any of the men were present, only women and children. Here houses were made of low stick walls with grass roofs and had a loft overhead where grain was stored. Smoke from the fire burning in the center

Polyvillion dome tent at Surma

kept out the mosquitoes. Their beds were six-inch-high platforms made neatly of mud which looked similar to cement. The better beds were nothing more than a flat board cut from a log with a short piece of wood for a pillow.

The Polyvillion (first made in 1964 in Teppi) was ready for shipping and would be our living quarters at Surma. I constructed two plastic skylights for the Polyvillion.

I spent a month at Surma with five volunteers from Michigan erecting the first Polydome. In March 1970, I realized the building was not moving along as fast as I had hoped and planned. Hauling sand proved a bigger task than we anticipated since there were still no Surma men willing to work for more than an hour or two at a time. There were no roads available in order to retrieve the sand fifteen miles away; therefore, many trailer and tractor tires were deflated going over the rough and thorny terrain. Only the women and children carried water for us—never for money but for a small amount of salt. The women and young girls also did most of the stonework and worked the chicka while the older children watched over the babies. I admired the women for their willingness to work hard.

Progress on the buildings was slow and the five volunteers from Michigan had to do much of the hard work. But we had a great time and they learned quickly what was involved in building a new mission station. Sometimes I started my day at 5:00 A.M. and worked until midnight just trying to get everything done.

While on furlough in New Wilmington in 1970, the date December 17 sticks in my mind. On this day Dolly and I had gone shopping after lunch, and, upon our return, Dolly announced she had a headache and was going to lie down. About twenty minutes later I went upstairs, found her tossing on the bed, and was unable to awaken her. I called the doctor and he came immediately. An ambulance arrived and took her to a hospital in New Castle, Pennsylvania, where a spinal tap was performed. After running many tests the next day, the doctor suspected that Dolly had a brain tumor and he sent her to the Northside Hospital in Youngstown, Ohio. Here it was confirmed that she had a big tumor that had grown into the large bone on top her head. An operation was scheduled for December 29 involving the removal of part of this bone and the insertion of a plate.

Our return trip to Ethiopia was put on hold. Dolly was at peace about the procedure and we prayed together that God's will be done and that we might be faithful witnesses no matter what happened. (December 17, 1970, marked the twenty-fourth anniversary of our mission work in Africa.)

How different Christmas 1970 in the mission house where we were staying was compared to the prior year in Surma by ourselves. With Dolly and I on furlough, our entire family, including grandkids, met in New Wilmington. At this time Ed and Dorothy had a small son, Edward III; Penny and John had their newborn son, Chad; and Bill came from Troy, New York, with his wife, Carolyn, where he was continuing his master's degree at Rensselaer Polytechnic Institute. Ron traveled from Rochester, New York, where he was attending the Rochester Institute of Technology. Leah, Tom, and Ginny were all students in New Wilmington, Pennsylvania.

By Christmas Eve the children arrived and the girls went shopping to buy their mother a wig. On Christmas morning we called Dolly and all sang, "We Wish You a Merry Christmas." For four years we had been planning this Christmas when we would all be together, but it was not to be. Leah was in charge of Christmas dinner, and afterwards, we all went to the hospital lounge to take Dolly her gifts. Many visitors stopped by to cheer Dolly, but often they left with their own spirits lifted instead. The people at the hospital and in the whole community prayed for Dolly, sent food to the mission house, and sent money for my projects. Many pastors visited and many cards were received. Even the blood for her surgery was supplied by members of a Presbyterian church near Pittsburgh, Pennsylvania.

The night before Dolly's surgery, she was in good spirits. Ron, Tom, and Ginny came to see their mother and we all held her hands and said prayers by her bedside. There were no tears. Even without hair, she was not embarrassed for us to see her.

Surgery lasted five hours. Bleeding was hard to control and three pints of blood had to be administered. The doctor couldn't tell if there was any brain damage at the time of surgery. After two hours in recovery, she was taken to intensive care, and when I was permitted to visit, I was delighted that she recognized my voice and tried to answer me. During the night she was put in an oxygen tent, and her eyes and face became badly swollen.

The doctor had told Dolly that the left side of her body would be paralyzed after surgery, but as the days passed I could see improvements. Not only had she started opening her eyes and sitting in a chair to feed herself, but she had some feeling in her left leg and eventually in her left arm. The hospital was willing to let me stay with her as a nurse's assistant, and I performed physical therapy on her arm and leg as soon as she was released from the ICU. For the next three weeks, I spent fifteen hours a day with her and started a therapy to keep her joints loosened. As Dolly's sister, Virginia, stated, "You just won't let her die."

After one month, Dolly was taken by ambulance from Northside Hospital to Hillside, a rehabilitation hospital in Warren, Ohio. There they discouraged me from staying with Dolly, saying that she would be more inclined to try things for herself without my presence. Here they started both physical and occupational therapy and had her working on sanding a wooden fish plaque that she was planning to take back to Ethiopia. A bar connected her arms and when she moved the right arm to do sanding, the left one would move also, giving it the exercise it needed.

While Dolly was in the hospital, I continued speaking and showing slides at various churches in the area, but most of my time was filled with trips to and from the hospital. For the first ten days, Dolly was tired and depressed at the rehab hospital. She had an especially rough time when her left leg got badly swollen with a superficial phlebitis above the knee. But after a week in bed with hot packs, she made a good comeback.

One evening the end of January, I arrived to find Dolly waiting for me in a wheelchair in the hall outside her room. She was very tired and, since the medical staff here was not adequate, she waited impatiently for me to put her into bed. When I left at the end of visiting hours, she was crying. This was the only time I left her in tears. The verses, "In everything give thanks: for this is the will of God in Christ Jesus concerning you," (1 Thess. 5:18 KJV) and "we know that all things work together for good to them that love God," (Rom. 8:28 KJV) came to mind.

At Northside Hospital, we had a wonderful time and things went well. It wasn't hard to give thanks then. Here at the rehabilitation hospital, it was harder to be thankful. If only I could see and know what God wanted us to do.

In an article titled, "Pollocks Originate a New Dome Building for Remote Mission Posts," there was this insert: "The following story was written by Dolly Pollock shortly before going on furlough last summer. Now, just before their return to Ethiopia and quite unexpectedly, Dolly had an operation to remove a large brain tumor. She is presently convalescing in a rehabilitation center in Ohio. Pray for us for Dolly's recovery, the family, and the future."[33]

As days passed, Dolly became stronger. She rode a stationary bike, tried to walk, and attempted to write some letters. At various times, though, she dealt with swelling in her head and her left leg, and twitching in her left arm. I didn't know if the twitching was a good sign, but at least it was an indication that the nerves and muscles were working.

I noticed Dolly's memory was excellent for things that happened before her hospitalization but mixed up with what happened since. One of the nurses suggested that I hadn't accepted the fact that Dolly's left arm might not return to normal use, but I had faith that it would and felt that it was too early to predict. In fact, besides not having use of her left arm, some of the therapists felt Dolly would never walk again.

At first it had been decided that Dolly would be fitted with special shoes and a brace, but by February she attempted to walk with the aid of a three-legged cane and handled herself so well that she never wore the shoes. At this point I was able to bring her home on weekends. The last weekend of February was especially good; I not only took Dolly to the mall to purchase a blonde wig, but we also attended church that Sunday.

At the beginning of March, the staff did a review of Dolly's progress and I was called in to get the report. Her leg was doing fairly well, but they doubted the arm would ever function again. They thought I was wrong to encourage her, but I indicated that I didn't agree with them.

One day shortly after the review, there was a surprise. The staff saw Dolly move her left arm slightly. The head of the physical therapy department commented, "I just cannot believe it. It is the first time I have ever seen a miracle! I've never seen anything like it before. A few weeks ago she couldn't even sit up alone."

Friday, March 19, 1971, was a red-letter day. Dolly was discharged from the hospital and told to "go live it up." She had been a patient at the rehab hospital for over eight weeks, and a patient in the two hospitals for a total of ninety-four days. Dolly said, "In all those ninety-four days I never had a bedsore. I am sure that I was borne upon the wings of your prayers."

Dolly's arm seemed to be improving. Perhaps it was due to all the therapy she was doing at home. Besides some hand-grips I made for Dolly to exercise her shoulder, I rigged up many other gadgets to help improve her mobility. I read everything about therapy that I could get my hands on, and for the rest of her life I would be giving Dolly therapy to help her improve.

It wasn't long before the doctor gave us the good news that Dolly would be able to return to Ethiopia. We immediately started planning for our return trip in July or August. In the meantime, I felt that a trip would be good for Dolly, and in May we tallied up over fifteen hundred miles traveling to Rochester, Buffalo, and Troy, New York; to New Jersey; to the Program Agency of the Mission Office in New York City; and on to Bethlehem, Pennsylvania. Upon our return, Dolly's doctor instructed us to make arrangements with the hospital to have a plate put in her head. But as it worked out, the doctor was unable to insert the plate because the brain had moved and any disturbance would be a setback for Dolly. So the decision was made not to insert the plate.

A letter written in April 1971, by Harold Kurtz, secretary of the mission program, to Dolly and me expressed how he had been "following Dolly's progress with prayers and praise and has been so thankful for the miracle of recovery" that she had experienced. He was anxiously awaiting word from the checkups which Dolly was soon to have with her doctor and from the rehabilitation hospital. He was greatly relieved that it looked as though I would be able to return and continue with my work in Ethiopia.

In response to Harold's letter, I wrote: "She is getting some return now and is able to pick up an item from the table with some effort. . . . As things look now we should be able to return to Ethiopia in July or August. . . . This may work out so that we will be able to take over at Surma."

Surma school

Since the McClures had lived in tents at Surma for three years, the second dome there was to be used for their house. Due to Dolly's surgery, this dome was put on hold—or so we thought. We eventually learned that high school students from Good Shepherd Mission School in Addis Ababa volunteered their spring break to do a ten-week work camp to build the McClures a Polydome.

It looked like things were falling into place when Dolly was cleared by her doctors to return to Ethiopia and our visas had been extended. On September 17, 1971, we left New York City for Cairo where we picked up our visas. I was anxious to get back on a construction job.

The McClures had established an airstrip, studied the language, and gathered materials at Surma. Permanent buildings were begun in 1971, and in 1972, I put up a school and clinic there. The Surma school, different from the others we built, was a pre-fab building (twenty-two foot by forty foot) with sections of asbestos panels made and bolted together in the workshop at Ghimeera. For the Surma house, we were using burnt brick instead of stone. Local materials were used for construction.

About this time, I made a request to Harvey Hoekstra to come and tape some Surma music. MAF flew Harvey in from Teppi and we taped the Surma girls singing and dancing. Also, Harvey and I made a tape in Surma called, "The Origin of Sin and God's Remedy." It was good to have some gospel tapes available for the people there. Our goal was to lead the Surma people to a personal relationship with God with them choosing their own worship forms.

In 1973, we finished the clinic at Surma and had a great time singing and dancing to the tape player—a real old-time hoedown. I had dropped down to 125 pounds, probably due to hard work in the extreme heat.

In the summer of 1973, son Bill and his wife, Carolyn, arrived from Schutz School (where they were teaching for two years), and son Ed and his wife, Dorothy, arrived from the States. Ed worked on panels for the gable ends of the Surma school and clinic (tons of gravel and thousands of bricks), Bill and Carolyn worked on the village wiring at Ghimeera, and I worked everywhere, as I recorded in my diary.

The destination for our vacation in October 1972 was South Africa. While en route, we stopped in Kenya and met up with the U.N. representative in charge of ACROSS, the Association of Christian Relief Organizations Serving Sudan. ACROSS, based in Nairobi, ministered across the border to the Sudan in evangelism, education, relief, agriculture, and health. The U.N. representative had heard that I was being laid off and was interested in recruiting me to help the organization with the rebuilding of clinics in the South Sudan.

In February 1973, ACROSS invited me to visit Juba, Sudan, to discuss locations and building plans for their clinics. Should I stay on in Ethiopia until retirement or should I go to Juba to join up with ACROSS as a mission builder? With uncertainty in Ethiopia, I was tempted to consider their offer. Back in 1969, Colonel Gaafar Nimeiri, a Muslim who seized power in a military coup, had taken control of the Sudan government, forbade political parties, and arrested many of the head politicians. Independence was stripped in the south and Islamic law imposed. In 1971, then Major-General Nimeiri became president. In 1972, he declared a ceasefire with the rebelling southerners and signed the Addis Ababa Agreement establishing self-government in the southern Sudan provinces.

On the trip to Juba that February, ACROSS introduced me to their head personnel to discuss future plans. Their minister of education assured me there was much we could do to help them. I found everyone in a holiday spirit celebrating Unity Day, the one-year anniversary of the signing of their peace treaty between the government of the Democratic Republic of the Sudan and the Southern Sudan Liberation Movement. Since Ethiopia had played a major role in the peace agreement between northern and southern Sudan, both the Ethiopian Emperor Selassie and Sudan President Nimeiri were in attendance for the celebration. I was thrilled to be within arm's length of men of such high prestige. There were more than 250 Shilluks on the docks and 150 more at the airport who came from Malakal to see the leaders, and many recognized us. The army greeted me and I felt that everyone was glad to have us back. (Peace endured for only eleven years before hard-line government policies created new conflicts in 1983.)

On March 1, 1973, while we were visiting the Sudan, the news spread quickly that Palestinian terrorists had taken the American ambassador and the deputy chief of mission hostage in Khartoum. Emperor Selassie and President

Nimeiri's visit was cut short as their attention immediately focused on the catastrophe. When the terrorists didn't get their demands, both hostages were killed. Sudanese officials arrested the terrorists, tried, and eventually convicted them on murder charges.

A couple of months later, in May 1973, I spent several days on a survey trip as a consultant in key centers in the southern provinces of Sudan. It was on this trip that I had the opportunity to observe the condition of some of the mission stations that I had built.

We started out from Ghimeera. As we cleared Sudan customs and flew over Nasir, I was curious to see that the mission buildings were still standing there after many years of war. We stopped in Malakal and were happy to see that all the old mission houses were in use. But a trip to Doleib Hill was a different story. Although a lot of work was in progress, sadly, all that was left of the two brick houses after the civil war were the walls. Things were badly damaged.

Also, Obel, my first job in the Sudan, had been destroyed and flattened to the ground by the northern army—including the destruction of all forty-five of my buildings at the Teachers' Training School. I couldn't find even one whole brick left. On this trip, I was with Mr. Kiplagat, the deputy general secretary of the National Christian Counsel of Kenya (NCCK), and he asked me how I felt about the destruction. I responded that out of the twelve ministers on the South Sudan High Executive Council, seven had been mission schoolboys. I expressed that, "the building of men is more important than the building of buildings. It had accomplished the purpose for which they were built." Interesting enough, their minister of education had been the last headmaster at the Obel training school that I had built.

While I was at Obel, many of the natives traveled from Doleib Hill for a reunion celebration. Everyone was glad to see us and gave us a big welcome, and I even enjoyed a good talk with my friend Adwok from Doleib Hill. It surprised me that I was remembered by so many, as they called out, "Jal Dong OK," the name they had given me in the early days. In their native tongue, they shouted, "You have come!"

I responded, "I am here." They remembered me as the Shilluk warrior—he who killed the hippo and the lion. The workmen on the buildings gave me credit for teaching them their skills. When I spoke of retiring the following year, Deputy General Secretary Kiplagat stated, "You cannot leave—you belong to Africa." (Mr. Kiplagat later became the Sudan ambassador to France.) Many also came to see us at the hotel, including the Nuers from Ler.

Physically the people in the South Sudan were never worse off, but spiritually they were never better. The church had grown, and the people were working together and handling their own affairs. I felt it was better that they be in charge and we work with them. We could see how mission work had changed. When we first went to the field in 1946, we were doing pioneer work where the local pastors and leaders worked under the missionaries or side by side with them as Christian brothers. The mission workers knew the people and their language. But as time passed, mission work became a community development endeavor—more just technical help and training.

Plans had to be altered on our survey trip to the South Sudan. Not only was our plane grounded due to engine trouble, but some hyenas ate the tire off the tail wheel of the plane in Malakal. It was several days before a new tire was sent from Khartoum and we were able to continue on our trip. In the meantime, I attended a full communion service at a Shilluk church with lots of young people. I walked along the river and saw the old *Omdurman*, the first steamer we used back in 1947 to traverse the Nile, still in use.

With our new tire, we continued on. Our next stop was Pibor where we met friends from the Murle tribe and saw the

old mission site. The hospital was still in fair shape, but the
Arcon house was badly wrecked and the Swart house was
down. The shop had walls but no roof. I was informed that
three hundred people had been baptized the prior week.

For a short time, we stopped in the village of Akobo where
the merchants gave us a big welcome, and then it was back to
Malakal where we refueled. Weather problems delayed us
here, allowing time to talk about clinics and visit the native
market where we once again met old friends, including many
Shilluk women. From Malakal, it was on to our final destination, Juba, and to the ACROSS house where we reviewed
everything I had learned on my trip in the Upper Nile. From
Juba it took five hours before arriving back at Ghimeera. It
had been a good trip, but I was glad to be home.

COMMUNITY DEVELOPMENT

In 1973, we had been in Ethiopia ten years. By this time,
due to lack of funds, there had been a cut in overseas church
work and mission workers were brought home. With fewer
missionaries and personnel, the need for new buildings was not
as great. Because of this, when the necessary buildings of the
I. K. project were completed, emphasis of my work switched
from mission builder to community development. Where life
was hard, I tried to use technology to help the tribal peoples
improve their lifestyle. Wherever they requested help, it was a
challenge for me to find answers in books or seek out someone
knowledgeable on the subject.

My "jack of all trades and repairman for many" image
continued to be tested: I poured a new terminal for a truck
from Jimma that had a broken battery terminal; repaired the
front fork on a bicycle for a boy from town; helped the station
foreman discover the cause of a power outage in one of the

houses; sewed leather soles on Dolly's shoes; and made a solar stove for Omo. Besides these jobs, I tried to entice the bees inside my homemade beehive since they were creating problems in our mango tree, worked at getting my handmade soap to the right consistency, and made a drying rack for food. I experimented with making neat's-foot oil from boiling shin bones and cow feet, worked on repairing wheelbarrows, and made and installed the clinic turnstile. Horticulture interested me, and I budded a tangerine to an orange tree and cleft-grafted an apple onto a guava tree.

Since most tools were hand powered like those used by early pioneers, in my "free time" I designed an affordable sturdy frame saw for the locals called a bow or bucksaw. The twenty-one-inch blade for this saw cost just two dollars in Addis Ababa and the frame was made from native guava wood. Also, we experimented with other hand-powered tools: an ancient device made from a sapling stick, a leather thong or strong cord, and a wooden block called a bow drill; a bench-vise combination called a shaving horse popular for its sit-while-you-work feature; and a tub wheel, the ancestor of our hydraulic turbine once used in America as gristmills. Some of these tools were as old as the hills, yet as new as the morning's sunrise in this community.

In June 1975, I wrote in my diary, "Happy days." Dolly and I had been married thirty-four years. By October I started making up the triangles for our octahedron windmill towers at the base shop in Ghimeera. These thirty-foot towers were taller and stronger than the ones currently in use and had room for a pump underneath. Each tower was comprised of one-inch steel tubing bolted together into six octahedron modules, and if properly constructed should withstand wind speeds up to one hundred miles per hour. The tubing was lightweight and easily transported by plane to isolated areas.

Ethiopia, a land of many beautiful waterfalls, was a natural for water-powered grain grinding mills. It was foolish to use powered machinery during this time of fuel shortage when there was so much wind and water power available. I had received a notice from son Tom, which stated that he was planning to come to Ethiopia the following summer and would get college credit helping me with community development. I decided I would let him take over the Omo wind-driven grinding mill. I later received word that he decided to join the marines.

In the mountainous area of Ghimeera, the eight-foot annual rainfall had a tendency to leach out soil nutrients. Another one of my jobs in community development was teaching organic gardening in order to replenish the soil. We found that in most cases, those who had well-fed souls were the ones who were willing and eager to accept new ideas for providing food for well-fed bodies.

In October I worked with Appropriate Technology Unit (AT Unit), the Christian Relief and Development Association in Addis Ababa, on problems that had been sent to them. Development problems could be brought to this center with the assurance that the staff would strive to find solutions. The AT Unit provided information, suggested materials and personnel to use, and was a link between communities with similar development projects. They had many sources of assistance: village development workers, village craftsmen, government ministries, international aid organizations, missions, churches, voluntary agency personnel, and many others. The AT Unit also assisted by sponsoring seminars, providing a resource library, making useful reports available, and visiting projects.

One interesting project I researched was bamboo piping. Since my time was so limited, I commissioned John Morgan from Village Technology Innovation Experiment (VTIE) in

Addis Ababa to come and run my experiments at Ghimeera. My goal was to alleviate having to hand-carry water to the villages for domestic use, and to show that bamboo could be used as a piping material to carry water for irrigation of crops. A manual titled, "Bamboo Piping—An Experiment in Mezan-Tefari" (AT Unit Report, 1974) stated that at every thirty to eighty centimeters, the hollow bamboo stem was interrupted with inter-nodes that restricted water flow, so I fabricated a simple drilling bit to rid the bamboo of these nodes to allow free flow of water. To connect pieces of bamboo, local rawhide from cows and goats (and later inner tubes) was wrapped and tied at the joints. As the skins dried, they shrunk and formed a tight fit.

Bamboo, common in Ethiopia, grew to fifteen meters high and commonly had an inside diameter of up to forty millimeters. This size could handle a flow of twenty-four liters per minute, which was enough water to supply the needs of one acre of land. Since villagers were very frugal in their use of water for the household, one forty-millimeter bamboo pipe to a village tap could serve up to five hundred people.

Using the results from our experiments, John wrote up a report on bamboo piping, and I gave Appropriate Technology permission to print up an instructional manual for anyone who was interested.

"The harvest is plentiful but the workers are few," He told his disciples. "Ask the Lord of the harvest, therefore, to send out workers into his harvest field" (Matt. 9:37–38 NIV). At this time, we were sure that the folks back home were hearing many disturbing facts about the situation in Ethiopia. Many of them were true.

By May 1975, the Communists were taking control. I relinquished my guns at the request of the police, but before doing so, I threw my ammunition in the garbage pit. The police started to burn houses on our mountain in search of Finny Combs, the witch doctor. There was some shooting near our house and the body of a one-year-old child was found drowned in the channel. Not only were Bibles being burned in schools, but we weren't allowed to meet in churches. Often the church buildings were burned and the church had to go underground. No more than four or five could meet at any one place. Foreigners were being watched and accused of any irregularity. These truly were days of testing for Ethiopian Christians.

Eventually Emperor Haile Selassie was overthrown. We were told that in case of evacuation, all Presbyterian missionaries should exit their mission posts and go to the fourth floor of the Hilton Hotel in Addis Ababa. The U.S. ambassador knew our plans and we were told to always keep a small suitcase packed. Even though we were making plans like we were going to stay forever, I started selling off my personal goods.

In the meantime, our windmill project at Omo was not being neglected. We had completed twenty more windmill heads since our return to Ethiopia. In July we had spent some time at the Omo River Post, where there were two young volunteer couples helping with agriculture by irrigation. The new Dacron sailcloth that I had brought back with me from the States had greatly improved the efficiency of the Polomo mill.

There were many problems in this land, but we gave praise for the fact that during the past month, the little church at Ghimeera had been packed—two hundred people inside and fifty outside. The services seemed to be getting longer and longer, and one day it continued until after one o'clock in the afternoon. Forty new believers were baptized and 160 more had asked for training. If the Bible had been translated into their tribal language, it wouldn't have been useful since, unfortunately, many of the natives were illiterate. But truly the fields were "ripe for harvesting" (John 4:35 NRSV).

At Ghimeera, Dottie Rankin, a Presbyterian missionary in charge of the village schools, visited a small group which was meeting together on the Sabbath day. She inquired about what had happened to the witch doctor who used to live in that village. The witch doctor had been notorious for refusing to allow Christians to cross his property on their way to the waterfalls just above his place. Someone said, "He's here," and pointed to the back of the room. Dottie strolled back and, sure enough, he was there without his normal witch doctor garb or hairdo. It was amazing that he shook the hand that she extended, for in the past he would never allow a female to touch him—especially a white one. The congregation laughed and laughed and the witch doctor did too! We trusted that it was for joy!

Years later, after the Communists left the country and the church came out from underground, it was discovered that some of the witch doctors had become Christian. And to think that not long ago when a native was sick, the witch doctor took a little hair and some fingernails, plus all the evil spirits of the sick person, and put them in a magic charm. This charm was worn on the arm of the sick person. Donning a funny mask, the witch doctor performed a strange-looking dance to scare away the evil spirits. Costing the ill person two cows, this ritual didn't necessarily make his illness any better but he was afraid that he would be a lot worse without it.

November 7, 1975, had come and gone with no notice this year. There was no time nor family around to celebrate my sixty-third birthday. For the first several months of 1976, I was working on windmill parts (new type of swivel for heads, windmill tails), octahedron towers, and Omo dome houses. By March we had 706 pounds ready for MAF to ship to Omo. These were small windmills where the owners could live near the mill.

Tom, Ginny, and Leah arrived home that June 1976, and things really moved in the shop. Leah, then twenty years old, planned a class for seven sixth-grade girls at the Ghimeera shop teaching them to make knitting needles. I got busy welding the heads for the needles.

———•◆•———

For several years, the Ethiopian situation had been deteriorating and Ethiopia was in complete anarchy. It was every man for himself. We were living on the edge and had to have faith enough to be ready for what the next chapter held. Three planeloads of my freight was impounded at the Mizan Tefari airport and it got harder to ship goods and travel. It took more than one month to get the freight released. Word was received on the RT that Don McClure Sr., who initially was responsible for Dolly and me entering the mission field back in 1947, was shot and killed by Somali guerrillas in a raid at Gode in southeast Ethiopia.

The local farmers' association at Ghimeera was getting more and more demanding. They came to my shop and informed us that we could not move, sell, burn, or give away any of our personal belongings at the house or any of the tools and windmill parts in the shop. It brought to mind Hebrews 10:34 saying that you were actually joyful when all you owned was taken from you knowing that better things were awaiting you in heaven—things that would be yours forever.

While ruled by Emperor Haile Selassie, Ethiopia got all its military equipment from the United States. But the Ethiopian military officers overthrew the emperor in 1974. Socialism and its utopia promises of land for everyone, plenty of money, and every man working and sharing with his neighbor, seemed to be failing. Why, you ask? Perhaps it was the Chinese or Russians who were in Ethiopia acting as advisors or the Cubans who were reportedly training a peasant guerrilla army to crush the forces of imperialism. Big power struggles led to assassinations of the ruling group and mass execution of the opposing groups. Ethiopia's hunger and illiteracy were paving the way for a quick move from socialism to communism.

In February 1977, the Carter administration halted military aid to Ethiopia. We knew that it was likely we would have to give up our home in Ghimeera. We had mission approval to use the Omo River Post as base in order to continue the windmill project, and just a week before our move, we were assured that we could continue using our home and shop until March 1978.

Then on a Sunday morning, May 1, 1977, we heard a report by the mission secretary on shortwave radio informing us to take our large suitcase and plan not to return to Ghimeera due to the leftist military government socialist revolution. We packed and took the MAF charter flight the next day—and even as Abraham—not knowing where. We were kicked out and had no idea what the future held, but we knew who held the future. We walked by faith looking for another door to open, knowing that in our life with Jesus Christ, every ending has a new beginning.

At that point we were still expecting to move to the Omo River Post to set up our base of operation to continue windmill work. After a quick trip to Addis Ababa to pick up parts that had been on order at a machine shop, we went on to Omo. By then MAF planes were at risk of being nationalized and we realized our days were limited. MAF was making plans to evacuate their people and planes from Ethiopia. This would leave us with no means of transportation to the mission posts, so there was no choice but to leave.

In the twelve days at the Omo Post, we managed to erect seven more Cretan-style windmills on Geleb land and see the natives clearing the land and digging irrigation ditches in order to plant their crops by irrigation. It was satisfaction enough when one of the first baptized Christians in the Geleb tribe expressed in his farewell with the few English words he had learned, "Thanks for the bumps [pumps]!" We had asked for a two-week stay, but MAF requested that we leave a few days earlier. Actually we left on MAF's last day of flying. The police thoroughly inspected each suitcase down to the smallest tube of toothpaste—seeking to find hidden gold, guns, or other contraband. Or was it curiosity to see what sort of strange things these peculiar foreigners carried? We were allowed to take only those suitcases which would fit into one flight of a small Cessna.

Shortly before leaving Ethiopia, I reread the book of Jeremiah. It was amazing how things that had happened in Jerusalem in Jeremiah's time were going on in Ethiopia at this time—some good and some bad. God had said to me as well as Jeremiah, "don't be afraid of the people, for I, the Lord, will be with you and see you through," (Life Application Bible, The Living Bible, 1977) and He always has. A missionary's job is to work himself out of a job, but if I walked in faith, I knew there would always be another one waiting.

Bye-bye, Ethiopia. Leaving here was similar to leaving the Sudan: we were thrown out with a lot of work remaining and not knowing what God had planned for us. We did not think our work was completed, but God said, "Go." It was difficult leaving the only home we had ever known in Ethiopia—especially since the fruit trees we had planted from seed were just beginning to bear nicely. But we would rejoice if others used the fruit from our trees instead of them being cut for fuel and planted over with corn.

So on to Addis Ababa we went, where the guest house was full. Here we sorted; packed; shipped; got shots, visas and tickets; closed out our bank accounts; and changed our mailing address. It was so difficult to express our many farewells. Our secretary suggested that we go on to Egypt where Leah was teaching at Schutz School in Alexandria. Our youngest daughter, Ginny, on her way home to Ethiopia for the summer, instead ended up staying at Schutz as the director of their summer activities program. There were a million jobs to do at Schutz and I helped with the electrical repairs, maintenance, and built a walk-in refrigerator for the school. Then it was on to London and New York City to go over our plans at the mission office.

We were to be on furlough in the United States until the end of November. Since we had to come home to the United States early, we thought we would retire, then return on a volunteer basis. We had a reentry visa for Ethiopia, good for one year, if the situation stabilized by then.

Life always is and always will be a venture into the unknown. In August 1977, after thirty-one years of service, another chapter of our lives had ended and a new one was about to begin. Our newsletter announced the surprise that we were back in Pennsylvania. Folks kept asking us how we could smile. We had left behind all the belongings that we had accumulated in our home and workshop for over thirteen years, including many partially completed windmill heads.

We were fortunate to be back home in time to attend the New Wilmington Missionary Conference. The theme that year was most appropriate for us: ". . . for we walk by faith, not by sight" (2 Cor. 5:7 NRSV).

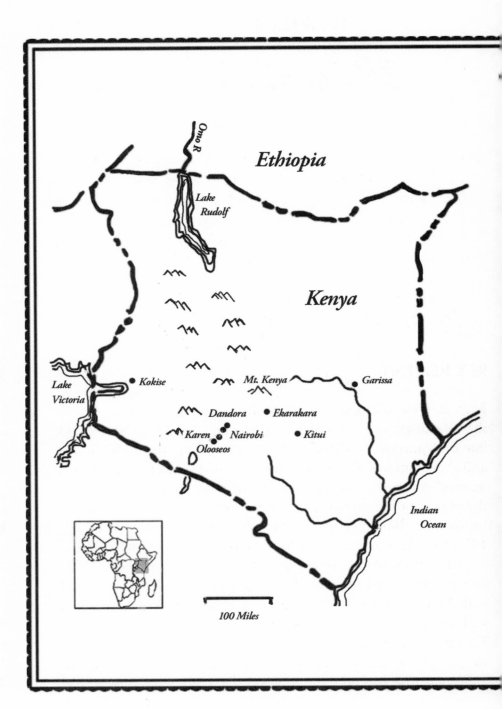

Omo R

Ethiopia

Lake
Rudolf

Kenya

Lake
Victoria

• Kokise

Mt. Kenya   • Garissa

Dandora   • Ekarakara

• Karen   Nairobi   • Kitui
Olooseos

Indian
Ocean

100 Miles

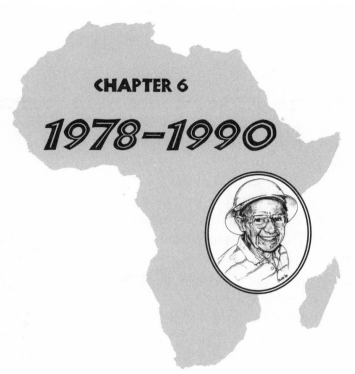

CHAPTER 6

1978-1990

"Oh, God of all creation, Bless this our land and nation."

—first line of the Kenyan national anthem

RETIREMENT

Back in New Wilmington, Pennsylvania, we settled into one of the apartments in the mission house. This mission house had but one purpose and that was to accommodate missionaries and their families while on furlough. Most often the house was in need of repairs, and I could almost hear a sigh of relief from the place upon my arrival. Sometimes there was a car available for our use, but since there was none at this time, we bought a 1970 Impala and made the rounds to visit all of our children.

My insatiable quest for windmill information took Dolly and me on a study trip to Brace Research Institute (associated with McDonald College) in Montreal where I talked with windmill specialists. On the return trip, we stopped in Vermont at Topsham and Ryegate Presbyterian Churches to check out the steeples that I had worked on some twenty-five years ago. What a nice surprise to find them in good shape after so many years.

In the fall it was time to hit the road again—this time a trip west to take youngest daughter, Ginny, to school at the University of Northern Colorado to study nursing. We tallied up 3,780 miles round-trip.

Back at our apartment in the mission house in Pennsylvania, I organized my Ethiopian photos and, since there were many requests to speak, I started booking talks. I felt no sense of completion after being thrown out of Ethiopia and was having difficulty getting excited. One day while working on a talk to present to Sunday school, I was tempted to call and cancel. I just wasn't motivated. But I had to kick the dust off my boots and move on. By evening God had spoken to me and I came up with an idea for my talk. As I always said, "God is good to me."

CHRISTIAN INDUSTRIAL TRAINING CENTER—KENYA

On the first of November 1977, we traveled to New York City to work on retirement papers. How timely that, while there, the volunteer office received a cable from the National Christian Council of Kenya (NCCK) inviting us to go to their country for a year. Perhaps windmills! And winter in Kenya sounded great! But as the Lord willed, there were many questions we needed to have answered before we could make the decision to go.

It was shortly after my sixty-fifth birthday in November that a note came from the mission office in New York City with a copy of a letter from the NCCK confirming their request. I was needed to do research and development on low-cost windmills that would be used to pump water for domestic and small irrigation projects in arid parts of Kenya.

In Nairobi I would be commissioned with a view towards establishing a windmill production unit at the Christian Industrial Training Center (CITC), operated by the Anglican Church of Kenya. In this effort I would seek to draw on the experience and expertise of other persons and agencies, both inside and outside Kenya, who had an interest in windmill development. Due to retirement, I now would be serving in a volunteer status and living on pension and P.U.T.T. funds instead of regular missionary appointment.

Back in 1975, the CITC was approached by an engineering professor at the University of Nairobi requesting that they fabricate a simple wooden-pole, cloth-sail windmill. Besides this request, other orders of different specifications and designs followed—all one-time jobs for CITC, purchased mainly by the National Christian Counsel of Kenya.

There was a great deal of interest in the development and application of what was termed "appropriate technologies" in Kenya. With an increased emphasis on harnessing natural resources of energy worldwide, Kenya tried to produce and erect windmills in various districts but with little success. According to the Windmill Production Unit Proposal (August 1978), it was believed that the most effective way to spread these alternative technologies was to introduce some of the more obviously beneficial products, like windmills, in rural areas. There were a number of research and demonstration centers appearing on the Kenyan scene, and CITC was one of them.

By 1977, CITC had manufactured fifteen windmills that were placed in strategic positions throughout the country. They had enough experience to form the basis for further research and production, and hoped to identify within a three-year period a more or less optimum windmill design that could be modified to suit locations having varying wind and weather conditions. During this research time, the windmills would be gainfully employed for village and small irrigation projects. Production and installation would be a major part of the project but certainly not the end. Maintenance and repair teams needed to be trained and would be critical to keep the mills up and running. So overall, the plan called for a properly organized production unit which could manufacture and arrange for sales and follow-up services, and they hoped to make a profit immediately.

This windmill project at CITC would be guided by a subcommittee composed of UNICEF, NCCK, CITC, International Development Research Centre (Canada), Faculty of Engineering at the University of Nairobi, Africa Inland Mission Technical Division, and Oxfam. The committee was responsible to the Board of Management of the CITC.

I was informed that my goal for the next year was to train Kenyans to build windmills using CITC plans. I suspected there would be very little room for originality on my part. It would have been difficult for CITC staff to travel, inspect, and maintain all the windmills in running condition so they requested that I be responsible for these duties.

December 17, 1977, was the thirty-first anniversary of the day we boarded a ship to sail to the Sudan to begin our mission work back in 1946. And here we were preparing for another chapter of our lives. This one was different though. I referred to it as "Retire, Retread, and Second Harvest." It was once said that a good Christian never puts his sword in the sheath but is always ready for the second harvest.

There were oh so many acronyms: we were going to Kenya under a church program named VIM (Volunteers in Mission), to answer a request from NCCK (National Christian Council of Kenya), seconded by CITC (Christian Industrial Training Center), and financed by P.U.T.T. (Pollock's Unfinished Tribal Training).

On January 3, 1978, we left for Kenya. Our stop in London allowed time to visit with Peter Frankel at the Industrial Training Development Group and then on to Cairo where daughter Leah met us. Since we were instructed not to go to Kenya until we had work permits, we busied ourselves ten days at Schutz School in Alexandria, Egypt, where Leah was working. There was always work to be done there.

While waiting for our Kenyan work permits, we applied for a Sudan visa so we could visit the capital city of Khartoum and see old sites and friends. It was good to be back in the Sudan for a week-long stay, but the ubiquitous bullet holes were a testament to the unsettled conditions there, and, besides, it brought back memories of being thrown out of the country in 1962.

During this waiting time, we also managed to squeeze in a side trip to the lovely tropical islands of Seychelles in the Indian Ocean. Normally Dolly did a good job of keeping my hair trimmed, but with no hair clippers available on this trip, we had to make alternative plans. One day I paid a dollar to have a scissor cut sitting on a chair outdoors under a tree in Victoria, the capital city of Seychelles. Normally a haircut was no big deal, but this was the first time that I had gone to a "barbershop" in over twenty-five years.

Kenya was different from other countries where we had worked. Its leaders were Christian and they welcomed outside help as long as it did not take jobs away from native Kenyans.

In February we arrived in my favorite African city, Nairobi. This tourist town was home to many game parks and the Christian Industrial Training Center was located in its suburbs.

When I arrived, CITC had windmills set up, but none were in working order. I spent time reading their windmill file and realized they had a lot of problems—or should I say— opportunities. There were still many requests for new mills, but first I had to determine what repairs were needed on those that were broken down. Also, we had to consider cost, ease of operation, and output, and agree upon a finalized standard efficient windmill design before proceeding with production.

In order to learn from each model produced, we needed to manufacture only one machine at a time, each one incorporating new variations. For this prolonged research program on windmill development, rigorous field and lab tests would be required. It would be imperative to maintain efficient records in order to give successive researchers involved in this program the past history of each windmill.

Similar to some parts of the Sudan and Ethiopia, Kenya did not have enough rainfall to grow crops. But I knew it was possible to use windmills to pump water from drilled or dug wells, lakes, and catchment beds. I knew that the wind was free and eternal, unlike oil. Along with the need for water, there was a need for education in irrigation and a need in technical training for building and repairing windmills, water-wheels, hydraulic rams, pumps, and storage tanks.

Our apartment in Nairobi was located on the second floor over the workshop of the Christian Industrial Training Center. In very limited space, here 144 boys spent two years learning a trade in blacksmithing, carpentry, welding, and painting. When the power tools were running, the noise was devastating. But when the school was out of session, it was peaceful and quiet. Fortunately, my work frequently took us away from the school to study, repair, and install windmills.

Out the window of our apartment on the street below we could see the one-room mud houses where the local families resided. One latrine served the whole block, with children mostly using the drain ditch. Many city dwellers hauled water from a central tap where women stood in line to fill their bucket or pot late into the night. I could better understand why a cup of cold water given in Jesus' name, when just a cupful, meant so much. But it was all relative. Just five minutes away in the valley of Mathari, conditions were much worse. Thousands lived in cardboard and plastic shanties with no water or sanitation.

I cut iron for an octahedron tower at CITC and displayed it for the staff to see. For one week I taught the instructors how to build one of these windmill towers, hoping to replace their crude three-legged wooden style with this taller model that could better catch the wind.

Dolly enjoyed being a part of CITC and some of the boys thought of her as their new mother. We found the beautiful school prayer that hung in the chapel most appropriate:

Jesus, master carpenter of Nazareth
You have through wood and nails worked out man's full
    salvation
Use well your tools in this your workshop, that we who come
    to you in our rough state
May be changed to a truer beauty by your hand.

One day we traveled from Nairobi to the Catholic mission at Ekarakara where there had been a request for a mill on a site ten miles away. CITC had a mill ready to set up, and this would be my first mill installation for the training school. The locals and I worked hard all day on the prep work: clearing the site, digging holes, mixing concrete for the anchors, and anchoring the tower base. We worked straight through until 4:00 P.M. before I stopped to have even a drink. By 6:00 P.M. we had the tower base and anchors in place.

How we appreciated the meal that the priest at the Catholic mission prepared for us, although I wasn't even close to being satiated with the amount that was served to me. I was elated when I discovered that it was just the first course and that there were five additional courses coming.

Six weeks later we returned to set up the Ekarakara mill and were entertained by hippos as we camped in the garden along the river. Everything we touched was filled with sandburs, but eventually the mill was up. I had concerns about this type of tower since it really wasn't a tower but only a four-inch pipe column. Using my safety belt only made it more difficult to tie on the sails. If we made more of this kind of mill, I knew I wanted to make changes.

To support the two one-thousand-gallon water storage tanks at Ekarakara, the locals built a platform on poles five feet above the ground. The next day there was no steady wind, just gusts, and the mill only ran for short spells. We started to pump at noon and at 6:00 P.M. the men went home and left the mill running with the tanks a little over half full at twelve hundred gallons. From my tent I could see that the mill was running at thirty rpm. Suddenly I heard a cracking of timber and discovered that the platform under the tanks was going down. I ran to cut off the mill and opened a drain valve which prevented the platform from collapsing completely.

It was no surprise to me that this platform had collapsed. It wasn't sturdy enough to hold the weight of the water tanks, and I knew that the locals would have to redesign and make the platform stronger. When full, the tanks weighed over eight tons, but the locals had no concept of the weight of water. While installing the Ekarakara mill, various alterations and improvements were carefully noted for consideration in future manufactures. It was a poor design, it didn't work, and we never built another one.

The next morning we broke camp and two of the men carried the gin poles (a pulley used for erecting mill towers) for a distance, crossing the river bed. At this point I loaded the lengthy gin poles onto my truck with the ends extending way beyond the front and back. On the rough road, they whipped about and made driving difficult. One time the truck got stuck in the sand, and another time, it got high centered (stuck with all four wheels off the ground). This time I was unable to move and was blocking a busload of men on the road. Thank goodness, they got out of the bus and helped push while I steered.

Windmill board meetings were talk, talk, talk, and already I felt that one year of banging heads would be enough. It brought to mind Rudyard Kipling's poem, "If": "If you can keep your head when all about you are losing theirs and blaming it on you."[1] Every windmill plan and change needed to be carefully reviewed by CITC and I felt very restricted. Sometimes tempers got hot. Each group on the subcommittee had their own ideas and it was challenging to coordinate all of them. There was no use to promote windmill work because the school wouldn't give me the men that I needed nor let me bring in volunteers.

Often I watched the CITC instructors from my office window and could see that they were becoming knowledgeable about windmills. I went out to help only if it were absolutely necessary. I felt it was best to let them proceed without my help, but in retrospect, it didn't work. When I checked on the two octahedron towers that the school was building, I discovered nothing fit. They didn't follow the plans, therefore the angles were not accurate.

Since my assignment included a lot of traveling and field work, I was given a Chevrolet Luv pickup truck to use. I designed and built a cover for the back of the truck in order to store and lock my tools and haul camping supplies. I got a Kenyan driver's license and needed to familiarize myself with driving on the left side of the road and shifting with my left hand.

At the beginning of July 1978, the CITC chairman of the board flew me a short distance east of Nairobi to the Garissa mill project to check on the operating condition of five crude early-style windmills. Unfortunately, we found them all in bad shape. The welders had done a poor job and left much to be redone. They did not have enough trained men to proceed with production without someone checking closely on their work. None of the windmills had been working for the past year and one had been washed away in a flood. Another one of the Garissa mills had to be dismantled in order to avoid being swept away in the river, but it was in good condition and would be erected again as soon as the weather permitted.

Approximately every fifteen years, there was an extremely heavy flood in the Garissa mill area and there had been one in 1977. Before the flood damage, the farmers were impressed by the windmills and, if we could follow up with sturdier models, more people would want them. But at this stage it was important to get the old windmills back into action in order to keep the farmers' interest. I planned to rebuild three of the heads at Garissa to replace ones that were inoperable.

At the end of July, we left Nairobi with all the windmill paraphernalia needed to install the rebuilt heads at Garissa. Along the way we stopped at a park to camp for the night. Here we were reminded of the wilds of Africa: an elephant walked thirty feet from our truck, a lion ran through the grass a short ways from our tent, and, before breaking camp, five rhinoceros congregated nearby. Later that same day we saw water buffalo—so all we needed to complete the "big five" animals of Africa was the leopard—but no luck.

Danger was always present. While stopped for lunch along the road, a gang of bandits surfaced the hill and headed straight towards us. I instructed everyone to return to the truck immediately. I knew the bandits would have no qualms about killing us; in fact, I had learned on the news that people had been killed along this very route. With everyone on board the truck, I floored the accelerator and sped in the direction of the bandits. As they ran, the group split wide open allowing us to pass. Amazingly enough we were able to get away without any trouble.

At Garissa we rebuilt heads, rotor, and tail, and put them back on the old towers. All the windmills at Garissa needed some kind of repair work and were bad advertising. We needed to do experimentation followed up with design improvements.

The village of Dandora, another of the CITC projects, was an urban self-help housing project composed of lower-income families struggling to construct new homes. High building costs and the daily expense of city living competed for the little money the locals earned, with nutritional concerns completely overlooked. Early in 1977, Nairobi City Council's Dandora Development Project received a promise of financial support from UNICEF to develop not only a demonstration fruit and vegetable shamba (small garden) but also a nutrition center within the urban community. The National Christian Council of Kenya was asked to supervise.

The objective of the urban demonstration garden and the adjoining nutrition center was to give free instruction to each member of the community in simple, productive methods of intensive, organic gardening, small pond fish culture, and raising of small livestock. It demonstrated how a family with little land could meet its nutritional requirements and provide the community with a new market of fresh, low-cost food. The final goal of the project was to obtain self-sufficiency and to demonstrate maximum land usage at minimum cost from the acre of land comprising the shamba. The hope was to encourage suburban neighbors to take advantage of the little open space around their homes, to lower their food budget, and improve their health by planting kitchen gardens. It was hoped that the shamba and the nutrition center would aid considerably in the economic struggle of many of the families.

In addition, to help establish an irrigation system, UNICEF made a donation to purchase a CITC wind pump, plastic pipeline, and materials to construct a storage tank on the shamba. The wind pump would pump water from an old forty-foot-deep stone quarry in order to irrigate their gardens. In October 1978, we picked a site for the mill and in January we took the thirty-foot octahedron tower-Polomo mill with cloth sails out to the site and set it up. By the end of the month the mill was pumping quite efficiently.

But one day the mill was left unattended, and rain, accompanied with a strong wind, bent the top of the tower. The mill had to be taken down, brought back to the center for repairs, and replaced with a commercial mill. I was very disappointed. I wrote in my diary, "The commercial mill is pumping so well now they don't know what to do with all the water." We eventually discovered the cause of the trouble with the Polomo mill.

One evening Dolly and I left CITC and went into town to hear Dr. Richard Leaky, the noted anthropologist, speak. Dr. Leakey had made important discoveries in eastern Africa concerning the origin of the human species. His father, Dr. Louis Leakey, a noted paleontologist who had worked in Kenya, was asked in 1966 by Emperor Haile Selassie to organize an expedition to Ethiopia. Emperor Selassie had hopes that Dr. Louis Leakey would make an exciting "find" in his ancient country. "Dr. Leakey's arrival at the Omo River Post in Ethiopia was the first step in fulfilling the emperor's request," Morrie Swart tells in her book, *The Call of Africa*. According to Swart, it became known as the Omo Research Expedition and was located approximately forty miles north of our mission station in Ethiopia. Both Leakeys were involved in the project and stored their equipment at our mission station at Omo. How privileged I was to learn that I had kept my supplies in the same storehouse with these world-renowned scientists!

On August 22, 1978, President Kenyatta, the first president of the Republic of Kenya, died. I remembered seeing Kenyatta in a parade back in 1948 during the time of the Mau Mau, the secret movement composed of Africans who wanted to end European colonial rule in Kenya. I was amazed how this Christian country expressed their reverence and literally closed down for twelve days while the body laid in state. Church choirs sang hymns during the viewing, and all bars, movies, nightclubs, and other forms of entertainment were closed. Only religious music was played on the radio and television.

On August 31, many VIPs were in town for the funeral and because of the mobs of people present, we chose to listen to the service on the radio. Dr. Daniel arap Moi was installed as second president of the Republic of Kenya and we were present when he honored St. Andrew's Presbyterian Church in Nairobi with his presence by reading the scripture lesson. The bulletin stated, "As you know, when the good Lord took the soul of our beloved father of the nation, the late Mzee Momo Kenyatta, to rest with him, all Christians in Kenya gave you a new name of Joshua, who took over leadership of the people of Israel from Moses."

Many people were interested in windmills and I had a Polomo mill with octahedron tower pumping at the Nairobi Trade Show in September. It was great advertising for the CITC mills, but what good was advertising if there were problems with production?

Tourism was a major contributor to Kenya's economy—especially travelers desiring to view and photograph wildlife. On several occasions while in Kenya, we took advantage of some of the local sights. One weekend we traveled north of Nairobi to one of the big parks and spent a night at the Ark Lodge. Deep in the mountain forest, at seventy-five hundred feet, this glassed-in lodge overlooks a water hole (with natural salt lick) where animals pass by throughout the night. The glass allowed for a close-up view of elephants, warthogs, hyena, Cape buffaloes, giant forest hogs, rhinos, bushbucks, Senet cats, and Colobus and Sykes monkeys that entertained us with their presence. A "spotter" kept watch throughout the night and buzzed our rooms when he saw something of interest. At 2:00 A.M. we were notified that a rhino had made an appearance.

One time we stayed overnight at the Outspan Hotel with its beautiful gardens and spectacular view of Mt. Kenya. Lord Baden-Powell, the founder of the Boy Scouts, had a home located next to the hotel where he spent the final days of his life.

On another trip we stayed at Treetops, a lodge also located in a park north of Nairobi. It was unusual in that its rooms were built on poles in the tops of Cape chestnut trees. Here we climbed the tall stairs and could view, from our beds, animals that came to drink at the small lake. An interesting note is that years before, Princess Elizabeth was staying at Treetops when she received word that her father,

King George VI of England, had died. Princess Elizabeth then became Elizabeth II, Queen of England.

The CITC had an office located at Kisumu in the Lake Victoria area, and in April 1978, we traveled from this office over one hundred kilometers to the Kokise Agricultural Training Center. At the village of Kokise, they were interested in two windmills. The site for one of the mills was located halfway up a hill and I couldn't help but wonder if, instead of using a windmill to pump from Lake Victoria, it might be better to try a well. But in November 1978, a six-bladed, cloth sail windmill was installed and initially it worked quite efficiently. But there were mechanical faults within the mill and it was decided that the whole windmill tower needed to be disconnected and the faults needed to be corrected. It was the same problems as Dandora: CITC didn't use the proper materials to construct it nor did they control it properly. Another base had to be made and the pump rod straightened before erecting the mill again.

What pleased me most at Kokise were the two schoolgirls who came to my tent and said "thank-you" for the hard work. If we managed to get water to the top of the hill, it would be the girls and women who would benefit the most since they were the ones who carried the water up the hill from the lake.

From our tent at Lake Victoria that night, we viewed a storm below the dark clouds at Mt. Homa. The brilliant sky glowed with the illumination of St. Elmo's fire, a phenomena visible only in complete darkness occurring during thunderstorms or other times when electrified clouds are present.

Months later we received word that the octahedron tower I had originally put up at the Kokise Agriculture Center had buckled and collapsed. Octahedron towers were taller, lighter, and easier to transport, but the many bends and angles of the tubing created problems for the students at CITC.

Unfortunately, the specifications weren't followed and the material used was too light. Since the octahedron tower was my design, I took the blame for its collapse and the chairman of the committee decided it was time for me to go.

In an attempt to correct the situation at Kokise, I planned to erect a commercially made mill from South Africa—that was until I was informed they no longer wanted a windmill. Due to the mill's many problems, the bishop of the Anglican church promised to replace it with a diesel pump. Replacing mills with diesel pumps was common for the Anglican church all throughout Kenya. Unfortunately, the mill that I had ordered from South Africa had already been shipped to Nairobi and would leave P.U.T.T. holding the bill, including the six hundred dollars for trucking. At Kokise one of the foremen from CITC and I dropped the tower, took it apart, and tied it into bundles ready to be shipped back to Nairobi. No one would help us unless I paid them high wages, so we did it ourselves. What a day and what a group to work with! I wrote in my diary, "Someday I'm going to lose my patience."

After the conclusion of another windmill committee meeting, I felt like I was wasting my time and was a fool for coming to help at CITC. Perhaps I should have stayed in the States to enjoy my retirement. I felt like the man in the middle, being pulled at one end by the supplier of the windmills and at the other end by the new windmill owners.

On the first of February 1979, I got a cable from Penny saying my dad had died. I got a call through to Canonsburg and talked to Mother. I learned that Dad was to be buried on February 3. I was the oldest of the eleven children and Mother always turned to me. I felt that she really wanted me to be there, so immediately Dolly and I got packed for a trip to the United States. God had given Mother peace and strength, and she was taking it well. All five of my brothers and four sisters were present, plus many friends and family. I was proud of our family lineage with its 101 direct descendants.

Dad's funeral in Canonsburg was different from the last funeral I had attended. Not only were there no pallbearers, but the hearse took the coffin on to the cemetery while the service was being held at the funeral home. I would have preferred to have his body at the funeral home service and also with us in the chapel at the cemetery. I particularly noticed how impersonal it felt when the pastor didn't mention Dad's name during the entire service. I didn't like these changes. Several days after his funeral, I helped my five brothers sort Dad's clothes and clean out his shop in the basement.

On February 18, we returned to Kenya and were glad to be back where it was warm. While I was gone, work on the CITC windmill had stopped. Evidently they were afraid to continue on their own without more training and it was an omen of what would happen once I left here for good.

It was no real surprise to me that due to difficulties, including lack of both training and preparation for mass production using advanced technology, the management committee of CITC agreed that the windmill project should be discontinued for the time being. As a consequence, I found out in the beginning of March that our time would be terminated with CITC in May—which happened to be when Dolly and I had plans to leave anyways. I suspected this meant that CITC would give up building windmills permanently.

It wasn't long before I went to the NCCK and confirmed that we were finished at the training center. I was informed that the chairman of the windmill production committee felt that the project wasn't progressing fast enough and wasn't making enough money. CITC minutes revealed the same: "The figure on account showed that windmill production is on the red. And it has strains with other production items. Therefore the windmill production objectives are not fulfilled."

I let the management committee know I wanted to finish up the three mills we were currently working on before leaving in May, and the staff was cooperative. The NCCK felt it was important to do a postmortem on the project in order to identify what was learned and which aspects of the project were particularly deficient. Unfortunately, my involvement with the CITC windmill projects was not successful but then I wasn't naïve enough to think that every mission project would be. I knew that I might fail in one but succeed in another.

On April 11, there was a farewell party at CITC for us. As I had requested, there was work to be done on several projects before my departure. In the last few weeks, on April 19, 1979, we arrived at the Maasai Rural Development Center at a place called Olooseos, run under the auspices of the Presbyterian Church of East Africa.

Olooseos, thirty-five kilometers from Nairobi, had marginal rainfall of about forty inches per year with frequent droughts. The inhabitants of the area were nomadic Maasai who depended on livestock for their livelihood. At the request of the local leaders, a church had been started here in 1968, and three full primary schools were in operation, with four more under construction. (Reverend Lowrie Anderson, previously mentioned in the chapter on the South Sudan, started work here.) The objective at Olooseos was to help the Maasai people realize their potential, improve their way of life, and hence help themselves. To achieve these objectives the center was broken down into four branches: medical, agriculture, education and evangelism, and outreach.

At Olooseos we found a fourteen-foot Dempster windmill from Nebraska that had been in pieces for ten years, with no one available to erect it. I located some of the windmill parts in a shed, but others had to be dug out of the grass and weeds outdoors. After reworking the parts and erecting it, the mill looked good and was functioning from a deep 168-foot well. Approximately twenty hours per day, it pumped one hundred gallons per hour to the main tank at the center. This was near well capacity.

Shortly after my mill work at Olooseos I received a letter from the director there stating, "When we see the wheels turning and water being pumped out of the hole, we feel like it is the wheels of heaven pouring blessings on to us." Everyone was delighted and I noted in my diary, "Time to let the young men take over."

In addition to the CITC windmills, there were other windmills being produced. Back in 1976, the Industrial Training Development Group (ITDG) out of Reading University in London had initiated a plan to develop a windmill that could be built and used in third-world countries—one flexible enough to cater to the particular needs and resources of different countries in Africa. This plan was started and inspired by our Omo windmill project in Ethiopia. I had been involved with the planning of this project through the years and stopped in London whenever possible to be updated on its progress. Six countries were requesting ITDG windmills and Kenya was one of them.

The Kenyan series of windmills, named Kijito, was a relatively simple construction with an emphasis on efficient operation. Initially these Kijito mills cost more than an equivalent size diesel engine, but once the payment was complete, they would have an economical machine not reliant on imported fuels. "Help Reduce Kenya's Oil Bill By Buying a Kijito Windmill," the ad stated. "Wind pumps can solve many of your water pumping problems. Wind is not imported, it will not run out, and it's free!"

By the end of April 1979, we had finished our work and felt that we had made an improvement to the Kijito Kenyan windmill. It was a successful business and the much-improved model was being manufactured right there in Kenya, with many of them exported to other countries. I declined an invitation to work for Kijito producing windmills after my departure from CITC.

After scrubbing up my tools at CITC and turning them over to the storekeeper, I cleaned out my part of the shop. There was no sign that anyone had ever worked on windmills there. Dolly was thinking, "Good, now you can retire."

But three days before we were to leave our tour of volunteer service in Kenya, the moderator of the Presbytery Church East Africa invited us to go on a survey trip to review the Kitui Mission Rural Development and Evangelism Projects, the center of the outreach. He told me that this was a part of our presbytery outreach he wanted me to see and help with, if possible. That was a full day, leaving at 6:30 A.M. and returning at 10:30 P.M. The Kitui district was one hundred miles east of Nairobi and over very rough roads. Many of the Kamba, the fourth largest tribe in Kenya, lived here and were a gentle, loving, and friendly people. Instead of the spear and shield, the Kamba tribe used bow and arrows. "Could this be another door opening with one of God's opportunities?" I wondered.

Only two-fifths of Kenya had enough rainfall to raise crops and the Kitui district was in a marginal area. For seven years the district had a drought and there was not enough rain for these subsistence farmers to raise crops. It was so serious that Christians from Nairobi took food to Kitui and held prayer meetings. The needs were scattered in approximately a dozen villages around the Kitui district and that day, we managed to visit five of the villages that were asking for help. They said, "We can do the work but we need someone to tell us what to do and how to do it." The need was great: churches, schools, staff houses, water wells, dams, pumps, and help with agriculture were all on the list. I firmly believed that it was better to develop a good life for the local people in the villages instead of them fleeing to the inner-city shanty towns to find work.

In May 1979, after settling up CITC accounts, we turned in the keys and were on our way to the United States. Upon our arrival in New York City a large group of mission personnel gathered to see the mission office present Dolly and me with a citation for our many years of service on the mission field. Normally, once a month, they held a luncheon to honor retiring missionaries, but this one was different—a brown bag lunch just for Dolly and me since they were catching us on the run. Penny met us in Pittsburgh with four of our grandkids and then it was on to the mission house in New Wilmington once again.

The duration of May was spent seeing my mother, our families, children, and grandchildren. "It is nice to have a chance to get to know the little ones," my diary revealed. "What a fun time we had today. Nothing but fun, fun, fun." There was plenty of food and games and the grandkids enjoyed sleeping in tents in the backyard. Sunday morning twenty of the family went to church on Father's Day. What a grand Father's Day present.

It wasn't long before the P.U.T.T. committee gave us their thumbs up for our return to work with the Presbyterian Church of Kenya. But I have always been good at thinking up excuses. I said, "Lord, I am retired. Let someone else go. There is too much work and I cannot do everything. I am old, send a younger man."

But the Lord said to me, "You can not do everything but you can do something." So we prayed about it and the decision was made to return to Kenya.

While in the United States, time permitted me to reroof the Canonsburg house and I noted in my diary, "I can still carry an eighty pound bundle of shingles up the ladder—although it is a little harder than it was twenty-five years ago." I also noted that, while laying shingles that day, I had done over two thousand knee bends and my legs were stiff.

In the fall of 1979, Dolly and I left Pennsylvania and traveled by car to New Mexico State University where I was registered for a course in windmill technology. Our son Tom and a mission worker, Bob Kraft, would be joining me to take the course. During the six-thousand-mile round-trip out west, we toured the Dempster windmill plant in Nebraska in order to price mills to be used in Kenya and stopped in New Mexico to do research on passive solar houses.

Mornings for the sixteen students in the windmill course were filled with lectures and book learning, while the afternoons were spent on site taking apart old mills, cleaning, and repairing them. One day during this course I showed the students how to cut a fresh cowhide into strips and use it to attach the wood blades to the spokes. We finished rebuilding an old mill and had it running, and it looked great. I was proud to graduate with a certificate for successful completion of the curriculum in windmill technology, since it was the only "diploma" I had ever received.

After returning from New Mexico, I tallied up the number of miles we had traveled since arriving home from Kenya. We had driven 12,695 miles and due to my obsession with numbers, figured that the cost of the car and all the expenses averaged twenty cents per mile.

At a P.U.T.T. meeting at the end of October, my windmill order and estimates were approved. Now it was time for us to return to work at Kitui in Kenya with the Presbyterian Church of East Africa, and we did it by way of the ITDG in London.

Arriving back in Kenya, there was time to kill before the Presbyterian Church of East Africa was ready for us to begin work on their program at Kitui. In the meantime we were happy to help with the installation of some windmills in Nanyuki, a large village north of Nairobi. This project evolved into an ecumenical effort with people from many organizations helping. Also, I helped a team put a head on three mills in Wajir, a very hot and dessert-like part of Kenya, where three windmills were erected at a therapy hospital for crippled children. A group of dedicated Italian Christian women not only ran the hospital, but they also oversaw the operations of a government tuberculosis clinic across the road. This collection of volunteer helping hands was hard to explain or understand, but they all worked hard and enjoyed it. Surely the Lord was there.

One Sunday in November at Wajir, our boss insisted that we work. I disagreed. I felt strongly about Sundays being the Lord's Day and a day of rest. He was the boss on this job so we worked, but we didn't have God's blessing. Things did not go well. I wrote in my diary, "My week has been spoiled since I worked on Sunday. It hasn't been a good week. So many things have gone wrong." By the time the next Sunday rolled around, it was good to have a day just to read, sleep, and write letters to our seven children.

Another adventure was about to begin as the Pollocks and mission worker Bob Kraft arrived at Kitui on December 5, 1979. We were grateful to the Presbyterian Church of Kenya, Nairobi Presbytery, for the pleasant little two-bedroom house at the edge of town they had rented for us, and we began setting up house-keeping. The apartment had a kitchen, dining room, and running water, but was without electricity or telephone. Even though our furnishings were nothing more than a camp cot and a charcoal burner, it was still more than many of the locals had.

Traveling around the seventy-mile Kitui district was slow going since we had to rely on the *mattau*, a pickup truck that was used for public transportation. There were no schedules, so this method of traveling was very unpredictable and ran only when full. When making the one-hundred-mile trip from Kitui to Nairobi, it stopped at every little village along the way, and several times in between, for a total of fifty-one stops. It took six hours to go 165 kilometers—a good way to develop patience.

I was always amazed at the way the Kenyan Christians witnessed for their Lord. One day we were traveling by van from Nairobi to Kitui with a Presbyterian prison chaplain. Due to a heavy storm we were detained for forty-five minutes, and it wasn't long before the chaplain passed out brochures and preached a sermon. They seldom missed an opportunity to evangelize for the Lord.

The first days at Kitui were spent getting acquainted with Christians, inspecting sites, and listing needs. We visited shops to find out what materials were available and their cost. Our time was filled with surveying plots, drawing plans, making estimates, and getting government approval before beginning our projects. Kitui was different from many of our other mission projects since we were not here to introduce Christianity.

We were grateful for the patient help and valuable wisdom of the elderly Rev. Silas Muchina, the pastor who initiated the work at Kitui and oversaw twelve to fourteen churches. Indicative of the type of person he was, one time Silas had his suitcase stolen in Nairobi. My reaction would be to complain and report it to the police. Silas's first thought was to pray that God would forgive the thief.

The most urgent need at Kitui was water—with some villages three to four miles from the nearest water source. Water was carried on the backs of women or donkeys and laundry was done at the river. Cattle and sheep had to be driven many miles for water each day, and school children had to carry their own daily drinking water. In a good year light rains fell in the fall, with heavier rains in the spring. With the heavier rains there was a lot of runoff and the need for dams. One of our jobs was to help find sites for the dams and to build storage tanks at the schools to catch rainwater.

The local Christians at Kitui wanted to share part of their meager belongings with us (if only a chicken, a few eggs, or a banana) and sometimes we were overwhelmed. When we arrived home late, it wasn't unusual for them to come bearing a gift, perhaps three ears of hard corn and three green oranges, or a bowl of goat stew and green bean leaves. We always accepted with a thank-you, knowing full well they were giving up part of their evening meal. The extended stomachs of their children were testament to that. The next day we would make a special effort to return the gift with nutritious food.

Christmas in our rental house in Kitui had its own unique special blessings. Son Bill and his family arrived from the States for a six-week visit and set up their tent under a mango tree. Bill scrounged up a thorn tree branch for our Christmas tree and his two daughters made the trimmings. After a service at the chapel, we prepared a goat dinner (the only meat remaining at the butcher shop) with side dishes of cabbage, potatoes, and mango. A call came from son Ron in New York with the news that I was Grandpa once again—this time to their new son born three days before Christmas. It was the best kind of Christmas present.

At the Presbyterian Church of East Africa (PCEA) office in Nairobi, I was surprised to learn I had a female boss for my project officer. This was a first for me. Plans for the Kitui Mission Rural Development and Evangelism Projects had been completed so I could start designing and making estimates for the buildings.

At the end of December, I went to check out the Kitui site. Work had begun there by the Presbyterian Church of East Africa in 1976 at the request of the local people. The three acres of land that the mission purchased from the government was grown up with brush and some large trees dotted the land. This land would provide a location for a home for the project director as well as a nursery school, six staff houses, a hostel for students, and a site for a new larger church building. Son Bill, Bob Kraft, and I drew up the plans and were in favor of building the new church on a large flat rock there on the compound.

In the meantime a chapel was being used at Kitui that had been converted from an old post office building. Although this church was very small, it had several active members who were dedicating a lot of their time and effort. Some of the pastors had twelve to fourteen churches in their parish and the only way they kept them running smoothly was with the help of strong lay groups. In some families both the husband and wife preached.

During the church services, when asked if there were any special song requests, members frequently gave their testimony along with the song. Sometimes it was a song the person had been inspired to write. I was pleased to see that the twenty-four new Swahili songbooks that we bought in the States were in use at the Kitui church. I wrote in my diary, "The singing is much better now that there are enough songbooks to go around." The Kitui church was much like the Macedonian churches that Paul speaks of in 2 Corinthians 8:2–4: ". . . for in a severe test of affliction, their abundance of joy and their extreme poverty have overflowed in a wealth of liberality on their part. For they gave according to their means, as I can testify, and beyond their means, of their own free will . . ." (RSV). There is an old East African saying: Giving flows from a good spirit as a river flows to the lake. Giving is not a matter of great possessions; it is a matter of the heart. The river gives of its waters to the lake even though the waters of the lake are many times greater.

The new year arrived while I was sleeping. Son Bill worked on plans for the Kitui projects and I made up the drawings and estimates. Also, Bill made a map of the Kitui area including names of any new places.

On a day in January 1980, I felt good sharing with my diary, "Another day when everything fell into place. All the right people in the right places at the right time." I felt we were getting much better cooperation at Kitui than we did from the CITC projects. The people here were ready to listen.

PRESBYTERIAN CHURCH OF EAST AFRICA—KITUI

In the early 1960s, the Major Mission Fund, a cooperative mission program under the Presbyterian Church, supported national and international programs and projects in evangelism, medical work, theological education, general education, and self-reliance. Kitui, the center of the outreach, was the gracious recipient of some of these funds and acquired land in the town for the project. Besides Kitui, six other sites had been identified as recipients of the Kitui Major Mission Fund and land was acquired.

On January 20 we drove twenty-three kilometers to Kamuti Utonyi, one of the Kitui District projects, to complete construction on a church. The main road to the church was rough and dusty as we followed behind a herd of cattle and goats, along with many of the locals who walked five or six miles to attend the service. The church, sitting prominently on a hill, had been constructed of cement blocks made by its members. Throughout the week this house of worship was used as a school and was in need of doors and windows.

As we entered, we were greeted by the singing of a twenty-girl choir (sharing only two songbooks) and noted that women in brightly printed dresses and head scarves were in the majority. The pews were comprised of school desks with attached benches (each seating three people) made by the students from local trees that grew nearby. With one hundred people present, many had to sit on the floor in the back of the church. Not only was the cement work unfinished, but the metal windows had no glass or catches. Regardless, it made me feel good to see them making the most of what they had.

Here at Kamuti Utonyi, students used the Nairobi Bibles to read Scripture. There was a real need for Bibles at this time, but we had to wait until more were printed and shipped from America. An elderly lay leader gave the sermon, and a man and woman took the offering using long poles with a bag attached to the end. I could not understand a word of the two-and-a-half-hour service but I liked the way they said it. Thirty-five people signed up to be members of the new church that day. Basically they seemed delighted to just have a building in which to worship—and Christ was there.

A trip to Nzukini Primary School, another one of the Kitui District projects with the PCEA, revealed that it was in operation but needed doors and windows. Could it be that a student body of two hundred was housed in two rooms with only two teachers, and one of these was a U.T. (untrained teacher)? Each child stood as we entered the room and I felt the teachers did an amazing job with keeping so many students under control. The children brought bottles or gourds filled with drinking water to school and were requested to bring a small stone each day to be used for gravel when the concrete floor was installed in the school building. Women had to carry water several miles to the school, and to alleviate this trek, we built a cement tank to collect rainwater from the gutters we had installed.

It wasn't long before villages in the Kitui area organized their people and erected multipurpose halls to be used for schools and worship as well as community meeting places. Unfortunately they ran out of cash before completion, but funds from donations given by friends in the United States helped pay for doors and windows. Working with people who have taken this much initiative on their own was really a joy. Besides housing for a social worker, evangelist, and a handicraft teacher for the area, a youth hostel was needed. In order to raise money to complete this project, I was trying to come up with an idea for a cash crop. Two PCEA-sponsored primary schools were already in operation here.

From the primary school, we traveled to another of the Kitui projects, the pump house at Kathungo. People here had not requested aid and I had no knowledge of this village. One day I was traveling past Kathungo and noticed a large tank off the side of the road in the bushes. Eventually I learned this tank was two miles from the river up a two-hundred-foot hill.

After talking with one of the old men in the village, we were informed that there was a diesel pump down by the river. Evidently this pump was installed in 1973, and worked until 1977. How great it would be if the water could be pumped to the village tank and eventually to the villages.

The old man took Bill and me to the spot where we could see the Lister diesel engine within the pump house. We had no key to get in but could see through the wire that it had been a gift from UNICEF. After getting the key, we were able to start and prime the diesel, but it wouldn't pump water.

At Kathungo I learned that there were three wells in the sand out in the river. We dug through sand and silt and knew that the wells needed to be cleaned. We managed to get the diesel pump working well enough to know that it was repairable. We soldered #60 mesh wire around the foot valve to allow water to flow through, but at the same time, prevent sand from entering. Over a period of three months, I supervised this job and we were able to locate all the parts that were needed to make the necessary repairs. The village chief gave me a crew of men to make major repairs to the seven leaks in the two-mile PVC pipe between the pump and the tank. Since these leaks were caused by exposure to sun and erosion, the crew followed the pipe to the river and the wells, and buried the pipes deeper in the shamba.

Money was collected from the locals, Nairobi Presbytery made a donation, and we used contributions given by churches in the United States for this project. Besides my own, many peoples' efforts and funds went into this project: son Bill; Bob Kraft; the government water department of Kitui; the local community; and officials and laborers. In Kenya this is referred to as *harambee* (Swahili for pulling together)—everyone putting his shoulder to the wheel and pushing together in real Kenyan spirit. With the combined efforts of the Kitui water engineers, we managed to pump six to seven hundred gallons of water per hour into the tank on the hill. The project was working well and before leaving Kitui, we turned it over to the local men.

Plans for Zombe and Mulundi, additional Kitui projects, were approved by the health department. Pastor Silas felt that Mulundi was high priority and suggested a multipurpose building (church/school) since there were so many people but no church. This whole area, although available, was expensive and marginal as far as food was concerned. Due to drought, no crops succeeded for six years prior to 1977, and people were fed from government supplies. New projects, including wells, better farming, and grain storage would help prevent a reoccurrence of this in the future and it was estimated that three hundred thousand dollars would be needed over three years. This entire venture was an outreach of faith on the part of the PCEA.

When enough gravel had been collected by the people at Mulundi, work began laying the foundation for the multipurpose building. Since Mulundi was a new area and we had very few workers, the prison chaplain connected me with a prison official in Kitui who offered use of the prisoners to make the cement blocks that were needed. After purchasing cement from the local merchants, I sent the sacks to the prison and two thousand blocks were made.

Unfortunately, I could haul only fifty blocks with each trip from the prison back to the job site. After one month of hauling blocks, we had made thirty-five trips. As I unloaded the blocks at the worksite at Mulundi and starting back with my empty truck, I offered rides to the women on their way to market with their heavy loads of bananas or sugar cane on their backs. I became known as the "free mattau." An evangelist rode along with us and had a message in Kamba (the local language) for the ladies as they loaded and unloaded their goods. The truck on loan from the CITC helped tremendously with the Kitui projects by freeing us from reliance on public transportation and rented vehicles.

Zombe, another Kitui project, was a new area where land had been acquired but work had hardly begun. It was to be a center, the outreach for the area. Churches and a multipurpose hall were planned, as well as staff houses for an evangelist, extension worker, and dispenser. A demonstration farm was to be set up here to teach better farming methods. The river was one and a half miles away and water was the most urgent need. My job was to organize, plan, and survey for reliable water supplies.

One evening at Kitui, someone stole supper from our charcoal grate that Dolly had been cooking at our back door, kettle and all. Four boys and a crippled shoemaker were suspect, and eventually our kettle was found. The group was taken to the police station and a report made that I had to sign. Later I received word of the date and time to appear in court. At the end of April, the case was heard and I had my kettle returned to me—a lot of trouble for one little saucepan but necessary to maintain law and order in the area.

After obtaining all the information at the various Kitui sites, I met with the Presbytery of Nairobi to report on the projects. When asked how long it would take to finish the Kitui projects, I responded that there could be no conclusion. My goal was to plan and initiate projects in order for others to take over. Africans were adding to Christianity at the astonishing rate of sixteen thousand believers a day. These new Christians needed our help in many ways, not just money.

On June 1, Nzukini School held a farewell get-together for us where I was made a Kamba warrior and given a bow, arrows, and quiver. They said, "You have been on the front lines helping us fight our enemies: poverty, disease, and ignorance."

I was pushing hard to get done all that I could before leaving Kitui. I had hoped to be finished before this time. On June 5, we turned things over and left Kitui; we praised God for health and strength during our entire time there. After a stop at Amsterdam, we were met by Penny and four of our grandchildren in Pittsburgh.

I say my time spent on the Kitui projects in Kenya was one of the most rewarding experiences of my life, not because it was easy, but because of the Christian fellowship. No longer was my work directed by a committee of expatriates or missionaries, but it was the local Christians telling me what they needed and my helping them to accomplish it. I felt very much a part of the group. With their great need for water, we were able to assist the natives in repairing old wells and pumps and introduce the idea of cisterns for storage of the occasional rain that fell.

On March 15, 1980, a letter written to friends announced,

This is an official notice that we have retired. Our P.U.T.T. committee and the Canonsburg church have served most faithfully all these years. Now they plan to discontinue as our forwarding organization. Please send no more funds through them for us. The past two years we have continued on as volunteers in mission. Upon our return to the States this summer we have no plans for returning to Africa in the near future. We suggest that you, dear and faithful friends, find other projects and people to support as faithfully as you have us!

After ten years in existence, we were closing down the P.U.T.T. account. I wrote in my diary, "It has been a good ten years but everything must come to an end. Thank-you Lord." There were substantial monies remaining in the account and I suggested that any remaining funds be given to the Presbyterian Church, Nairobi Presbytery, for their outreach work—not only for Kitui but for new church centers in and around Nairobi.

That summer we received news that daughter Ginny had gotten married. Then in August we celebrated another daughter's wedding—this time Leah's. Many mission friends from Egypt, Sudan, Ethiopia, and Kenya were present for this wedding that was held at the Seventy-fifth New Wilmington Missionary Conference. This was the first wedding that Dolly and I were able to attend of our six married children.

On our trip out west for Ginny's graduation from college that summer, we visited our supporting churches. Many wanted me to recommend a mission project they could support—both large and small. Maybe it was a Sunday school class that was willing to donate money for a door or window, or perhaps money to help provide Sunday school materials for children. Often it was these donations that allowed the PCEA Kitui projects to move forward, and oh so many times we said our thanks to the Christian friends for supporting them. Our prayer was that some of these friends would go to Kenya to see the work going on in the Kitui district—not just to Nairobi and the big game parks but the real nitty-gritty of the Lord's family there. As written by Margaret Mitchell in *Gone with the Wind*, "What the eye does not see, the heart cannot feel."

On January 20, 1981, my diary revealed: "What a day this was with the Reagan inauguration and the photo finish of the release of the fifty-two American hostages from Iran. . . . This is the first time I watched an inauguration and the first time I have been in the United States for one since 1945. It is good to be an American." My mood changed when President Reagan was shot on March 30.

During our eighteen months in Kenya we saw the beginning of a revival with people turning to God. Nowhere had we seen such a love of the Lord among such needy people as in the Kitui district. In a letter written to me in 1982, it stated, "Your names are mentioned whenever discussions about Kitui come about. We praise the Lord for your love, concern, and accomplishment

during your time in this country. We have realized that sometimes services rendered by elderly people surpass those given by
younger people who have not experienced many difficulties—
especially in developing nations." Another letter written in
1986 expressed, "Your time at Kitui left a landmark. . . ."

A letter from the Rev. Bernard Muindi, secretary general of
the Presbyterian Church of East Africa, expressed our feelings,

> *You have said that although you are in the States, your hearts
> are still with us in Kenya. This is indeed a very valid state-
> ment because we know that you think very much about the
> work in this country, especially Kitui area where you spent all
> your time when you were in this country. The way you
> handled the situation is very much appreciated and we are
> convinced that what you did in that short period continues to
> speak though you are away from here.*

HOUSE BUILDING

After retirement, many friends asked what we planned to
do with our time. I replied that I was going to help our kids
build their homes. It wasn't long before Dolly and I bought a
house trailer to use as our residence. Often our extended family
met on weekends and camped out at the particular house where
we were working. "It was great to work with the family again
and we had a lot of fun. The nine grandchildren were busy and
enjoyed playing together," I shared with my diary.

Son Ed and his wife, Dorothy, had bought an acre of land
fifty miles north of Washington, D.C., and started construction in 1976. Daughter Penny and her husband, John, bought
a house near Pittsburgh and we helped them build a large
addition in 1980. Also in 1980, son Ron and wife, Bev,
bought a farmhouse near Rochester, New York, that they
planned to remodel and expand. When son Bill and wife,

Carolyn, returned to the States after teaching at Schutz School for two years, they bought a small farm near Rochester, New York, and built a home on it in 1981. In addition, Dolly and I wanted to find a place to settle where we could build our retirement home.

Each of these projects had their own unique set of challenges and opportunities. The three new homes were interesting because they incorporated different approaches to make them energy efficient. Ed and Dorothy's home is a sun-tempered hexagon. They used the hexagon shape since it has less external wall area for the same-sized house than a rectangular house, making the heating and cooling loads smaller. Sun-tempering is achieved by maximizing the window area on the south side to provide for solar heating in the winter. The eaves of the roof are made wider than standard practice so that the windows are shaded in the summer to reduce the cooling load. Since natural gas was not available, Ed and Dorothy went with a heat pump. Heat pumps were fairly new to the residential market in 1977, and these early systems were not very efficient when the outdoor temperatures dropped below forty degrees. Ed added a wood-burning furnace which was ducted into the air handler of the heat pump. When the outdoor temperatures dropped below forty, they switched over to the wood furnace.

Bill and Carolyn took a more aggressive approach to energy efficiency. They built their solar house into the south side of a hill so that most of it was below ground. Their house is a single story half-circle. The rooms on the south side—kitchen, living room, and study—all have large south-facing windows which are no different from those in a conventional home. Since the bedrooms on the north side are below the ground, they do not have the standard type of windows. To provide light for the bedrooms the family room in the center of the house is an atrium with a large clerestory (south-facing windows at the roofline). The bedroom windows all open on to the family room, providing them with natural lighting. One of the especially attractive features of this house is the large mosaic of a lamb lying with a lion which Bill created for the family room floor.

Because the ground temperature at Bill's house stays at fifty-five to sixty degrees the year round, there is no cooling load and the heating load is small. Most of the small heating load is supplied by solar heat collected through the clerestory windows in the family room and the south windows on the front of the house.

On the whole, this unusual solar house has worked well. At one time, there was a problem with condensation in the closets in the summer since there was little air circulation and the walls are in contact with the cool earth, but insulating the walls and using louvered closet doors corrected this problem. In 1985, after four years, the house was completed using volunteer help, and Bill and family had a house dedication with more than one hundred in attendance.

Bev and Ron's house, built before 1900, was not conducive to energy efficiency, although they added a greenhouse on the south side. I have helped Ron with his renovation work over the years. One incident that happened when we were working on the addition to their house shows how God has protected our family through all of our years of construction. Their house has a rubble stone foundation consisting of loose rock stacked without mortar between the rocks. At one end of the house we had dug out the sand to add a basement room below the addition. Ron and I were standing in the hole near the old basement wall when he noticed sand streaming out from the cracks between the rocks. He said, "I think we should get away from the wall because the way that sand is coming out reminds me of a dream I had last night. In the dream the wall fell down." No sooner had we gotten to the other side of the hole when the entire end of the basement wall fell over. Fortunately, the house was well built and continued to stand even with no support under the one end wall.

Dolly and I considered several possibilities as we looked for a site to build our retirement home. When Ron offered us a part of his lot in Pittsford, New York, outside Rochester, we accepted, since it filled most of the criteria we had established for our search. It was a good spot and I liked the idea of having a workshop in Ron's barn.

Our house was being designed by sons Bill, Ron, and Ed, and their job was to estimate what materials were needed and get them at the best price. In September 1982, after much red tape, the plot plan for our passive solar home was approved by the town engineer. Because of the moisture problems in Bill and Carolyn's house, Ed suggested we stay above ground and build a super-insulated house with high performance windows. Dolly insisted that she wanted a regular-looking house with windows on all sides.

Standard homes built to code have 3 ½-inch-thick walls with an insulating value of R-13 and R-38 in the ceiling. Our house started out with six-inch walls, but after adding insulation board on both sides, it made the finished walls R-40 and the ceilings R-60. This is a little more than specified in the design but the cost of the insulation was minimal. Because the house is so tight we installed an air-to-air heat exchanger to ventilate it.

Most of the windows on our house are on the south side, but at Dolly's request, we put small windows on the east and north sides (the garage is on the west side), and used windows fitted with Heat Mirror. This is a thin film placed between two layers of glass that has a metallic coating on it to reflect heat. Heat Mirror also reflects a great deal of the solar energy, so on the south side we used quad-pane windows—windows with two layers of thin film between two layers of glass.

To provide more light and solar energy to heat the bedrooms on the north side, we used south-facing clerestory windows. The slope of the ceiling over the bedrooms was designed so that the winter sun is reflected down into the rooms. In the center at the front of the house we incorporated a small greenhouse for Dolly's plants. The wall between the greenhouse and the living room is solid concrete and during the day the sun heats this wall, and the energy released from it helps to heat the living room. The house is a single story slab-on-grade. The floors in the kitchen and office on the south side of the house are tiled, which enables the concrete beneath the floor to be heated by the sun during the day and keep the rooms warm at night.

The kitchen sink and washing machine in our home share common walls with the bathroom, both as a way of reducing construction costs and to reduce the energy losses from the hot water pipes. Hot water is preheated in a solar breadbox water heater, a tank painted flat black that is placed in an insulated box behind one of the clerestory windows. The water is heated to final temperature by an instantaneous electric water heater.

Our house was originally wired for auxiliary resistance heating. The only units we hooked up were the radiant heating panel in the kitchen and the small heater in the greenhouse. The balance of the heat needed on cloudy cold days is provided by a small air-tight woodstove, which I use to burn about a half a cord of firewood each winter. My total electric house uses an average of 640 kilowatts and costs me $92.00 per month.

Since we intended to continue our volunteer projects over-seas, one important criteria for the design of our home was being able to turn off all utilities and walk away free from worry that pipes would freeze. One winter Ron monitored the house while we were away and, even with sub-zero temperatures outside, the inside temperature never went below forty-five degrees.

In the fall of 1981, Mother was taken to live with my
brother Jack. Mother had been living alone in our house in
Canonsburg, Pennsylvania, since my father's death. In
September I went to Jack's home in Canonsburg and was
relieved to see that Mother had good accommodations and
that she seemed to be content. Dolly and I had a pleasant visit
with her and as we were saying our good-byes, Dolly told
Mom that everything was going to be all right. Mom smiled
and said, "I know it is." The next day, as Jack was preparing
to take Mom to a doctor's appointment, she dropped dead at
the door.

————•◆•————

At the beginning of the new year, 1982, Dolly and I left for
the island of St. Croix where daughter Leah and her husband,
Dave, were working with the Lutheran Social Services of the
Virgin Islands. There were three cottages for the children at
Queen Louise Home (the orphanage where they worked) as
well as a nursery for babies. Part of the time Leah and Dave
worked in the cottages with the children, with their remaining
time devoted to maintenance work.

During our two-month stay, Dolly and I helped put addi-
tions on one of the cottages and assisted with enlarging the
nursery. Our accommodations were great here—a beach house
twenty feet from the sea and we felt like we were really living
it up. While in St. Croix, we flew over to St. Thomas with
Leah and Dave for a weekend. Not only did some of their
Wycliffe friends give all of us accommodations in their hillside
home overlooking the bay, but they also lent us their car to
tour the island. The beginning of March we were feted with a
farewell party by the staff of the children's home.

After our return from St. Croix, we prepared our
Canonsburg house in Pennsylvania to sell. This involved digging

out old books that had been stored in a trunk in the cellar some fifty years, with many of these books printed in the 1800s. We also sorted old papers from stored dirty cartons and burned the rest in the fireplace. After packing our African "trophies" and slides, I typed a list of our old Victrola records that were also stored in the cellar, most of them recorded before 1920.

Back at Pittsford, New York, in May, we were informed of an old barn that had fallen down due to the weight of heavy snow. If we cleared the site, we were welcome to have the lumber, including some big oak beams. It was a big job but I liked the idea of having the barn wood and beams available for later projects. (I used this wood to panel the study and a loft in my solar home.)

In August 1984, the Canonsburg house sold. That November Dolly and I traveled down to Pennsylvania with a U-Haul to load our goods and bring them to our new home being built in Pittsford.

I was unable to wrap my gift to Dolly that Christmas—eight hours of my time working on our new house. In January 1985, Dolly and I slept and ate in it for the first time. That spring I rototilled a garden, planted fruit trees, installed a strawberry ring, made a compost bin, and planted grapes at our new home.

Passive solar home in Pittsford, New York

We planned to transfer our membership from our church in Canonsburg, Pennsylvania, to the First Presbyterian Church in Pittsford, New York. We chose this church not for something that it had, but for something it lacked. Mission work was of utmost importance to me and this church had a lot of room for improvement. My goal was to introduce the importance of church mission work and share with the members the rewards that can be gained when giving their time, talent, and treasure.

In October I gave the Thanksgiving messages at Polk Presbyterian Church and at North Sandy United Presbyterian Church, both in Pennsylvania. In November I also gave the Thanksgiving message at Emanuel Presbyterian Church, where some thirty-nine years prior, Don McClure gave the message that called us into mission work.

AROUND THE WORLD—VOLUNTEERS IN MISSION

In July 1986, Dolly and I started making plans for our trip around the world, a gift to each other for our forty-fifth wedding anniversary. Our October 1986, newsletter expressed our sentiments:

> Here we go again! Yes, we are returning to the mission field for a short term of volunteer service, to visit and help dear ones working in the outback of Australia and in Africa.

> Forty years ago we left for Africa, sent on our way by Chartiers United Presbyterian Church of Canonsburg, Pennsylvania, and Chartiers Presbytery in Pennsylvania for, what was called in those days, a short term, three to five years.

> This time it is the First Presbyterian Church of Pittsford, New York, and the Genesee Valley Presbytery doing the sending

with their prayers and blessings, but for a shorter time, only three to four months.

At first we thought we are much too old. But now we hope this might be an opportunity for a second harvest.

When we left years ago for our time of career service, we left behind a house that we had just begun building in Pennsylvania with only the outside brick work and roof completed. We left that shell and came home on our next furlough and completed it.

This time we are already living in our passive solar house while we work on it. The inside is still not finished with the kitchen cabinets, carpeting, and painting still needing attention. As we did before, we are trusting God to keep our house for us until we return to complete it.

God is calling us to high adventure and a life of great discovery! Minor things will have to wait. Our life span is much too short and our days too limited.

This time we do not go by freighter as we did the first time, but we fly from Rochester on November 13 with one day stops to visit family in Chicago and son, Tom, in Los Angeles. [Tom had graduated from college and was working for Rockwell International in Los Angeles studying the aerodynamic loads on the space shuttle.] From Los Angeles we fly on to Hawaii and New Zealand to visit friends and then on to Australia to meet daughter, Leah and her family, (who work with Wycliffe Bible Translators) and visit some of their tribal work. We expect to be back to Leah and Dave's home in Darwin, Australia, by Christmas.

Leaving Darwin on January 15 and going by way of Harare, Zimbabwe, we plan to arrive in Nairobi, Kenya, on

January 24. In Kenya we hope to spend some time with the Presbyterian Church of East Africa, visit Reverend Bernard Muindi and his parish in Nyeri and their community development center, and go to the Christian Industrial Training Center where we lived and worked. Also, we want to visit Reverend J. R. Swart, a former colleague who is now working with the Orma Tribe, one of the hidden people groups where the Bible is being translated into their language for the first time.

Please hold the ropes by upholding us in prayer, as so many of you did the first time we went out to Africa. . . . We plan to return in March 1987, via London and Toronto, Canada.

I remembered the story of Paul in Damascus and how his followers held the ropes and lowered him over the wall. Once again we needed someone to hold the ropes. The people at the First Presbyterian Church of Pittsford, New York, were getting excited about our going to Australia and on to Africa. I gave the Minute for Mission testimony and the children's sermon, and the pastor sent us off with a prayer. How great it was to see excitement in a church that previously had little foreign mission involvement.

Not only were we looking forward to spending several days with directors of Wycliffe Bible Translators, meeting our twelfth grandchild, and visiting an Aboriginal mission station in the outback, but also we planned to revisit the Christian Industrial Training Center and the Olooseos project at Kitui. When I left Olooseos several years ago, money was available to drill another well and I had the second windmill to put up. This time I would be following up to see what had been accomplished. At Nyeri we would be helping Reverend Muindi, the former secretary general of the PCEA, with his parish of fourteen churches. There was a possibility that I would be helping with some building at the East Africa Training Center in the village of Karen outside of Nairobi.

[For those of you who have seen the movie, *Out of Africa*, Karen Blixen's (the white settler and author of *Out of Africa*) old house is still there at Ngong Hills.] Also, on our return trip to the United States, we expected to spend a few days in London at the ITDG with the engineer who worked on windmills with me.

On November 13 we left Pittsford, New York, on the initial leg of our trip around the world. After a stop in Chicago for a family visit, it was on to Los Angeles where we enjoyed time with son Tom and visited with retired missionaries at a mission retirement home. Even though our flight from Los Angeles arrived in Honolulu, Hawaii, at 2:30 A.M., we were up early and took a bus to the historical Kawaiahao Church. This church, known as the Westminster Abbey of Hawaii, was founded in 1820 and is the first acknowledged place of Christian worship in Honolulu. Here the message was given in both Hawaiian and English. The impressive service sounded somewhat like Pentecost, with the singing and the Lord's Prayer given in a mixture of languages.

From Honolulu it was on to the less-commercialized island of Kauai, where we were fortunate to meet up with the Krafts, missionaries from Egypt in years' past. Touring one day, we saw a quaint little church on the end of the island that had tombstones of early missionaries to Kauai. The posted sermon topic was "Between Despair and Repair, is Prayer." It made us think of all those back home holding the ropes and keeping us in their prayers.

We took a boat up the Wailua River through beautiful tropical Hawaii to the Fern Grotto near the center of the island, the wettest place on earth. The record for one year was seven hundred inches of rain, and true to tradition, it rained on us.

From Kauai we flew back to Honolulu to make our six-and-a-half-hour flight to tropical Nadi, Fiji, during which time we flew over the international dateline and lost one whole day.

Here we retired to a quiet motel with enticing fresh beds and caught up with sleep before booking a tour of Fiji.

The tour took us through the valley to the coastal village of Veiseisei (which translated, means dispersed) where a monument had been erected for early missionaries who gave their lives. A large church was being erected to honor John Wesley, the first missionary to arrive in 1835. Forty-seven percent of Fijians at the time of our visit were Christians, a large portion Methodist, and all were a part of the Pacific Conference of Churches. We took a ride over twisting roads up to Sky Park, twelve hundred feet above sea level, to get a panoramic view of the bay where Fijian canoes first landed centuries ago. Our tour guide, who gave praise for the early missionaries, was the first one we had met who had the courage to witness for Christ to an entire busload of tourists. We visited villages and saw local crafts and beautiful orchid gardens. We never realized there were so many orchid varieties and that many of them were shipped to the United States. After only twenty-four hours in Nadi, Fiji, we boarded our flight to Auckland, New Zealand.

Auckland, New Zealand, was an amazing city where most all the shops closed at Saturday noon and didn't reopen until Monday morning. Supposedly, this was time set aside for families to be together. What a wonderful idea—except for this time. Since we had missed both breakfast and lunch, we hoped to find a snack bar at a railway station close by. Upon inspection we found nothing. When we asked where we could buy something to eat the reply was, "It is Sunday, isn't it?" We were told we either had to eat at home or fast.

This time of year, New Zealand was lovely and green with many herds of sheep—ten times more sheep than people. Most of Auckland was built on hillsides, and we could see the church steeple from our hotel. Because of our late arrival, we attended the evening service at St. Andrew's Presbyterian Church. After the service, there was a time of Christian fellowship over a cup of tea. While there, we met a lady who had once served as a missionary nurse with the Sudan United Mission in the 1940s under Dr. Ronald Trudinger (our son Ronald's namesake.) Dr. Trudinger had served for a short time with the Upper Nile Mission of the Sudan. This was the same doctor that met us when we arrived in Malakal, Sudan, back in January 1947. Again, small world!

The next day, our tour bus took us to Rotorua, the cultural center of the Maori people. Our tour bus driver told us that he called his bus "the Rambo warrior" since he drove it over the twisting switchback bends. I told him not to worry and then shared the story of the preacher and the bus driver with him. In heaven, the preacher was assigned a very small room, but the bus driver's room was very spacious. When the minister asked St. Peter why, he was told that during the sermon many people fall asleep, but when they get on the bus, they begin to pray!

At another tour bus stop, we walked through the first part of Waitomo Caves and found them to be similar to many of the caves we had seen in America. We wondered why they were called Glow-worm Grotto. Then we were loaded into a boat and moved along in total darkness. As we looked up at the ceiling, the lights of thousands of glowworms revealed themselves—like viewing the Milky Way through branches of leafless trees.

Switching from tour bus to regular bus, we traveled down the thermal valley. The thermal craters illustrate the raw power of nature. Several contain boiling springs which were probably formed by violent explosions perhaps eight hundred years ago. At the time they were being used to heat water and generate electricity. We continued past the beautiful snow-covered Mt. Ruapehu with some of its peaks reaching up to 2,797 meters.

Briefly, we stopped at the town of Turangi and passed an interesting building with large sculptured letters on the outside:

"Church of the Cross," Anglican, Methodist, and Presbyterian. We were told that the Presbyterian Church of New Zealand was comprised of 500,000 members in 1,637 congregations.

After spending a night in Wellington, we took a ferry ride from the north island to the south and boarded a train to Christchurch. In Christchurch we checked into the historic Clarendon Hotel where Queen Elizabeth II had stayed during her early visits to New Zealand. How surprised we were to learn that our room was the exact one where the queen had been housed. Upon asking the cost of the room, we were dismayed to learn that this suite was used as a regular hotel room at the same cost as the others. How could that be—with its red plush chairs, royal tea cups, plus the loveliest view of the memorial park along the Avon River? The sad part was that this lovely edifice was scheduled to be torn down the following year and replaced with a modern high-rise. We spent an unbelievable three days in the lovely surroundings of Christchurch before flying to Sydney, Australia.

With the harbor bridge and the opera house, Sydney has one of the world's most beautiful harbors. The opera house, taking twenty years to build, cost $102,000,000. Unlike lush, green New Zealand, Australia this time of year was harsh, dry, and hot. After another twenty-four-hour train ride traveling northwest into central Australia, we met Dave and Leah in Alice Springs, where we took lodging in a mission house for one week. From the mission house, we traveled to the outback—two hundred miles southwest to the Aboriginal mission station of Ernabella where Wycliffe was working on Bible translations. Mission work here was started by the Presbyterian Church in 1937.

From Ernabella we stayed two nights in central Australia at the popular tourist attraction, Ayers Rock. Here Leah, her husband, and I accepted the challenge and made the climb up the huge (1½ miles long and 1,000 feet high) loaf-shaped rock formation and signed our names in the book at the top.

From Alice Springs we traveled north by car en route to the Summer Institute of Linguistics (SIL) Headquarters in Darwin where Leah and Dave resided and worked for a branch of Wycliffe. We gladly offered ourselves for six weeks as volunteers at the SIL post and marveled at the translators as they translated the Bible into many different languages. Wycliffe had an international staff with teams working in twenty language areas. In the past fifty years, Wycliffe had worked on more than one thousand languages in forty-five countries of the world, yet, at that time, there still remained about three thousand languages without God's written word. The goal was to reach the entire world by the year two thousand.

It was a real blessing to be with our daughter and son-in-law, and be able to watch our two grandsons open gifts and enjoy a typical Australian holiday meal of fish and chips on the rocky seashore at sundown that Christmas of 1986. Also, it was perfect timing to be there and have the thrill of watching our twelfth grandchild blow out his first birthday candle.

When it was time to leave Leah, Dave, and our grandsons, we flew south from Darwin to Alice Springs. Here we boarded the night train for a twenty-four-hour trip to Adelaide on the southern coast of Australia. With just enough time, we caught the Overland train for Melbourne and received a warm welcome from Christian friends at every stop.

Southwest of Melbourne, we toured the rugged southern coastline area—one of the most picturesque coastlines in the world. Here the strength of waves crashing upon the high banks along the shore formed column-shaped rocks. The most famous of these rock formations is "The Twelve Apostles" at Port Campbell.

At Port Campbell, we visited the Uniting Church and became familiar with its mission work. The Uniting Church, the third largest denomination in Australia at the time, was ten years old and formed when Congregational, Methodist, and Presbyterian churches joined together. The name Uniting was used with hopes that other churches would join them in the future. We worshiped in some of their churches and visited their head office in Melbourne.

From Melbourne we traveled north to Canberra, the capital of Australia, and on to Sydney. At Sydney we caught our plane to Zimbabwe and refueled in Perth on the west coast of the Australian continent. Flying time from Perth to Zimbabwe was a little over fifteen hours (7,949 miles) and a third of the way around the world. At a stopover in Harare, the capital of Zimbabwe, we arrived once again to the warm Christian fellowship at the Harare Christian College. From Zimbabwe it was north on to Nairobi, Kenya.

So many times, it seemed like we kept running into our past. In Karen, outside of Nairobi, we stayed with Dr. Alfred Heasty, the son of Presbyterian missionaries with whom we lived on our first trip to the Sudan in 1947. Dr. Heasty was part-time school doctor and part-time school teacher at the Nairobi Evangelical Graduate School of Theology, a three-year-old school with forty-four students. The school is located on an old pig and chicken farm in Karen and most of the buildings were in need of repair and adjustment.

Once people there discovered what I could do, there weren't enough hours in the day. I worked on purifying the water in one of the wells and helped add a room for a dentist's office. The students' apartments were the old chicken runs, and the dining hall, kitchen, and chapel were in what had been a dog food factory. This was one of two schools in Africa offering graduate work for pastors and meant that these pastors wouldn't have to go to America to study. Often times when the students left Africa for the States, they didn't return.

One of the students at the graduate school was Pastor Gahamya from Uganda. As a boy, he experienced government uprisings in his country. One time, the army came into his village and pointed their guns at him. One of the militia said, "Dig your grave. We are going to shoot you." His grandmother saw what was happening and said to the soldier, "These boys are young and still have their lives to live. Shoot me instead." So the boys dug their grandmother's grave and buried her. Gahamya became a Christian and a pastor and graduated from the Nairobi Evangelical Graduate School of Theology.

In Nairobi, we met many dear American and Kenyan friends in the distressed area of Pumwani where we once had lived and worked. We visited other Presbyterian work in Ngong where Johnson Muchira, the principal of CITC, invited us to his new home. I commented, "I can't believe you built this by yourself." It was very similar to an ancient palace. Johnson had written to me in the United States asking us to come and advise him on his water needs at the graduate school in Karen. The work would not be completed before leaving for home, but I was relying on the next group of volunteers to complete it. We were privileged to be a part of it.

At Kitui we revisited some of the projects and shared praise with the Christians for what God had done. As Dr. Wanjau, the moderator of the PCEA stated, "Your work in Kitui has grown from strength to strength. They have in Zombe a village polytechnical school, a high school, a dispensary, and a tree nursery." At Olooseos, where I had put up a sixteen-foot windmill, there was a four-acre garden, with the produce being sold in Nairobi. It was here that I had sent a second windmill to be erected.

We were asked to speak many times on our world trip. In a speech I gave at CITC, I expressed my happiness at the change since I had been there last, "I am glad to see you are giving girls a chance. It may mean that you fellows will have to work a little harder to keep up with the girls."

We had an opportunity to visit Stanley Ndog, a minister who we had worked with some years ago in Kitui. We remembered him as an evangelist, but this time he was ordained and pastoring in twenty-nine churches. Five evangelists assisted him, plus the lay leaders in each church. He, his wife, and five children greeted us with warm hugs and a meal of fried eggs, bread, butter, and tea.

Also, we spent a weekend with Rev. Bernard Muindi, former secretary-general of the PCEA, and found his work at Nyeri outstanding—but way too much for any one preacher. Not only had he initiated a weaving project for women, but he was raising funds to complete a church that had begun in 1970. He, too, took us to his home for a Kenyan meal. In both these cases, we ran into major obstacles trying to locate our friends, but we persevered and it was wonderful the way the Lord connected us.

We were thinking of our trip home as our six weeks as Volunteers in Mission in Kenya were coming to an end. In May 1987, we took off from Nairobi for the American continent via London, where we met up with friends before crossing the Atlantic Ocean to Toronto, Canada. Two of our sons met us in Toronto and took us on the last leg of our journey back home to Pittsford, New York. It was a beautiful blessed trip and we decided that the world was not so big after all.

Reflecting, we were welcomed by Christians everywhere, as we visited churches and mission projects, and worked as Volunteers in Mission in both Darwin, Australia, and Nairobi, Kenya. We were proud of the fact that this was the 150th year of the Presbyterian Church involvement in global mission work, located in eighty countries at this time, but were a little sad that the Presbyterian Church had sent so few

Dolly, Reverend Muindi, and me at the Nyeri Inn

career missionaries out in the past twenty years. More than 80 percent of the Presbyterian Church (U.S.A.) career missionaries serving overseas at this time were due to retire within six years. Instead of career missionaries, the church was sending out temporary workers who wanted to get the feel of overseas service before making a life commitment, but we knew there was still a need for career missionaries in order to have some continuity. Many career missionaries were lost when doors closed in the Sudan, Egypt, and Ethiopia following government changes and political turmoil. Due to lack of finances, many were not reassigned to other countries and took assignments with other Christian groups.

Our church in Pittsford extended us a warm welcome home as we caught up with the latest news of church friends and events. Since our home was not big enough to accommodate very many, on the Fourth of July, six of our seven children and their families converged at our new house with tents in tow. A phone call to daughter Leah in Australia had the voice of our seventh child on the speaker phone forty-five seconds after dialing, hearing as clearly as if we were next door. I thought, "Praise God for modern technology!"

Upon our return, the Lord provided a lush garden with plenty of vegetables to enjoy, freeze, and share. Besides the garden, I continued working on our passive solar house, helped son Ron put a new addition on his home next to ours, and was involved in building a home as a memorial for our retired minister to be used by those in need.

———————•◆•———————

In August, once again, we were en route to the New Wilmington Missionary Conference—this time the 82nd. One week after returning home from the conference, we turned around and headed back to New Wilmington for a youth work camp to repair the decayed area of the arches of the amphitheater that we had built back in 1957. Once again I would be working with Dr. Ed Fairman, who had been director of the conference for twenty-five years.

The New Wilmington missionary newsletter of October 1987, stated that "after twenty-nine years of snow and rain, the Auditorium was showing signs of needing repair." Once again my title was "work boss" and I instructed my work campers to do all the preliminary work: sand the arches; place brown aluminum covers over the arches to protect them from wind, rain, and snow; and top the covers with flashing. These procedures would allow the bottoms of the arches to dry out before the next step of repair. A second work camp, anticipated for the spring of 1988, would deal with the application of the chemicals to treat the arch dry rot and start to reverse the decaying process. And yet another camp sometime before the 1988 missionary conference would be needed to fill the dry rot areas with epoxy and complete the job.

I felt good celebrating my seventy-fifth birthday, and, at my physical, I got an "all clear" from my doctor. He expressed, "It shows what clean living and hard work can do!"

In a flashback, we realized that Christmas 1987 was very different from the prior Christmas in Australia. It helped us see the truth in the words of the hymn, "In Christ there is no east or west, in Him no south or north, but one great fellowship of love throughout the whole wide earth."[2] It really confirmed our feelings of the miracle of Christian fellowship!

TRAVEL WITH A DIFFERENCE

In March 1988, our youngest daughter, Ginny, blessed us with grandchild number thirteen. My response was, "He is a fine looking boy." Shortly after her grandson's arrival, Dolly discovered a lump in the right groin area and I took her to the hospital to have the lymphomas removed. This lymphoma was a treatable form of cancer and our family felt that she would be cured.

As the Presbyterian Church in America celebrated its two hundredth birthday, Dolly and I started planning for a mission trip to Asia with an organization called Travel with a Difference led by Art Beals. Instead of traveling to the big tourist attractions and the finest resorts, the "difference" in our travels would be touring through lesser-developed countries and visiting orphanages, mission hospitals, schools, and social welfare projects. One little setback—I was diagnosed with a double hernia and had surgery which involved eight staples inserted across my belly. The doctor's instructions to avoid lifting anything heavier than five pounds, I'm afraid, fell on deaf ears. A week later at Dolly's first chemotherapy treatment, the doctor gave his permission for her to travel. So, at the end of December 1989, we met up with a tour group of twenty travelers in Seattle to begin our trip to Asia.

With stops at Tokyo and Bangkok, we totaled over nine thousand miles before arriving at Kathmandu, the capital of Nepal. Nepal, 95 percent Hindu, had many Buddhist temples, most of them old and in bad shape. No missionaries were allowed in Nepal but the United Mission of Nepal had been working in the country for thirty-five years and it was interesting to hear its history. We traveled to the home of a Nepalese pastor and after removing our shoes, we joined the crowd and sat upon mats on the floor for the two-hour service. Here the churches were often an extension of a house.

On the first day of the new year, 1990, our tour group traveled by bus east of Kathmandu to one of the mountain trails along the Nepal/Tibet border. Since the trail was too difficult for Dolly to climb, I found a road she could manage and we walked up one mile to watch the sunrise over the Himalayas. Looking back, this was the highlight of our trip.

Not far from Kathmandu, we visited the medieval town of Bhaktapur and had lunch on the top floor of one of the many old pagodas. On the Nepal border, we toured handicraft shops of the Tibetan refugees' resettlement camp and visited the United Mission of Nepal hospital where thirty-eight Christian groups from around the world worked together.

We traveled an hour from Kathmandu over incredibly poor roads to visit a leprosy hospital. In many places, the road was too narrow to pass and had a drop-off of one hundred feet or more with no guardrails. One consolation was that the mountains were all neatly terraced and planted. Here our group ate lunch with the hospital staff while they told us about their work. I wasn't fond of the local food and, unfortunately, most everyone came down with diarrhea.

Our next stop after Nepal was an area of Calcutta, India, referred to as the Black Hole of Calcutta. This sector of Calcutta housed one hundred thousand people who lived in an area the size of three football fields, and sickness, filth, and suffering were ubiquitous. We were told that 35 percent of the food of India was consumed by rats and cows. It was in this area that Mother Teresa, a Roman Catholic nun, dedicated herself to the "poorest of the poor" in one of the most crowded, poverty-stricken places on earth. In 1950, Mother Teresa founded the Missionaries of Charity, a religious order that provided care and comfort to the poor in Calcutta, and in 1979, she received the Nobel Peace Prize for her work.

From Calcutta we took a flight to Dhaka, the capital of Bangladesh. Bangladesh stretches from the Bay of Bengal in the south to the Himalayas in the north, with the Ganges River one of three main rivers flowing over the flat plains and dividing the country. Bangladesh had been part of Pakistan until its independence in 1971. In Dhaka, we were bused into the countryside to visit the College of Christian Theology, an interdenominational school supported by various church groups. Our tour group also visited refugee camps which many had called home for the past ten years, with little hope of the political problems that sent them there being resolved.

From Bangladesh it was on to Bangkok, the capital of Thailand. Southeast of Bangkok on the Thailand border, we stopped at the U.N. refugee camps. Many Christian groups were successful in the running of these camps, including World Concern.

Diarrhea continued to be a problem for all twenty members of our tour group. With only a squat toilet on the bus and no water to flush, life was most interesting. Did I mention the bus made no rest stops?

Eventually, we arrived in the town of Hua Hin in Thailand, the final stop on our Travel with a Difference tour.

It was here that Dolly and I decided to go to the hospital in hopes that we could get medicine to ease our diarrhea problem. Since they were unable to diagnose the cause, we were prescribed three kinds of medicine, thinking that surely one would work. On January 11, our Travel with a Difference group had a debriefing, a farewell dinner, and disbanded in Hua Hin. But Dolly and I had plans to continue on.

The two full days by train to reach Kuala Lumpur, the capital of Malaysia, was not exactly what we had expected. Instead of individual cabins in our sleeper car, there were rows of berth end to end along both sides of the car with only curtains to pull. After two days in the same clothes, we were ready for a change.

From Malaysia it was on to Singapore for eight days, where we connected with Paul Hoekstra, a friend from our days in Ethiopia who had invited us to come and help him with his World Cassette Outreach project. This outreach had a soundproof taping room where they also did duplicating.

Singapore, an island smaller than New York City, was very clean with all its parks, lawns, and trees neatly trimmed. Since land was scarce and expensive here, many tall apartment buildings housed the multitudes. Two hundred years ago the Chinese came to Malaysia and Singapore. But at this time, most of the people spoke Malay and English, with even the older ones forgetting Chinese.

Because of the traffic problems in Singapore, there was a high tax on cars coming into the country and the government only allowed a certain number to enter. To prevent traffic jams in the morning, people coming into work had to purchase an extra permit. Driving was on the left side and many roads were wide and one way.

Since Singapore was short on water, it caught a lot of its own rainwater and bought a supply from Malaysia. The many drain ditches helped to recycle the water.

Friends from Michigan, counselors at the China Methodist School for two thousand students in Singapore, gave us a tour. We delighted in being part of the Thanksgiving service at the beautiful Kampong Kapor Methodist Church where they were celebrating their ninety-sixth anniversary. As we toured the city, the bright decorations revealed that it was Chinese New Year. In August of 1990, Singapore planned a celebration for its twenty-fifth anniversary as a republic.

From Singapore we took a flight to Madras on the southeastern coast of India en route to Kodaikanal. In my journal I made note that this Singapore airline was the best that I had ever flown, and this is significant considering all the miles I had under my belt. The crew was neat, sharp, and very polite, and I was impressed.

There is no other place on earth like India. It is a land that manufactures rockets and satellites, but where eight out of ten of its inhabitants have never traveled faster than oxen can pull their carts. At this time it had 850 million people with 35,000 babies being born each day. Of its inhabitants, 81 percent were Hindu and 58 percent were unemployed.

In Madras, I summoned an auto rickshaw to take us to the railroad station. What a rat race! It was rush hour and buses, cars, motorcycles, oxen carts, cows, and people were weaving in and out of traffic with the sounds of horns tooting, clanging bells, and the roar of engines. I knew I wouldn't like the job of a traffic policeman here, waving his white glove in the middle of the intersection, and darting in and out as the traffic went by. In America you have the right of way, but here you had to adapt to every man for himself. Eventually we arrived at the railroad station and two attendants took more than three hours to prepare the tickets for our trip.

On January 24, 1990, we boarded the train in first class to find that our two-bunk cabin left a lot to be desired. Little did we know that we had to pre-order our bedding, so we ended up laying our heads on cold leather for a long, hard night.

At our stop we not only had to dicker for a taxi but had to push to get it started. It was difficult to see around the rough, narrow mountain road with its many sharp bends, necessitating frequent use of the horn. (My theory was that the constant horn blowing was the cause of the low battery and the reason why the cab would not start in the first place.)

With one turn after the other, the taxi climbed from one thousand to seven thousand feet throughout our one-hundred-kilometer trip to Kodaikanal. Finally we arrived at our destination, the International Mission School started back in 1901 for mission kids. Due to the spread of malaria, the school was later moved from the valley to a hill overlooking Kodai Lake. It was an interesting school with buildings stacked one above the other going up the hill and completely circling it. Since the school was located on a hill, many steps were necessary to access it and everyone seemed to keep fit from all the exercise. Five hundred students in grades kindergarten to high school attended classes, with students and staff from forty countries. I was familiar with Kodaikanal since Presbyterian missionaries have sent their children to this school for many years.

Kodaikanal is a resort town with many hotels and inns. Thousands come here on holiday—mostly Indians but also many Hindu. On January 26, Republic Day in India, crowds dressed in their best clothing and bands played in parades. I awakened to see a bright red horizon from my window and quickly dressed to make the five-minute walk up the trail to the ridge. Standing on the trail at dawn at seven thousand feet, looking at the lights on the flat plain six thousand feet below, the horizon seemed to be perfectly flat for 180 degrees around me. Then a tiny red spot appeared. It grew larger and larger, and three minutes later, the sun was a bright ball of fire.

A local golf course in Kodaikanal got my attention. At one point not only did the course have the golfer play across a road, but each of the greens had fencing to keep cows from entering. If your ball hit a fence post, you got three extra shots, and if it landed on a cow patty, you got three extra strokes!

On the descent from Kodaikanal we retraced our route down into the valley. Cars, trucks, buses, bikes, and ox carts competed for space. Even elephants walked the roads. Here many fruits and vegetables were grown by hand or with the use of oxen. How practical that some of the grain was distributed on the roads to have cars and trucks run over it and do the thrashing.

From Kodaikanal we traveled by way of Madurai and Madras to Vellore. Vellore was a dirty city with 200,000 living within its limits. There were no first class hotels in Vellore, and streets were crowded with lots of horns blowing, just like most other Indian cities. Vellore started out as an old temple encircled by a fort, complete with moat. A lot of history was connected to the city, but not many tourists visited here.

It was in Vellore that Dolly developed a sore, swollen leg all the way from her hip to her toes. It had been progressively getting worse for the whole day and we decided to take her to a mission hospital and have it checked. I called home to Dolly's doctors in the United States, and they instructed the hospital to give Dolly chemotherapy. The decision was made that she should remain for treatment for a few days, so I was given a cot and bunked down in the room with her. (This was the first time I stayed overnight in a hospital.) My bed, a sheet of metal with a very flat pad on top—and no springs—made the sound of thunder when I moved.

There were many cost-cutting procedures at this Christian hospital in Vellore: after meals, we were expected to keep our cup and flatware and wash them ourselves, the shower water ran across the floor to a drain in the corner, and hot water was only available in the afternoon when the sun was out. Otherwise, hot water had to be carried to the rooms and a pitcher was used to pour the water over the patients' bodies. There was a belief here that you could only use water that had never before touched the body, and it was a poor method of conservation.

The hospital in Vellore was a big operation with 540 doctors and approximately 3,800 staff. There was a strange dichotomy here: inside the hospital grounds, lovely flower gardens delighted the eye, but outside the hospital wall was filth and crowded streets. For a long time, I had wanted to see this hospital, but I never expected to see it like this: up close and personal. In fact, back in 1951, when working at the Tanta hospital in Egypt, I had received an invitation to come to Vellore to build this hospital.

So now, of course, I was especially excited to tour the maintenance part of the hospital and learn that it was self-contained. With its own steam boilers and generators, the hospital made half the oxygen it needed (which was about 87 percent pure) and purchased the rest. Water for the hospital was pumped from a well at the river and stored in large tanks under the engineering building. The water for laundry and the wards was heated by solar panels on the roof. It was an impressive setup.

While Dolly was being treated, I had an opportunity to tour the Vellore Christian Medical College associated with the hospital. This college was started in 1900, with just one bed, and on the day of my tour, it had accommodations for 1,285 patients and was the best in all of India. Here it was mandatory for each class to have at least twenty-five female students.

In order for morning devotions to be piped in, the rooms at this mission hospital were wired with speakers connected to the chapel. Every afternoon an Indian lady chaplain named Noksangdrila (meaning "off with your head") came to visit Dolly and have prayer. Her grandfather, a headhunter with a volatile temper, was a prestigious man in his village with thirty heads to his collection. He had three wives and two sons, and Noksangdrila's father was the first son of the first wife. As a boy, her father ran away to the jungle, where he ate fruit and herbs, made a hammock, and slept in the trees away from the wild animals. Eventually he met a missionary who fed him and taught him the alphabet. Noksangdrila's father gradually learned to read Matthew and Mark, was sent to school, and became a preacher. He married a Christian girl and they named their daughter "off with your head." Her evangelizing would have made him proud.

At the beginning of February, I went to visit the Family Village Farm north of Vellore, a home where children, newborn to eighteen years old, were raised and trained in their own school. The Family Village Farm was started in 1969, and at that time had 168 children. Boys worked on the farm and took care of the chickens, while the older girls were taught tailoring. By the age of eighteen, all the children were prepared for life.

Because of Dolly's illness our trip had to be shortened. It wasn't long before we took a flight back to Calcutta to begin working our way to Bangkok, Thailand, where we would depart for our flight to the United States. One report indicated that Air India was the world's riskiest airlines, and I felt that their airport was the worst in the world. For transportation in Calcutta, I hired three auto rickshaws and one bicycle—all in one morning. I soon learned that it was more economical to hire one driver and have him wait for me in between stops.

In a run-down part of Calcutta, we were taken to the third floor of an old building to visit an orphanage named the International Mission of Hope. We particularly wanted to come to this orphanage since a member of our church back home had adopted a baby from here. I had never seen so many babies at one time and in one place. Every room was full of babies—some in beds and many lined up on the floor. Babies were being fed, some were having their diapers changed, and others were being bathed. We were told there were approximately 160 babies here at the time.

From Calcutta we continued to work our way back to Bangkok, with a stop at Dhaka (once again) for three days to give Dolly a rest. Here soldiers surrounded our Japanese hotel and were stationed at all entrances and at the elevator doors on every floor. In Dhaka we visited the World Cassette Outreach which broadcast gospel programs over the radio in the area. The cassette program director had written six hundred songs in the local language—ones with rhythm that the people knew and words they understood. World Cassette Outreach worked at the same studio with World Vision where they dealt mainly with sponsoring children.

On February 13, after fifty days of traveling, we started our long and arduous trek home to the United States. From Dhaka, Bangladesh, we had an overnight stop in Bangkok. February 14 I titled, "The Longest Day." The flight from Bangkok to Seattle, Washington, totaled over fifteen hours, including the stop in Tokyo, and we were ready for a good night's rest. Considering all the hours gained and lost in flight, our day totaled thirty-five hours. In order to give Dolly time to rest, we stayed in Seattle for a couple of days. On February 16, son Ron and family met us at the Rochester airport and took us home to Pittsford.

DOLLY'S DEATH

At home it was common for Dolly's leg to swell and become painful. Not only was she having chemotherapy treatments, but eventually she started radiation treatments five times a week. Pills every four hours controlled the pain, and she was spending most of her time in bed. Often she just hurt all over. By the middle of May, Dolly was weak and had lost fluids. Since she was unable to attend church, I was going alone.

One day in the beginning of June, Dolly fell, and I had a difficult time getting her back into bed. Daughter Ginny called an ambulance and she was taken to the hospital. At the hospital, she was on IVs constantly and tests were run. The report on her scan was not good. The lymphoma had spread throughout her body, and because she was so weak, nothing more could be done. We were told she might live for another six months, or she could die at any time. Doctors suggested that we take her home and have home-care hospice.

On the way home from the hospital with Dolly, thoughts raced through my head. I prayed, "If a train would just hit me now then we could ride into the sunset together." In prior times Dolly had confided in me that she hoped the Lord would take her first. She loved all of her children dearly but did not want to live in their homes and have them be caretakers.

At home most of my time was spent writing up notes and labeling the seventeen rolls of film that I had taken during our Travel with a Difference trip. Dolly got weaker and weaker, and would awaken many times throughout the night. The hospice care ladies were available, but Dolly called out to me for help. Of course, I wanted to be there every time she called. Sometimes the children relieved me so I could catch a nap. On June 15, I wrote in my diary, "God gives me strength for each day and each hour." On this day, Dolly's sisters from Chicago and a brother from Ohio arrived to visit, and Dolly was coherent and chatted with them. The next day son Tom and his wife arrived from California. Since Leah was in her eighth month of pregnancy, she was unable to fly from Darwin, Australia, to be by her mother's side and had to say her good-byes by phone.

Dolly continued to deteriorate, with her breathing getting harder and her blood pressure dropping. I gathered the family together to plan her funeral. Dolly loved flowers so we decided to accept flowers from all those wishing to send them and would plan other memorials. We called our pastor and had prayer around Dolly's bed. At 9:15 P.M. on Saturday, June 16, I was with Dolly as she took her last breath and went home to be with her Lord.

At 10:30 P.M. the funeral directors arrived for her body. I took one side of the draw sheet and helped move her from the bed to the stretcher. Then I helped maneuver her through the door, wanting to be with her until she left the house. The following day, Sunday, our whole family attended church where everyone was shocked to hear the news.

Immediately calls had to be made to Global Mission, the Presbyterian office in Kentucky, various churches, family, and friends to inform them of Dolly's death. Plans were made with the funeral home, and son Ed made up memorial posters titled, "Missionary to the World, Wife, Mother, Grandmother" of Dolly's life to display at her viewing. Son Bill worked on a letter to be sent out informing everyone of her passing.

"A sad day," I wrote in my diary on June 19. "A beautiful service. I'm sure Dolly would have been happy with it." She would have been especially pleased to know that our longtime friend, Ed Fairman, spoke at the service representing both the Global Mission and the New Wilmington Missionary Conference. The many floral arrangements sent by friends and family seemed so natural for someone who loved flowers and gardening as much as she did.

There were many memorials in Dolly's memory. One was the Anderson Auditorium stage apron at Westminster College where the New Wilmington Missionary Conference was held. Another was the Dolly Marie Pollock Memorial Fund at the First Presbyterian Church in Pittsford, New York, which purchased the following items: cabinets for church tape cassette library in Kenya for PRM International; a tape player with solar panel for Aboriginal work in Australia; new songbooks for the Nuer tribe in the South Sudan; tape players and batteries for the Surma project in Ethiopia; and a donation to Mission Aviation Fellowship. Besides these memorials, there were more: the New Wilmington Conference Endowment Foundation; Hospice Home Care; Wycliffe Bible Translators; Christian Broadcasting Network; Sujay Welfare Society (Calcutta orphanage); International Mission of Hope (Calcutta); American Bible Society; Gideon Memorial Bibles; Camp Good Days (for children with cancer); and the Christian Medical College in Vellore, India, where Dolly was hospitalized during our round-the-world trip.

Almost immediately after Dolly's death I busied myself planting a garden and drew up plans for a gazebo that I planned to build in my yard in her memory. And with sadness, came joy. It wasn't long before daughter Leah presented me with my fifteenth grandchild. As usual, that summer I attended the New Wilmington Missionary Conference where Dolly's death was the topic of conversation. The end of August was a difficult time when Dolly and I would have celebrated our forty-ninth anniversary. "My mind has been going over some of the wonderful memories I have of those years," my diary revealed. In a letter I stated, "After fifty years as a team it is hard now to pull the load alone. God has carried us over many rough roads before, and I know He is with me as I go on alone."

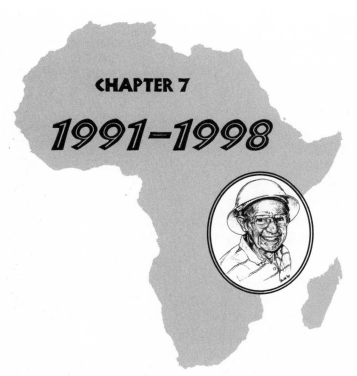

CHAPTER 7

1991-1998

Let us not become weary in doing good, for at the proper time we
will reap a harvest if we do not give up. Therefore, as we have
opportunity, let us do good to all people . . .

—*Galatians 6:9–10 (NIV)*

CHRIST'S GLOBE-TROTTER—
REACHING THE WORLD USING VOLUNTEERS

Back in 1977, with the Communist takeover and our expulsion from Ethiopia, I had "retired." For the next twelve years, Dolly and I traveled the world to faraway places with strange-sounding names, engaged in volunteer work. But after Dolly's death in 1990, I switched my focus and started to recruit volunteers to help me with short-term mission projects throughout the world.

In the middle of December 1990, once again I left Rochester, New York, this time meeting up with daughter Leah and family in the city of Cairns on the northeastern coast of Australia. Due to her pregnancy, Leah had been unable to attend her mother's funeral and we felt the need to connect. With a pop-up camp trailer in tow, we had plans to spend ten days traveling across northern Australia on our way to their home in Darwin.

Along the way, we toured an Aborigine village in the town of Boroloola and familiarized ourselves with their customs. From Boroloola, it was on to Leah's home in Darwin. Here I worked on maintenance projects at the Wycliffe Summer Institute of Linguistics Center where Leah and husband, Dave, worked. Besides maintenance projects, I was surprised to find myself back in the pulpit building business when I decided to build one for a group starting a new church here.

After six weeks in Darwin, I headed back towards the United States. At a stop in Perth on the west coast of Australia, I attended a church service and was introduced with a new title, Recycled Missionary. I guess it was an accurate description since I had theoretically retired in 1977.

From Perth, I headed west and started the long trip across the Pacific Ocean, completing my second trip around the world. Since I was passing through Nairobi, Kenya, I stopped and reconnected with many old friends at the Christian Industrial Training Center and had a great welcome back from the staff. At this time, the Sudan Literature Center in Nairobi was in the process of printing Nuer songbooks and I inquired about contributing the first five hundred copies as a memorial for Dolly. I liked the idea of spreading memorials all over the world for Dolly since she viewed the world as her home.

Back in Pittsford that summer of 1991, on the one year anniversary of Dolly's death, I wrote in my diary, "Dolly went to be with the Lord a year ago today. It has been a lonesome year. I still miss her." Also, that summer Dolly and I would have celebrated our fiftieth wedding anniversary and once again my diary heard my laments, "We were married fifty years ago today. There is really nothing to celebrate. I think back over many happy memories but that does not help now. I am lonely and life is not the same."

I went to the New Wilmington Missionary Conference a few days early that summer to make and install panels on the inside of the lower arches of Anderson Auditorium. This finished the project I had started back in 1987 to repair and restore the auditorium.

Upon my arrival at the conference, I strolled into the NWMC office located in the basement of the United Presbyterian Church across the street from the Westminster College campus. Here I learned, much to my surprise, that I had been booked to give the sermon for the following Sunday. Reality set in when I saw my name displayed on the billboard in front of the church, and once again I had to "let go, and let God."

It was a Thursday, and I had just one day to decide on a topic to be put in the bulletin. On Sunday morning, while I stood in the pulpit and delivered my message, I was very aware of the clock at the back of the sanctuary. I had been informed that my sermon would have to end promptly at noon because it was being broadcast on the radio.

GRACE MEMORIAL HOSPITAL—WAGNER, BRAZIL

New opportunities always seemed to crop up. Specifically, I was asked to be work boss and organize the renovations needed at the Grace Memorial Hospital Nurses' School in Wagner, Brazil. The school was reopening after twenty years. This hospital had been a Presbyterian institution since 1916 and was founded and run for sixty years by the Presbyterian Church (U.S.A.). Currently it was being run by the medical doctor and nurse team of Jonas and Janet Araujo.

In the early 1970s, a financial crisis in the Presbyterian Church caused support to this hospital to be withdrawn. Rather than abandoning the people in one of the most poverty-stricken areas of northeastern Brazil, Jonas, the medical director, and Janet, the director of nursing, opened a small clinic in another location and continued their medical missionary work on faith alone. Since no mission organization supported them, they depended solely on contributions from churches in the United States, but often these contributions were sporadic.

Fourteen years later, with the help of friends in the States, Janet and Jonas reopened Grace Memorial Hospital with plans to convert the former student nurses' dormitory into a fifty-bed ward for women and children. I traveled to Brazil to do a thorough survey of the needs, materials, and prices for all the repair work needed there. As you learned from my prior projects, I liked to give them names.

This one I labeled Operation RAVE:

> **R**-ebuild for Christ
> **A**-ttempt great things for God—
>   expect great things from God
> **V**-olunteer with a mind to work
> **E**-ncourage others

At the beginning of October 1991, I made the long flight to Rio de Janeiro, a city I felt was more dangerous than Calcutta, India. Here, not only did the hotel have its room keys on chains to wear around the neck, but there were special safes in each room to hold valuables. Once upon a time, Rio was a beautiful city, but now its lack of maintenance resulted in a plethora of garbage and filth. Sex movie theaters and girls lined the streets, and because of the street boys, we were told not to wear our wristwatches.

From Rio I flew north to Salvador, a shoreside city built on hills, and then traveled by bus on rough road through rolling countryside to the nurses' school at Wagner to begin my survey of the project. As I approached the site, my eyes scanned a long, one-story building badly in need of paint and repair. A picket fence which highlighted the front was in need of complete rebuilding. The interior, which was to be our home and workplace, was in no better shape, and in some cases worse. Bathrooms were useable, but toilets were unable to accept tissue without serious consequences, and some needed to be flushed with a bucket of water.

At the hospital, I talked with Jonas and Janet concerning future plans, measured, calculated, examined, made drawings, and listed materials that I would need to make the repairs. I soon learned that the needs here were great and that the people were suffering from eleven years of drought.

I took pictures of the compound to take back home and display when making appeals for support from U.S. churches. This project would provide opportunities for volunteers of all ages, and all types and levels of skills, with the cost of materials estimated at fifteen to twenty thousand dollars. I knew if I returned to the States and made a request for twenty thousand dollars, I would be turned down. To make it more manageable, we hoped to have eighty people, groups, or churches contribute a gift of $250 each to cover the full cost of the materials.

Unlike most missionaries, Janet and Jonas ran a small farm in an attempt to be self-sufficient and keep their personal support separate from the financial needs of the hospital. Any overproduction went to the compound. But lack of water was a deterrent and they yearned for some type of irrigation. For years they dreamed of having a windmill.

With my years of experience building windmills in Ethiopia, I decided to make that dream come true. A few days after completing my survey at Grace Memorial, I visited the blacksmith shop, and in five days, using scrap iron, I made a windmill to irrigate land on their farm. Janet contributed to the project by sewing up the eight sailcloths. (In 2002, I received word from Janet saying the windmill is still up and running.)

Even though my volunteers and I would not be able to converse in Portuguese, our actions on this project would speak louder than words. We were fortunate we would have an interpreter who was a missionary and who had worked with New Tribe's Mission in Brazil for the past twenty-eight years. We planned on taking our hand-cranked tape players with the solar panels to share the New Testament in Portuguese. As always, my excuse for taking on this type of project was to repair the buildings. But in reality, it was the evangelism that I was most interested in.

After reading morning devotions, on October 17 (Dolly's birthday), I had a revelation. With needs so great here, was there a possibility that God would be willing to help me rebuild this hospital just like he helped Nehemiah rebuild the wall around Jerusalem?

A year later, in October 1992, I left Rochester to begin the Brazil work project. When purchasing materials, I was introduced firsthand to the high inflation in the country. The $20,000 in traveler's checks that I exchanged netted me 14,358,000 cruzeiros, but I quickly learned it didn't go very far.

I arrived in Wagner on October 6 in time to greet the first group of volunteers, a total of twenty coming in stages and staying from two to four weeks. It was a good group with a lot of skills.

In order to convert the old nurses' dormitory at the hospital, there was much work to be done. Our volunteer crew dug right in: they repaired floors, rewired the building, put in new pipes, put new tile on the walls and floors in the kitchen and bathrooms, repainted inside and out, and rebuilt the fence. Not only was work accomplished, but the group also made contact with the local people and participated in the local Presbyterian church.

It was springtime and the hard work was exacerbated by the heat, but the crew endured. The grass was green, trees were in full bloom, and lilies were popping up though the hard earth. Bugs and locusts that arrived with the mild spring weather were attracted to our lights and managed to get in our hair and under our collars. One morning we swept them up by the shovels full.

Locusts whined as they flew overhead in the mornings and evenings, and the air was full of swarming ants. This time of year, the female ants were filled with eggs, and the local girls collected them in jars to take home, remove their wings, and eat them.

After one month to the hour, on November 6, the last of my work crew had left. I felt a lot had been accomplished during that month. The next day I visited the hospital for one last time. It was a beautiful spring morning in Brazil with the lilies, acacia, and frangipani all in full bloom. What a thrill it was to walk through the hospital building and see the newly painted walls and ceilings, freshly varnished doors, new tile on the kitchen and bathroom walls, and clean shiny floors.

Then I stepped outside to see the white walls and bright yellow trim, and across the lawn, the new fence with its white columns and green pickets. The facility which was once dull and unsightly now glistened inside and out. This had all been done in one month with my team of volunteers, God's help, and many faithful prayers from folks back home. As I turned over the keys to Jonas and Janet, I took one last photo and remembered that it was my eightieth birthday. My team couldn't have given me a better present.

In a newsletter printed by Grace Memorial Hospital Janet commented, "The people here loved the Americanos. . . . They were amazed, simply open-mouthed that you would come from so far and work so hard, for free, and at your own expense! What wonders the Christian love accomplishes!" *(See photo section.)*

SURMA TRIBE—ETHIOPIA

By the end of January 1992, I was on my way for another missionary adventure and felt just as strong as I did when I left for Ethiopia thirty years ago. We had first reached the Surma Tribe back in the 1970s as part of the mission outreach program, but because of war in Ethiopia and the Sudan, the tribe was uprooted from Surma and driven into the mountains. Since most of their mission station had been stripped away, I had received a letter requesting that I return to Ethiopia to salvage what we could of the old Surma post and consult on building plans for a new one.

The Surma Tribe, fifty to sixty thousand in number, covers a large area of southwestern Ethiopia along the Sudan border. It was in this area that *National Geographic* photographers had taken photos for an article published in their February 1991 issue (as well as in the February 2003 *National Geographic*). Originally it was determined that the location for the new Surma post be at the village of Kibish. Eventually I traveled there to select a site and locate a good supply of water.

Sitting on a log with some Surma men at Kibish, I took off my hat, exposing long locks of hair. As one of the men reached for a lock and started to braid it, it was apparent to me that I was long overdue for a haircut. The Surma have no hair on their bodies—not even eyebrows—so they were intrigued.

I had fun with two girls who came over to shake hands. The first girl had a firm grip and squeezed my hand, so I squeezed back until she let go. The second girl found this amusing, so she tried it. Then the men discovered our little game and wanted to participate. So, one by one, I challenged a dozen men. Some of them were much bigger than me, but none defeated me. I was surprised at the weak grip of the men compared to the women, but this was explained by the fact that the women did most of the work.

For entertainment, the girls at Kibish joined hands and encouraged the Surma men to dance inside their circle. Some of the girls had two sticks that they clapped together while singing. Now and then a stick was dropped on the ground in front of some of the men. The number of sticks in front of each tribesman represented the total number of stick battles he had won. (Stick battles, fierce fights between two tribesmen, were fought in front of women to prove their bravery.) In order to keep track, each tribesman noted a victorious battle by putting a notch in a tree.

Notches on tree indicate number of stick battles won

The village of Kibish was large and it wasn't long before a huge crowd gathered around and pleaded for my hat, shirt, belt, shoes (even the laces), and razor blades. They particularly wanted the razor blades in order to shave their hair into the intricate patterns they wore on top their heads. Not believing I was without razor blades, they asked how I shaved. I pulled out my battery-operated shaver and showed them.

At Kibish we had a successful meeting with the Surma chief, Dolata, to plan our work. We would focus our attention on education, agriculture, and medicine, along with evangelism at the new post. As far as we knew, there was not one Christian in the tribe. I prayed that when I returned to the States, I might be able to find a church to adopt them.

After spending a couple of months helping to plan the Surma station, I started for home. I praised the Lord for this opportunity to return to Surma and help make plans for the new Kibish site.

Summer arrived in Pittsford, New York, and once again my plans included the New Wilmington Missionary Conference in Pennsylvania. I left three weeks early and, in the sawdust of Anderson Auditorium in front of the old stage, I laid out the ellipse of the new apron and the new ramp.

When I requested volunteers for the job, a new approach was tried. Ten churches were contacted and requested to send a team of workers for just one day. It required a little more coordination with a different daily work group, but I didn't have any concerns about overworking my crews. I knew they wouldn't be coming back the next day!

The stage extension in Anderson Auditorium was completed in two weeks and was dedicated as a memorial to Dolly during the conference. The board of managers presented me with a plaque that I mounted at the top of the stage ramp indicating that the stage apron was in her memory.

Me with village chief, Dolato, and locals at Kibish

With so much to do and so little time, I didn't like giving grass a chance to grow under my feet. I often felt hurried to get things done, forgetting to wait for God's perfect timing and His schedule for us. If I got ahead, then things did not go as He had planned. Other times it was hard to keep up and I would get a little out of step and fall behind. Sometimes I found it difficult to walk with God. I had to remind myself to be still before the Lord and listen for that small voice that knew my every need before I asked. When I became impatient I found this quote by Helen Keller uplifting:

I am only one, but I am one.
I cannot do everything, but I can do something.
And I will not fail to do what I can do.[1]

*My four children born in
Africa help move
Surma domes*

In January 1993, my goal was to help relocate what was left of the buildings at the original Surma post (including two geodesic domes) and move them to their new site. I was excited at the prospect of many of the original buildings being recycled. I was told it couldn't be done, that it would be impossible to move the buildings, but this gave me more incentive to try. Also, it was a chance to show the Surma that I still cared and wanted to help.

Eventually we learned that the government wouldn't give us permission to relocate the original Surma post at Kibish like we had originally planned, so we had to regroup and come up with an alternative plan. It was decided that the new location would be at the village of Tuligit. The four of my children born in Africa—Bill, Ron, Tom, and Leah decided to help their dad with this impossible mission. I wrote in my journal, "I have a perfect crew for this job. I am glad the family came to help me with this project. With the equipment or lack of it, it is dangerous work."

No one lived at the old Surma post at this time and the airstrip was grown up with brush. Our plan was to hire a helicopter to take us to the old site and, in nine days' time, disassemble the buildings and be ready to airlift them to the new location at Tuligit.

It had been twenty-four years since the Pollock family was in Ethiopia together and it didn't take long before we were enjoying the fun times of camping at the job site and bathing in the river. But this wasn't just a hardship tour; this was a deluxe hardship tour. Our family, plus the two Surma boys I had hired, lived in tents and battled rain, mud, and wind and ate MREs (Meals Ready to Eat) surplus from the Middle East War. Heating the MREs and doctoring them up with salt and hot sauce made them a lot more palatable.

When they heard we had arrived, a few of the Surma men came down from Tuligit bearing gifts of chickens and eggs. We had a good visit and they expressed their appreciation that we had come back to salvage what we could of their old station. "This land is not only ours, but yours too," they said.

As always, I felt that if it were an easy job, let someone else do it. But the Surma job was one of the hard jobs, and I had to depend on God's help to accomplish it.

After nine days at the old station and with a lot of difficulty, we had the buildings disassembled. The helicopter returned and it was quite a sight to see the trusses and some of the purlins from the old buildings hauled in a net dangling from a thirty-foot rope underneath the plane. It took twelve trips—each carrying one thousand kilos—to transport the ten tons of building material over the mountain by HeliMission helicopter to the new site at Tuligit. Some of the dome triangles got twisted and bent in the move and had to be welded.

By the middle of March 1993, I felt like I had done all I could to help plan the new post at Tuligit and was leaving it in good hands. John Haspels would take on the reassembly project. It was time to move on.

HeliMission helicopter

On my way home to the States I made a side trip to Belfast, Ireland. Belfast was sheep country; in fact, they almost had as many sheep in the fields there as they did in New Zealand.

I had been invited to Belfast to make a survey of renovations needed for a hall at the Townsend Church located here. The friends who invited me offered wonderful accommodations with breathtaking views all the way across the sea to Scotland.

Due to the violence between Protestants and Roman Catholics, there were still guns and tanks at checkpoints all throughout Belfast, and scanners and computers were being used to detect questionable license plate numbers. It appeared that Northern Ireland had security more under control now than in years previous.

I attended the Townsend Church in Belfast and checked out everything from ground to roof to see what renovations were needed on the large hall behind the church. One thing for sure—the old slate roof needed to be replaced. Tentative plans were to bring a work group here to help with renovations the following year.

After eight wonderful days in Northern Ireland, it was time to leave. By the spring of 1993, I had been away from home a total of eighty-three days, and for the last four Sundays, I had been in four different churches, in four different countries, on three different continents.

The warm welcome home and interest from my hometown church in Pittsford, New York, made me feel good. Many more people were becoming interested in mission work.

Not long after my arrival home, I received an invitation to serve on the administrative board of an exciting new organization called SERVE (Sending Experienced Retired Volunteers Everywhere). It was discovered that, for the most part, retirees are an untapped source in churches. The idea was to recruit those who were retired, and, through the use of a computer database, match skills with mission service opportunities in the United States and overseas. Although targeted at retired volunteers, anyone interested in volunteer work could join. Many of my future mission trips were sponsored through the SERVE organization.

As my birthday rolled around, I wrote in my diary, "My passport says that tomorrow I will be eighty-one, but from the way it looks to me, I am 18."

Two years later, in March 1995, I went back to visit the Surma people. At Tuligit a lot had been accomplished since we had air-dropped the domes back in 1993. One of the domes that had been transported by helicopter was nicely erected into a two-story residence. It was great being back again at the church service under the trees. (Since then a church has been built using local materials.)

NILE THEOLOGICAL COLLEGE—SUDAN

The South Sudan rejected the Northern Sudanese government's attempt to keep their people and resources under the north's control. Many people in the south had died of war-related causes in the past ten years, and between four and five million persons had been displaced from their homes. The hostile and oppressive fundamentalist Muslim government in the north had engaged in aerial bombing of villages and markets in the south. Some villages had only 30 percent of the population remaining. As one Sudanese Presbyterian pastor said, "The war has become our great teacher. It has taught us to find Christ on the path of much suffering."

In spite of continued strife and civil war in the South Sudan, the Christian Church was growing rapidly. Because we had introduced Christianity here, they looked to us for help as the mother church. The greatest need was training new pastors and church leaders.

In 1991, the Sudan Theological College was formed as a Protestant college to train Presbyterian ministers and lay members. Seventy students matriculated here, with many of them receiving scholarships funded in part by mission giving of congregations and presbyteries of the Presbyterian Church (USA). Initially the classes met in a rented house in Khartoum, the capital, but later it was opportune that the old Khartoum North Girls' Boarding School offered the Sudan Theological College use of some of their unused buildings. Most of the buildings at the old school were badly in need of repairs and renovations.

On my way to Ethiopia in the beginning of 1993, I stopped in Khartoum, Sudan, to make a survey of this Christian girls' school. It was urgent to get the building work planned as soon as possible. In the beginning of 1994, with the help of forty volunteers, I planned to go as an ambassador to the Sudan to complete this work and share God's love.

The Presbyterian Church had started many of the mission stations in the Upper Nile region. Since I had built many schools, clinics, and other buildings in the fifteen years we were there, I was referred to as "the man who built the Upper Nile."

One afternoon we were invited to the theological college to meet some of the students. The director of the college introduced me to the group and said, "This is the man that built the first school on the island of Wanglel in 1949. I was one of their first schoolboys. If it hadn't been for that school, I would not be here today." It was amazing what one little cattle boy out of the bush could do if he had a chance. Those mission dollars were well spent.

Right after Christmas 1993, my volunteers and I left for the Sudan to supervise work at the Khartoum North Girls' Boarding School. Our task was to refurbish the unused buildings there into an office, two large classrooms, a computer room, and a guest room.

Since there was little hope that the government would give us permission to build a seminary in the predominately Muslim north, we had to come up with a generic name to fool them into thinking that this project at the girls' school had no Christian affiliations.

We called this project Operation Ful Sudani, the Arabic name for "PEANUT."

P-ray for the Sudan Theological College
E-ncourage
A-chieve
N-urture
U-nite
T-rust God

The building to be refurbished was a wreck. There were so many jobs: shoring up the roof; putting up new ceilings;

plastering the walls inside and out; installing new wiring, plumbing, and phone lines; installing water coolers and ceiling and attic exhaust fans; and painting the entire building. Not only did twenty-two volunteer workers rotate in and out every couple weeks, but the seminary students helped in the afternoons after their classes.

The older mason I hired to help with the project wanted more money. After inquiring what he needed the money for, he replied, "To feed my three children." I informed him that I had seven children. But he outdid me when he retorted, "But I have three wives!"

In the middle of January 1994, one of my volunteers and I were welcomed at a Nuer church service with open arms. Here they remembered me as the builder of their schools. You could hear the church building moan as those in attendance squeezed to overflow, with many standing outside at the doors and windows.

At the beginning of February, I attended a United service at a nearby church. Refugees came in from some of the camps (over three hundred), and I shook hands with almost all of them. One lady remembered me and called out, "Jal Dong OK!"

While in the Sudan, I visited five refugee centers north of Khartoum. These people had been displaced from the war-torn South and many had not been home in a decade. I couldn't even imagine the hardships that they had been subjected to. No one knew how many Southern Sudanese lived in these camps.

The Salema Camp, located one hour from Khartoum, was typical and covered seven square miles. Families were crowded in a single room mud shack which often was completely open on one side. Facilities were minimal and there were no schools. I saw a few chickens and an occasional thin goat, but there were no trees or other greenery. There were times in the desert area of Khartoum that the refugees were tempted to give up Christianity and become Muslim when bribed with food to feed their children. But because they refused to give up their Christ, they were paying a terrible price.

These camps were too far from Khartoum for the refugees to walk, and bus fares were too high so there was little incentive for them to try to find work. Without education, land or water for farming, and little opportunity for work, the future of these people in the camps was indeed bleak. This meant an entire generation was without education.

By the end of February 1994, seven weeks after the start of the theological college project, everything fell into place. Almost magically the dilapidated building was turned into two beautiful classrooms, two new offices, and a guest room. At this time we packed up and turned the work over for others to finish. (The name of the Sudan Theological College was eventually changed to the Nile Theological College.)

I don't want to fool you into thinking that this project was without glitches. There were visa delays, injuries, thefts, and even a volunteer who was picked up by the security officers for taking photos outside the college grounds. Of course, this project was humanly impossible in the allotted time. But God had chosen us and He had things planned. We always had the right people with the right skills at the time when they were needed, allowing the job to be completed on time. Approximately one hundred people at the farewell dinner party gave me a wood carved box, an ebony cane, and a beautiful photography book titled *The Nile,* as departing gifts. (I didn't plan to ever use the cane.)

After completion of the Nile Theological College project, I traveled to the South Sudan for the New Sudan Christian Council (the church council that had been formed by the merger of the presbyteries from both North and South Sudan). This council had made a request that I design and supervise the reconstruction of a storehouse for United Nations refugee supplies that had been erected improperly at their distribution center in Nimule, on the southern border of the Sudan. Since Nimule had been bombed by the northern air force three days before my planned arrival, I was sent to a U.N. refugee camp at Pakelle on the Uganda border.

The fifty-by-one-hundred-foot metal storage shed, which I was to construct, was to be made from six two-and-a-half-ton shipping containers—a real challenge since there were no tools or equipment available. Most of my workers were Sudan refugees whom we fed one meal of rice and beans per day. Peter, an orphan who walked forty kilometers from his refugee camp, was very thankful to have work.

Two of the workers were Shilluk from Doleib Hill and one told me that his grandfather had worked for a man named Jal Dong OK back in 1948. The Shilluk's grandfather had shared a song with him that the workers used to sing about Jal Dong OK's haircut. Imagine his surprise when I said that I was Jal Dong OK! I was now working with third-generation Africans!

From Pakelle, on Easter day, I traveled twenty-three kilometers to attend a refugee camp church service. This church, built by the refugees, was made of mud blocks and reed roofs and was a good example of how their strong faith supplied hope for the future. Here Scripture was read in four languages.

After the service I visited several other United Nations refugee camps and discovered that services were in progress at all of them. The number of refugees here was also staggering. Upon entering the camps, I saw many tents and small shelters covered with plastic. Wherever there was a well, there was a long line of refugees waiting their turn to get water. It was obvious that the refugees were being grouped according to tribes and languages. Sadly, many of these camps had been in existence for over five years and had become established villages. I shared with my diary, "It has been good to be here at this time of trouble to get a real feel for what is going on, to see, and to hear."

"The Nile Theological College is the only theological college for pastoral training operating in Sudan, serving a rapidly growing church of over five million Christians," stated an article written about their first graduation in December of 1995. Typically graduations in the States are joyous occasions, but at the first graduation ceremony of the Nile Theological College, pandemonium erupted as family and friends rushed to congratulate the students as they received their diplomas. Reverend Bill Anderson's wife, Lois, exclaimed, "T.I.A.: This Is Africa!"

A couple of years later in February 1996, I returned to the Nile Theological College for a five-week project to renovate one of the old buildings into a school library and reading room. Daughter Penny and two other ladies from the United States, volunteered to help me. But the new Muslim government, being anti-Christian, made it as difficult as possible for the ladies to get visas to enter the country. Eventually tourist visas were granted, and the ladies arrived and brought books with them to be used at the college. Because I was short on volunteers, I hired Nuer boys off the street to help with this job. The library included a checkout/return desk, a separate area for reference books, and a veranda that we enclosed and made into a quiet reading room for the students. Since one of the volunteers was a librarian, we were able to catalog and organize the books for the new facility.

GHIMEERA, ETHIOPIA

In the early 1960s, part of the Fifty Million Fund of the United Presbyterian Church was designated for outreach to the untouched tribes in southwest Ethiopia. For fourteen years,

Dolly and I were instrumental in helping to open up new stations there and felt that those mission dollars were well spent. During this time, we were based at the Ghimeera Mission Station and it was here that we built our first real home. But, in 1977, during our expulsion from Ethiopia, we not only had to leave our completely furnished house, but we had to leave behind a fully equipped workshop as well. After the communist takeover of the Ethiopian government, Ghimeera was nationalized and the facility was poorly maintained.

When we first came to Ghimeera in 1963, there were only three churches in the synod. When we were expelled in 1977, there were approximately six to eight churches. Many Christian groups were forced underground, but in spite of the war, the church remained alive. In fact, some grew. Amazingly enough, at this time in 1995, the synod had 13 parishes, 75 churches, and 293 preaching points.

After the overthrow of the Marxist government and fall of Communism in 1987, many of these missions and churches were returned to the Christian communities, but were badly in need of renovations. Such was the case at Ghimeera. The Washington Presbytery in Pennsylvania had a partnership with the Kaffa Bethel Presbytery in Ethiopia and requested that I return to Ghimeera, Ethiopia, to assess the needs of the station there. At this time (the end of 1991), the Kaffa Bethel Presbytery in Ethiopia was using Ghimeera as their headquarters and for a guest house.

I dubbed this project Operation RETURN.

R-eturn to Ethiopia
E-ncourage local people
T-ogether we can
U-pdate for Christ
R-emember God is with us
N-ow is the time

Thirty years had passed since I first went up into the Ethiopian mountains, but like Caleb who was eighty-five when he went back into the mountains (Josh. 14 RSV) I felt ready and strong. Due to the manner in which we were put out of Ethiopia in 1977, I was not looking forward to returning to Ghimeera. I wanted to remember things as they were when we left. Also, because of the years spent here with Dolly, I didn't look forward to returning on my own. But the good news was that the doors were opened in Ethiopia once again. This time I would be able to go anywhere, at anytime, and take all the photos I wanted. I knew there was a need and I prayed that I would show Christian love to those who were trying to rebuild Ghimeera.

At the government town of Mizan, I met many people running down the road shouting, "Pollock is back!" It was a joy to be welcomed by the station workers and our many Christian friends there.

After fourteen years of war, I wondered what shape our former house was in. No maintenance had been done, but it had stood up quite well. Its good shape was probably due to its having been used by the Communist party as a guest house for their leader when he visited. All the trees had been cut down and gardens had been planted on the hills. I knew that when the rains came, it would take the topsoil all the way down to Egypt. The furniture, except for the dining table, was missing, along with the light fixtures, switches, and many of the doors.

We were hoping to salvage any remaining equipment in my old shop and at the station shop, but after inspecting, I was discouraged to see that most everything was missing or damaged. A four-foot chain saw frame and some windmill parts were all that we found. All my tools, including saws, planers, and generators were gone.

I spent some time talking to Benyam, the first and only ordained pastor in the Ghimeera tribe, and the executive director of Kaffa Bethel Presbytery. Benyam happened to be one of the schoolboys who had worked in Dolly's garden to earn his school fees many years ago. Dolly used to pray that one of her sons would become a minister and I believe God answered her prayers. Benyam and I discussed many topics, and I learned that the local church that had burned was rebuilt and a new bigger church was being planned to hold the crowds.

After the church went underground fifteen years ago, new churches emerged much stronger in the area. Some were meeting in small groups in homes and a lot of good had come from all the suffering. The translation of the New Testament in the Ghimeera tribal language had been completed and the first printed copies had arrived. I committed to look into having some Scripture tapes made to use with the tape players and solar panels for those who could not read in the village.

Often I stuck my neck out to get things started. Once I had Operation RETURN planned and organized, I let it go. It was always interesting to see how God worked out the details. This time I had twenty-one volunteers from churches all over the United States, including five pastors (one was Dr. Earl Johnson Jr. from my hometown church). At Ghimeera these pastors planned to visit congregations to teach and share with evangelists, elders, and pastors in the local area. We were not going to Ghimeera to reestablish the old mission station. Instead the group of volunteers would strive to recondition the old termite-infested mission buildings and make repairs so these buildings could be used by the local presbytery as offices and training facilities. This was to be completed between January 8 and March 10, 1995.

Sometimes I longed for some of the dumpsters used on construction sites in the United States. But people in these third-world countries have no need for them since they don't live in a disposable society. Nor were there any do-it-yourself stores to buy building supplies. But I believed wisdom was the ability to find an alternative, and I had to find alternatives on most of my projects.

There were many jobs at Ghimeera, and my volunteers and I started to renovate the whole station: repairing wiring in the hopes that a new generator might be found; replacing broken window glass; shoring up some of the floors; rebuilding some of the foundation; and removing the front wood veranda on one of the houses and replacing it with a stone wall and concrete floor. Also, there were damaged ceilings, kitchen cabinets that were destroyed by rats and water, rotten floors, damaged roofs, and a septic system that needed attention. We fixed all these problems besides replacing a front porch, installing new gutters, and painting the outside.

"The house looks almost like it did when we lived here," I told my diary. This house not only made good accommodations for Earl Johnson and me while on this project, but we used it as an office as well. Overall, my crew did a splendid job. It was an adventure for each and every volunteer. I praised God that all of the work was completed and the volunteers were kept safe and in good health.

On March 8, work with my crew was finished; I turned in the tools and the key and paid off my workers. By March 10, the last volunteer had left and Operation RETURN ended. I had a meeting with the committee and offered to return in 1996 to repair the clinic and put up a new school for evangelists' training. In actuality, this work was done by another group of volunteers.

Before going home to the United States, I stopped off at the village of Lokichoggio in the northwest corner of Kenya on the Sudan border. Presbyterian church leaders there requested my help to draw up plans for the development of a new United Nations base camp in order to get relief supplies into the South Sudan. The south had its supply line cut off by the northern

army and many mission groups were working with the U.N. at
Lokichoggio, the jumping-off point for their large cargo planes
taking in the supplies.

At Lokichoggio I laid out sites for a storehouse, office, and
living quarters for staff and guests. I cut windows and doors
into a large metal ocean shipping container for the office,
covered it with a metal roof, and put grass over the roof to
help keep the inside cool. While at Lokichoggio, I lived in a
World Vision tukl and did my own cooking. I had a lot of time
alone to think and dream of all the places in the world where
I had worked and all the things I had done. Suddenly it was
unbelievable to me: to think that all I had to offer God were
my two hands.

U.N. cargo plane at Lokichoggio

Back home in New York, I spent one week in the middle of July 1995, at New Wilmington, Pennsylvania, supervising a crew to upgrade and repair the electrical system at the Anderson Auditorium on the Westminster College campus. The old wiring was thirty-eight years old and the rewiring specifically involved pulling approximately two miles of new wire.

It was while serving at the ninetieth annual New Wilmington Missionary Conference that Dr. Alfred Heasty, my missionary friend and medical doctor to the Sudan, became critically ill and died. Dr. Heasty knew that he was dying but wanted to come to the conference one last time. He felt there was no better place to be. I had worked with his father, Dr. Alfred Heasty Sr., for forty years in the Sudan.

During the fall of 1995, I spent two weeks in October speaking at churches in the Detroit, Michigan, presbytery. God brought Joshua 13:1 to my attention. He was saying the same to me as He said to Joshua: You are well advanced in years, and all have not heard. There still were a lot of unreached people who had not heard that "old, old story of Jesus and His love."

On October 1, World Wide Communion Sunday, my friend from Ghimeera, the Reverend Benyam Aerma, was the guest pastor at my home church in Pittsford. Benyam was studying in the States for the year. At the conclusion of the service, an announcement was made of the establishment of the Ted and Dolly Pollock Mission Endowment Fund in recognition of life-long service to God and Christ's mission to those in need throughout the world. I wrote in my diary:

This was a real surprise. I did not expect anything like it. I was glad that three of my children were there. They knew about this before hand. This could not have happened if it had not been for Dolly and the seven children. They should

*have most of the credit. In all of this I want God to have the
glory. I thank Him for the wonderful wife that I had. I
thank Him for each one of our children. . . . I am proud to
be their father.*

Interest from this fund was to be used to help finance mission
projects worldwide.

By my eighty-third birthday in November of 1995 I had
covered much of the world, but I continued to make plans.
The next project on my agenda was Operation ADURA in
Ethiopia in January and February of 1996. Here I hoped to
rebuild one of the dilapidated buildings into a badly needed
clinic and guest quarters.

ADURA CLINIC—ETHIOPIA

A-llowing
D-eliverance
U-sing
R-econstruction
A-t Adura

In 1961, a mission station had been opened up at the
Adura river post in the lowlands of the most western tip of
Ethiopia near the Sudan border. Started by Mr. and Mrs.
Charles Jordan, the goal of this Presbyterian endeavor was to
provide ministry for the Nuer Tribe located there. Boundary
lines between eastern Sudan and western Ethiopia split this
tribe in half, and, with tribe members on both sides of the
border, it was especially difficult to work with them.

Since the evacuation of many missionaries in 1977, there had
been no resident missionary at Adura. When MAF operations

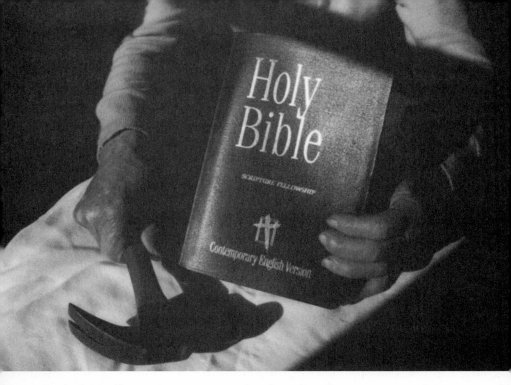

All I had to offer God were my two hands. (photo by Erin Reeve, the youngest Adura volunteer at fifteen years old)

resumed in Ethiopia after the fall of Communism, a nurse in Gambela suggested that she would be willing to make regular half-hour MAF trips to Adura in order to supervise their clinic.

Christians started clearing the tall grass from the former airstrip and I was contacted to arrange a work project. During six weeks at Adura, our goal was to take apart several of the old buildings at the site and use the salvaged concrete blocks and lumber to rebuild the former nurses' house into a clinic and guest room. A clinic would be a great blessing to many of the people in this isolated part of Ethiopia and also to the refugee camp close by. Currently a mud hut was being used as a clinic and many of the Nuers had to wait in long lines for medical treatment. In March of 1995, the nurse and I flew to Adura for a brief survey trip to check out the possibilities.

Even though Operation ADURA was organized under the auspices of SERVE, we not only included retirees but had volunteers from ages fifteen to eighty-three. There would be two groups coming for a period of three weeks each, and we would use as many local Nuer workers as possible.

At the end of December 1995, I left New York City to begin my journey to Adura. After a stop in London, it was on to Addis Ababa, Ethiopia, where I spent ten days gathering supplies for the project. It would be challenging to try to get volunteers and supplies into this very remote site.

At Addis Ababa I met up with the first group of volunteers. Chuck Jordan, who started the Adura post in 1961, would join our group and be pastor to the volunteers and Nuer workers.

Many from the Nuer Tribe came running to greet us as our plane touched down on the unpaved, crater-filled landing strip. One word to describe this location was primitive. There was no electricity or refrigeration, but thank goodness, the locals had dug a latrine for us before our arrival. The village nurse, a male, resided in a mud hut on the compound, and we decided to set up camp near him. Encircling the compound was a tall grass fence, not only for privacy, but also for protection from the wind. Inside the fence a large mango tree supplied welcome shade for our tent city. Nearby we found the remains of an old refrigerator and, laying it on its side, we used it as a prep table for our meals. Our makeshift stove was salvaged from the concrete top of a charcoal cooker that we set on blocks and fueled with scrap wood.

Walking around the old station, you could see foundations where buildings had once been. The many foxholes were indications that a military group from the Sudan had made headquarters here and that a big battle had taken place.

Conditions at Adura were very rough. The river was used for both bathing and drinking, but we quickly learned that the purification tablets were not effective in killing the "bugs." It was imperative to boil the water before drinking in order to prevent Ethiopian revenge. Rationing water became the norm.

The heat was almost unbearable and I was dragging a little. Swarming flies were a major source of irritation and caused some scratches on my leg to become infected. My legs swelled and became painful, resulting in the Nuer clinic dresser giving me penicillin shots three times a day. Since I could barely walk, I started to wonder if this might be my last mission endeavor. I felt like Job.

Sundays were long at Adura. After attending the early morning church service, there wasn't much to do. The choices were to stay in your tent in the natural sauna or sit outside under the mango tree and swat flies.

Workdays were long too, but in an exhausting kind of way. Work was hard as we tore down one of the dilapidated buildings at the site and salvaged as much of the concrete blocks and lumber as possible. When I saw there was a shortage of good concrete blocks, I collected reinforced concrete fence posts and concrete beams from other buildings in order to use them in our new clinic. As soon as the old roof was propped up, we used these blocks to reinforce the cracked, leaning clinic walls. Eventually the walls were completed and fitted with door and window frames. Bullet holes in the corrugated roof, due to the fighting, were patched and the roof was painted.

By the middle of January I wrote in my diary, "The volunteer crew and the Nuers are getting into the swing of things." It wasn't long before one of the locals slaughtered a cow in our honor. For fun, two of my grandchildren who joined me on this trip made a solar cooker of cardboard, foil, and grass, and baked a cake for the sweet sixteenth birthday of my youngest volunteer.

Toward the end of January, we attended a Nuer church service. This church was under construction and being enlarged to twice its original size. Walls and some of the tall center poles for the roof were up, and mud seats were completed. Considering that the roof hadn't been built yet, church was held early in the day before temperatures got too hot to sit in the sun. It was a full house with 320 in attendance. At the end of the service, a line formed in order that everyone could shake hands and it was exciting to see the vitality of this Christian community.

Our pastor, Chuck Jordan, found that there were churches scattered throughout this area, and he wrote that all of them "had enthusiastic choirs with homemade rhythm instruments and drums." He felt God was doing great work with the Nuers.

In January 1996, three weeks into the project, thoughts of home filled the minds of the first group of volunteers. It was time for their replacements to arrive and the fresh work crew would have plenty to do.

The second group of volunteers arrived and immediately delved into constructing doors and window shutters, repairing the floor, and painting many of the bare walls. They finished up the Adura project on time, within their allotted three weeks. Was it another one of God's miracles? I think so.

By February 20, I packed up, turned in the keys to the new clinic, and traded the old shirt that I was wearing for the local blacksmith's fishing spear. This was to be added to my memorabilia in my "museum" back home. I bid a fond farewell to Adura, and on a stop at Addis Ababa, I treated myself to a savory, succulent New York T-bone steak. "What a meal after six weeks at Camp Adura," I informed my diary.

At the Ninety-first New Wilmington Missionary Conference in June 1996, a dinner was held for retired missionaries. "There are not many of us left," I informed my diary, "only nine here. We are almost an extinct breed. I have served more years than anyone here." In July the wiring repair that began in 1995 on the Anderson Auditorium was completed.

Adura clinic before (above) and after (below)

OPERATION SIMBA

S-outhern Africa
I-nternational
M-ission
B-uilding
A-dventure

Sometimes God waited a long time to find someone dumb enough not to know that it couldn't be done. Or did God plan my life this way? Moses was already eighty years old when God sent him to Egypt and he still worked another forty years. Caleb was eighty-five and still ready to go back into the mountain. And Joshua was well-advanced in years. The Bible doesn't say much about retiring. I had something in common with these men as I approached eighty-five in 1997. It had been a long road from my childhood as a poor little kid in the horse and buggy days to the high tech of the nineties.

As soon as I returned home from one trip, it wasn't uncommon for me to start packing for another. Often times I thought of the immortal John Wesley's Rules for Living:

Do all the good you can,
by all the means you can,
in all the ways you can,
in all the places you can,
at all the times you can,
to all the people you can,
as long as you can.[2]

In the first four months of 1997, God's plans for me included a trip to the southern part of Africa to work on two projects: one, to help build a church in the Glen Norah area of

Harare, Zimbabwe, and the other, to build a staff house at the Justo Mwale Theological College in Zambia.

GLEN NORAH CHURCH—ZIMBABWE

At the beginning of 1997, I arrived in Harare, the capital of Zimbabwe, to supervise a team of volunteers whose goal was to build a church for the Glen Norah congregation of the Church of Central Africa Presbyterian. We had thirty working days to do it. Located in the suburbs of Harare, the Glen Norah church had been given a piece of land by the local town council with the stipulation that the church be built within a specified period of time or the land would revert back to the council. I knew it was an impossible feat for me. God could do nothing for me until I recognized the limits of what was humanly possible, and then let Him do the impossible.

The eight-member volunteer construction crew sent by SERVE for this project (including their executive director and their projects director) was graciously welcomed to stay in the local homes of members of the Glen Norah congregation. While staying in one of the local homes, I quickly realized that I was wasting too much time traveling back and forth to the worksite. And besides, I felt like I needed to be at the job site 24/7 to stay on top of things. In order to do this, I moved into an eight-by-eight storeroom at the worksite and used it as my field office and living quarters. ". . . I have learned, in whatever state I am, to be content" (Phil. 4:11 RSV).

The church members' desire for a place of worship was so great that they all volunteered to help us work. When I arrived, footers had already been dug for the building and footer pads poured. Church women with children strapped to their backs prepared lunch for all the workers, joyously singing the entire time.

While at Harare, I attended a United Church service in the area. What a service it was! With just one pastor in the pulpit, the service started at 10:30 A.M. and continued for three hours and forty minutes. After a fifty-minute break, there was an hour for Communion. Whole families attended the service together, including children and babies, and after three hours the children were restless. I must admit, so was I.

We were fortunate to have water and electricity on site most of the time at Harare, but unfortunate on those days when the mud and rainwater collected two to three inches deep on the concrete floor. Everything on this project was done by man and woman power. All the bricks were unloaded by hand and tossed, along with shovels full of mortar, to a worker up on the scaffolding.

Five weeks (thirty working days) later, the brick walls were up, the cement asbestos roof was on, concrete floors were poured, the doors and windows were completed, and the inside walls were plastered in the 460-seat church. The church location was ideal since the cross at the top of the gable in front could be viewed from both roads leading into it.

In mid-April, two thousand people attended the all-day church dedication. The keys were turned over and the Outreach Foundation of the Presbyterian Church presented a plaque to the congregation, acknowledging that the church building was a gift from the children in America. Amazingly enough, the entire construction costs of the building had been raised by thousands of PC(USA) boys and girls during their vacation Bible school in the summer of 1996. I had learned to expect great things from God.

JUSTO MWALE THEOLOGICAL COLLEGE—ZAMBIA

While visiting with daughter Leah and her family in South Africa for a month, I indulged in hot baths and slept in a real bed. Then it was time to move on to my next SIMBA project in Zambia.

On March 10, 1997, I arrived in Lusaka, the capital of Zambia in southern Africa, with plans to construct a staff house at the Justo Mwale Theological College in six weeks time. The college, property of the Reformed Church in Zambia, was located about ten kilometers east of Lusaka. Many of the sixty students were being sponsored by their sending churches.

The fifteen SERVE volunteers for this project resided on campus, and work hours were scheduled from nine to five, six days a week. Students at the school would be available to lead daily devotions for the volunteers after lunch.

When we arrived, the concrete pad for the floor of the staff residence had already been poured. Before coming to Lusaka, I had received a plan indicating eight-inch outside walls and four-inch block inside walls. But instead, without the approval of an architect or structural engineer, walls were being built with six-inch block and the windows had been increased from six feet to eight feet. This meant that half the weight of the roof would be over the windows, and it made me feel very uncomfortable.

Besides these concerns, masons were poorly trained and the sun-dried cement block was an inferior grade, with some already cracking. The foreman had purchased sand for making mortar, and, after testing it, we discovered it was 95 percent mud.

Things didn't get off to a good start, and I was ready to walk off the job and leave the site. The idea of wasting my time and mission dollars was unsettling to me. And besides, I didn't think it was right for my volunteers to be responsible for this building. It was not safe. It brought to mind Abraham Lincoln's saying, "He has the right to criticize who had the heart to help."

The following morning, the principal of the school approached me with a signed letter saying that the school would be responsible for any resulting cracks due to the wrong choice of blocks. I agreed to go ahead with the project with the stipulation that I had the right to make some design changes. I exchanged the lintels for a reinforced concrete band, and pipe posts were put under the veranda roof.

Although it was a good school and met the need for training church leaders, there were many problems with sanitation and maintenance needing to be resolved. Their open garbage pits and poorly designed septic system needed to be changed to a closed pit system in order to cut down on rats and malaria-bearing mosquitoes. The open pits also risked contaminating the drinking water from the wells in close proximity. There were other problems too: leaky faucets caused a water shortage, and the Stone Age axes used to clear the jungle for the septic system were much too inefficient.

Except for the concrete pad, all the remaining building work, walls, and roofing were completed by the volunteers and, once again, in the allotted time. On April 21, a tea was held and the principal of Justo Mwale Theological College thanked me and my team for all our effort.

———————◆———————

In November 1997, an open house was held at my home in Pittsford, New York, in honor of my eighty-fifth birthday. At times life seemed like a jigsaw puzzle. There were so many pieces. Each activity, each decision, and each event was a piece of the puzzle.

Sometimes we look at the puzzle pieces and become overwhelmed. We wonder how they will all fit. I learned that I needed to trust God and just watch in awe as He put the pieces in place.

When people ask me if I ever faced danger in my life overseas, I make reference to the riots, mobs, guns, spears, and lions I had frequently encountered. However, I felt the most dangerous moment in my life occurred the beginning of 1998 right in my own home.

On January 7, at 9:00 P.M., my doorbell rang. The man standing in the doorway asked if he could use my phone to call a tow truck and motioned to a car with its lights flashing parked by my mailbox. As I turned to let him in, another man stepped up, put a gun to my back, and said, "We want money." With the gun still in my back, three more men entered and began to rip the phone out of the wall and tear my house apart. For fifteen minutes I talked to the man with the gun, saying that I felt sorry for him and that he had problems and needed help. "You can shoot me," I said, "but it would do you more harm than it would me."

Finally they all left without harming me, taking nothing more than my wallet and one hundred dollars in cash. Evidently none of my other possessions were of value to them. "Even though I walk through the valley of the shadow of death, I fear no evil, for thou art with me . . ." (Ps. 23:4 RSV). Just how God intended to use that piece to touch the lives of those men or to change my life was not clear yet, but it was the first of many pieces which formed the picture that was to be made in 1998. From it I learned that I cannot hide from danger, but I can trust God to bring me through no matter where I am as I try to follow His plan for my life.

Other times it took years to see how some of the pieces would fit together. In 2002, I received a delightful letter from Gordon Kunde, one of the volunteers of the Agamy work camp in 1955 (see Agamy, chapter 4). Back then Gordon had worked alongside other American and Egyptian college students to build a conference center in the Egyptian desert on the coast of the Mediterranean Sea.

Before: Campers working on chapel foundation of conference center

After: Conference center at Agamy forty years later

In April 1998, Gordon traveled to Egypt on business and was able to visit the conference center at Agamy. Gordon remarked in his letter:

I was overwhelmed to not only find the place, but to be treated as a friend of Christ. . . . The original building is now the first floor dining hall underneath the chapel. That our original motive had survived, grown, and continues to bear fruit after all these years made me feel that I was a part of something much bigger. . . . Working as a volunteer builder in Egypt had been the catalyst for my life as a citizen of Christ in a wider world.

*Entrance to
conference center*

CUAMBA CHURCH—MOZAMBIQUE

During Mozambique's bloody sixteen-year civil war, tens of thousands became refugees in the neighboring country of Malawi. Here Christians shared the good news of Jesus Christ with the refugees. But as they returned to their homelands to start anew in Mozambique, the simple churches that they were building from local materials could not be finished. They faced difficulties: iron sheets for the roofs were too expensive, roofing timber was hard to acquire, and it was difficult to transport materials to the construction site. All of this impeded the growth of the Lord's work and help was needed.

With an invitation from the Presbyterian Church of Mozambique, my goal that March and April of 1998 was to organize a five-week mission trip to the town of Cuamba in northern Mozambique. My plans were to build a thirty-by-sixty-foot church with the help of five volunteers from my hometown church, two daughters, and two grandsons, and the assistance of the local people of Cuamba. The land had been paid for and plans were approved by the government. God had carried me over a lot of tough places and I had faith enough to believe He could do another miracle. I knew I was dreaming, but if God supplied funds and volunteers, it could be done. I was always expecting the unexpected.

On March 25, 1998, I left Rochester, New York, to start the four-day trip to north central Mozambique. The last nine hours of the trip riding on a filthy, old wreck of a train that stopped at every fence post to pick up and drop off passengers was especially memorable.

Shortly after my arrival in Cuamba, I went to the site where the new church was to be built. Besides clearing the land, the locals had made and fired thirteen thousand bricks of the thirty thousand that were needed for the project. I got prices on materials, met with the mayor and the head of religion, and had a welcome for all the volunteers. After the footers were dug, the local pastor announced that it was their custom to have a church service. During the service a "cornerstone" was placed under the spot where the pulpit was to be located.

Local church members helped place eight inches of stone into the footers before we poured the concrete. I ordered a door, windows, and timber for the thirty-foot trusses from a local carpenter shop. Since there were no plates to connect the trusses, we scavenged until we found an old abandoned pickup truck and tediously cut the needed plates from the truck metal. Not only did the volunteers get calluses cutting plates for the trusses, but they worked hard making arbors for doors and rings for reinforcing. We were constantly trying to straighten out bent nails and work with the badly-bowed lumber from a local sawmill. We worked side by side with the natives, including the pastor, his wife, and many of the church women, to build a church that they so badly wanted.

By April 11, in twenty-two days, all the door frames and seven windows were set, all twenty-one trusses were made and put up, all the brick work was completed, and the roof was on. We proved over and over again that "many hands make light work."

By April 23 our project was looking good. The only unfinished job was the outside plastering which had to wait for more funding. We met with the church leaders and took photos beside the front door before packing up. I wrote in my diary, "It took a lot of mission people working together to do this project. . . . The tears in their eyes as we departed on the train were signs enough of their deep appreciation for our help." The ten-thousand-mile flight from Mozambique to Miami gave me seventeen hours to catch up on my sleep.

After arriving home I received an announcement in the mail of the inauguration of the new church which we had the privilege to help build at Cuamba. I replied saying that it was most unfortunate that we could not attend. I stated, "The whole team of eleven of us will be with you in spirit on November 18! Pictures bring back fond memories of laying the cornerstone and reading of the scripture." I was reminded of several Scriptures. ". . . built upon the foundation of the apostles and prophets, Christ Jesus himself being the cornerstone" (Eph. 2:20 RSV). "Behold, I am laying in Zion a stone, a cornerstone chosen and precious, and he who believes in him will not be put to shame" (1 Pet. 2:6 RSV).

PRAYER HOUSE MISSION—SOUTH CAROLINA

Prayer House Mission in Summerton, South Carolina, held its first services in a small vacant house in 1976. In 1980, with only twenty-eight hundred dollars, a church was constructed using many volunteer man-hours. Unfortunately, in 1989 the church was destroyed by Hurricane Hugo.

In 1990, on the eleventh anniversary of Prayer House Mission, the Lord blessed them with another church, built on the same two-acre site using volunteer labor. But as their pastor described it, "the Lord kept on blessing, the devil kept on messing." Unfortunately, on June 1, 1997, early on a Sunday morning, the word spread quickly that the church had burned to the ground. This church was not only in an area known for heavy Klan activity, but it was in an area that had the largest concentration of burned black churches in the United States. It was one of fifty churches that had fallen to arson in the past few years.

Help was needed once again. This time Interfaith Rebuilding Partnership of Cambridge, Massachusetts, an organization involved with construction projects for southern churches struck by arson, came to their aid. Through this organization, a youth work camp was planned at my church in Pittsford to travel over eight hundred miles to Summerton, South Carolina, for two weeks at the end of June 1998. This work camp was spiritually based to provide an interfaith experience and promote cultural diversity. Several other adults and I would travel with the youth to help rebuild this Prayer House Mission.

When we arrived, the main job was to finish putting Sheetrock on the ceiling and walls of the sanctuary. Besides kitchen duties, there was painting, ditch filling, assembling air-conditioning ducts, nailing floor underlay, and general cleaning up. When we finished up on Friday afternoon of the first week, the sanctuary was ready to be taped and mudded by a professional dry wall person.

For some rest and relaxation, the first group of volunteers headed off to the beach at Charleston to celebrate the Fourth of July and a job well done. Arriving back in Summerton, the volunteers packed up and passed on advice and tools to the second group of volunteers arriving. At the end of our second work week, we all left and felt good knowing that the church was scheduled for completion by early fall and that we all had a part in its fruition.

———◆———

From 1991 to 1998, I was involved in thirty-two projects, in twelve countries, on four continents. It was back in the early nineties that the editor of the *Ethio-Re-Echoes* (formerly known as *Ethio-Echo*), a newsletter containing information about missionaries and mission work in Ethiopia, first dubbed me with the title "Christ's Globe-Trotter." It is amazing how the name has stuck. "It is getting harder and harder to live up to this title of Christ's Globe-Trotter," I wrote in my diary that summer of 1998.

At times it was hard to fit the pieces together, but I continued to try. In 1999, I began to compile information for writing a biography of my life and to do so meant that I had to put many speaking engagements and trip opportunities on hold. I began the arduous task by organizing all my mission project files in chronological order. Thank goodness, I had been a notorious pack rat and had saved everything, and, fortunately, I had kept journals since 1947. In order to share with others what God has done in my life, we used eighty-one of them in writing this book.

Since Dolly shared in so many of my projects, it was more difficult to do the writing without her. But I felt that it was the most important project I could complete and worked full-time on it.

Like my other projects, I gave this one a name: Operation BOOK.

B-iography of
O-verseas
O-utreach for the
K-ing

Working with hundreds of volunteers on dozens of projects in countries around the world, I have helped build foundations that continue to bring witness for Christ. Just like the title of the old hymn, I had always said, "I'll go where you want me to go, Lord, I'll do what you want me to do." It was exciting to be handpicked by God for unique tasks. Having so many people on my team with a wide network of prayer support keeps me going. I give Christ the glory who gives me strength and power.

This world is not my home. I'm just passing through. Someday the Lord will call and a little chariot will swing down and take me to my real home. I do not know the date, but being in my ninety-second year, I am preparing for my final journey. When He calls me, I will answer. I'll be somewhere working for my Lord. Then He will be looking for someone to fill my shoes.

Anne and Ray Ortlund, in their book, *You Don't Have to Quit*, state: "Only one life, T'will soon be past, Only what is done for the Lord will last."[3]

EPILOGUE

Looking back at what I've done, I never dreamed I would still be pounding nails for the Lord in the year 2005.

In August 2001, on the southern tip of Mozambique in the town of Mabilibile, I arrived with a team of twenty volunteers to rebuild a church. This church had burned during their civil war and the members were meeting under a tree. As project manager, my job was to take the fourteen concrete columns and the concrete slab floor that were remaining after the wars and turn them into a viable church. There was no electricity or running water, and with the closest building supplies four hours away, it was a formidable task to complete this project in just three weeks time. With mission accomplished, a grand dedication was held and a marble plaque placed by the front door identifying the church as a SERVE project built with funds from Presbyterian churches in the United States for the glory of God.

For many years I have attended the New Wilmington Missionary Conference held in Anderson Auditorium on the campus of Westminster College in Pennsylvania. In May 2002, I organized a work project with volunteers and in one week we replaced the old concrete floor at the entrance of the auditorium.

On September 1, 2002, a grand celebration was held at the First Presbyterian Church of Pittsford, New York, in honor of my ninetieth birthday. Well over one hundred friends and family gathered to commemorate this milestone and enjoy a native Ethiopian lunch of watt and anjera. It was a day of fellowship with skits, family slides, and memories shared by many of my volunteers—a day I'll always treasure.

In July 2003, I traveled to Africa once again—this time to build a church in north central Mozambique in the village of Ribaue. My group of volunteers (many from my home church) and I were shocked to discover that the fifteen thousand blocks plus gravel and sand promised by the local community of Ribaue had not materialized. With great disappointment, my volunteers and I gathered up our supplies and left, saying that we would return when they were ready for us. The agreement was that we would help them build their church, not build it for them.

Fortunately, within days, I found another community that was ready to build a church and the entire project was moved to the seaside community of Pemba, about one hundred fifty miles away on the Indian Ocean. Here the local congregation was meeting in a small thatched-roof mud structure with backless bare logs for seats. Using the handmade concrete blocks and lumber stacked neatly in the back courtyard of the church, volunteers and I, along with some of the local young men, transformed the materials into a house of worship in five weeks. A dedication was held to hand over the new church to the Presbyterian Church of Mozambique and a plaque dedicating the church in memory of my wife, Dolly, was hung on the front.

Time marches on, and, as we completed my memoirs in the summer of 2004, I continued to make plans for the future. I am currently working on a project for the Tumutumu Hospital in Kenya and look forward to a fiftieth year reunion for the

Agamy volunteers in Egypt in 2005. How could I have done more? How can I encourage more people to go or to pray and hold the ropes at home? There are still so many people left to reach for Christ.

NOTES

CHAPTER 1
1. Joseph McFarland, *20th Century History of the City of Washington and Washington County* (Richmond: Arnold Publishing Co., 1910).

CHAPTER 3
1. Thomas Winburn and Edwin Fairman, *Africa and the United Presbyterian* (New York: Commission on Ecumenical Missions and Relations, UPC-USA, 1959), 16.
2. Albert Roode, "Facts from the Foreign Mission Field," *Christian Union Herald* (1948).
3. Roy Grace, "Addressing a Service in South Sudan's Newest Mission Station," *United Presbyterian* (1950).

CHAPTER 4
1. Margaret Neal, *Women in Mission, One Hundred Years* (Washington, Penn.: Washington Presbyterial, 1976).
2. Thomas T. Winburn and Edwin B. Fairman, "Africa and the United Presbyterians" (Commission on Ecumenical Missions and Relations, UPC-USA, 1954, booklet).
3 Ibid.
4. Margaret Crawford, *The Sudan: Its Land and People* (New York: Commission on Ecumenical Mission and Relations, PCUSA, n.d.), 65.
5. A. C. Forrest, "Egyptian Evangelicals: A New Life Stirs," *Presbyterian Life* (1969).
6. Edwin Fairman and Marion Fairman, "Miracle of Agamy," *Ecumenical Echoes* (1970).
7. Edwin Fairman, pamphlet "The Nile Project" *(Christian Union Herald*, 1955).

8. Willis A. McGill, pamphlet "Work Camping in Egypt" (Board of Foreign Missions, 1956).

9. Edwin Fairman, "The Nile Project."

10. Edwin Fairman and Marion Fairman, "Miracle of Agamy."

11. Michael Boyland, ed., "Presbyterians Praying through the Window 111," Presbyterian Center for Mission Studies (September 1997): 43.

12. Dave Hackett, "Old Testament Translation Effort Launched for the Murle People of Sudan," *Global Prayer Digest* (1999).

13. Marion Fairman, *Remember What You Have Received* (New Wilmington, Penn.: New Wilmington Missionary Conference, 1979).

14. New Wilmington Missionary Conference, brochure "Good News for the New Wilmington Conference" (New Wilmington, Penn.: New Wilmington Missionary Conference, n.d.).

15. "Sudan," *World Book Encyclopedia*, vol. 18 (1988).

16. "Mt. Kilimanjaro," *World Book Encyclopedia*, vol. 11 (1988).

17. J. L. Anderson, ed., *Light* (American Mission, 1963).

18. "Missionaries Told to Vacate Sudan," *Presbyterian Life* (1963).

CHAPTER 5

1. *Ethiopia, General Information* (Addis Ababa: Press and Information Department, 1958).

2. Commission on Ecumenical Mission and Relations, brochure "Mission through Medicine" (United Presbyterian Church [USA], 1962).

3. Carl Karsch, "An African Adventure," *Presbyterian Life* (1967).

4. Lillian Huisken, personal communication, quoting the *Sudan Daily*, 28 February 1964.

5. Ann Rowe, "Circuit Rider with Wings," *Ethio-Echo* (American Mission United Presbyterian, 1972).

6. Dolly Pollock, "Pollocks Originate a New Dome Building for Remote Mission Posts," *Ethio-Echo* (1971).

7. Ibid.

8. Ibid.

9. Karsch, "An African Adventure."

10. Pollock, *Ethio-Echo* (1971).

11. William Muldrow, "Work Begins with Teshenna People," *Ethio-Echo* (1965).

12. William Muldrow, "Reflections on a Year with the Teshenna Tribe," *Ethio-Echo* (1966).

13. Ibid.

14. Ibid.

15. Ibid.

16. Edythe Draper, *Living Light* (Wheaton, Ill.: Tyndale House Publishers, 1972).

17. Richard L. Scheffel, ed. *ABC's of Nature* (Pleasantville, N.Y.: Reader's Digest Association, Inc., 1984).

18. Morrie Swart, "Medical Clinic and Bible Teaching Begin for the Gelebs at the Omo Post," *Ethio-Echo* (1966).

19. Morrie Swart, "Swarts Make Home in Geleb Country," *Ethio-Echo* (1965).

20. Ibid.

21. Ibid.

22. Bob and Morrie Swart, "Food from Wind," *Ethio-Echo* (1965).

23. Bob and Morrie Swart, "Tails and Sails at Omo," *Ethio-Echo* (1975).

24. Peter Frankel, *Food from Windmills* (London: ITDG, 1975).

25. Bob and Morrie Swart, "Tails and Sails at Omo."

26. Harvey Hoekstra, "Missionary Family to Live Among the Mesengo People," *Ethio-Echo* (1964).

27. Ibid.

28. Harvey Hoekstra, "Hoekstra's Journey to Begin Godare River Post," *Ethio-Echo* (1965).

29. Harvey Hoekstra, "Volunteers Build Mission Post in the Forest," *Ethio-Echo* (1967).

30. Lois Anderson, *Ethio-Echo* newsletter (1967).

31. Mark Hoekstra, "Tie a Knot on Your String for Me," *Audio Scriptures International Newsletter* (April 1995).

32. Global Ministry, ed., "MAF, God's Surprises—Always Good!" video (Mission Aviation Fellowship, 2001).

33. Pollock, *Ethio-Echo* (1971).

CHAPTER 6

1. Rudyard Kipling, "If," line 1, *The Works of Rudyard Kipling* (Chatham, Kent, U.K.: Wordsworth Ed Ltd., 1994).

2. John Oxenham, "In Christ There Is No East or West" (1908, hymn); (Alexander Reinagle, 1830).

CHAPTER 7

1. Helen Keller, *The Story of My Life* (N.Y.: Bantam Classic Signet edition, 1988), 372.

2. Albert C. Outler and Richard Heitzenrater, eds., "Rules for Living," *John Wesley's Sermons: An Anthology* (Nashville, Tenn.: Abingdon Press, 1991).

3. Anne and Ray Ortlund, *You Don't Have to Quit* (Nashville, Tenn.: Thomas Nelson Publishers, 1994).

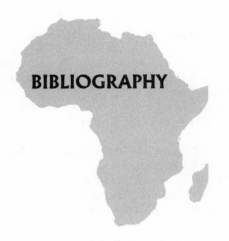

BIBLIOGRAPHY

Anderson, J. L., ed. *Light*. American Mission, 1963.

Anderson, Lois Anderson. *Ethio-Echo* newsletter. 1967.

Boyland, Michael, ed. "Presbyterians Praying through the Window 111," Presbyterian Center for Mission Studies, September 1997.

Commission on Ecumenical Mission and Relations. Brochure "Mission through Medicine." United Presbyterian Church [USA], 1962.

Crawford, Margaret. *The Sudan: Its Land and People*. New York: Commission on Ecumenical Mission and Relations, PCUSA, n.d.

Draper, Edythe. *Living Light*. Wheaton, Ill.: Tyndale House Publishers, 1972.

Fairman, Edwin. Report "Facts about the Sudan," 1956.

———. Pamphlet "The Nile Project," *Christian Union Herald*. 1955.

Fairman, Edwin and Marion Fairman. "Miracle of Agamy," *Ecumenical Echoes*. 1970.

Fairman, Edwin and Winburn Thomas. *Africa and the United Presbyterians*. New York: Commission on Ecumenical Mission and Relations, UPC-USA, 1959.

Fairman, Marion. *Remember What You Have Received*. New Wilmington, Penn.: New Wilmington Missionary Conference, 1979.

Forrest, A. C. "Egyptian Evangelicals: A New Life Stirs," *Presbyterian Life*: 1969.

Frankel, Peter. *Food from Windmills*. London: ITDG, 1975.

Freeman, David. *One of Us*. New York: Carroll & Graf Publishers, 1997.

Global Ministry, ed. "MAF, God's Surprises—Always Good!" video. Mission Aviation Fellowship, 2001.

Grace, Roy. "Addressing a Service in South Sudan's Newest Mission Station," *United Presbyterian* (1950).

Hackett, Dave. "Old Testament Translation Effort Launched for the Murle People of Sudan," *Global Prayer Digest*. 1999.

Hoekstra, Harvey "Hoekstra's Journey to Begin Godare River Post, " *Ethio-Echo*. 1965.

————. "Missionary Family to Live Among the Mesengo People," *Ethio-Echo.* 1964.

————. "Volunteers Build Mission Post in the Forest," *Ethio-Echo.* 1967.

Hoekstra, Mark. "Tie a Knot on Your String for Me." *Audio Scriptures International Newsletter.* April 1995.

Karsch, Carl. "An African Adventure," *Presbyterian Life.* 1967.

Keller, Helen. *The Story of My Life.* New York: Bantam Classic Signet edition, 1988.

Kipling, Rudyard. "If," line 1, *The Works of Rudyard Kipling.* Chatham, Kent, U.K.: Wordsworth Ed Ltd., 1994.

McFarland, Joseph. *20th Century History of the City of Washington and Washington County.* Richmond, Va.: Arnold Publishing Co., 1910.

McGill, Willis A. Pamphlet "Work Camping in Egypt." Board of Foreign Missions, 1956.

Ministry of Education. *Ethiopia, General Information.* Addis Ababa: Press and Information Department, 1958.

"Missionaries Told to Vacate Sudan," *Presbyterian Life.* 1963.

Muldrow, William. "Reflections on a Year with the Teshenna Tribe," *Ethio-Echo.* 1966.

————. "Work Begins with Teshenna People," *Ethio-Echo.* 1965.

Neal, Margaret. *Women in Mission, One Hundred Years.* Washington, Penn.: Washington Presbyterial, 1976.

New Wilmington Missionary Conference. Brochure "Good News for the New Wilmington Conference." New Wilmington, Penn.: New Wilmington Missionary Conference, n.d.

Ortlund, Anne and Ray Ortlund. *You Don't Have to Quit.* Nashville, Tenn.: Thomas Nelson Publishers, 1994.

Outler, Albert C. and Richard Heitzenrater, eds. "Rules for Living," *John Wesley's Sermons: An Anthology.* Nashville, Tenn.: Abingdon Press, 1991.

Oxenham, John. "In Christ There Is No East or West." 1908; Alexander Reinagle, 1830.

Pollock, Dolly. "Pollocks Originate a New Dome Building for Remote Mission Posts," *Ethio-Echo.* 1971.

Pollock, Ted. "Meet My Friends," *Christian Union Herald.* 1948.

Rowe, Ann. "Circuit Rider with Wings," *Ethio-Echo.* American Mission United Presbyterian, 1972.

Scheffel, Richard L., ed. *ABC's of Nature.* Pleasantville, N.Y.: Reader's Digest Association, Inc., 1984.

Sudan Daily. 28 February 1964.

Swart, Bob and Morrie Swart. "Food from Wind," *Ethio-Echo.* 1965.

————. "Tails and Sails at Omo," *Ethio-Echo.* 1975.

Swart, Morrie. "Medical Clinic and Bible Teaching Begin for the Gelebs at the Omo Post," *Ethio-Echo.* 1966.

————. "Swarts Make Home in Geleb Country," *Ethio-Echo.* 1965.

World Book Encyclopedia, vols. 11, 18. 1988.

INDEX